# The Tabernacle
## THE PRIESTHOOD AND THE OFFERINGS

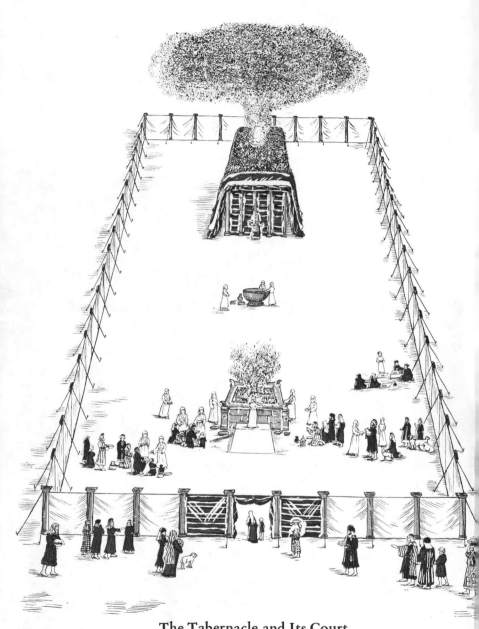

The Tabernacle and Its Court

# The
# Tabernacle
## THE PRIESTHOOD AND
## THE OFFERINGS

by

Henry W. Soltau

kregel
CLASSICS

Grand Rapids, MI  49501

*The Tabernacle, the Priesthood, and the Offerings*, by Henry W. Soltau.

Enlarged type, illustrated edition copyright © 1972 by Kregel Publications.

Published in 1994 by Kregel Classics, an imprint of Kregel Publications, P. O. Box 2607, Grand Rapids, MI 49501. KregelClassics provides trusted and time-proven publications for Christian life and ministry. Your comments and suggestions are valued.

**Library of Congress Catalog Number 72-88590**

ISBN 0-8254-3750-4 (pbk.)

10  11  12  13  14  Printing / Year  98  97  96  95  94

*Printed in the United States of America*

# Contents

## THE OFFERINGS

# List of Illustrations

These illustrations, based on descriptions in the Old Testament and on archaeological discoveries, are artists conceptions of the Tabernacle, its furnishings, and events with which it was closely associated when it played an important part in the daily lives of the children of Israel.

**The Children of Israel Encamped by the Waters of
Elim before Journeying to the Wilderness of Sin**

# Memoir

HENRY WILLIAM SOLTAU, the author of *The Tabernacle, the Priesthood, and the Offerings,* was born in the year 1805. When a youth he was under serious religious impressions, and was for a long time groping after salvation. At Cambridge University he was a regular attendant at church; sought the society of Christian men; went to hear the best preachers; and by good works and prayers hoped to attain to eternal life. In those days a clear gospel was rarely preached; and the earnest cravings of the soul after *reality* remained unsatisfied.

When his University career was ended he came to London, entered the legal profession, and became a Chancery barrister. After tasting the pleasures of London life the whole of his religious impressions were cast off, and he plunged into all the gaiety and amusements of the day. His attractive manners, sparkling wit, keen intellect, and extensive literary acquirements, made him a favourite in society. A bright career of worldly prosperity was opening up before him; the world was welcoming him as one worthy of its honour. But "the Lord had need of him," and the way was being prepared for his deliverance, though he knew it not. God was allowing him to have his own way, till at length he felt like the

Israelites when they lusted for flesh, and God gave it to them *to the full.* He loathed the excitement and pleasure afforded by the scenes of gaiety in which he moved, and yet had no power to stop himself; *seeming* happy to those around him, whilst at heart he was wretched.

In the beginning of the year 1837 tidings reached him of the illness of his mother, and he prepared to go to Plymouth to see her. Whilst packing his portmanteau he felt convinced that he should only arrive home to find his mother dead. There was nothing alarming in the letter, but he began to realize it was God's voice to him. The tedious coach journey was accomplished, and, as he had surmised, his mother had departed. Falling down on his knees by her coffin alone that night he cried out, "Lord, thou must save me, or I am lost for ever." That was a *real* prayer.

Shortly afterwards he was led to Christ through the preaching of an earnest servant of God in Plymouth, and from that day to him "*to live was Christ.*" He turned his back there and then on the world, and gave up his profession that he might devote himself to the study of the Scriptures and to the work of the gospel. There were at that time many earnest and godly men in Plymouth with whom he was thrown ; and these met daily for the study of the Scriptures and for prayer. He thus became trained in the work of the gospel, and entered on a new career of unswerving devotion in the Master's cause.

For several years his labours were confined chiefly to Devonshire; and through the whole of the county he went preaching Christ crucified, and ably ministering the word of God amongst Christians. Plymouth, Exmouth,

Bideford, and Barnstaple were the chief centres of his work for a time. Latterly, on going to Exeter to reside, the sphere of his influence widened considerably. His name is specially associated with the prophetic meetings held in London, in Freemasons' Hall, in the years 1865 and 1867; and his visits to Dublin, Glasgow, Birmingham, Hereford, and Taunton, will long be remembered by those who were privileged to meet him and hear him speak.

His teaching was remarkable, not only for its clearness and depth, but also for its close adherence to Scripture, thus proving how much he lived in communion with God. The great central truths of Salvation through the cross of Christ, and of the Second Coming of the Lord, were ever present to his mind, and pervaded all his teaching. Fearless in his denunciation of what he believed to be error; intensely solemn in his warnings of the power and the consequences of sin; an unflinching standard-bearer of the gospel of God's grace, and yet most tender in ministering the truth of God to stricken ones—he was the means of strengthening the hands of many a feeble one, and of preserving from the snares of the adversary many of God's people.

His last visit to London was made in the autumn of 1867; and although symptoms had then appeared of the disease that so soon after laid him altogether aside, he relaxed none of his energies.

On the Lord's-day he gave no less than six addresses, one of them being delivered in the open-air in Soho Square. He touchingly referred to the days long gone by when he, as a young man of fashion, was well acquainted with that locality; narrating the incidents that had led to the great change in his life, and then testifying to the happiness and blessing of the period of his life since spent in the Lord's service. Fervently he appealed to the numbers of young men crowding around him to turn their backs on the world and sin, and come boldly forth for Christ. It was past ten o'clock that night before he had finished his work; and it was amongst the last of his days of public service for the Lord.

Very shortly afterwards paralysis supervened, which gradually exhausted his mental and physical powers. So gradual was the progress of the disease that for seven years and a half he remained amongst his family, though unable to take any active part in the work of the Lord. During this long trial of patience and faith no murmur ever passed his lips. His peace was unbroken, and his mind unclouded by any fear or doubt. He always delighted to hear of the Lord's work, especially that portion in which his own children were engaged. In July, 1875, he quietly passed away, falling asleep in Jesus to await the day of resurrection.

The Encampment of BENJAMIN, EPHRAIM, and MANASSEH

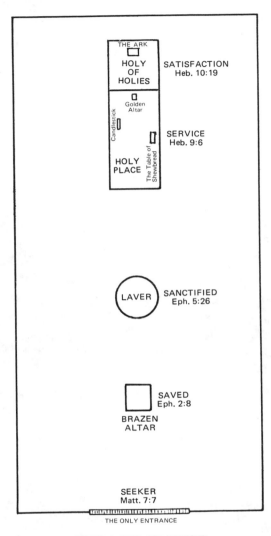

The Encampment of SIMEON, REUBEN, and GAD

The Encampment of ASHER, DAN, and NAPHTALI

MOSES, AARON AND HIS SONS

The Encampment of ZEBULUN, JUDAH, and ISSACHAR

**Diagram of Tabernacle with Position of Tribes**

Offerings for the Tabernacle

# THE
# TABERNACLE

THE tribe of Levi was divided into three families,
under his three sons, Gershon, Kohath, and Merari.
Each had his own separate place of encampment around
the Tabernacle, and to each was committed a peculiar
charge and burden. The Merarites, who encamped
on the north, watched over, erected, and carried all the
solid framework of the building, the pillars of the surrounding courts, together with the sockets of silver and
brass.

The Gershonites pitched towards the west, and had
under their care the curtains, hangings, and coverings
of the Tabernacle and court, which they also bore on the
journeys : whilst to the Kohathites, whose camp was
south, were allotted the charge and carriage of the holy
vessels. Thus was all distributed among these three
families of Levites, and the burden of one was kept
distinct from that of another.

In like manner, we may divide the truth under three
heads : the solid foundation and framework, without
which the Tabernacle itself could not be spread abroad,
portray the great verities on which the whole of salvation rests, viz : the Person of Him who is God and
Man, the eternal, unchanging, and unchangeable Son
of God, Jesus Christ, the same yesterday, and to-day,
and for ever.

The varied colours, as well as costly materials, of
which some of the beautiful draperies were fashioned,
attracted and pleased the eye of the beholder, both by
their brilliancy and tasteful arrangement.   So does the
eye of faith explore and delight in the display of God
manifest in the flesh.   The character and ways of Jesus,
and His blessed work accomplished on the cross, reveal
Him to us, and make Him manifest as the Son of God.

The holy vessels of different forms and adapted to
different uses, but all to one end—that Israel might have
access to God—represent the priestly offices of Christ,
which depend on the glories of His person, and result
from the perfection of His work.

In pursuing the subject, this subdivision will, in
measure be retained.   But, though prominence be given
to one aspect or portion of truth, yet the Spirit of God
would always have us contemplate the one undivided
Christ.   If His character be displayed, it is in order that
He may be revealed.   If His offices are more particularly before us, it is that we may " know HIM."   The
soul is not nourished by mere abstract statements of the
character, or even of the work of the Lord.   HE is the
living bread: His *flesh* and *blood* must be eaten, as He
says, " As the living Father hath sent me, and I live by
the Father; so he that eateth ME, even he shall live
by me."—John vi. 57.

When Moses received directions from God respecting
the Tabernacle, the order in which the vessels and parts
were enumerated, was different from that in which they
were subsequently made.   Thus the Ark, the Shew-
bread table, and the Candlestick were first described to
him; then the Curtains, Coverings, Vail, and Door; after
that, the altar of Burnt-offering, and Boards, and Bars,
of the Tabernacle.   In the order of construction, the
Curtains, Coverings, Boards, Bars, and Sockets—in
fact the whole Tabernacle was first fashioned before
the Vail and Door, or any of the vessels were made.

The order followed in this exposition will be, first.

to consider the various Curtains and Hangings, and the
Courts formed by them : and subsequently, the Boards,
Bars, Pillars, and Sockets ; first the Gershonite, and
then the Merarite charge. In doing so, the Vail has
been selected by way of commencement, because we
have a distinct Scripture in the New Testament,
directing us to its typical signification. " The Vail, that
is to say, His flesh."—Heb. x. 20. And if we can, by
means of this key, unlock some of the hidden treasures
contained in this type, we shall be better able to arrive
at the true interpretation of the other parts.

## THE VAIL

" And thou shalt make a vail of
blue, and purple, and scarlet, and
fine twined linen of cunning work:
with cherubims shall it be made."
—Exod xxvi 31

"And he made a vail of blue,
and purple, and scarlet, and fine
twined linen : with cherubims
made he it of cunning work."—
Exod. xxxvi 35

FINE TWINED LINEN.—One material only is specified in
the construction of the Vail, " fine linen :" the blue,
purple, and scarlet, were simply colours. Upon this
ground-work of fine linen these colours were displayed ;
so that the observer would be first arrested by the beauty
of the blue, the depth of the purple, and the brilliancy
of the scarlet, before he perceived the material, over
which these tints were spread. Does not this aptly
exemplify that wondrous truth, " God was manifest in the
flesh ?" " The Word was made flesh, and dwelt among
us ; and we beheld His glory, the glory as of the only-
begotten of the Father, full of grace and truth."

The Wife, in Rev. xix. 7, is represented as having
made herself ready for the marriage supper, and it is
added in the succeeding verse, " To her was granted,
that she should be arrayed in fine linen, clean, and white :
for the fine linen is the righteousness of saints." ver. 8.
Here a twofold, yet united, aspect of the truth is beauti-

fully presented: the Church makes herself ready, and
yet she is clothed by another.   So in Rev. vii, 14, believers
are said to have washed their robes, and made them
white in the blood of the Lamb: while, in chap. i. 5, it
is written " Unto Him that loved us, and *washed* us from
our sins in His own blood."   We may view the saint as
clothing or washing himself; for he may be regarded as,
by faith, appropriating to himself the precious blood of
Christ; or, we may consider the work as all accomplished
for him by the Lord Jesus, through the grace and mercy
of God.   The word " righteousness of saints " is remarkable, being in the plural number; it may be rendered
' *righteousnesses*;' the fine linen displaying every form of
bright and holy purity; righteousness in every aspect;
according to that beautiful word " Thou art all fair, my
love: there is no spot in thee."   But whence were these
garments derived?   If we turn to Jer. xxiii. 6, " This
is His name, whereby He shall be called, Jehovah our
Righteousness."   Jehovah Jesus is the righteousness of
the saints.   He is the spotless robe; they are clothed
with Him; they stand accepted (graced) in the Beloved.
God has made Him to be unto them " righteousness,
sanctification, and redemption," and His name is placed
upon them; as, in Jer. xxxiii. 16, Jerusalem on earth
will have " Jehovah our Righteousness " as the name
whereby *she* shall be called.

The fine linen of the Vail seems, then, especially
to present to us " the Righteous One," who in His
life of toil and sorrow, and most especially in His
death of shame and suffering, manifested that unsullied
purity, that perfect obedience, and that delight in
accomplishing the will of His Father, whereby He
has earned for Himself a name, which is above every
name, the name of Jesus; " who was made sin for us,
that we might be made the righteousness of God
in Him."

# THE COLOURS

BLUE.—This ranks pre-eminent, being always the first mentioned in the frequent enumerations of the colours given in the latter chapters of Exodus. It attracts, without dazzling the eye ; and the epithet *lovely* is very appropriately attached to it. It is seen spread over the expanse of heaven, of boundless extent. When the thunder-cloud *vails* the sky, and the tempest bursts in fury on the earth with its desolating power, this serene colour is concealed ; but we hail its gradual reappearance as a sure presage of the returning calm, and of the sun's genial beams. It is peculiarly a heavenly colour ; and throughout these types, is closely linked with *gold*. Thus in Exod. xxviii. 6 and 15, the word " and " is omitted between the gold and blue ; so that the passages may be read as follows : " They shall make the ephod of gold, blue, and purple ; the curious girdle of the ephod shall be of gold, blue, and purple, &c. Thou shalt make the breast-plate of gold, blue, and purple, &c." The same order is precisely repeated in chap. xxxix. 2, 5, 8, the "*and*" being again omitted between the gold and blue. Taches of gold were inserted into loops of blue, connecting together the curtains of the Tabernacle. Laces of blue, passing through rings of gold, fastened the breast-plate to the ephod, and a lace of blue bound the golden plate to the mitre of the high priest. The golden vessels of the sanctuary, with the exception of the ark, were all covered with a cloth of blue. If the gold was a type of the glory, majesty, and eternity of the Son of God, blue will fitly represent the grace and love He manifested as declaring the character of God. "God is love." So inseparably and exclusively is this blessed attribute descriptive of Him, that He affirms it to be His very nature. It is not of earth. As the blue vault of heaven, with its vast

dimensions, defies our puny measurements, so the
breadth, and length, and depth, and height of the
love of Christ passeth knowledge. The thunders of
God's wrath and holy indignation against sin, may for
a time, seem to obscure His love. But "His anger
endureth but a moment." Judgment is "His strange
work," for "He delighteth in mercy."

The dark cloud only intimates a passing storm, needful,
it may be, to purify the air. Compared with the azure
depth beyond, it is but superficial and momentary. And,
since we have known the full outpouring of His wrath
upon His Son, no cloud, however black, can cross our sky,
without the heavenly blue being seen in the bow, which
God has set there as a token of eternal mercy, that
judgment once poured out shall never more be repeated.

In looking at the Vail, the first colour, which would
draw the attention of the beholder, was the Blue. The
sinner's first glance of faith on the Lord Jesus recognises
Him as from above, " God manifest in the flesh," " the
only-begotten of the Father, full of grace and truth."
Grace is ever the attraction to one who is burdened with
guilt. The woman who was a sinner, Luke vii. 37—50,
despised and shunned by her more decorous neighbours,
broke through all restraints, to welcome Christ. She
heard that Jesus sat at meat in the Pharisee's house. God
had, in very deed, come down to visit fallen man : but
no thunders of Sinai, no fearful voice of stern rebuke,
no trumpet sound of judgment heralded His approach.
He came upon one errand, that of mercy. He made
known the depth of God's heart, and the woman felt
she had a claim above all others upon His compassion,
for she knew herself most guilty. Conscious of her
unfitness for His presence, and yet assured that her very
unfitness had brought Him down from heaven—loathing
herself on account of her sin, and yet aware that her
loathsomeness was her best plea to be in the company of
Christ, she rushed, unbidden, into that assembly ; all
considerations of propriety giving way before the one

engrossing thought, that it was her Saviour, her God,
who sat there, neglected by all but herself: and there
she remained, satisfied with her nearness to Him; lost
to all around her, her heart more broken, the more she
tasted His love; arrested by the heavenly beauty of Him
on whom she gazed. At length, she heard words
which could come from no lips but those of the Son of
God: " Thy faith hath saved thee: go in peace."
Well might she have exclaimed, "Thou art fairer than
the children of men: grace is poured into thy lips."
(Psa. xlv. 2.) She recognised the loveliness of the
blue.

It would be deeply interesting, to trace through the
Gospels this beautiful colour, exhibited in the ways of
the Lord, and above all, its intensity, in those last scenes
of anguish and distress, when He proved how He loved
us. But this may suffice to direct others into these
green pastures, and to the still waters, where refreshment and rest are found.

## THE RIBAND OF BLUE

As a confirmation of the typical import already proposed
respecting the colour, Blue, it may not be amiss to insert
here a short exposition of Numbers xv. 32—41, a peculiar ordinance, giving directions concerning the dress of
the children of Israel. One of that people had been
found transgressing a commandment of God by gathering sticks on the sabbath-day. He had, by this act,
violated the direct precept, " Thou shalt do no manner
of work :" and had he been allowed to carry out his
purpose, he would have broken another statute, " Ye
shall kindle no fire throughout your habitations on the
sabbath-day." For this offence he was stoned to death;
an early example of the severity of that law under which
Israel had voluntarily placed themselves, and which they
had promised to obey. He perished without mercy :

for the law knew no grace.  It demanded strict obedience ; and no plea of necessity or of ignorance could be
allowed in mitigation of its fearful penalty.  It was on
this occasion that the following directions were given by
God : " And the Lord spake unto Moses, saying, speak
unto the children of Israel, and bid them that they make
them fringes in the borders of their garments throughout
their generations, and that they put upon the fringe of
the borders a riband of blue : and it shall be unto you
for a fringe, that ye may look upon it, and remember all
the commandments of the Lord, and do them ; and that
ye seek not after your own heart, and your own eyes."
Ignorance of God is the fruitful source of disobedience.
The sabbath-breaker (who was but a specimen of the
whole nation) had sinned because he had forgotten God
and the great redemption out of Egypt, in which God
had made Himself manifest, both as to His holiness and
His mercy.   The Law made righteous demands on those
who were under its covenant.   It was " holy, just, and
good."   But, in its precepts, it made not a full display
of God's blessed character of mercy.   Grace and truth
did not come by it : they came by Jesus Christ ; and
there would be no power to fulfil the righteousness of
that law, or even to remember it, unless the heart were
first instructed in the goodness, love, and compassion of
God.   A little intimation of this blessed truth (which
was afterwards fully revealed under the new covenant)
is given us in the command respecting the riband of
blue.   That heavenly colour, figuratively directing the
beholder to the gracious character of God, was to be the
ornament of his dress.   The skirts of his clothing were
to remind him, as he walked, that he belonged to God,
who was holy, and who had redeemed him out of
Egypt by the blood of the lamb, and through the waters
of the Red Sea, unto Himself.   The Law, written and
engraven on stones, had proved ineffectual as to securing
obedience.   Even its threatenings of judgment prevailed
not to restrain the wilful purposes of the heart, which,

by nature alienated from God, only despised His judgments, and found an additional zest in sinning presumptuously against His word. It might be, that some intimation of His grace, kept constantly under the Israelite's eye, would remind him of those commandments of which he had proved himself forgetful.

This seems to be the purport of the fringe of blue riband. But, like all ordinances addressed merely to the senses, we know how it failed. The Pharisees enlarged the blue riband, in order that men might praise their scrupulous adherence to the letter of the law. They did it, to be seen of men; not that they might themselves look upon it, and remember all the commandments of the Lord. They fashioned their dress, in order to attract the notice, and gain the approbation of others; to get a character for sanctity, and separation from the world; and they had their reward. They were held in reputation among men. So, in modern days, a peculiar garb may be assumed, an outward appearance affected, an ascetic life practised, which will gain human applause; and he who adopts such will be hailed as a heavenly man. But, if the heart be not first right with God; if the affection be not set on things above, and that on the ground of resurrection with Christ, and the life hid with Christ in God; all these outward observances are mere Pharisaical displays, and nourish, instead of mortifying, the flesh.

The every-day garments of the Israelite were to be adorned with this memorial of the God who had redeemed him, and to whom he especially owed his allegiance. The believer is constantly to keep in view his heavenly origin, and to remember, he is not of the world, even as Christ is not of the world. He should gaze continually on the face of Him, who has manifested the love of God in giving His life for his redemption. God, in the gift of Jesus, has proved that love is inseparable from holiness; and if we reflect His character, we shall, in our ordinary ways, display something of the grace and purity, which pre-eminently shone forth from the Son of God. As holy brethren, partakers of the heavenly calling, we have to consider the Apostle and High Priest of our profession, and thereby we shall be more and more conformed to His likeness, and adorn the doctrine of God our Saviour. The heart first, and the eye next, can only be kept from lusting after the things of the world and of the flesh, by being fixed on heavenly things.

The touch of faith drew out cleansing virtue from the border of His garment, who was truly the Heavenly One; and as we, by faith, hear, see with our eyes, look upon, and handle, the Word of life; as we exercise our every spiritual sense in contemplating Christ; so shall we be practically holy, and have the adorning of the hidden man of the heart, in that which is not corruptible, but which will be made manifest in the meek and quiet spirit, which is, in the sight of God, of great price: " That ye might walk worthy of the Lord unto all pleasing, being fruitful in every good work, and increasing in the knowledge of God." " As ye have therefore received Christ Jesus the Lord, *so* walk ye in him.—Col. i. 10.; ii. 6.

The Blue colour in the vail, and other hangings of the Tabernacle, may therefore, without assuming any fanciful interpretations, represent the gracious and holy character of God, who is Love, as displayed in the Lord Jesus.

THE SCARLET.—As blue is peculiarly the colour of the heavens, so, scarlet is the gorgeous colour belonging to earth. The flowers, the produce of the soil, display its brilliant tints. We do not look above to find it: but it meets our eye when we contemplate the flowers of the field. The Word of God also employs this colour as an emblem of royalty. The beast, and the woman in the Revelation, are both represented as scarlet. Not that the scarlet of itself, denotes evil; but because the kingdoms of the world were held under their regal sway

And, when the Lord Jesus was, in mockery, hailed as king, the soldiers of imperial Rome clothed him with a scarlet robe.* Matthew xxvii. 28.

This colour, in the Vail, seems therefore to typify the perfect human kingly glory of the Lord Jesus. He was, by birth, of the royal line of David ; David's son, as well as David's Lord. He was *born* King of the Jews ; having title to the throne, and sovereignty of the world, not only by descent, but He was truly a king, by virtue of his own intrinsic excellency.

At his creation, Adam had dominion conferred on him by God. All things of this earth were put under him. But he debased himself by giving credit to one who was classed as of the beasts of the field ; for it is written of the serpent, to whom man yielded his allegiance, that " he was more subtle than any *beast of the field*, which the Lord God had made." Gen. iii. 1. Adam was not indeed deceived, as Eve was ; but he participated in her sin, and thus both parents of the human race for ever lost their legitimate place of authority.

A true king would neither come in his own name, nor accept his kingdom from any, but from God. Too exalted for ambition ; satisfied with the favour of God, and owning no other as Lord over him ; contented to be His servant, in meekness and righteousness would he triumph. Combining mercy and truth in all his actions, and uniting boldness and courage with pitifulness and courtesy, he would scatter away all evil with his eyes, and would plead for those who are appointed to destruction. Liberal of heart and having a bountiful eye, he would give bread to the poor and needy. Unerring with his mouth as to judgment, a divine sentence would ever proceed from his lips. In the light of his countenance

---

* NOTE.—In the Gospels by Mark and John, the robe is said to be PURPLE : in Luke, no colour is specified, but it is simply called a gorgeous robe. The difference between scarlet and purple, according to the present estimation of these colours, seems hardly to have been recognised of old. But the royal purple of the ancients was what we should now term scarlet, or, it may be, crimson — Purple, in our days, inclines strongly to blue

would be life; and his favour, as a cloud of the latter rain.  These are some of the leading features of the royal character, portrayed in the Word of God: and such was the Son of Man.

The blind beggar discerned, in the despised and rejected One, the true Son of David.  He saw the royal colour; whilst others, who had eyes, perceived it not.  And the woman of Canaan put Israel to shame, for she, though a dog, recognised her royal master.  Once, for a moment only, the multitude owned their meek and lowly King.  They caught a transient glimpse of His majesty and glory.  But soon they lifted up, in shame and dishonour, on the tree, Him whom they had welcomed, a little while before, as their rightful sovereign.  Never did His glory shine forth more resplendently, than when His crown was thus trampled under foot.  Never did the Royal One so prove His own majesty, as when disowned by all, and even cast off by God.  The exaltation of the cross was His one step to the throne of God.  He manifested Himself, when hanging on the tree, so glorious and so worthy, that no place was high enough, but that at the right hand of Jehovah: no name sufficiently dignified, but "the name that is above every name."

The true dignity of man was blessedly maintained and exhibited by Christ when tempted of the devil, as recorded in Matt. iv. 1—4.  Eve, when surrounded by all that bespoke God's care and kindness, mistrusted His love, and believed the insinuated lie of Satan, viz: that God had withheld the best fruit lest she should become, by eating it, like Himself.  Her ambition was stirred; she desired to be greater than she was.  Her eye also was attracted by the beauty of the fruit, and her heart received the whisper of the enemy.  She gave credit to the devil in preference to God.  She took and ate, and gave to her husband, and he did eat: and the dignity and honour of the creature, Man, was voluntarily surrendered to the unclean apostate spirit, Satan.  "Dust thou art," was all that could now be said of the fallen lord of creation : and there was no power in him to regain his lost greatness.

Let us now mark the contrast displayed by the Son of God. In a wilderness, surrounded by wild beasts, an hungered, and apparently deserted by God, Satan desired, if possible, to induce the blessed Lord to act independently of His Father ; to provide Himself with the bread which He needed for His sustainment, by a simple act of His own power. But he answered the tempter, not by asserting His dignity, as being Himself God, but by keeping His own subject place as man. He proved Himself thus above the control of the circumstances in which He was placed, and above yielding even to His own need. Again assailed by the enemy with the suggestion as to whether God's Word were true, and therefore, would it not be well to test its faithfulness ? He not only maintained His perfect reliance on that Word, but proved His obedience to its commands. And when, as a last device, the tempter spread out before Christ such a vision of earthly glory as human eyes had never beheld, and sought, by that enticement, to allure Him from His allegiance to God; the Lord, taking, for a moment, His kingly seat of judgment, drove the wicked one from before Him ; at the same time preserving His humble, yet happy position as a worshipper of the Most High. Throughout this wondrous scene the kingly colour, the scarlet, is most manifest.

Two Hebrew words are united in all the passages in Exodus relating to the Tabernacle, where our word, *scarlet*, occurs. The first of these, (tohlahgh,) is translated *worm* in the following texts: " The son of man, which is a worm." Job xxv. 6. " I am a worm, and no man." Psa. xxii. 6. " Fear not, thou worm, Jacob." Isa. xli. 14. The other word, (shahnee,) is of doubtful signification. Some suppose it to mean *double-dyed*. In the margin of Proverbs xxxi. 21, *double garments* is the rendering suggested instead of scarlet, where the Hebrew word occurs. In Isa. i. 18, both words occur separately. "Though your sins be as scarlet, (shahnee,) they shall be white as snow: though they be red like crimson, (tohlahgh,) they shall be as wool." In this verse, perhaps, the first word, (shahnee,) is used to imply the *depth* of the dye ; and the latter, (tohlahgh,) its glaring colour, *red*. Others suggest, that the two words used together, express the kind of insect, (coccus,) from which this colour was extracted. It is remarkable that our most brilliant dye is procured from it.

Is there not some deep instruction to be gained from these Hebrew words? On the one hand, do they not teach us, that, however gloriously attired through human agency, however dignified with human greatness, the robe of honour, after all, is but the produce of a worm, and covers but a worm? And we read in Isaiah xiv. 11, that the king of Babylon, who is hereafter to be clothed with regal splendour and dignity heretofore unknown on earth, so as to exceed even his predecessor Nebuchadnezzar, the king of kings, in greatness and glory, will be brought down to the grave, where the crimson worms will be his bed and his covering.

On the other hand, does not this word *worm*, or the scarlet colour derived from it, instruct us as to the humiliation of the blessed Lord? He made Himself of no reputation, when He took upon Him the form of a servant, and was made in the likeness of men. He who was equal with God, was found in fashion as a man. The blue of the heavens was connected with the scarlet of the worm. And at length, on the cross, in the depth of His self-abasement, and under the judgment of God, He exclaims, "I am a worm, and no man ; a reproach of men, and despised of the people." But what a glorious display of the perfect Man was this! How that dazzling colour has been, as it were, expressed : so that now we behold it on the throne of the Majesty in the heavens.

Purple.—If we were to place the blue and the scarlet side by side, without the intervention of some other colour, the eye would be offended with the violent contrast; for, though each is beautiful in itself, and suitable to its own sphere, yet there is such a distinction, we might almost say opposition, in their hues, as to render them inharmonious if seen in immediate contact. The purple interposed, remedies this unpleasing effect: the eye passes with ease from the blue to the scarlet, and vice versa, by the aid of this blended colour, the purple. The blue gradually shades off into its opposite, the scarlet; and the gorgeousness of the latter is softened by imperceptible degrees into the blue. The purple is a new colour, formed by mingling the two: it owes its peculiar beauty alike to both: and were the due proportion of either absent, its especial character would be lost.

The order of the colours, blue, purple, scarlet, repeated at least twenty.four times in Exodus, is never varied. The scarlet and the blue are never placed in juxta-position throughout the fabrics of the Tabernacle. Does not this intimate a truth of an important character? Would the Spirit of God have so constantly adhered to this arrangement had there not been some significant reason for it? Are we not hereby taught a very precious fact respecting the Lord Jesus? He is God and Man: and we can trace in the Gospels all the fulness of the Godhead, as well as the dignity and sympathy of the perfect Man. But, besides this, in His thoughts, feelings, words, ways, and actions, there is an invariable blending of the two. Many mistakes and errors would have been avoided, in the Church of God, if those, who have undertaken to write or speak on this subject, had been subject to the definite words of Scripture, instead of adopting abstract reasonings upon the divinity and humanity of the Son of God. .The Christ of God is the object of our faith; not a nature, or natures, but Himself. He was born of the Virgin, though HE eternally existed as the Son of God: HE died on the Cross, though He is the Mighty God. The importance of this little word HE, cannot be over-rated. The Apostle John was so intimately acquainted with his Lord, that in his first epistle, he constantly refers to Him, without mentioning His name; as if assured that the hearts of his readers would be so filled with the same blessed object that occupied him, that they would at once know to whom he alluded. See especially chap. iii, 2—7.

In contemplating Christ, it is well ever to remember the first syllable of His name, as given us in Isaiah ix, 6. "WONDERFUL:" and part of this marvel is, that in Him are combined the deep thoughts and counsels of God, with the feelings and affections of man. In Him there is no incongruity; in the days of His flesh, and on the cross itself, He was "*the same*," the "I AM," the Son of God, Jesus Christ, the same yesterday, and to-day, and for ever. He could say, whilst on earth, "The Son, which is in the bosom of the Father." When speaking to Nicodemus, in that memorable meeting by night, He said, "No man hath ascended up to heaven, but He that came down from heaven, even the Son of Man which is in heaven." And subsequently, when some of His disciples murmured at the difficulties raised in their carnal minds by His words of life, His answer was—"Doth this offend you? What, and if ye shall see the Son of Man ascend up where He was before?" (John vi, 61, 62.) Such words as these, from the lips of the Son of God, should silence our fleshly reasonings, and cause us to bow down and worship, instead of attempting to fathom that which is unfathomable. Vain of our own conceit, we try, with our puny resources, to sound the depths; and fancy, when we have run out our little line, that we have reached the bottom. We cut and square systems of divinity, and stamp, with our imprimatur, as orthodox, the theology of this or that divine; and all the while, lose sight of HIM, in whom are hid all the treasures of wisdom and knowledge. Man can applaud his fellow; for, in so doing, he praises himself. He can approve the sayings of another; for, thereby, he constitutes himself a judge. And thus, in the divinity of the day, we shall find that creeds, confessions of faith, and writings of the Fathers, really assume the place of the Word of God: and orthodoxy consists, not in holding what God says, but in subscribing to articles drawn up by fallible man.

Three instances are recorded in the Gospels, of the dead being raised to life by Christ : Jairus's daughter, the widow of Nain's son, and Lazarus of Bethany. Together, they afford us a complete display of His mighty power : for, in the first case, death had only just seized its victim ; in the second, the sorrowing mother was on her way, to commit the body of her only son to the grave , in the third, the corpse had already been deposited some time, and had become corrupt in the tomb. In each of these remarkable scenes, the colours of the Vail may be traced. We can have no hesitation in recognising the *Blue*, in the manifestation of the love of God, when His blessed Son, at the entreaty of the sorrowing father, went to the house, to heal the dying child. On the way, the message came to the ruler, " Thy daughter is dead : why troublest thou the Master any further ? " Little did they, who spake these words, understand who that Master was ; or the depths of trouble, in which He would be overwhelmed, in order that the dead might live. They knew not that God was present with them, manifest in the flesh : but He at once stilled the fear of the damsel's father , thus doing what none but God could do ; commanding peace into his bosom, in the very presence of death. Again, the voice of the Mighty God sounds forth, to hush the boisterous grief of those who had no hope, saying " Weep not: the damsel is not dead, but sleepeth." But they perceived not who it was that thus spoke. Death was to them a familiar sight ; they knew its power : but they laughed Christ to scorn. Ought not the believer exactly to reverse this ? In the presence of the Lord, he may well laugh death to scorn.

Lastly; how were the power and the grace of the One
from heaven made known, when He spake those words—
"Damsel, I say unto thee, arise ! "

Let us now turn to the *scarlet* in this beautiful picture.
Who but the Son of Man, would have pursued the path
of kindness and sympathy, notwithstanding the rude
scoffs, with which His ready love was met? and who,
but one that knew what exhaustion and hunger were,
would have added, to this mighty miracle, the command
"Give her something to eat"? And does not this also
exhibit to us the *purple?* With sympathy and love for
the child, deeper than the mother's, and yet present in
the scene as one who was Lord in it, and above it ; He
can call the dead to life, and at the same moment, enter
into the minutest want of the little maid. The mere
human beings who were present, even the very parents,
were so overpowered with what they had witnessed, and
with the joy of receiving back the dead one to life, that
their human sympathies failed. None but God could
thus have abolished death : and none, but He who was
God and Man, could so have combined power, majesty,
grace, sympathy, and tenderest care.

The next instance already alluded to, depicts in few
but full sentences, the beautiful tints of the Vail. Un-
solicited, the Son of God went to the city where He
knew the stroke of death had fallen, and had inflicted
another wound upon a heart already stricken with grief.
He timed His visit so as to meet, at the gate, the
mournful procession, bearing to the grave the only son
of a widowed mother. If any hope of God's interference had at one time cheered her whilst she watched
her dying child, all such hope must now have fled. A
little interval only remained, and the earth would close
over her lost son. But attracted by the very extremity
of the case, He, who declared the Father, drew nigh.
With the authority of God, He touched the bier, and
arrested the bearers in their progress to the tomb. Struck
by a sudden consciousness that they were in the presence

of One who had a right to stop them on their way, they
stood still ; they did not, like the attendants on the dead
in the former case, laugh Him to scorn ; and therefore,
they had the blessing of witnessing His mighty act.  He
commanded the young man to arise from the bier, as He
ordered the child to arise from her bed ; and in like
manner He was obeyed.  " He, that was dead, sat up,
and began to speak."  Here, then, the heavenly colour
was evident ; so that even they that looked on, said,
" God hath visited His people."  But the heart of Christ
was occupied with the mother as well as with the son.
As the voice of the risen youth reached His ear, He
knew how the widow felt as she heard it.  Himself
undistracted by the exercise of His life-giving power, yet
fully occupied in sympathy and grace with the yearning
of the mother to embrace her son, and thus to assure
herself of the reality, which even the evidence of her
eyes and ears scarcely enabled her to credit, He gave
completeness to the scene by delivering him to his
mother.  Here was the perfection of human sensibility,
such as no man could have exhibited in such circumstances, unless that man were also God.

But perhaps the most complete manifestation of " the
Word made flesh" is to be found in John xi., if we
except, as we must always do, the Cross, where all was
marvellously concentrated.  It seemed to the sisters as
if the Lord had strangely disregarded their urgent message : for, He still abode at a distance, and allowed not
only death to bereave them of their brother, but the
grave to close upon his remains.  His very reply to their
announcement, (" Lord, behold, he whom thou lovest, is
sick,") contained in it a paradox which they were unable
to comprehend, and which the subsequent circumstances
apparently falsified ; for, His answer was, " This sickness is not unto death, but for the glory of God, that
the Son of God might be glorified thereby."  And yet
He tarried till death had, for four days, retained its
victim.

Thus, love and truth in Him who is Love, and who is the Truth, for a while appeared to have failed ; but in reality the glory of God was the more to shine forth in His Beloved. It was, to Mary and Martha, as if the Vail had suddenly lost its colours. The short suspense, however helped them to discover fresh and deeper beauties in that curiously wrought fabric.

What mingled feelings occupied the heart of Christ, when, seeing the grief of Mary, and of those around, He groaned in the spirit, and was troubled! He grieved over their unbelief and ignorance of Himself: and yet He wept in sympathy with them, and sorrowed for the very sorrow which His presence might have prevented. Who could have shed tears in such circumstances but Christ? Had a mere man been gifted by God with the power to raise the dead, he would be so eager to exhibit that mighty power, and thereby to still the mourners' grief, that he would be unable to weep whilst on the way to the grave. He must be more than man who could display what man in perfection is. The tears of Jesus are precious, because they are those of true human feeling : but they are most precious because they flow from the heart of Him who is the Mighty God. And when those tears plenteously fell from His eyes, all questions as to His love were at an end ; and even the Jews exclaimed, " Behold, how He loved him." Again another groan burst from Christ as He drew nigh to the sepulchre : for, not only was his heart sorely pained because of the inroad that death had made in this once united family, tearing asunder the most cherished human relationships; but it may be also that the cave, with its door of stone, presented to Him in anticipation the sepulchre to which he was fast hastening, and that fearful death upon the tree where He for a season was to experience the forsaking, even of His God, whose bosom had been His dwelling-place from all eternity. This second time He groaned *in Himself*.

As with authority He had touched the bier, so now He commanded that the stone should be removed. But Martha interposed her objections ; and though she owned Christ as Lord, and had heard, from His lips, the wondrous words, " I am the Resurrection and the Life," yet she believed not that there could be a remedy for one who had already seen corruption. It was then that Jesus reminded her of the message he had returned when they sent to inform Him of Lazarus's sickness— that it should not be unto death, but for the glory of God, by answering, " Said I not unto thee, that, if thou wouldest believe, thou shouldest see the glory of God?" God's glory was ever His object : and to accomplish that, He had been content to bear the questioning of those dear to Him, who could not understand why He had not at once come to their aid.

The sepulchre was now laid open ; and Jesus lifted up His eyes from that receptacle of death to the heaven above, resting His spirit in the bosom of His Father, and audibly expressing His dependence on Him, before he cried, with a voice of almighty power, " Lazarus, come forth." What a wondrous blending was here of subjection and authority, of obedience and command, of " the opened ear," and of the great " I Am."

The dead, hearing the voice of the Son of God, came forth. The corrupting corpse stepped out in life. What a moment of astonishment and delight must that have been to the sisters, as well as to their brother ! But here again the Lord alone entered into the minutest details of this astonishing act of His power. He saw, or rather felt, (for He loved Lazarus,) that His friend was still encumbered with the relics of the grave ; and He left it not till others awoke from their surprise, to perceive the clothes that bound and troubled the risen one, but gave another command, " Loose him, and let him go."

Jesus is the second man from heaven, made like unto His brethren, yet not of the earth, earthy; that Holy thing born of the Virgin, partaker of flesh and blood, yet incorrupt and incorruptible; in Him are inseparably united God and Man; yet He is the One Christ, manifesting that which is altogether new, viz.: the perfect blending of all that is of God, with all that is proper to man. Nor can we ever contemplate Him, unless we keep in view the mystery of His person. God, in sending His beloved Son, has given to man and angels a new object of attraction. He enables us to behold the brightness of His glory; yet in such a manner, that we are not terrified or struck down by the sight. We can also look upon man in perfect union with God. All such expressions as, "the Divinity being in abeyance," "the Divine nature sustaining His human nature," "Divinity enshrined in humanity," and the like, are attempts to explain to human understanding, that which can only be received by faith: they are the efforts of intellect to grasp that which is beyond human scan; and in measure falsify the great truth, "The Word made flesh."

The Jew saw no beauty in Christ to admire: he could only perceive an afflicted man of sorrows. The believer, at the same moment beheld His glory, the glory as of the only-begotten of the Father, full of grace and truth. The type we have been considering especially teaches these truths: for, all the colours were curiously wrought with the fine linen, so as form one mass of cherubim; a vail instinct with life and power, manifesting glory and beauty.

It will be seen that, in Exodus xxxvi. 35, the word "with" is in italics before "cherubim:" the vail being so fashioned as to present nothing but cherubim. Much has been written on these emblematical figures; and the reader will find the subject more fully expounded in the work on the Holy Vessels before mentioned, under the article, "The Mercy-Seat." Many have supposed that the Church is symbolised by the cherubim in Exodus. But the fact of their forming the vail seems to preclude

this interpretation. As the vail shadows forth Christ in
the flesh, we cannot suppose that any type would be
given representing the union of the Church with Him
then; as, before death, the corn of wheat abode alone:
it must die, in order to bring forth fruit. The union of
the believer with Christ is in life, quickened together
with Him; seated in heavenly places in Him. He was
the *substitute* in death; but He is the last Adam, the
head of the new family, and source of its existence
in resurrection.

The lion (one of the four faces of the cherubim) is
classed with the king, against whom there is no rising
up, in Prov. xxx, 30, 31; and is also described as going
well, and being comely in going; and as strongest
among beasts, turning not away from any. Majesty,
strength, and courage, are therefore here typified.

The ox, in addition to its well-known character for
patient enduring labour, is also recognised in Scripture
as knowing its owner; herein it may prefigure the
persevering resolution of Him who unflinchingly set His
shoulder to the arduous work committed to Him by His
Father, and who always recognised His Father's will,
and delighted to do it.

The way of an eagle in the air is alluded to in
Prov. xxx, 19. as too wonderful to be known: referring
probably to the astonishing extent and accuracy of its
vision as to things of earth, when poised aloft; and to
its swiftness of flight when the object of its search is
discovered. Fit emblem this of Him, whose eyes search
the depths of the heart, and who is as rapid in discovering
where the lawful prey is, as in delivering it from the
power of the destroyer.

These three faces, combined with the human face
and form, completed the cherubim: for all this power,
labour, activity, and quickness of perception, were put
forth under the control and guidance of perfect wisdom
and sympathy. Wings were also spread abroad
over the surface of the vail, proceeding from the

cherubim; denoting the heavenly origin and unearthly ways of the Son of Man, who was "from above," and who could say, even while here, "The Son of Man, who is in heaven."

The vail, blue, and purple, and scarlet, and fine twined linen, and cherubim was made " of cunning work," or, as it might be translated, "the work of a deviser." It was skilfully wrought with wisdom and cunning device; a matchless fabric, copied from a heavenly pattern, and never again to find its equal on earth : type of Him who said "A body has Thou prepared me." Gabriel's words to Mary betoken the wonder of Immanuel's birth. "The Holy Ghost shall come upon thee, and the power of the Highest shall overshadow thee. Therefore also that holy thing, which shall be born of thee, shall be called the Son of God." She conceived in her womb, and brought forth a son, and called his name Jesus. He was the Son of the Highest, and to Him, the Lord God gave the throne of His father David : and He shall reign over the house of Jacob for ever: and of His Kingdom there shall be no end. (Luke i. 28—35.) Wondrous mystery ! the Virgin's Son, and yet the Son of God : the Son of the Highest, and yet inheriting the throne of His father David : the Child born, the Son given; His name, Wonderful, Counseller, the Mighty God, the Everlasting Father, the Prince of Peace : Jesus, Immanuel, to whom every knee shall bow, and who is the object of the church's contemplation and worship on earth; and the subject of eternal song in glory for ever. May we ever be filled with reverence and godly fear, when speaking or meditating on Him. The precincts of the tabernacle are holy ground: and before we view the great sight of God manifested in the flesh, we must loose the shoes from off our feet.

The Hebrew word, translated Vail, is, according to Gesenius, derived from an unused verb signifying to *break*, and in a secondary sense, to *separate*. It is called the Vail *of the covering*. (Exod. xxxix. 34 : xl. 21.

Num. **iv.** 5.) It was hung up, in order to separate between the holy place and the most holy, and also to cover or hide the ark, (Exod. xxvi. 33 ; and xl. 3.) And when the tabernacle moved, the vail was taken down, and thrown over the ark as its first covering. As long as the Lord Jesus was in the flesh, His very presence on earth declared the impossibility of any one approaching God excepting Himself, or unless having His perfectness.—He stood as the Perfect Man, who alone was fit to appear before God; the standard weight of the sanctuary. Any one, weighed against Him, was found wanting. His perfect righteousness placed in dark shade the uncleanness of all men. The measure of His stature declared the utter insignificance of all human attainments. His fulness proved man's emptiness. The white and glistening purity of His character, exceeding white as snow, put to shame the filthiness of all that was born of woman·

Thus, the very display of the Perfect One on earth, showed the impossibility of any approach to God, unless some way could be devised, whereby the sinner could draw near, clothed in garments equally unsullied. Man, both Jew and Gentile, had made it plain that he was by nature a sinner, and had come short of the glory of God : and the presence, amongst men, of One who was fit for that glory, only rendered the melancholy fact more apparent. The vail, as it hung on its golden pillars, precluded entrance into the holiest: the ark and mercy-seat were hidden, instead of being laid open to public gaze.

The whole ritual of Jewish worship, under the law, was one that served to maintain the distance between God and the creature. Bounds were set about Sinai, so that not even a beast must touch it: and the people felt, their safest place was far off. One tribe alone was permitted to encamp around the tabernacle: one family alone of that tribe was singled out to be allowed to enter the holy place: and one man alone of that family had access to the holiest; and that, only once a year, and with such preparations, and fearful ceremonies, as must have inspired him with dread, lest, in the very act of approacn, through some omission, he might incur the judgment of the Most High.

The incarnation of the Blessed Lord, and His subsequent sojourn here, presented in themselves no gospel to the sinner: the requirements of a holy God were only made more manifest. A vail unrent, a mercy-seat without blood, might indeed exhibit what the glory of God required, but could not advance the ruined sinner towards that glory, or throw open the way of access.

## THE RENT VAIL

EACH dispensation, as it succeeded that which went before, only the more shut up man in the hopelessness of his misery. It left him manifestly worse at the close, than it found him at its commencement. The Law and Prophets effected no deliverance; the former, instead of proving a remedy for sin, became its strength; the latter were slain and persecuted, and afterwards their memory was honoured by the children of those who had so used them, and who thought themselves better than their fathers. At length, in the fulness of the time, God sent forth His Son, made of a woman, made under the law. The second man, the brightness of God's glory, appeared on earth. Still, nothing was effected. He came into the world, and the world was made by Him, and the world knew Him not. He came unto His own; and His own received Him not. The world, in the stupidity of its brutish ignorance, caused by sin, recognised not its Lord. Israel, still worse, conscious to some extent of His presence, wilfully despised and rejected Him, treating Him with the scorn and derision, which devils dared not to offer.

"The Word, made flesh," dwelling among men, and going about ceaselessly doing good, was not the fullest manifestation of the love of God. Man himself felt rebuked by the presence of the Holy One, rather than attracted ; he might, for a moment, be startled at the glory, beauty, and grace, manifested in Him whom the vail typified : but soon the contrast with himself made him hate the perfect One. The *way* into the immediate presence of God was not made manifest as long as the vail remained unrent. Two things had to be accomplished. God must declare His love after such a manner that the mouth of every gainsayer might be stopped, and man be left without excuse ; besides which, a way of access must be prepared, so that the vilest sinner covered with all his filthiness, might, without one attempt at self-amendment, be welcomed to the presence and heart of the Father. To effect these objects, God counted nothing too costly. The Wonderful One for whom He had prepared a body, and whom He had sent into the world, whom he delighted to contemplate, and on whom His eternal love rested with unabated fulness and complacency, was bruised, and utterly marred in death. But who can tell the feelings of His heart, when, compelled by His love to us, He spared not His own Son ? Or, who can tell the sufferings of that Son, when bruised by the hand, and pierced by the arrows, of the Almighty ?

The following is the record, in three Gospels, of the rending of the Vail :—

Matt. xxvii. 46—52.—"And about the ninth hour Jesus cried with a loud voice, saying, Eli, Eli, lama sabachthani ? that is to say, my God, my God, why hast thou forsaken me ? Some of them that stood there, when they heard that, said, This man calleth for Elias. And straightway one of them ran, and took a sponge, and filled it with vinegar, and put it on a reed, and gave him to drink. The rest said, Let be, let us see whether

Elias will come to save him.   Jesus, when he had cried
again with a loud voice, yielded up the ghost.   And, behold, the vail of the temple was rent in twain from the
top to the bottom : and the earth did quake, and the
rocks rent; and the graves were opened."

Mark xv. 34—38—"And at the ninth hour Jesus cried
with a loud voice, saying, Eloi, Eloi, lama Sabachthani?
which is, being interpreted, My God, my God, why
hast thou forsaken me?   And some of them that stood
by, when they heard it, said, Behold, he calleth Elias.
And one ran and filled a sponge full of vinegar, and put
it on a reed, and gave him to drink, saying, Let alone :
let us see whether Elias will come to take him down.
And Jesus cried with a loud voice, and gave up the
ghost.   And the vail of the temple was rent in twain
from the top to the bottom."

Luke xxiii. 44—46—"And it was about the sixth hour,
and there was a darkness over all the earth until the ninth
hour.   And the sun was darkened, and the vail of the
temple was rent in the midst.   And when Jesus had
cried with a loud voice, he said, Father, into thy hands
I commend my spirit : and having said thus, he gave up
the ghost."

Although it was the vail of the *temple* that was rent.
yet it is to be remarked that in the Epistle to the
Hebrews, where we have the explanation given what
the vail typified, "that is to say, His flesh," reference is
alone made to the *tabernacle*.

The temple embodied in its type, a dispensation
beyond the present, and cannot be so exclusively used
as a shadow of heavenly things, while the Church is
passing through this world, like Israel in the wilderness.
Throughout this epistle, no allusion is made to the
existence of the temple, although in fact it was then
standing: and the rending of the vail is made to have the
same import as the passing away of the earthly tabernacle:
(compare Heb. ix, 3, 8, with x, 20.)   It may also be
observed, that the Ark was the only vessel of the

Tabernacle, which was, as originally made, placed in the Temple, the other vessels being all fashioned anew; and the Vail was also the only hanging which preserved an analogy between the temple and the tabernacle. It seems to have been perpetuated in the temple, to the end that it might be thus significantly rent.

In the Gospels of Matthew and Mark, as above quoted, the same expression is repeated, "rent in twain from the top to the bottom." The only type in which God Himself, represented by His own act, the great and most wonderful truth respecting the death of Christ, viz: that He, with His own hand, smote the Lord Jesus. Many are the allusions to this in the Old Testament Scriptures, " He that is hanged is the curse of God." (Deut. xxi. 23.) " THOU hast brought me into the dust of death." (Psa. xxii. 15.) "THINE arrows stick fast in me, and THINE hand presseth me sore." (Psa. xxxviii. 2.) "All THY waves and THY billows are gone over me." (Psa. xlii. 7.) "THOU hast laid me in the lowest pit, in darkness in the deeps. THY wrath lieth hard upon me, and THOU hast afflicted me with all THY waves. THY fierce wrath goeth over me; THY terrors have cut me off." (Psa. lxxxviii. 6, 7, 16.) "It pleased Jehovah to bruise Him: He hath put Him to grief." (Isaiah liii. 10.) "Awake, O sword, against my shepherd, and against the man that is my fellow, saith Jehovah of hosts; smite the Shepherd." (Zec. xiii. 7.) This was, to the Blessed Lord, the most terrible element in the cup of judgment which he drank. The grape was trodden in the winepress of the fierceness and wrath of Almighty God. The corn of wheat was bruised between the upper and nether millstone of His righteous indignation. The oil was beaten from the olive, under the heavy pressure of His hand. When the Lord was crucified, we behold all the powers of hell, earth, and heaven, arrayed against Him. He was lifted up between earth and heaven; the fountains of the great deep spouted up their billows from beneath, and the windows of heaven poured down the water-spouts of Divine vengeance from above.

In the death of Christ, we have marvellously combined Satan's power; man used as the instrument in killing the Prince of Life; God smiting Him; and yet no one took His life from Him. He laid it down of Himself, with the same power by which He took it again in resurrection; and this, in obedience to the command of His Father.

No human hand rent the vail in twain ; neither was it torn from the bottom towards the top ; but a hand from above rent it from the top to the bottom. Access to the heaven of heavens was to be laid open ; no love and no power could either have devised or accomplished this, but the love and power of God.

In the Gospel of Luke, the rending of the vail is mentioned as if it had occurred during the three hours of darkness, and before the Lord Jesus gave up the ghost. May it not be, that in accordance with the *order* of this Gospel, (which is rather a spiritual than a chronological order,) it is so inserted, to direct our thoughts to the fact, that during those hours of darkness, the hand of judgment from God lay in unmitigated weight on the soul of the Lamb of God ? The period was one, during the whole of which, He was being rent from above.

In Luke, also, the expression " in the midst" is substituted for " from the top to the bottom." Here, another blessed feature is added to the truth typified by this act of God. The vail hung upon four pillars ; and the ark was placed in the centre of the holiest ; so that, the vail being rent in the midst, from the top to the bottom, a way of approach was made *directly* to the very centre of the mercy-seat, where, between the cherubim, the God of glory dwelt. It was not a *side* access, but the shortest and most direct that could be made, to the fore-front of the ark.

The rending of the vail made an entire change in the dispensation. Up to that time, the tabernacle and priesthood, connected with the law, stood in their integrity. Heb. ix. 8 states, that as long as the first tabernacle was standing, the way into the holiest was not made manifest. Not that the tabernacle was actually standing when the vail was rent, but, as the Greek expresses it, it had yet a *standing*, or existence, dispensationally; for the first covenant, with which it was connected, had not waxed old and passed away. When however, the vail was rent, all the exclusive privileges which the law had established, were abolished; distinctions in the flesh were at an end : the first covenant, with its ministration of death, was for ever superseded by the second, established upon the blood of Him whom the vail typified. The same hand that rent the beautiful fabric which hitherto had concealed the holiest of all, opened simultaneously the graves ; one act of God laid open the way, even from the ruin and death caused by sin, up to the height of His own glory. Henceforth no human priest was needed to stand between the sinner and God. No steps of approach were prepared in order that, by slow degrees, the unclean might be gradually fitted to draw nigh. The way from the grave to the glory was but one step ; by the blood, through the vail, the sinner, however guilty, however unclean, might at once with boldness take his place before the throne overshadowed by the Cherubim of Glory.

Creation also heaved in convulsive throes, for " the end of the world" had come : and all that was old, and which could be shaken, was to be removed, to make way for the new heavens and the new earth, wherein dwelleth righteousness. True, this blessed consummation has not yet arrived : God still waits to be gracious ; but the whole period which has elapsed since the death of the blessed Lord, has only been one of long-suffering : for, the Cross stood, in the counsels of God, at the end of all things ; and the believer himself is able, by faith, to say, " If any man be in Christ, (to him there is) a new creation : old things are passed away ; behold, all things are become new : and all things are of God " (2 Cor. v. 17, 18).

The vail of the tabernacle divided between the holy and the most holy places. (Exod. xxvi. 33.) The sons of Aaron, the priests, ministered in the holy place : the congregation of Israel had no access into it. The high priest alone entered the most holy, and that only once a year. All believers in Christ are not only worshippers, like Israel, but priests. " Unto Him that loved us, and washed us from our sins in His own blood, and hath made us kings and priests unto God and His Father." Rev. i. 5, 6.

The exhortation in Heb. x. 19, contemplates this priestly standing of believers ; they have liberty to enter into the *holy places* (see original) through the rent vail, the new and living way, which Jesus has newly made. The passage beautifully expresses the two thoughts of life and newness, inseparably connected with this way, in contrast with the old covenant and its ceremonial observances of dead works, which never advanced the sinner a step nearer to God. Besides this, access is *in the blood;* because, not only is the way made, but the worshipper himself has a perfect priestly sanctification thereby, and is perfectly fit to draw near to God. The holiest, also, was thrown open ; and though there can only be one Great High Priest, the Lord Jesus Himself, yet all believers, seeing they constitute the royal priesthood, have the same high-priestly standing, as regards their nearness of approach to God in the holiest.

# THE PILLARS OF THE VAIL

Exod. xxvi. 32.—"And thou shalt hang it upon four pillars of shittim wood overlaid with gold: their hooks shall be of gold, upon the four sockets of silver."

Exod. xxxvi. 36—"And he made thereunto four pillars of shittim wood, and overlaid them with gold: their hooks were of gold; and he cast for them four sockets of silver."

THE pillars of the vail were four in number (Exod. xxvi. 32 ; and xxxvi. 36.)   Unlike those on which hung the curtain for the tabernacle-door, they had no capitals ; thus they lacked the ordinary architectural completeness of a pillar.   May not our thoughts be directed by this, to the contemplation of those Scriptures which speak of the Lord as *cut off*? (Isa. liii. 8.)   " Who shall declare His generation ?   For He was cut off out of the land of the living."   And Psa. cii. 23, 24, " He shortened my days : I said, O my God, take me not away in the midst of my days ! "   And yet the very fact of this seemingly abrupt termination of the life of the Lord Jesus, in the days of His flesh, has made Him to be unto us " wisdom, righteousness, sanctification, and redemption :" a fourfold perfection, meeting our fourfold need ;  to which possibly the number of vail-pillars may allude.

# THE CURTAINS OF THE TABERNACLE

Exod. xxvi 1—3 —" Moreover thou shalt make the tabernacle ten curtains of fine twined linen, and blue, and purple, and scarlet; cherubims of cunning work shalt thou make them.

"The length of one curtain shall be eight and twenty cubits, and the breadth of one curtain four cubits: and every one of the curtains shall have one measure.

"The five curtains shall be coupled together one to another; and other five curtains shall be coupled one to another."

Exod. xxxvi 8—10—"And every wise hearted man among them that wrought the work of the tabernacle made ten curtains of fine twined linen, and blue, and purple, and scarlet: cherubims of cunning work made he them.

"The length of one curtain was twenty and eight cubits, and the breadth of one curtain four cubits: the curtains were all of one size.

"And he coupled the five curtains one unto another: and the other five curtains he coupled one unto another."

THE framework of the tabernacle was made of boards of shittim-wood, overlaid with gold, standing in sockets of silver. Over these boards which enclosed an area of 30 cubits by 10, were thrown two sets of curtains, and two coverings, forming what may be called the roof of the building, and hanging down over the back and two sides. The first and innermost set of curtains are emphatically called " The Tabernacle."

" Thou shalt make the *tabernacle*, ten curtains." Exod. xxvi. 1. " The work of the *tabernacle*, ten curtains." Exod. xxxvi. 8. " And it shall be *one tabernacle*." Exod. xxvi. 6. Also xxxvi, 13. " curtains of goats' hair, a covering upon the tabernacle." " The tabernacle and the tent." Num. iii. 25.

Upon reference to these quotations, it will be found, that the word *tabernacle* is used to express the set of ten curtains, whilst the word *tent* has reference to the eleven curtains of goats' hair, which were thrown over this first set. The Hebrew word, translated *tabernacle*, means a dwelling-place, and is exclusively confined to the thought of this structure being God's dwelling-place. In our translation, we find the words " tabernacle of the congregation " constantly occurring; but, in almost every instance, the Hebrew has the words " *tent* of the congregation " : for, this building was their tent of assembly ; and God's tabernacle or dwelling-place.

Ten curtains were first made, each 28 cubits in length, and four cubits in breadth. Five of these were subsequently joined together ; thereby forming one curtain, 28 cubits in length, and 20 in breadth. The other five were similarly joined together, forming a second curtain of like dimensions. The materials used in the manufacture of this fabric were precisely the same as those which formed the vail; a different arrangement, however, is adopted as to the *fine linen*. In the vail, the *blue* first meets the eye; and the fine linen is last in the series. In these curtains, the fine linen stands first, succeeded by the blue and the other colours. The vail, we know from Heb. x. 20, was a type of the Lord Jesus in the days of His flesh, and was rent when He yielded up the ghost. The curtains, fastened together by golden taches, seem to foreshadow Christ in resurrection. The same glorious display of God and man, wondrously united, meets the eye of faith, whether the blessed Lord be contemplated when sojourning on this earth, or raised to the right hand of the Majesty on high. Indeed, He cannot be known upon the throne of God, unless He has been first revealed to the soul as the Crucified One on earth. He that ascended, first descended. He is the unchanged and unchanging One. " Jesus Christ, the same yesterday, and to-day, and for ever." Resurrection added to Him no new perfections; for He was, while on earth, the Resurrection and the Life. He was ever perfect. The blue, purple, and scarlet, were as bright and gorgeous in the vail, as in the 10 curtains of the heavenly roof. The fine linen was as spotless in the one, as in the other. The Cherubim of Glory were manifest in the *cunning work* of both. The same blessed name of Jesus, bestowed on the Lord at His incarnation, is again the "name above every name" given to Him on His exaltation.

Even when His days, like the shadow declined, and when He was withered like grass, at the very moment of His death, the Father pronounced Him to be the *same*, the Jehovah who, of old, had laid the foundation of the earth. Compare Psa. cii. 25, with Heb. i. 10. "And Thou, Lord, . . . . . . . ." &c.

Fine linen, which formed the groundwork, on which the beautiful tints of the vail were displayed, was also the material of the curtains. The Holy One, whose flesh saw no corruption, was unchanged by resurrection: for mortality was never attached to Him. He alone had, and has, incorruptibility and immortality, though crucified and slain. "I am the First and the Last, and the Living One who became dead, and behold, I am the Living One for evermore." Rev. i. 18. Wondrous mystery, to be received alone by faith : and as the priests walked barefoot in the tabernacle, so must we, with reverent and worshipping hearts, tread on this holy ground.

It has been already observed, that the fine linen is put first in the description of the curtains; whilst the blue is first in that of the vail.

Is not this the order, in which the Holy Spirit instructs as to Christ in humiliation and in glory? The eye of faith is first directed to that mystery, God manifest in the flesh; the Word made flesh. The heart is attracted by the blessed truth, that the Child born to us, and slain for us, is the Mighty God. The heavenly colour stands pre-eminent in the vail. The other marvel is, that there should be a Man upon the throne of God. So, the fine linen, which especially sets forth Christ as the righteous Man, is pre-eminent in the curtains.

The five curtains, which were joined together in their breadth, defined the extent of the holy place, 20 cubits: for, the vail, which separated the interior of the tabernacle into two parts, the holy and the most holy, was to be hung up under the taches. These taches being golden clasps fastened into loops of blue, and thereby uniting the two curtains, each formed of five breadths, one curtain covering the holy place, 10 cubits of the other covering the most holy, and the remaining 10 cubits hanging over the boards of the west end of the tabernacle. It may be, that the explanation of the number five is found in Heb. vii. 26, "Such a high priest became us, who is holy, harmless, undefiled, separate from sinners, and made higher than the heavens." Under the shelter of this glorious Priest, we dwell, and have access, as priests to God, into the holy and most holy places; which, by reason of the vail being rent, now form but one undivided tabernacle. Of the two holy places, formerly separated one from the other by the vail, the holiest was especially the dwelling-place of God alone. None dared intrude thither; not even the priests themselves were allowed to pass within the vail. No worship was carried on there; no human voice was ever heard within its precincts. In fearful majesty the God of Israel dwelt between the Cherubim of glory. And though, once a year, the high priest was directed to enter, yet he could not draw nigh without blood. And the object, for which he was commanded to approach the mercy-seat, was in order to appease the wrath of God, offended by the sins of Israel. But the clasped curtains of the roof betokened that the tabernacle was *one;* and in due time, the rending of the vail proclaimed it. Christ crucified, Christ the power of God, and the wisdom of God, is like the golden tache in the loop of blue. He links heaven and earth together. He gives the worshipper entrance to the immediate presence of God. All distance and separation are gone. The sound of prayer and praise; the cry of distress, and the voice of melody, are presented and heard in the holiest of all.

The curtains, like the vail, were a mass of cherubim. In the latter, these emblematic figures of glory were marred and rent asunder; for, it pleased Jehovah to bruise His Son. "He made His glory to cease, and cast

His throne down to the ground. He shortened the days of His youth, and covered Him with shame." Psa. lxxxix. 44, 45. But in the former, that is the curtains, we behold again the same cherubim of glory, spreading their wings on high, and forming the lofty ceiling of the tabernacle ; a firmament of expanded feathers, composed of the blended tints of blue, purple, and scarlet, on the pure white ground of fine linen. Various are the references in the Psalms to this sheltering canopy. For instance—" I will abide in Thy tabernacle for ever : I will trust in the covert of Thy wings." Psa. lxi. 4. " He shall cover thee with His feathers : and under His wings shalt thou trust." Psa. xci. 4. " Hide me under the shadow of Thy wings." Psa. xvii. 8. " How excellent is Thy loving-kindness, O God ! therefore the children of men put their trust under the shadow of Thy wings." Psa. xxxvi. 7. " Because Thou hast been my help, therefore, in the shadow of Thy wings will I rejoice." Psa. lxiii. 7. " In the shadow of Thy wings will I make my refuge." Psa. lvii. 1.

The blessed Lord Himself, during all His life on earth, abode under the shadow of the Almighty. He dwelt in the secret place of the Most High, till that awful hour when refuge failed Him, and He had to exclaim, " I am cast out of Thy sight." Jonah ii. 4. " Lord, why castest Thou off my soul ? Why hidest Thou Thy face from me ?" Psa. lxxxviii. 14. " My God, my God, why hast Thou forsaken me ?" Psa. xxii. 1. " But the God of peace has, through the blood of the everlasting covenant, brought again from the dead that great Shepherd of the sheep." Heb. xiii. 20. And now, in the holy places not made with hands, Christ is the covert, the hiding-place, the refuge, the defence, help, power, and joy, of all those who trust under the shadow of His wings. The secret place of the Most High, the Holy of Holies, this glorious pavilion, covered with the feathers of the Almighty, is a safe and quiet resting-place for the wearied saint. The strife of tongues enters not there; no terror by night; no arrow that flieth by day; no snare of the fowler, or noisome pestilence can reach one that is sheltered there. Death may be at the right hand, and yet shall not come nigh. The young lion and the dragon can there be trampled under foot. Love, wisdom, patient tenderness, and almighty power, combine to form a fitting shelter.

The comforting passage in Heb. vi. 18—20. refers to the security found in the Holiest. There is no place of safety, short of that within the vail. The Eternal God alone is our refuge : thither we have fled, through the *rent* vail. There, *hope*, not deceitful or fluctuating, but sure and stedfast, is laid hold of, and becomes actual certainty to the soul : for Christ is there, the forerunner. Rapid has been His course, having broken the gates of brass, and cut in sunder the bars of iron. He has taken the prey from the mighty, and ascended from the lower parts of the earth far above all heavens. And now, He has entered for us into the very presence of God ; the sure pledge, that every one, whose hope is fixed on Him, shall likewise obtain this everlasting glory. We may, with confidence, brave the storms and tempests of this world, and the buffetings of Satan ; seeing we have hope, as an anchor, fastened in the holiest. But let us not think that the word *hope* expresses uncertainty ; in human language, it is often used to convey the thought of chance or doubt ; so that we hear, all around us, such expressions as, hoping for salvation, hoping to go to heaven, &c., the utterance of unbelief : whereas, in the Scripture use of the word, hope always implies assurance; and he who hopes, patiently waits for that which he knows he shall obtain.

There were six cities in the land of Israel, appointed by God, to which the man-slayer might run for protection, when pursued by the avenger of blood. The three, which lay on the west of Jordan, were each set upon a hill ; Kedesh, in Galilee, in Mount Naphtali ;

Shecem, in Mount Ephraim ; and Kirjath-Arba, which
is Hebron, in the Mountain of Judah : Josh. xx. 7
These were priestly cities. A way was to be prepared,
so that the guilty person might have no difficulty in
reaching the nearest city of refuge. If an Israelite, or a
stranger, by accident as it might be called, killed his
neighbour, as for instance, " when a man goeth into the
wood with his neighbour, to hew wood, and his hand
fetcheth a stroke with the axe to cut down the tree, and
the head slippeth from the helve, and lighteth upon his
neighbour, that he die." Deut. xix. 5. he must at once
raise his eyes from the scene of his calamity, and look
for the nearest city of refuge. God had provided that it
should be conspicuous on every side. He must then
hasten, with all speed, along the prepared way to that
city, and pause not till he found himself within the
threshold of its gate. A cry for mercy to the avenger
of blood, would be unheeded ; a plea that his crime
was unintentional, would be of no avail. The sword of
vengeance would inevitably fall upon him, if he delayed
to hasten to the refuge. To spend, in entreaties and
prayers, the precious time which yet afforded him
opportunity of reaching the only place of safety, would
be madness. He must *flee* from the approaching wrath.
God had established the place of mercy : safety was in
that alone. Moreover, the slayer had, by inheritance,
no title to a dwelling-place within that city. His crime
and danger were his only plea ; and marvellously enough,
his very misery placed him, through the merciful provision of God, in association with the holiest of God's
people. He was raised from the rank of an ordinary
Israelite, or from the outcast condition of a stranger, to
be a fellow-citizen with the priests of God.

These shadows of truth are more than fulfilled in the
merciful and rich provision made by God for the salvation of the sinner. The dwelling-place of the Most
High becomes the city of his refuge, his everlasting home.
On the mercy-seat he beholds the blood ; sure pledge

that wrath has been appeased, that the avenger of blood has buried the sword of justice in the heart of another on his behalf. The ground on which he stands, within the holiest, is as a rock under his feet; for the blood of the atoning victim has also been sprinkled there. The great High Priest is likewise present, Himself the forerunner, the first that has tasted the joy, and entered into the rest, the blessed rest of that eternal salvation which He has obtained for others. From the ruin, degradation, and death, entailed on him by the Fall, the sinner is raised into a standing of perfection, glory, and life, to be a king and a priest, to go no more out, to be an heir of God, and joint-heir with Christ. The cry of terror and distress is exchanged for the song of victory and joy; holy worship and ceaseless praise take the place of vain regrets and unhappy murmurings. He, who looked back over the past with fearful forebodings, dreading the rapid advances of well-merited vengeance, now sees goodness and mercy *pursuing* him all the days of his life, Psa. xxiii. 6 (in the Hebrew), and gazes with unspeakable delight upon Him who has opened the way into the holiest through His own death, and is seated there, crowned with glory and honour.

These are some of the many blessed truths which seem to be crowded together in the types of the tabernacle. Ever and anon fresh aspects of the glories of salvation present themselves to the soul; even as to the eyes of the priest in the sanctuary, mingled gleams of light and beauty shed their radiance from the gorgeous curtains and golden boards, lighted up by the cloud of glory which covered the mercy-seat.

# THE LOOPS AND TACHES

"And thou shalt make loops of blue upon the edge of the one curtain from the selvedge in the coupling; and likewise shalt thou make in the uttermost edge of another curtain, in the coupling of the second.

"Fifty loops shalt thou make in the one curtain, and fifty loops shalt thou make in the edge of the curtain that is in the coupling of the second; that the loops may take hold one of another,

"And thou shalt make fifty taches of gold, and couple the curtains together with the taches: and it shall be one tabernacle."—Exod. xxvi 4—6

"And he made loops of blue in the edge of one curtain from the selvedge in the coupling: likewise he made in the uttermost side of another curtain, in the coupling of the second.

"Fifty loops made he in one curtain, and fifty loops made he in the edge of the curtain which was in the coupling of the second: the loops held one curtain to another.

"And he made fifty taches of gold, and coupled the curtains one unto another with the taches: so it became one tabernacle."—Exod. xxxvi 11—13

FIFTY taches, or clasps of gold, linked together the innermost or beautiful curtains of the tabernacle. Fifty taches of brass coupled the goats' hair curtains. By the former, one tabernacle—by the latter, one tent was made. The vail, which divided the interior into two unequal portions, was hung up under the taches. As long as that vail remained entire, there might be said to be two tabernacles; thus, in Heb. ix. 1—7, where this building is looked at before the rending of the vail, we read of the *first*, wherein was the candlestick, and the table, and the shewbread; and the *second*, or holiest of all, into which went the high priest alone, once every year. At the same time, there was an intimation that the whole interior was but one holy place, in the fact of the curtains that covered, being connected by the taches, and forming one tabernacle, and one tent above it.

All priestly service is now conducted in the holiest. Heaven itself is the place where Christ appears in the presence of God for us. There is no intermediate place of acceptance; but a man is either a sinner, short of the glory of God, and as such, outside, and infinitely far off; or, he is made nigh by the blood of Christ, and presented in Christ, faultless in the presence of that glory in the holiest of all.

The fifty taches of gold may be so many distinct presentations of the glories of Christ, expressed in His various names and titles, as seen crowned with glory and honour upon the throne of God.

The taches of brass may exhibit the same names and titles as appertaining to Him when He was on earth, the second man, the Lord from heaven; as it will be found that the brass is used as a type of the Lord on earth in suffering and trial; while the gold has a resurrection aspect of the same glorious One. He has, as risen from the dead, retaken His own glorious titles; having, for the joy set before Him, endured the cross.

The brazen taches seem appropriately to knit together the curtains of goats' hair, which proclaim to us His sorrows and sufferings on the tree; while the golden taches, as appropriately coupled together the beautiful curtains, which manifest Him as received up in glory, because of the perfection of His labour and service in suffering on earth.

The following are fifty names and titles of the Blessed Lord, which were His alike when on earth, as now in the glory above.

1. The Mighty God
2. The Almighty
3. Jehovah
4. The Son
5. The Son of God
6. The Only-begotten of the Father
7. The First-born of every creature;
   (or) born before all creation
8. The Word
9. The Beginning
10. The Wisdom of God
11. The Power of God
12. The Image of the Invisible God

13. The Brightness of God's glory
14. That Eternal Life
15. The First and the Last
16. Immanuel
17 Jesus
18. Messiah
19. The Lord
20. The Lord of Glory
21. The Prince of Life
22. The Prince of Peace
23 The Everlasting Father
24 The Creator
25. The Sustainer
26. The Holy One of God
27. The Same
28. Wonderful
29. Counsellor
30. The Son of Man
31. The Seed of the Woman
32. The Resurrection
33. The Quickening Spirit
34. The Light
35. The Truth
36. Righteousness
37. The Way
38. The Sun of Righteousness
39. The Day-Star
40. The Amen
41. The King of Kings
42. The Heir of all things
43. The Root of David
44 The Offspring of David
45. The Shepherd
46. The Lamb of God
47. The Rock of Ages
48. The True Witness
49 Shiloh (or the Sent One)
50. The Redeemer

It must not be supposed that the above glorious list of names and titles of Jesus is given as a definite interpretation of the type. But every true-hearted believer will own that each of these names is a golden link, uniting together heaven and earth, connecting God with His people, and enabling Him to spread out a heaven of glory, into which He will receive the royal priesthood, and where already true worship is in spirit carried on. Each tache of gold, or of brass, was carefully numbered and guarded by the Levites ; for if but one had been wanting, the curtains of the tabernacle or tent would have been insecurely united.

God has committed to His Church all truth connected with the glory of the work and person of His Son. The Church of the Living God is the pillar and ground of the truth. It is the blessed responsibility of each member of that body carefully to watch and guard every—even the smallest—portion of the truth, which testifies of Christ. Error and weakness will result if anything be lacking, as to what is held respecting the Lord Jesus. If one link in the golden chain be weak or deficient, the strength of the whole is impaired.

## THE CURTAINS OF GOATS' HAIR

WE have now to consider the other set of curtains, viz. those of Goats' Hair, which were thrown over the beautiful curtains already described. It will be observed that these of goats' hair, like those, were made in breadths of four cubits each : instead however of there being only ten such breadths, as in the former set, there were eleven. Six of these were joined together, forming one curtain ; and the other five, joined in like manner, formed the second. The sixth, or additional breadth, hung down over the front of the tabernacle The length also of these curtains was greater than that of the former set, being 30 cubits instead of 28. A cubit of this additional length hung down on each side of the tabernacle, so as completely to cover up the cubit of the golden boards which had been left exposed; the beautiful curtains falling short by a cubit each side. The boards of the tabernacle stood 10 cubits high on the north and south sides; the space which separated them being the width of the tabernacle, was also 10 cubits. A curtain therefore 28 cubits long, thrown over the top, and falling down each side, would leave a cubit on each side of the golden boards exposed: whereas one of 30 cubits long would exactly cover up the whole. This explains the meaning of the somewhat obscure passage. "A cubit on the one side, and a cubit on the other side, of that which remaineth in the length of the curtains of the tent, it shall hang over the sides of the tabernacle, on this side and on that side, to cover it." Exod. xxvi. 13.

The sixth curtain, or breadth, which hung down in front of the tabernacle, was doubled back so as to hang like a bag: the same expression being used, "Thou shalt *double* the sixth curtain in the forefront of the tabernacle," as in Exod. xxviii.16, respecting the breast-plate, which was doubled or folded in the form of a bag, so as to receive within it the Urim and the Thummim. This additional sixth curtain being thus allowed to hang down in front, the other five breadths exactly corresponded with the five breadths of the beautiful curtains beneath; and the taches of brass, which linked together the goats' hair curtains, precisely reached the same place, so as to be immediately above the taches of gold, which united together the innermost or beautiful curtains.

The 12th verse may present a difficulty to the reader. "The remnant that remaineth of the curtains of the tent, the half-curtain that remaineth shall hang over the back side of the tabernacle." The meaning of this is, that half the curtain, which was formed of the five breadths of four cubits each joined together, hung down over the back or west end of the tabernacle, so as to

**The Blood of the Passover Lamb Being Applied to the
Posts of the House of an Israelite Family**

**A Household of Israelites Eating
the Lord's Passover in Haste**

cover up that extremity ; for the width of it would be exactly 20 cubits ; ten of which would reach over the top, from the taches to the end of the tabernacle ; and the other ten would fall down from the top over the west end, so as to reach the ground.

The material of which these curtains were made, was goats' hair ; probably of a fine texture, like the modern Cashmere shawl. In the original, the word " hair" does not occur.

It will be found that the goat was universally selected for the sin-offering in the great feasts under the law, when Israel was collectively represented and appeared before God.

In the beginnings of their months, Num. xxviii. 11—15, when the thin crescent of the new moon marked the commencement of another period of increasing light and blessing, fresh burnt-offerings were laid upon Israel's altar for a sweet savour to the Lord, and a kid of the goats for sin atoned for the darkness and evil of the past month; which though unknown to themselves, had been observed by Him who is of too pure eyes to behold iniquity. They should have abode before Him, fair as the moon : but as that light in the heavens had waned into darkness, so was their history one of brief hope and quick declension. And such alas! is the history of the Church of God, and too often, of the saints which compose it. One's life passes away in a series of revivals and declensions ; of bright purposes and intentions, ending in sorrowful failures and short-comings. Well for us is it that the value of the sin-offering, the memorial of that costly gift, abides for us before God, like one of the breadths of the goats' hair curtains.

Israel's year commenced with the appointment of the passover, Exod. xii. Intimately connected with this ordinance was the feast of unleavened bread. In Luke xxii. I, they are identified. Throughout the seven days of this feast, one goat for sin to make atonement was sacrificed, besides other offerings. The more the

unleavened purity and holiness of Christ is realised,
and the more He becomes the strength of our life,
and we feed on His flesh and blood, as on unleavened
bread, the more shall we find our need of Him as
"made sin for us." Israel, by feeding on the unleavened
bread, had to discover their own leavened condition;
and thus the goat for the sin-offering was daily provided,
to meet the uncleanness of their state; an uncleanness
made manifest by the very purity of the food on which
they were directed to feast. So it is with the believer. Not
only will the daily contact with the leaven of sin around
him cause that same leaven to work within; but the
more he walks in the light as God is in the light, the
more will he discover his own uncleanness, and find the
need of the blood of Jesus Christ (that one sin-offering)
which cleanseth us from all sin.

Another breadth of the goats' hair curtain may thus
have had reference to this feast of unleavened bread,
and its accompanying sin-offerings.

The next great feast of Israel, which followed the
passover, was the feast of weeks. It commenced with
the waving of a sheaf of first-fruits before the Lord. A
beautiful type of the resurrection of Christ; the corn of
wheat, which had fallen into the ground, and had died,
and had sprung up, bringing forth much fruit. At the
conclusion of the feast—the day of Pentecost of
Acts ii.—a new meat-offering, consisting of two loaves
of the fresh harvest, baked with leaven, was waved
before God: a type this of the presentation to God of
Israel's first-fruits on the day of Pentecost, when the
first portion of the Church of God stood risen with
Christ, one with Him in life eternal, and anointed with
the Holy Ghost sent down from heaven; a sample of
the whole body, to be completed at the Lord's return,
when the harvest shall be all gathered into the garner
of glory. But these first-fruits, these believers, were still
leavened with the presence of the old man, the old sinful
nature, and were still in their old corrupt bodies of death.

A sin-offering was therefore commanded for atonement. In Num. xxviii. 30, a kid of the goats, and in Lev. xxiii. 19, the same sacrifice connected with this new meat-offering, is in both places appointed.

The believer, though he be (by virtue of the death and resurrection of Christ) a new creature; though partaker of a new and everlasting life, derived from, and in union with the Lord Jesus; yet is burdened with the body of sin and death, and finds the constant lusting of the flesh against the spirit; an incessant warfare during all his abode on earth. That which is born of the flesh remains still flesh, irremediable in its corruption, with a mind at enmity with God, and which cannot be subjected to the law of God. Like some ferocious evil beast, it may be chained, but cannot be tamed. We cannot make a servant of this monster, or come to any agreement with him, any more than with the leviathan described by God to Job. "Will he make a covenant with thee? Wilt thou take him for a servant for ever? Wilt thou play with him, as with a bird?" (xli. 4, 5.) An evil beast, neither to be trifled with nor trusted.

It is of deep importance to the child of God, as regards both his peace and his walk, that the truth respecting the distinction and co-existence of the two natures, new and old, should be fully believed. They are denominated in Scripture, the new man and the old man; the former, after God, created in righteousness and true holiness; the latter, one's original existence, derived from the ruined fallen Adam, often called the flesh, in which dwells no good thing. Sin can never be eradicated. It abides as long as the flesh remains. No power of the Holy Spirit burns up or consumes it. Neither is there any possibility of converting that which is evil into good. The presence and power of the Spirit of God, by strengthening the new man, and feeding the soul with Christ, and deepening its value of the precious blood, enable the believer to repress and keep under the motions of sin, the energies of the old man.

Watchfulness, faith, and prayer, are as needful, up to the very end of the race, as they were at its commencement. Through the whole of this Pentecostal dispensation, the constant remembrance of the sin-offering is imperatively required, in order to preserve fellowship with the Father and the Son, and to give power, and to afford us a weapon of strength against the leaven still mingled with the new meat-offering.

Another of the six curtains of goat's hair may remind us of this aspect of the sacrifice.

A long interval elapsed in Israel's year between the feast of weeks, and the next general feast. It was not until the seventh month opened, that any special gathering of the people was appointed. But on the first day of that month was the feast of the blowing of trumpets. By this time, the labours of the harvest-field, of the olive-yard, and the vineyard were nearly over ; and the silver trumpets were to sound in the ears of the people, to call them from the busy cares and thoughts of earthly things, that had now occupied them some time, to rest in holy convocation before God, under the sweet savour of fresh burnt-offerings, and under the atonement of a kid of the goats for a sin offering. It was a joyful, as well as a solemn sound, that those trumpets gave forth. Their silver note supplanted the shout of the harvest-home, or of the treading of the wine-press ; and summoned Israel to the presence of their God, who had blessed their labours, and crowned their year with His goodness. Yet even in this scene of holy repose and worship, the sin-offering was needed. The convocation itself brought with it evil, and the blood of atonement must flow.

May we not learn from this, how needful it is to keep in remembrance the precious blood of Christ, in the midst of our very activities of service and labour for God ; and to seek to preserve as our first object, the soul in fellowship with the Father and the Son ; lest busy occupations, even though they be of the holiest kind, withdraw the heart's affection from the Lord, or usurp that place in our souls, which belongs alone to Himself.

" My son, give me thy heart," is one great command. " Keep thy heart with all diligence," is another. There may be much diligence in outward service, and yet the soul may have little fellowship with God, and be rendering but little true worship to Him. The blood of Christ alone keeps the way of access open for us : and as we are eating that meat indeed, and drinking that drink indeed, so are we abiding in God's presence.

This feast of trumpets, with its accompanying sin-offering, may have had its memorial in a fourth curtain of goat's hair.

On the tenth day of the seventh month, was the feast of Atonement. On that day alone, in all the year, a special sin-offering for atonement was appointed. Two kids of the goats, looked upon as one sin-offering, were presented before the Lord. One was selected by lot to be slain ; and the other to be a scape-goat. The blood of the one slain, was on this occasion, and on none other, carried by the high priest into the holiest, and there sprinkled upon the mercy-seat, and before the mercy-seat, seven times. Israel's sins of the past year were thus in type covered over, and blotted out from God's remembrance.

The high priest, after having completed the work of atonement within the tabernacle before God, then came out, and confessed over the living goat, the sins of the people ; at the same time laying both his hands upon its head, and thus typically transferring them to the animal ; which was then sent into the wilderness, never more to return ; and thus the sins reckoned to it were no more to be remembered. The object of having two goats for one sin-offering was, to convey to Israel assembled outside the tabernacle, the knowledge of what had passed before God on their behalf within the holiest. The disappearance of the scape-goat, bearing their sins, represented to them the fact that those sins had been blotted out from God's remembrance, by means of the blood sprinkled on the mercy-seat. The goat whose blood had been carried within the vail, was entirely consumed as a sin-offering without the camp. It may be that the goats' hair curtain, doubled, and hanging down in front of the tabernacle, was intended to keep a memorial of this day of atonement before Israel's eye. The doubling of the curtain, so that half faced inwards, and the other half could be seen from without, may have some allusion to the double aspect of atonement, set forth in the different uses of the two goats, the one sin-offering: the object of the one being solely for atonement towards God; that of the other being to express the result of that atonement towards Israel. The 9th and 10th chapters of Hebrews give us an exposition of the 16th chapter of Leviticus; but chiefly by way of contrast; comparing the inefficiency of the blood presented on that day for Israel, with the complete and eternal efficacy of the one offering presented by Christ—the offering of Himself. A more full explanation of this beautiful type is reserved for a future occasion, when the dress of the high priest will be considered.

As the worshipping Israelite could not draw near the tabernacle without observing the goats' hair curtain folded down in front; so has the believer ever to draw near to God with the full assurance that his sins and iniquities are remembered no more, and that the record of this blessed fact is preserved in God's dwelling-place, by the rending of the vail, the sprinkling of the blood upon the mercy-seat, the presence of the living High Priest, and the very construction of the tabernacle itself.

The last feast in the year was the feast of tabernacles— the feast of in-gathering—when Israel had only to rest, and rejoice in the blessing of God upon all their labours. Liberty, cessation from toil, mingled with solemn feasting and joy, marked this holy festival. There were also two remarkable things connected with it : first, the dwelling

ın booths : secondly, an eighth day added to the seven.
The booths were to be erected in remembrance of Israel's
deliverance out of Egypt, when their first resting-place
was at Succoth (booths.)   There seems also to be an
intimation of a future deliverance out of Babylon, in the
fact that " willows of the brook " were to be intertwined
with other trees to form these booths.   Psa. cxxxvii. 2,
alludes to the willow as a tree growing by the rivers of
Babylon.   The eighth day, "that great day of the feast,"
gave a resurrection character to this remarkable ordinance.
Throughout this feast, on each day, a goat was offered,
for a sin-offering.   And though the burnt offerings
declined in number from day to day, yet the sin-offering
remained the same.   The goat was considered sufficient
at the close, as at the commencement.

This feast of tabernacles is mentioned but once in the
New Testament, (John vii.)   The brethren of Jesus
urged upon Him to manifest Himself openly to the
world at this feast.   But He tarried behind in Galilee.
His time was not full come for shewing Himself to the
world.   The cross must precede that full time.   He
must be lifted up in order to draw all men unto Him.
However, after " His brethren were gone up, then went
He also up unto the feast, not openly, but as it were in
secret."   When there, He marked the lack of peace and
joy which should have filled that city of God, especially
at such a time.   He heard the restless questionings and
surmisings which disturbed the hearts of the people, and
" about the midst of the feast, He went up into the
temple and taught."   He still confined Himself to the
temple, and did not openly manifest Himself to the
world.   The Jews marvelled at His knowledge of letters
rather than at the deep subject which He taught.   Just
as in the present day the ear is attracted often by a sweet
sound of God's truth, whilst the heart is unmoved by
its solemn verities.   A preacher is wondered at, it may
be for his eloquence and earnestness ; whilst the all-
important doctrines which he enunciates are passed by.

The GREAT TEACHER sought in vain to direct them to the source from whence He Himself, as well as His doctrines proceeded, viz. to God.

At length, "in the last day, that great day of the feast, Jesus stood and cried, saying, " If any man thirst, let him come unto me, and drink. He that believeth on me, as the Scripture hath said, out of his belly shall flow rivers of living water. But this spake He of the Spirit, which they that believe on Him should receive : for the Holy Ghost was not yet; because that Jesus was not yet glorified." Ver. 37, 38, 39.

The man of sorrows discerned under the seeming prosperity and gladness around Him, aching, unsatisfied hearts. The best feast under the law, with its great day, had given no lasting peace or joy. The booths, at first green and fresh, were now withered and dead; the sun poured its scorching beams through their lifeless branches ; the burnt-offerings had dwindled down from thirteen to one. Though professing to know God, Israel was still ignorant of Him. The bounties of His hand, manifested in the full winefat and corn-floor, had not revealed, and indeed could not, the depth of His heart of love. Though in the promised land, the people had not entered GOD'S rest : they were still, as to their souls, wandering in a barren wilderness. " The feast of tabernacles" instead of being the crowning feast of the Lord, was but "a feast of the *Jews*." Wearied souls were still unsatiated, The True bread-corn had yet to be bruised, (Isa. liii. 10;) the wine had yet to be pressed from the grape, (Ps. xxxviii. 2;) and the oil had yet to flow from the beaten olive. (Isa. liii. 5.)

Was this closing feast all that could be reached under the law ? Was Israel to know no deeper spring of joy, no more lasting fountain of gladness than had been provided through this feast of tabernacles ? The pent-up heart of the blessed Lord could be restrained no longer. Straitened though He felt, till He should have accomplished His baptism of judgment, yet He could not look

upon this scene without pouring forth in anticipation the
stream of living water. So He stood in the midst of the
fading festivities, and cried, " If any man thirst, let him
come unto me and drink." " The Rock Christ" was
there with its great depths of life—" The wine and the
milk" were there, though Israel knew it not. Jesus
manifested Himself openly, as the fountain of living
waters for every parched sinner, in anticipation of the
time when the full tide of eternal life would flow from
Him, smitten by the rod of God's power and wrath,
over a waste desolate world.

The law, with its weak and beggarly elements, had
accomplished nothing. It could give no life, no righteousness, no peace ; and though bright gleams of future
glory shone out here and there from its types and
shadows, yet even those gleams of light could only be
discerned by those who had through faith, been raised
like Moses, above its grievous yoke ; and who had been
admitted into a friendship and acquaintance with God,
which the law could never give.

What a mighty cry of the blessed Lord was this!
How it must have sounded forth in the midst of that
city of unavailing solemnities, in the midst of those
multitudes, the mirth of whose hearts was but as the
crackling of thorns under a pot. And that cry which
then commenced was taken up again by the same
blessed One when brought into the dust of death. He
Himself said, I THIRST ; and having drank to the very
dregs the full cup of woe at the hands of God; and
having tasted the last bitter drop of hatred and malignity
at the hands of man, He said, "It is finished"—the
Rock was riven; the water of life burst forth. And still
from the glory itself the cry sounds forth, before the
closing day of judgment overtakes the world, "Let him
that is athirst come, and whosoever will, let him take
the water of life freely."

It was the eighth day when these memorable words
of Grace were poured from the lips of the Son of

God; a day especially typifying a resurrection period. The Lord Jesus therefore stands forth as Himself the resurrection and the life, and speaks of the Holy Spirit, which they who believed on Him should receive after He was glorified. That Holy Spirit, would be an earnest of the inheritance; both a pledge to the believer of the future glory; and also revealing the first-fruits of that glory to his soul. See 1 Cor. ii. 9, 10, 12. Even now through the blessed work and witness of the Comforter, the fruits of the promised inheritance are realised. "Wine that maketh glad the heart of man, and oil to make his face to shine, and bread which strengtheneth man's heart," are ministered from the glory to the way-worn pilgrim on earth. And though still toiling in the wilderness, he can say, "we which have believed do enter into rest." Heb. iv. 3. Already he has an earnest of the feast of tabernacles. And not only so, but he becomes through drinking of the smitten rock, himself a channel of living water to thirsty sinners round. "He that believeth on me, as the Scripture hath said, out of his belly shall flow rivers of living water." "The mouth of a righteous man is a well of life." Prov. x. 11. "The words of a man's mouth, are as deep waters; and the well-spring of wisdom as a flowing brook." Prov. xviii. 4. What a blessed contrast this to a throat an open Sepulchre; a tongue using deceit; lips concealing the poison of asps; and a mouth full of cursing and bitterness!

And what a wondrous change, to have rivers of living water flowing from within; instead of evil thoughts, murders, adulteries, fornications, thefts, false witness, and blasphemies, as the bitter streams which the natural heart can only pour forth.

But this "feast of tabernacles" has also a prophetic aspect to the believer, as well as to Israel in the future day of millennial glory.

By faith, we can even now look forward to that day when the Israel of God, the countless multitude gathered out of every nation, will be assembled in their eternal resting-place, around the throne of God and of the Lamb in his temple. The wilderness will be passed, the weariness, the hunger and thirst of the journey be known no more. The withering power of persecution, and fiery tribulation, will have ceased for ever. The cup of joy will be full; and blessed freedom from every temptation, whether of Satan or of the flesh, will be rejoiced in for ever. God's rest will be entered. There, the song will be, "Unto Him that loveth us,* and washed us from our sins in His own blood." The value of the sin-offering will then indeed be appreciated: and the power of that blood to redeem, to cleanse, to preserve clean, and to present the sinner faultless before the presence of God's glory, will at length be realised.

And now, as we journey on towards that resurrection-day, and rejoice in hope of the glory of God, faith's foretastes of the future will be mingled with a constant reference to Him who was made sin for us. The glory is inseparable from the cross; and the cross can never be severed from the glory.

One of the six goats' hair curtains may have been intended to perpetuate the remembrance of the sin-offering, as connected with Israel's last feast, that of tabernacles.

It may be remarked that, on the great day of atonement, another goat was offered for sin, besides that above mentioned. (Num. xxix. 11.) In the case of all the sin-offerings, sacrificed during the feast, the blood was not carried into the holiest, but was put upon the horns and poured out at the bottom of the altar of burnt-offering. Selected portions of the inwards were also burnt upon the same altar. The remainder of the victim became the portion of the priest. The only exception to this rule was the goat, (Lev. xvi.) the blood of which, being carried into the holiest, the whole sacrifice was

---

* This is acknowledged to be the correct translation. The original Greek according to the best Authorities having the word "*loveth*" in the present tense, instead of in the past, "hath loved."

burnt with fire outside the camp, and no portion consumed on the altar of burnt offering

The feasts above alluded to have also a prophetic character, bearing on the second coming of the Lord Jesus. But it is not the object of the present exposition to enter into this deeply interesting subject.

There were two other occasions on which goats were offered as sin-offerings for Israel, as a people : the one (Lev. ix.) on the consecration of the priesthood : the other (Num. vii.) at the dedication of the altar. In the former case, the priests, Aaron and his sons, having themselves experienced the virtues of the sacrifices offered for them by Moses, took their place of priesthood, on the behalf of Israel, on the last day of their consecration, an eighth day. In the latter, each tribe was represented by its prince ; and each prince presented precisely the same offerings and sacrifices at the dedication of the altar. Thus each Israelite could claim the value of the priesthood for himself ; the whole people having been identified with the sacrifices on the eighth day of consecration ; and the need of each tribe was equally expressed ; and each stood alike accepted, through the offerings presented at the dedication of the altar.

So it is, even now, as it regards the Church of God. Christ has loved it, and given Himself for it, (Eph. v. 25,) and this love, and the value of this sacrifice, is equally true towards each individual in the Church. He loved us, and gave Himself for us, Eph. v. 2. He loved ME, and gave Himself for ME, Gal. ii. 20. And if we measure the amount of our need and misery by reason of sin, each of us requires the whole virtue of the perfect sin-offering : the entire work of the great High Priest is indispensable for each, and each stands accepted in the Beloved, according to the full and unspeakable glory, dignity, and value of His person. Two other breadths of the second goats' hair curtain may have allusion to these sin-offerings, presented on the day of consecrations, and on the dedication of the altar.

Hitherto, we have considered the goat, as offered for a sin-offering on behalf of Israel collectively. The same animal might also be selected by an individual Israelite, for a burnt-offering, Lev. i. 10—for a peace offering, iii. 12—and for a sin or trespass-offering, iv. 28, and v. 6. Thus the whole eleven curtains of goats' hair may embody a memorial of every sacrifice presented by an Israelite, but especially of the sin-offering presented for the whole people. Breadth for breadth, the beautiful inner curtains were accurately covered up by the goats' hair. Indeed, the whole building was enveloped in this fabric ; as if to enunciate the great truth, that God could have no tabernacle amongst men, and could not display His glory and beauty in the midst of them, unless His dwelling-place proclaimed, in every part, the fact that sin and infirmity had been fully met by a perfect sacrifice : and even death had yielded up a record of purity and holiness, fit to be perpetuated for ever in His presence.

It has been before remarked, that these curtains of goats' hair are particularly specified as the *tent* ; while the beautiful curtains are called the *tabernacle.*

| | |
|---|---|
| Exod.xxvi 7 | To be a covering, (or rather) *tent*, upon the tabernacle |
| ,,    ,, 11 | Couple the *tent* together, that it may be one —xxxvi 18 |
| ,,    12, 13 | Curtains of the *tent* |
| ,,    ,, 14 | Covering for the *tent* |
| ,, xxxv 11 | The tabernacle, his *tent*, and his coverings |
| ,, xxxvi 14 | For the *tent* over the tabernacle |
| ,,    xl 19 | Spread abroad the *tent*, over the tabernacle |
| Num. iii 25 | The tabernacle and the *tent* |

A twofold object was attained by this construction. The tabernacle formed a dwelling-place for God in the midst of His people. It was also a tent, where they could congregate for worship, for help, and blessing The goats' hair curtains recording the fact of the kid of the goats having been slain for sin ; Jehovah was enabled to manifest His glory in the midst of His people, and to abide with them, notwithstanding their waywardness and evil.

Speaking from the tabernacle thus covered with its tent of goats' hair, God could say, "I have not beheld iniquity in Jacob : neither have I seen perverseness in Israel." The breath of the accuser was prevented from entering the holy places of God's dwelling : for an outspread record of abundant sacrifice proclaimed a full answer of atonement made to every accusation respecting sin : and the goats' hair curtains protected the tabernacle of God, breadth for breadth, from Israel's defilement. North, south, east, west, and heavenward, these eleven curtains witnessed to God's holiness, by proclaiming wide and far, that sin had been judged in the slain lamb ; that iniquity was covered ; and a hiding-place prepared, where the justified sinner was compassed about with songs of deliverance.

Also the tent of congregation was so fashioned as to keep in constant remembrance the important truth, that atonement must precede worship : and the priests themselves, who ministered in the holy place, might have learned, from the arrangement of the tabernacle, the order of our song of praise. " Unto Him that *loveth* us, and hath washed us from our sins in His own blood, and hath made us kings and priests unto God and His Father; to Him be glory and dominion for ever and ever. Amen." (Rev. i. 5, 6.)

# THE COVERINGS

"And thou shalt make a covering for the tent, of rams' skins dyed red, and a covering above of badgers' skins."—Exod. xxvi 14

"And he made a covering for the tent, of rams' skins dyed red, and a covering of badgers' skins above that."—Exod. xxxvi 19

THERE were two coverings : one of rams' skins dyed red, and another of badgers' skins ; besides the two sets of curtains, which formed the tabernacle and tent. The curtains were measured : the coverings were not. On referring to Rev. xi. 1, 2, " And there was given me a reed like unto a rod : and the angel stood, saying, Rise, and measure the temple of God, and the altar, and them that worship therein. But the court, which is without the temple, leave out, and measure it not ; for it is given unto the Gentiles : and the holy city shall they tread under foot, forty and two months." We perceive that, to measure the temple, &c., was synonymous with claiming it as a place valuable to God ; while the court, which represented the city, not being measured, was still, for a season, to be left in the hands of the Gentiles. In the type before us, the two sets of curtains being measured, would seem to signify that they were costly, and precious to God ; and being such, would have an eternal value : while the coverings were only provided for a time, having no intrinsic value in them, but exhibiting an outward appearance which eventually would pass away.

THE COVERING OF RAMS' SKINS DYED RED.—As the curtains of goats' hair are especially spoken of as a tent above the tabernacle, or beautiful curtains ; so the rams' skins dyed red are particularly mentioned as a covering above the tent, or curtains of goats' hair. Exod. xxvi. 14, " And thou shalt make a *covering* for the *tent* (of ) rams' skins dyed red." Exod. xxxvi. 19, " And he made a *covering* for the *tent* of rams' skins dyed red." Exod. xl. 19, " And he spread abroad the *tent* over the

tabernacle, and put the *covering* of the tent above upon it."
Num. iii. 25, "The tabernacle, and the tent, and the
*covering* thereof." 'Num. iv. 25, "The curtains of
the tabernacle, and the *tent* of congregation, his
*covering*, and the covering of the badgers' skins, that
is above upon it."

It will be perceived from these quotations, that, though
" the covering " sometimes includes both the rams' skins
and badgers' skins, yet the covering of rams' skins is, in
some instances, exclusively connected with the goats' hair
curtains. The latter, if the explanation of the type
already given be correct, perpetuated a precious remembrance of the sin-offering, as affording a shelter for God's
priests in their worship, and approach to God.

The covering of rams' skins dyed red, seems to depict
that outward aspect of affliction and sorrow, which the
blessed Lord presented to the eyes of men, so that they
considered Him to be marked out as a victim, under some
peculiar dealings of God's hand in judgment. Many
were astonished at Him ; " His visage was more marred
than any man, and His form more than the sons of men."
Isa. lii. 14. He was esteemed to be stricken of God,
and afflicted. Isa. liii. 4. Such was the estimation, in which
the Lord was held, by those who ignorantly gazed upon
Him when hanging on the tree ; not understanding that
the object, for which He hung there, was, that He might
bear our sorrows, and carry our griefs ; and not recognising, that God was there bruising Him for our
iniquities, and that, with His stripes, we are healed.
Men could not fail to perceive the covering of rams' skins
dyed red—the sorrow and death, in which the blessed Lord
was steeped. But they saw not the precious goats' hair
curtains beneath. They estimated not the unspeakable
value of His sighs, and groans, and tears, and death
upon the cross for sin. And so it is still. The Socinian,
the Neologian, can admire the ways and words of Jesus
in His life on earth ; can present Him as a perfect
specimen of what man should be. But the costly pre-

ciousness of His death is unheeded and unknown. The thought of sacrifice, and shedding of blood, is repulsive, instead of attractive, to these Satan-bound souls. They picture the blessed Lord on the cross as a hero, bearing sufferings and indignities from the hands of men ; they know Him not as the sin-offering, of unspeakable value to the sinner, and to God.

The expression, " dyed red," or reddened, seems to have the same import, as regards the rams' skins, as the word " red" has respecting the *heifer*, selected in that peculiar type described in Num. xix. In this chapter a *red heifer* was to be chosen for sacrifice. It was to be without spot or blemish ; ungalled by any yoke ; marked in its very birth, by its colour, for the slaughter ; while intrinsically pure and spotless. In like manner, the reddened rams' skins implied, that they had been taken from slaughtered victims.

## THE COVERINGS OF BADGERS' SKINS

Much question has arisen respecting the animal, in our translation called the badger. The Septuagint renders "tachash" ὑακινθινα, or skins of a *blue* colour. Upon comparing the conjectures of many writers on this subject, that suggested by the late Colonel Hamilton Smith seems to be the most probable, viz. that they were skins of a blueish-grey colour, from an animal of a stag goat species, common in the East. Be this as it may, this covering was not measured, and therefore has reference rather to the outward aspect than to the intrinsic costliness of the material. We read of badgers' skins being used for sandals, (Ezek. xvi. 10 ;) and throughout the details of the tabernacle, these skins were employed for external coverings to protect the vessels on the march from the sun or rain.

Again, referring to the estimate in which the Lord

Jesus was held by the unbeliever, we find it written of Him, " He hath no form nor comeliness : and when we shall see Him, there is no beauty that we should desire Him. He is despised and rejected of men. He was despised, and we esteemed Him not." Isa. liii. 2, 3. Persecution, opposition, rejection, a life of sorrow on account of the ruin and misery which He saw around Him ; the havoc that sin and Satan had caused ; a life spent in ceaseless watchings, prayings, fastings, and going about doing good, had wrought their results on the blessed Lord ; so that in Him, there was no beauty to attract the outward eye. And at length when lifted up in shame and ignominy on the tree, bearing in addition to the buffetings of men and Satan, the out-pouring of the wrath of God; men beheld One from whom they would rather hide their faces in dislike, than gaze upon in love and admiration. No one, who looked merely upon the rough badger-skin exterior of the tabernacle, would have conceived that it was the dwelling-place of God. The eye of faith alone be-held in Jesus " the glory as of the Only Begotten of the Father."

> The visage marred, those sorrows deep,
> The vinegar and gall,
> These were His golden chains of love,
> His captive to enthrall.

The priest who had title, by reason of his consecration through the blood, to enter within the holy place, saw around him only glory and beauty.

The Church of God, in her wilderness journey, strikingly presents the same features as we have been considering in this type. " I am black, but comely," she can say : black, as to outward appearance and the estimate formed by sense ; like the tents of Kedar, the rough dark camels' hair dwelling of the wandering shepherd; black, not by reason of evil or sin, but because the sun of persecution and tribulation in the service of Christ had marred all outward beauty : but comely within, as the curtains of Solomon, the curiously wrought tapestry of divers colours, resplendent with the beauty and glory of her Lord.

"I am black, but comely, O ye daughters of Jerusalem, as the tents of Kedar, as the curtains of Solomon. Look not upon me, because I am black, because the sun hath looked upon me." Cant. i. 5, 6. In Psa. xlv. the Queen, the king's daughter, is seen after the wilderness journey is passed. The way-worn exterior is no longer presented. It is a resurrection-scene of complete and eternal glory. "Upon thy right hand standeth the queen, in gold of Ophir. The King's daughter is all glorious within (her palace :) her clothing is of cloth interwoven with gold. She shall be brought unto the King in raiment of needle-work." Even now, Christ's estimate of the Church is, that she is as one pearl of great price, (Matt. xiii.) for the sake of which, He has parted with all, making Himself poor : for He "loved the church, and gave Himself for it, that He might sanctify and cleanse it with the washing of water by the word ; that He might present it to Himself a glorious church, not having spot or wrinkle, or any such thing ; but that it should be holy and without blemish." Eph. v. 25—27.

The tabernacle must have appeared, to the eye of a stranger, as a long dark coffin-like structure. So also must the ark, that Noah built as a place of refuge, have seemed to men around a strange ungainly black wooden building. Christ in His death, presents no object of attraction to the natural heart; while to the believer He is, by reason of that very death, altogether lovely. In like manner, the Church of God is as the filth and offscouring of all things to the world. But the Lord is able to say of her, "Thou art all fair, my love: there is no spot in thee."

False prophets in Israel wore a rough garment to deceive. In modern days, men have affected an outward garb of humility, and separation from the world : while beneath the serge garment and rope of the recluse, or the unadorned vestments of some nominal Christian sects, has lurked a heart of unsubdued pride, and an eager desire for human approbation. The flesh, to accomplish its own ends, can mortify itself. There may be a shew of wisdom in will-worship and humility, and neglecting of the body. But by these very things, the flesh may be satisfied. The true badger-skin exterior should be the result of the walk and ways of a risen heavenly man, in the midst of an unredeemed wilderness earth. We must be first transformed, by the renewing of the mind, into the likeness of Jesus, and walk according to the rule of the new creature, if we would not be conformed to this world. Gal. vi. 15, 16. The unregenerate earthly man may make a fair shew in the flesh; may become a devotee, and thereby pacify his own conscience, and gain the esteem of men. But the Lord seeth not as man seeth: for man looketh on the outward appearance; but the Lord looketh on the heart. And the day is fast approaching, when realities will take the place of false appearances. The true follower of Jesus will, by reason of fellowship with God, and a heart set on things above, unconsciously acquire a stranger, and pilgrim-like character. He will be little esteemed amongst men, and may have a Galilean name of reproach. But he is a king and priest to God, and will be soon manifest in the glory of his Lord. The blessed Lord Himself was despised, as of Nazareth. But this very name of contumely was one of distinguished holiness: for it implied entire separation to God.

# THE DOOR OF THE TABERNACLE

"And thou shalt make an hanging for the door of the tent, of blue, and purple, and scarlet, and fine twined linen, wrought with needlework.

"And thou shalt make for the hanging five pillars of shittim wood, and overlay them with gold, and their hooks shall be of gold: and thou shalt cast five sockets of brass for them."—Exod. xxvi 36, 37

"And he made an hanging for the tabernacle door of blue, and purple, and scarlet, and fine twined linen, of needlework.

"And the five pillars of it with their hooks: and he overlaid their chapiters and their fillets with gold; but their five sockets were of brass."—Exod. xxxvi 37, 38

THE hanging, which formed the door of the tabernacle, was made of the same materials as the vail, arranged in the same order, "blue, and purple, and scarlet, and fine twined linen." The only difference between the two was, that the latter was of cunning work, Cherubim: the former of needlework, without Cherubim.

The word, here translated *needlework*, is in some places rendered "work of the embroiderer." Exod. xxxv. 35: xxxviii. 23. Also "divers colours." (1 Chron. xxix. 2; Ezek. xvii. 3,) and once, "curiously wrought." Psa. cxxxix. 15. This word on the whole seems to mean, *minutely variegated*.

And probably the difference between this work and cunning work may be, that in the "door curtain," "gate of the court," and the under girdle of the high priest, where the word needlework occurs, the colours were skilfully intermixed : but in the vail and curtains, a pattern of Cherubim was cunningly or ingeniously embroidered.

The priests, who entered within the door of the tabernacle, alone beheld the cherubim of glory worked into the vail and roof of the tabernacle; whilst the worshipper in the court saw the same colours intermingled in the door-curtain. May not this be intended to teach us, that *every* worshipper of God recognises the beauty and perfection of Christ, as God manifest in the flesh, his eye rests upon the door-curtain. But the nearer we approach to God as His priests, the more intimate our fellowship with Him in heavenly places; the more shall we discern the glories of Jesus, and realize His power, majesty, and strength. He will be the one object that fills our soul, and under the shadow of His wings shall we abide. We behold the same beauteous colours, but the glory of the Cherubim also is displayed. Many a believer does not, as he should, realize his priestly standing before God. Hence worship, prayer, and praise, are often delegated to certain consecrated men, who by common consent, even of many of the Lord's people, are supposed to have a nearer access to God, and a power to handle holy things, which others in God's church do not possess. But the rending of the vail abolished the standing of an earthly tabernacle; destroyed all distinctions in the flesh; opened heaven itself as the only holy place; and directly Christ entered there in resurrection, "the High Priest of good things to come," the eternal redemption, which He had obtained, brought every believer equally nigh to God; so that now all are holy brethren, partakers alike of the same heavenly calling as their great High Priest. Christ is the door of Salvation. "I am the door: by me if any man enter in, he shall be saved." The door; not into an earthly sheepfold, nor into a nominal church, but the door to God; the door into light, truth, life, and holiness.

With regard to the colours, of which the door-curtain was made, they were the same as those which composed the vail and the curtains. The reader is referred to what has already been written on this subject, under the head of the Vail.

The following are the only places where this hanging is called the door of the *tabernacle*.

Exod. xxxv.—Where Moses enumerates the things which are to be made, he specifies, (v. 15,) the hanging

for the door at the entering-in of the tabernacle, or, as
it might be translated, the door-hanging, for the door
of the tabernacle.

Exod. xl 5  The hanging, the door of the tabernacle.

„  6  And thou shalt set the altar of burnt
offering before the door of the tabernacle, the tent of the congregation.

„  28  And he set up the hanging, the door
for the tabernacle.

In all other cases, where this hanging is mentioned, it
is called either the door of the tent (Exod xxvi. 36;
and xxxvi. 37,) or the door of the tent of the congregation. The reason of this may be, that this door
afforded an entrance for the congregation, by means
of their priests, towards God who dwelt within the
tabernacle; rather than a way of exit for God out of
the tabernacle. His place of abode was within that
holy building; His glory was displayed there; and His
blessed purpose was, to remain uninterruptedly dwelling
in the midst of the people.

The door of the tabernacle was, to the ordinary
Israelite, what the holy places were within to the
priests :—the place where God's presence was realized.
The altar of burnt offering was set at or before the door
of the congregation-tent. Exod. xxix. 42, and xl. 6.
God was to be approached only through sacrifice. The
door of entrance into His presence was closely connected
with the altar, upon which victims were constantly
burning; upon which blood was sprinkled, and at the
bottom of which blood was poured. In fact we may
say an Israelite had no dealings with God, according to
the prescribed ritual, except about sacrifice or through
sacrifice. If he came into God's presence, it was to
bring either a burnt-offering, a meat-offering, a peace-
offering, or a sin-offering.

His three yearly seasons of drawing nigh to God were
marked with numerous sacrifices. His basket of first-
fruits could be accepted only through the altar. The

sweet savour of a lamb slain, ascended morning by
morning, to God for him from that altar at the door of
the tabernacle.   And in the evening, when his daily toil
ceased, he lay down to rest under the shelter of the slain
lamb, again presented to God for him in the same place.
His sabbath was ushered in by additional sacrifices,
offered to God : and each opening month commenced
with fresh memorials of the great truth, that " without
shedding of blood there is no remission ;" and that
there could be no acceptance of any man's person, save
through the death of another.   Thus the true Israelite
would in spirit, spend his life at the tabernacle-door in
the presence of God.   So also the believer now, is to
know nothing in this world, but Jesus Christ, and Him
crucified ; to hear, see, walk, live, in the remembrance
of Jesus, and the preciousness of His blood; and thus to
abide continually before God.

The command to Abram was, " I am the Almighty
God : *walk before me*, and be thou perfect." Gen. xvii. 1.
" Enoch *walked with God*." Gen. v. 24.   And the precept
to Israel was, " Ye shall *walk after* the Lord your God,
and fear Him, and keep His commandments, and obey
His voice, and ye shall serve Him, and cleave unto Him."
Deut. xiii. 4.   Could we but keep in mind this triple
cord of responsibility and blessing ; to *live* in the power
and presence of Almighty God, so that we consciously
pass our days in His sight.   1. Thess. i. 3.   To *walk*
also in fellowship with Him, that His counsels, His will,
might be ours ; that we might delight in pleasing Him,
and dwelling in the light of His countenance ; and lastly,
to *follow* His guidance; to know the path He would have
us to tread, so that it might be as the path of the just,
shining more and more unto the perfect day.   Could we
thus realize by faith our high calling, we should taste
somewhat of that fulness of joy which is in His presence;
and dwell under the shadow of the Almighty, in security,
happiness, and peace.   As one of old sang, " I had
rather be a door-keeper (margin ; I would choose rather

to sit at the threshold) in the house of my **God**, than **to** dwell in the tents of wickedness." Psa. lxxxiv. 10.

This door-curtain was suspended by hooks of gold, from five pillars of shittim wood overlaid with gold, crowned with capitals or chapiters of gold. Thus the manifested beauty and glory of Jesus, as the door of salvation, the way to God, leads us to contemplate Himself, according to the five syllables of His name recorded in Isa. ix. 6, "His name shall be called Wonderful ; Counseller ; the Mighty God ; the Ever-lasting Father ; the Prince of Peace."

We gaze upon His work on the cross ; we hear His seven utterances from thence ; and we turn to see from whence this great sight proceeds, and bow, and worship *Him ;* the mystery—God manifest in the flesh ꓼ the Wisdom of God ; the Mighty God ; the spring and source of all things ; the commencement of the everlast-ing ages ; the Prince of Peace.

Each pillar, a type of Him, had its crowning chapiter. And the crowning glory of the Lord is, that He is Prince of Peace : the One by whom it is the purpose of God to reconcile all things to Himself : the One in whom He has even now reconciled us to Himself. We see Jesus, who was for a little while made lower than the angels, crowned with glory and honour.

Each of these door-pillars stood in a socket of *brass.* The vail pillars, and the boards of the tabernacle, stood in sockets of *silver.* The object of this difference may be to exhibit the truth, that Christ is the door by reason of His sufferings in death ; brass being used for the altar, on which the sacrifices were consumed ; and brass being the metal often used in Scripture, to denote power to endure or sustain the fire.

The following are the references in the Scriptures to the various sacrifices offered before the door, or before the tent of the congregation, before the **Lord**.

Burnt-offering of the Herd . . Lev. i 3
Peace-offering of the Herd . . ,, iii 1

# THE BOARDS AND BARS OF THE TABERNACLE

"And thou shalt make boards for the tabernacle of shittim wood standing up.

"Ten cubits shall be the length of a board, and a cubit and a half shall be the breadth of one board.

"Two tenons shall there be in one board, set in order one against another: thus shalt thou make for all the boards of the tabernacle.

"And thou shalt make the boards for the tabernacle, twenty boards on the south side southward.

"And for the second side of the tabernacle on the north side there shall be twenty boards:

"And for the sides of the tabernacle westward thou shalt make six boards.

"And two boards shalt thou make for the corners of the tabernacle in the two sides.

"And they shall be coupled together beneath, and they shall be coupled together above the head of it unto one ring : thus shall it be for them both; they shall be for the two corners,

"And they shall be eight boards,

"And thou shalt make bars of shittim wood ; five for the boards of the one side of the tabernacle.

"And five bars for the boards of the other side of the tabernacle, and five bars for the boards of the side of the tabernacle, for the two sides westward.

"And the middle bar in the midst of the boards shall reach from end to end.

"And thou shalt overlay the boards with gold, and make their rings of gold for places for the bars: and thou shalt overlay the bars with gold."—Exod. xxvi 15 —29

"And he made boards for the tabernacle of shittim wood standing up.

"The length of a board was ten cubits, and the breadth of a board one cubit and a half.

"One board had two tenons, equally distant one from another: thus did he make for all the boards of the tabernacle.

"And he made boards for the tabernacle ; twenty boards for the south side southward :

"And for the other side of the tabernacle, which is toward the north corner, he made twenty boards,

"And for the sides of the tabernacle westward he made six boards,

"And two boards made he for the corners of the tabernacle in the two sides.

"And they were coupled beneath, and coupled together at the head thereof, to one ring ; thus he did to both of them in both the corners.

"And there were eight boards.

"And he made bars of shittim wood ; five for the boards of the one side of the tabernacle,

"And five bars for the boards of the other side of the tabernacle, and five bars for the boards of the tabernacle for the sides westward,

"And he made the middle bar to shoot through the boards from the one end to the other.

"And he overlaid the boards with gold, and made their rings of gold to be places for the bars, and overlaid the bars with gold." Exod. xxxvi 20—34

THE frame-work or walls of the tabernacle were made of boards of shittim-wood, overlaid with gold ; each board stood ten cubits high, and a cubit and a half broad. Twenty of these, standing side by side, formed the south wall of the tabernacle ; and twenty, similarly placed, formed the north side. Six were placed at the east end, where also two additional boards stood in the corners, to give increased stability to the structure. The length of the tabernacle would therefore be twenty times a cubit and a half, or thirty cubits : the breadth, six boards of a cubit and a half, or nine cubits. To this must be added the thickness of the boards north and south, which (though not specified in the directions given to Moses) may yet be gathered to have been half a cubit. This may be ascertained by the following calculation. The first set of curtains was twenty-eight cubits long ; and when thrown over the golden boards, there remained a cubit on each side of them uncovered. These two uncovered cubits were completely covered by the next set of curtains, which were thirty cubits long. Exod. xxvi. 13. Allowing therefore ten cubits for the height of the boards on the south side, another ten also for those on the north side, making together twenty cubits, we have ten cubits left for the width of the tabernacle. Of this, the six boards at the east end will occupy nine cubits : and allowing a half-cubit for the thickness of the boards on the south and north sides respectively, we get exactly the thirty cubits, the full measurement of the goats' hair curtains, which are specified as entirely covering up the tabernacle.

Each of the boards terminated, as to the lower extremity, in two tenons, which were inserted into mortises in two sockets of silver. The boards were also sustained in their upright position, and linked together by five bars of shittim-wood, overlaid with gold, which ran through rings or staples of gold inserted in the boards. The middle bar of the five ran the whole length of the tabernacle, uniting all the twenty boards together. The other four bars, of which two were placed above, and two below the middle bar, are not described as running all the length, but perhaps only extended half the distance, viz. fifteen cubits each. A similar number of bars coupled the boards composing the north side, and also the west end of the tabernacle. On the whole therefore there were forty-eight boards, and fifteen bars. All these were made of Shittim wood, overlaid with gold.

Each board of shittim-wood, overlaid with gold, seems to pourtray the Lord Jesus Himself, the Son of God, the Son of Man. The shittim-wood, incorruptible wood, being a shadow of that great truth, that He "partook of flesh and blood;" "the Seed of the Woman;" "the Second Man;" "from heaven;" yet "the Son of David," "of the fruit of his loins;" and at the same time, "the Son of the Highest;" born of the virgin, "the Man Christ Jesus;" made "in the likeness of sinful flesh;" though, unlike any other man that ever lived on earth, incorrupt and incorruptible; having a body prepared for Him by God, in order that He might die; but without taint of mortality or death in Him.

The gold also presents the other great truth, that He is "the Mighty God;" "the brightness of God's glory;" "the only-begotten of the Father;" "the Son" from everlasting, and to everlasting. Each board of the tabernacle, each bar, each pillar, reiterates again and again these great verities, on which salvation depends, on which the whole basis of Christianity rests, and on which the new creation, with all its glories, subsists, viz. the person of the Lord Jesus Christ, the Son of the Father, made of a woman, God and Man, one Christ.

The boards are like the ribs of truth, the massive frame-work; without which no dwelling-place of God could be created; no meeting-place between God and man provided. If the wood could corrupt, or if the fine gold could become dim; if the taint of mortality, or mouldering flesh, be connected, by human theory or speculation, with the glorious Emmanuel; the tabernacle of God must tremble and totter : the great truths of salvation are shaken : and a mis-shapen mass of ruin takes the place of the divinely-ordered palace of the Most High.

Moses was enjoined by God, again and again, to make and rear up the tabernacle with its vessels, according to the pattern shewed him in the mount. He was not to speculate on the materials to be used, or the shapes or measurements. All was defined by God ; and accurately did he conform to the directions he had received, and the pattern he had seen. So that " as the Lord commanded Moses" is the closing sentence of approval, as each portion successively was erected or arranged by him : and finally, God manifested His presence in the cloud without, and the glory within, as a token of His full satisfaction in the work of His servant. (Exod. xl.)

A reasoning and speculative mind is inconsistent with a humble worshipping spirit. God has laid down His own definitions, His measurements and dimensions of truth. The Father alone knoweth the Son. It is our place reverently to bow, and believe what He has recorded touching the Lord Jesus. Uzzah may think that the ark of the Holiest is in danger; David having himself, contrary to God's word, fashioned a new cart to bear it. But Uzzah was not spared by God, though his motive might appear unobjectionable : and David was at the same time made to tremble, and solemnly rebuked by the sudden judgment.

One result of fashioning creeds and confessions of faith as the vehicles of truth, and not holding God's own word to be sufficient, is, that unholy hands are often stretched out, to defend or maintain these arrangements of human wisdom : and coldness and deadness of soul, and lifeless profession result, instead of the power and vigour of the truth in the souls of God's children, manifested in their life and conduct. Orthodoxy, as it is called, ever appeals to human writings and human standards, which however true, can never embrace the fulness of God's word, and which may be held in the head, and subscribed to by the hand, without any living faith or power of the Holy Spirit. When will the children of God learn that *His Word* is sufficiently full, and sufficiently accurate ?

The massive framework of the golden boards and bars formed a compact structure, over which the curtains and coverings were suspended. They were to the curtains what the poles are to a tent. They upheld and sustained the glorious display of the blue, purple, scarlet, and fine linen cherubim, as also the goats' hair curtains. Thus what the Lord Jesus Himself was and is, viz : Son of God, Son of Man—*that* He has made manifest in His life, and above all, in His death on the cross : and His blessed work there, derives all its unspeakable value, and eternal efficacy, from HIMSELF. It is faith in HIM that is Salvation. " God so loved the world, that He gave His only begotten Son, that whosoever believeth in HIM should not perish, but have everlasting life." " He that believeth on the Son hath life." John iii. 16, 36. May there not be a tendency to separate too much the *work* of the Lord Jesus from His *person* ? to preach the death of the blessed Lord, without sufficiently preaching also the Lord Himself ? The Apostle determined not to know anything among the Corinthians, but Jesus Christ and Him crucified. I Cor. ii. 2. And his great object of pursuit, for his own personal blessing and joy, was to know Him. Phil. iii. 10.

The boards and bars have the same relation to the tabernacle itself, as the truth contained in the first two chapters of the Epistle to the Hebrews has to the rest of the Epistle. In the first and second chapters, the great foundations of faith are laid. The Lord Jesus

Christ is presented to us as the Son; the brightness of God's glory, and the express image of His person; the Son of the Father; God, the Creator—the Sustainer of all things; and who will change all things. He is also presented to us as the Son of Man, partaker of flesh and blood in order to die; the first-born from the dead, all things put under Him; anointed above His fellows; not ashamed to call them brethren. On these great truths respecting Christ, depend all the other great verities connected with the value of His sacrifice; the glory and power of His priesthood; the eternal salvation, the eternal redemption, and the eternal inheritance, which are obtained for us by His own blood. The Apostle also in the Epistle to the Colossians, unfolds the majesty, fulness, and glorious pre-eminence of the Lord Jesus: because the believers to whom he wrote, were in danger from philosophical speculations, and Judaising teachers. The completeness of their salvation; the loftiness of their standing; and the unbounded treasures of wisdom and knowledge within their reach, all resulted from the dignity, power, and glory of Him who was their Head.

We shall find that every false doctrine, which affects the faith or calling of the believer, may be traced to some misapprenension or error respecting the Lord Jesus Himself. If a bar, or board, or ring were wanting, the whole strength of the tabernacle would be weakened. It would cease to be a firm compact building, fitly framed together.

There is one verse respecting the corner-boards, which is of difficult interpretation. It runs thus in our translation : " And two boards shalt thou make for the corners of the tabernacle, in the two sides. And they shall be coupled together beneath, and they shall be coupled together above the head of it unto one ring : thus shall it be for them both : they shall be for the two corners."— Exod. xxvi. 23, 24.

And they were coupled beneath, and coupled together

at the head thereof unto one ring.  Thus he did to both of them, at both the corners."—Exod. xxxvi. 29.

The latter part of this description may be translated thus:

And they shall be doubled (or twinned) beneath, and together they shall be (finished or perfected) upon its head to the same ring.  Thus shall it be for those two ; for the two corners they shall be.  Exod. xxvi. 24.

Exod. xxxvi. 29, is precisely similar.

The word *doubled* is the same word, whence *twin* is derived.

The difficulty of this passage is, *First*, the meaning of the boards being *doubled beneath*.  *Secondly*, the meaning of the words, upon *its* head.  *Thirdly*, the same ring: or, to one ring.

The general description of the boards, (Exod. xxvi. 15—17,) and the words " Thus shalt thou make for *all* the boards of the tabernacle," and the fact, that the corner-boards are reckoned with the other western-boards in verse 25, " they shall be eight boards," would seem to imply, that these corner-boards were the same size and shape as the others.  If this be so, they must have stood in the corners of the tabernacle, at the north and south sides, at the western end, and may have been grooved (or twinned) into the other boards from beneath to the top, where a ring or staple may have bound them to the sides and end of the tabernacle.  However this may have been ; the object of these corner-boards was, to add strength to the whole structure, and knit the sides and end together.

Our thoughts naturally turn to the two occasions on which the Lord is spoken of in Scripture, with reference to the corner :

Isa. xxviii. 16.—" Behold, I lay in Zion, for a foundation, a stone, a tried stone, a precious corner-stone, a sure foundation."

Psa. cxviii. 22.—" The stone, which the builders refused, is become the head-stone of the corner."

Here we have presented to us, a corner-stone as foundation ; and a corner-stone crowning the building : the beginning, and the end : the whole strength of the edifice depending on the firmness of the foundation corner-stone ; and the whole compactness, and knitting-together of the building as one, depending on the head-stone of the corner. God laid the foundation in the death of His Son : He completed the building in His resurrection. The walls of living stone rest securely on this Rock of Ages, and are bound everlastingly together by the top-stone. The corner-boards of the tabernacle may have some reference to these blessed truths.

## THE ATONEMENT MONEY

"And the Lord spake unto Moses, saying, when thou takest the sum of the children of Israel after their number, then shall they give every man a ransom for his soul unto the Lord, when thou numberest them ; that there be no plague among them, when thou numberest them.

"This they shall give, every one that passeth among them that are numbered, half a shekel after the shekel of the sanctuary : (a shekel is twenty gerahs :) an half shekel shall be the offering of the Lord.

"Every one that passeth among them that are numbered, from twenty years old and above, shall give an offering unto the Lord.

"The rich shall not give more, and the poor shall not give less than half a shekel, when they give an offering unto the Lord, to make an atonement for your souls.

"And thou shalt take the atonement money of the children of Israel, and shalt appoint it for the service of the tabernacle of the congregation ; that it may be a memorial unto the children of Israel before the Lord, to make an atonement for your souls."—Exod. xxx. 11—16.

We have another metal presented to us, in the construction of the tabernacle—Silver.

The word in the Hebrew is frequently translated *Money*. It was indeed, the precious metal ordinarily in use, in all transactions of buying and selling : and even at this day, in many countries, it is the current money of the merchant. Francs, dollars, thalers, scudi, are all coins of silver : and mercantile transactions are generally

calculated in one or other of these coins, in most of the
countries of Europe, and indeed of the world.

We have two memorable instances in Scripture, where
life was bartered for silver ; Joseph for twenty, and the
Son of God for thirty pieces. The idea therefore, of
price or value, especially attaches to this metal. It ranks
also with us, as one of the precious metals : and though
not displaying the brilliant glory of the gold, it is yet
especially beautiful, by reason of its soft purity and
unsullied whiteness : and like the gold, it corrodes not,
and wastes not in the fining pot, though subjected to the
intense heat of the furnace.

The silver, used in the construction of the tabernacle,
was all derived from the Atonement money.

The whole range of God's truth rests upon two great
verities :—the Lord Jesus, the Son of God, the Son of
Man—and His work of atonement on the cross.
Throughout the history of God's ancient people, type
after type, and shadow upon shadow, reiterated the
absolute necessity of atonement. And while the Law
prescribed commandments, to obey which, Israel fatally
pledged themselves, it at the same time, contained abundant ritual observances, which testified to man's incapa-
bility and need, and prophesied of One, who while they
were yet without strength, should, in due time, die for
the ungodly. As a covenant of works, it was a ministration of death. But to one who was really a child of
Abraham, it must have shone out, like the face of Moses,
with a prophetic glory; and have pointed onwards to the
Lamb of God; in whom all the shadows of good things
to come passed into substance.

This type before us, of the atonement-money, preached
a very clear and blessed Gospel. It told out the great
truth, that birth in the flesh availed nothing. An Israelite
might trace up, in unbroken succession, his descent from
Abraham, or from one of Jacob's sons. Still, that
sufficed him not, if he desired to be entered on the roll
as one of God's soldiers and servants. The Jews, in

the time of the Lord, could say, " We be Abraham's seed :" and the Samaritan sinner claimed Jacob as her father.  But they were captives of the devil, and of fleshly lusts ; and their human pedigree had not raised them out of the dominion of sin.  God had therefore enjoined, that, whenever Israel were numbered as His people, every man must give a ransom for his soul.  The price was fixed by God Himself.  Each man, whether poor or rich, must bring the same.  One could not pay for another ; but every one must tender his own ransom-money, of pure silver, and of perfect weight.  "Half a shekel, after the shekel of the sanctuary, (a shekel is twenty gerahs,) a half-shekel shall be the offering of the Lord." (Exod. xxx. 13.)  Other Gospel truths here shine out.  When the question came to be one of ransom ; the poor and the rich, the foolish and the wise, the ignorant and the learned, the immoral and the moral, stood on the same level.  Each person was estimated by God at the same price.  He proved Himself no respecter of persons.  And so it is still.  The third chapter of the Epistle to the Romans defines the state of every one in the whole world, and levels the way for the Gospel.  John the Baptist prepared the way of the Lord by his voice, calling all to repentance, declaring all to be in one condition, needing change of heart.  And the Lord Jesus began to speak of the great salvation to hearts thus prepared.  The chapter above referred to makes the path straight for the proclamation of justification through faith in Christ, by pronouncing that all are under sin ; that every mouth must be silent ; that all the world is guilty before God ; and that there is no difference between the religious Jew, and the irreligious Gentile : for, "all have sinned, and come short of the glory of God."

Another truth enunciated in this type is, that salvation must be an individual, personal matter; between the soul and God.  Every man has to bring his own half-shekel.  One of the devices of Satan, at the present day—and it is spread far and wide—is the way in which he obscures this truth, by inducing whole communities to believe they are Christians ; made such, either by baptism, or by some formal profession of religiousness ; and placing, in the lips of thousands, " Our Saviour," and " Our Father ;" and thus beguiling them into the thought, that they are included in a general redemption of mankind, which affects the whole human race. Con-stantly therefore, in speaking to persons, we find the reply :—O yes, we are all sinners : and Christ has died for us all.

Each individual Israelite had to present himself to the priest, bringing with him his own piece of money as a ransom : and his name would then be entered in God's book. The Lord Jesus, in the 6th of John says: " Except ye eat the flesh of the Son of Man, and drink His blood, ye have no life in you." Eating and drinking are actions which one cannot perform for another. The food, taken into the mouth, becomes one's own, and ministers strength and nourishment to the body. So, the death of Christ must be appropriated by each to himself. The soul has to say, *My* Saviour; *My* Lord ; *My* God. *I* have been crucified with Christ. Christ loved *me*, and gave Himself for *me*. Just as assuredly as the Israelite of old, had to eat the manna he had collected for his own sustenance; or according to his eating, to make his count for the lamb.

The half-shekel was to be of silver ; the unalloyed, unadulterated metal. Three things are probably here presented to us in type : the Lord Jesus as God—as the pure and spotless One—and as giving His life a ransom for many. The silver, being a solid imperishable pre-cious metal, may have this first aspect : its chaste white-ness representing the second ; and its being ordinarily employed as money or price, may point out its fitness as a type of the third.

The *weight* was also defined by God :—"the shekel of the sanctuary;" kept as a standard in the tabernacle; and perhaps bearing some stamp or inscription to authenticate it. Its weight was twenty gerahs. The half-shekel, brought by each man who desired to be numbered, was to be compared with this. God kept the just weight and the just balance ; and his priest would neither take dross instead of silver, nor receive less weight of the precious metal than was required by the Lord. With confidence the true-hearted Israelite, would ring out the silver sound, from his half-shekel before the priest : with confidence would he see it put into the balance. And, in the blessed antitype, with confidence does the believer sound out, in the ears of God, and of the great High Priest of His sanctuary, his full dependence on Christ and His precious blood. He knows that that price is up to the full estimate demanded by God. He has one standard of perfection and purity, against which He weighs the hearts, spirits, and actions of men. Every thing short of this standard, every one who fails to reach this sterling value, will be condemned; like the Babylonian prince, who was weighed in the balances, and found wanting. To come short of the glory of God, is to be in the distance and darkness of corruption and death. How wondrous the grace, which has pro-vided One, in whom we are raised from the depth of human misery, degradation, and ruin, to the height of the throne and glory of the Most High ! How passing knowledge, that love of God, which has not hesitated to plunge into judgment and wrath, His only-begotten Son, and to shed the blood of Christ like water, in order to redeem, from filthiness and sin, the worthless and the vile; and to number them among the hosts of light and glory, in the courts above !

There is a manifest allusion to the atonement-money in 1st Peter i. 18. " Forasmuch as ye know that ye were not redeemed with corruptible things, as silver and gold, from your vain conversation, received by tradition from your fathers ; but with the precious blood of Christ, as of a Lamb without blemish and without spot." An allusion, by way of contrast. What men consider

precious metals, and free frcm impurity and corrosion,
God calls " perishable" and " corruptible." He says,
that gold and silver " canker" and " rust."

The man who amasses wealth is an object of praise
and envy. " Men will praise thee when thou doest well
to thyself." (Psa. xlix. 18.) But in this epistle, gain is
denominated *filthy lucre.* The redemption, which God
has paid for us, is no amount of corruptible things, as
silver and gold. Lebanon is not sufficient to burn, nor
the beasts thereof sufficient for a burnt-offering. Nothing
less than the precious blood of Christ would avail. God
has valued our salvation at no less cost, than the pouring
out of His soul unto death.

The Hebrew word, from which the words *ransom*
and *atonement* are derived, has a variety of senses all
bearing on the same truth. Thus, we find, the word
includes the thought of *covering* over our sin ; as a
covering of pitch covers over the wood on which it is
spread. (Gen. vi. 14.)

The blood of atonement blots out the page of sin,
and hides it from the eye of God. The secret sins,
which have stood out in their glaring evil, in the light
of His countenance, are hidden by the blood sprinkled
on the mercy-seat. It also means, to *appease* or *pacify.*
Thus Jacob sent a present to (*atone* or) appease his
brother Esau. (Gen. xxxii. 20.) " The wrath of a
king is as messengers of death : but a wise man will
(*atone* or) pacify it." (Prov. xvi. 14.) " That thou
mayest remember, and be confounded, and never open
thy mouth any more, because of thy shame, when I am
(*atoned* or) pacified towards thee." (Ezek. xvi. 63.)

This is the sense of the word in the New Testament—
*propitiation;* God's wrath being appeased in Christ through
the shedding of His blood. 1st John ii. 2 ; and iv. 10.

*Pardon* and *forgiveness* are included in the word.
Deut. xxi. 8, " The blood shall be (atoned, or) forgiven them."

Hezekiah prayed, " The good Lord (atone, or) pardon every one." 2nd Chron xxx. 18. Also, to *reconcile.*

" A sin-offering brought in (to atone, or) to reconcile withal, in the holy place." (Lev. vi. 30.

" And when he hath made an end of (atoning, or) reconciling the holy place." Lev. xvi. 20.

" Poured the blood at the bottom of the altar, and sanctified it, to make (atonement, or) reconciliation upon it." Lev. viii. 15.

" So shall ye (atone, or) reconcile the house." Ezek. xlv. 20 ; also 15 and 17.

In the New Testament also, the word *atonement* is synonymous with *reconciliation.*

" To make reconciliation for the sins of the people." Heb. ii. 17.

" We have now received the atonement." Rom. v. 11 (Margin—Reconciliation.)

" Reconciling of the world." Rom. xi. 15.

" That he might reconcile both unto God in one body by the cross." (Eph. ii. 16.

"By Him, to reconcile all things to Himself." Col. i. 20.

*To put off,* or *expiate.*—" Mischief shall fall upon thee : thou shalt not be able to put it off." (Margin—Expiate.) Isa. xlvii. 11.

*To disannul.*—" Your covenant with death shall be disannulled." Isa. xxviii. 18.

*Ransom,* or, *satisfaction.*—" Deliver him from going down into the pit : I have found a ransom." Job. xxxiii. 24.

" A great ransom cannot deliver thee." Job xxxvi. 18

" Nor give to God a ransom for him." Psa. xlix. 7.

*Satisfaction.*—" Ye shall take no satisfaction for the life of a murderer." Num. xxxv. 31.

In the New Testament.—" To give His life a ransom for many." Matt. xx. 28 ; Mark x. 45.

Lastly : *To purge or cleanse.*—" Purge away our sins, for Thy name's sake." Psa. lxxix. 9.

" By mercy and truth, iniquity is purged." Prov. xvi. 6.

" This iniquity shall not be purged." Isa. xxii. 14.

" By this, therefore, shall the iniquity of Jacob be purged. Isa. xxvii. 9.

" The land cannot be cleansed of the blood." Num. xxxv. 33.

We shall perceive, from these various quotations, that the same Hebrew word translated *Atonement*, signifies also, Covering over; Appeasing; Forgiveness; Reconciliation; Expiation; Disannulling; Ransom or Redemption; Satisfaction; and Cleansing.

One sense of *our* word Atonement is, At-one-ment; two opposing parties being brought together in agreement as one. And the means whereby this is effected, the payment of a price, ransom or satisfaction. So, this beautiful type of the half-shekel of silver, shadows forth the precious blood of Christ, as the redemption price provided by God. And, when the sinner estimates its all-sufficient value in the presence of God, he answers the action of the Israelite in paying down the silver half-shekel; as it is beautifully expressed in 1st Pet. ii. 7 : " Unto you which believe, He is precious :" or, as it might be rendered, " He is the preciousness ;" your full satisfaction, and value also before God,

We have also another important aspect of truth pourtrayed in this type—viz. that redemption *brings* us to, and *fits* us for God. The Israelite, who paid his ransom-money, was numbered as a soldier and a servant for God. A place was assigned him in the battle-field: and he had his position in the camp, appointed with reference to the tabernacle, the dwelling-place of God in the midst of the hosts. From henceforth Jehovah was his Leader, his Lord, his King. In like manner, the believer is redeemed to God, by the blood of Christ, from the world, and from slavery to sin and Satan; that he may be a soldier and a servant of the Most High; to be led, guided, and sustained by Him, who has called him out of darkness, into His marvellous light.

Two other words deserve our notice in this passage. Exod. xxx. 13, 14. "Every one that *passeth* among

them that are numbered." and the word "*offering*,"
13—15.　The allusion, in 13, 14, is to the sheep
passing under the rod of the shepherd, as he numbers
them. Ezek. xx 37.　"I will cause you to pass under
the rod: and I will bring you into the bond of the
covenant."　The priest took the place of a shepherd,
counting the sheep of God's hand.　And as the true
mark of the sheep came under his eye, in the ransom-
money offered by each, he entered each in the book of
the covenant.　So the good Shepherd has laid down
His life for the sheep; and they are entered in the
Lamb's book of life, because the atonement-price has
been paid for each.

The word *Offering* is a peculiar word in the Hebrew,
signifying something that is lifted off the ground, and
presented on high; and is the word translated *heave-
offering*.　All the various offerings brought by the
Israelites, as contributions for forming the tabernacle,
and enumerated (Exod. xxv. 2—7,) are called heave-
offerings.　This atonement-money was a peculiar piece
of silver, separated off to God, and lifted, as it were,
from the earth, with the special object of being paid into
His treasury, as a ransom for the soul.　So has the Lord
Jesus been lifted up, first on the cross, to pour out His
blood a ransom for many; and secondly, He has been
exalted, and made very high, "to be a Prince and a
Saviour, for to give repentance to Israel, and forgiveness
of sins." Acts v. 31.

This ordinance was transgressed by David, as related
in 2nd Sam. xxiv., 1st Chron. xxi.　Israel had settled
down in self-contentedness and pride; David their king
and shepherd, himself drinking into the same spirit.
Satan, by God's permission, was allowed to tempt the
king, and provoke him, by whisperings of vanity and
self-exaltation, to number Israel.　The desire in David's
heart was, not that God might be glorified, and His
promise made manifest, in the vast increase of His people;
but that he, the king, might congratulate himself on the

number of his subjects. "Number ye the people, *that I may know*." "Bring the number of them to me, *that I may know it*." Joab, to whom the command was given, though himself an ambitious worldly-minded man, yet was keen-sighted enough to perceive, that this desire of his master was not of God. He even had some insight into David's sin. He looked upon Israel as a people belonging to Jehovah; and on David, as committing a trespass in having them numbered for himself. But, like all unbelievers, though he could point out the fault, he was not able to direct David to the remedy. He did not allude to the atonement-money.

One result of this numbering was, that even cities of the Hivites, and the stronghold of Tyre, were included in the tale; which could never have been the case, had the silver half-shekel been required. At the present day, unconverted inhabitants of earth are too often classed as of the Church of God, by reason of the same neglect, viz : that they are not required to confess openly their confidence in the precious blood of Christ, before being reckoned among the hosts of God.

David's heart soon smote him, after the numbering was completed : he fully confessed his own sin and folly; he at once cast himself on the mercies of God for pardon, and preferred being dealt with in chastisement immediately from the Lord, rather than fall into the hands of men. Accordingly, the plague, (which had already been threatened, in Exod. xxx. 12.) broke out amongst the people: and the destroyer stayed not his hand until the Lord, listening to the humiliation of David, and appeased by the burnt-offering presented at the threshing-floor of Ornan the Jebusite, said— "It is enough." David, in his intercession, manifests a soul restored to the Lord; and proves that he has discovered his former error: for, he speaks of Israel as sheep, and as the people of the Lord; whereas he had numbered them as fighting-men, and for his own glory.

Also the price of the spot for the altar is paid in

shekels of silver. There may be some reference in this, to the atonement-money. The apparent discrepancy, between the fifty shekels, mentioned as the purchase-money in 2nd Sam. xxiv. 24, and the six hundred shekels of gold in 1st Chron. xxi. 25, may be reconciled on the supposition, that the former money was paid for the mere spot, on which the altar itself was erected; whereas the latter, was the purchase-money for the whole place of the threshing-floor.

The blessed words—It is enough—were again, in principle, uttered by Jehovah from heaven, when He raised the Lord Jesus from the dead. Satisfaction had been completely made: the sword of vengance had been buried in the heart of God's own Son; the precious blood had been poured out; the full redemption-price had been rendered; and Jesus was raised from the dead; at once the proof of the perfect value of His own death, and to receive the due reward of His loving faithful obedience. "It is enough" may be a fitting superscription for the half-shekel ransom-money.

It appears that the question asked of Peter, (Matt. xvii. 24.) "Does not your Master pay tribute?" (or, according to the margin, the didrachma) had reference to this ransom-money. Probably the payment, which had been instituted in Exod. xxx. of a half-shekel, when the Israelites were numbered; had in course of time, been converted by the Jewish rulers into a kind of poll-tax, payable for the uses of the temple. Peter, with his usual readiness, or rather rashness, answered the question in the affirmative, without referring, as he should have done, to the Lord Himself for a reply. And when he was come into the house, Jesus anticipated his request for the ransom-money, (to the payment of which, he had just committed the Lord) by putting the question, "What thinkest thou, Simon? of whom do the kings of the earth take custom or tribute? of their own children, or of strangers?" The Lord thus addresses him as *Simon*, instead of Peter. The Apostle had relapsed into the natural man: and Jesus uses the name, which Peter had received from his earthly parents, instead of the new name, given him on his confession of faith.

Peter had forgotten the late glorious scene of the Transfiguration, when the voice had sounded from the excellent glory, "This is my beloved Son: hear ye Him:" and he had committed two errors. Instead of hearkening to Jesus, and learning of Him, he had acted on his own self-confident judgment: and instead of owning the Lord, as the Son of God, he had lowered Him down to the position of a stranger, or captive, from whom a ransom was demanded by God.

This serves to explain the Lord's question quoted above. Peter replies to it—to his own condemnation—"Of strangers." Jesus saith unto him, "Then are the children free." Jesus came to declare *the Father*. "He that hath seen me, hath seen the Father." He had come to redeem them that were under the law; that those who believed on Him might receive the adoption of sons. Liberty of sonship, and not the bondage of servantship, not the slavery of bondmen confined under rigid commandments, was the liberty that Christ came to proclaim. The law, even in its type of the atonement-money, did not intimate the blessing of sonship. Grace and truth, which came by Jesus Christ, placed the believer in the freedom of new birth; as many as received Christ, were born of God. But Peter had not yet received the spirit of sonship. The Holy Ghost had not yet been sent from the risen Christ; and thus the apostle mingled up and confounded adoption and bondage, and lowered the Son down to the position of a stranger.

This is an instructive lesson to our souls: for the spirit of bondage is constantly working within us. It is of the flesh; of nature. It springs from Simon, the Son of Jonas ; instead of from Peter, a child of God. If we have known God, or rather, are known of God, we are no longer aliens or strangers, but

children and heirs; and the spirit of slavery cannot
dwell with the spirit of the Son. Law and grace can
never be united.

The Lord Jesus, having claimed for Himself and Peter
the liberty of children, adds: "Notwithstanding, lest we
should offend them, go thou to the sea, and cast a hook,
and take up the fish that first cometh up; and when thou
hast opened his mouth, thou shalt find a piece of money,
(a stater:) that take and give unto them for me and
thee." Thus, one piece of silver, brought up from the
depth of the sea, was paid into God's treasury; in which
piece Jesus and Peter were both included. There seems
to be a wonderful significance in this. The sea yielded
up the precious ransom-money. The depths, with their
billows and waves of wrath and death, were, so to
speak, the birth-place of atonement. Jesus rose not
alone, but inseparably linked on with His Church—one
with Him in all His own preciousness—presented in
Him to God in glory—laid up and hidden in God's
treasury above.

Whatever God's demand against Peter, the blessed
Lord was involved in the same demand: Peter's responsibility became Christ's:—"for me and thee:"—
and thus is Jesus now in the presence of God for
us, to answer every liability; to render payment in
the full for all our infirmities and sins; to save, to the
very end, all that come unto God by Him. He has
bound us up with Himself, in one bundle of life: and
we can never look upon Him now, without also
beholding, in union with Him, the whole ransomed
church of God, one precious piece of silver in God's
temple above.

" And thou shalt make twenty boards on the south side southward.

" And thou shalt make forty sockets of silver under the twenty boards; two sockets under one board for his two tenons, and two sockets nnder another board for his two tenons.

" And for the second side of the tabernacle on the north side twenty boards.

" And their forty sockets of silver; two sockets under one board, and two sockets under another board.

" And for the sides of the tabernacle westward thou shalt made six boards.

" And two boards shalt thou make for the corners of the tabernacle in the two sides.

" They shall be eight boards, and their sockets of silver, sixteen sockets; two sockets under one board, and two sockets under another board."—Exod. xxvi 18—25

" And he made boards for the tabernable; twenty boards for the south side southward.

" And forty sockets of silver he made under the twenty boards; two sockets under one board for his two tenons, and two sockets under another board for his two tenons.

" And for the other side of the tabernacle, toward the north corner, he made twenty boards.

" And their forty sockets of silver; two sockets under one board, and two sockets under another board.

" And for the sides of the tabernacle westward he made six boards.

" And two boards made he for the corners of the tabernacle in the two sides.

" There were eight boards, and their sockets were sixteen sockets of silver, under every board two sockets."—Exod. xxxvi 23—30

" And the silver of them that were numbered of the congregation was an hundred talents, and a thousand seven hundred and threescore and fifteen shekels, after the shekel of the sanctuary.

" A bekah for every man, half a shekel, after the shekel of the sanctuary, for every one that went to be numbered, from twenty years old and upward, for six hundred thousand and three thousand and five hundred and fifty.

" So were all those that were numbered of the children of Israel, by the house of their fathers, from twenty years old and upward, all that were able to go forth to war in Israel.

" Even all they that were numbered were six hundred and three thousand and five hundred and fifty."—Num. i 45, 46

" And of the hundred talents of silver were cast the sockets of the sanctuary, and the sockets of the vail; an hundred sockets of the hundred talents, a talent for a socket.

" And of the thousand seven hundred seventy and five shekels he made hooks for the pillars, and overlaid their chapiters, and filleted them."—Exod. xxxviii 25—28.

THE silver, derived from the atonement-money of the numbered Israelites, was chiefly appropriated to the sockets of the tabernacle.   Each board stood upon two sockets ; two tenons, at the extremity of each board, dropping into holes or mortises in the two sockets. As the number of the men that paid the ransom-money was 603,550, half of this (viz. 301,775) is the number of shekels, because each man paid half a shekel ; and as there were 100 talents, and 1,775 shekels, the hundred talents forming the hundred sockets, must have been obtained from the 300,000 shekels.   That is, 3,000 shekels would form a talent or socket ; and each socket would contain the ransom-money of 6,000 men, 3,000 shekels : and each board, therefore, stood upon the ransom-money of 12,000 men ; for each board stood in two sockets.

The whole massive framework of the tabernacle stood, as to its foundation, upon the atonement-money paid by the hosts of Israel.   Each man could affirm, that the very dwelling-place of God rested on the ransom-money which he had paid for his soul.   He could look upon the sockets, and say—my silver half-shekel has gone to make up the hundred talents, of which they are formed.   May we not, in like manner, say that the new creation of God, His everlasting dwelling-place in glory, rests upon the redemption of the Church ?   If one ransomed sinner were to fail of reaching the heavenly city, a living stone would be wanting in the super-structure : and there would also be a defect in the very foundation of the city itself.

Redemption is the basis on which God builds the new heavens and the new earth   The precious value of the blood of Christ will be made manifest in every part of the new creation.   All will tell out the costliness of the price that has been paid : and the very dwelling-place of the Most High, heaven itself, owes its stability to the ransom-money that has been provided for the redemption of each individual saint

The unspeakable value of the cross will be proclaimed throughout eternity, from every part, from every glorious feature of the new creation, as well as from every inhabitant of the heavenly city. The kingdom that cannot be moved, derives its stability and firmness from the foundation on which it rests.

The foundation of the *temple* has truths connected with it, in striking analogy with those typified in the foundations of the tabernacle, of which we have been speaking. Mount Moriah was the spot where the Lord provided for himself a lamb. Two great truths of redemption were manifested; first, in Abraham the father, offering up his only-begotten son : next, in the substitution of the ram provided by God instead of the sentenced victim, Isaac. It was therefore a place whereon redemption was stamped in marked features : Moriah, the land of vision, where this great sight was to be seen : Jehovah-jireh also, the Lord will provide Himself a lamb.

Besides this, the same spot was afterwards the threshing-floor of Ornan the Jebusite ; a place from whence wheat was gathered into the barn. It was here also that the angel of the Lord sheathed his weapon of slaughter, by reason of the burnt sacrifice, and the word *enough* pronounced by God. Thus the foundation of the temple was laid on a rock, remarkable as having been a place where a substitute had been provided by God ; where the sword of judgment and justice had been sheathed ; and where a sufficient atonement had been made.

The silver sockets of the tabernacle proclaimed the same truths. And it will be found that God has laid the beams of His chambers of glory above, in the deep waters of death, which rolled over the soul of His blessed Son, the Lamb of God ; the Rock laid as a foundation.

The corner-foundation-stone has been already alluded to, when considering the corner-boards. It may be well however, again to refer to the passages in Isaiah and the Epistle of Peter, as we are contemplating the sockets of the tabernacle, the foundations on which that building of God rested. The whole passage in Isa. xxviii. v. 14—19, should be read together.

"Hear the word of the LORD, ye scornful men, that rule this people which is in Jerusalem. Because ye have said, We have made a covenant with death, and with hell are we at agreement; when the overflowing scourge shall pass through, it shall not come unto us : for we have made lies our refuge, and under falsehood have we hid ourselves. Therefore, thus saith the Lord GOD : Behold, I lay in Zion, for a foundation, a stone, a tried stone, a precious corner-stone, a sure foundation : he that believeth shall not make haste. Judgment also will I lay to the line, and righteousness to the plummet: and the hail shall sweep away the refuge of lies ; and the waters shall overflow the hiding-place. And your covenant with death shall be disannulled, and your agreement with hell shall not stand : when the overflowing scourge shall pass through, then ye shall be trodden down by it. From the time that it goeth forth, it shall take you : for morning by morning shall it pass over, by day and by night : and it shall be a vexation, only to understand the report."

The spiritual rulers of Israel, like the Pharisees in the days of the Lord, had built up a refuge of their own, an elaborate structure of self-righteousness, resting on a foundation of pride and self-will, and constructed of religious observances, and conformity to the traditions and commandments of men—a refuge of lies, a hiding-place of falsehood, and having no other than a sandy foundation. (Matt. vii. 26.) The superstructure and the foundation were alike as to materials : vain, rotten, unstable ; the work of man from beginning to end.

In contrast with this, God laid in Zion the mountain of holiness, for a foundation, a stone, the firmness and everlasting stability of which He had tried, like silver tried in the furnace: a precious corner, the costliness and value of which, God alone could estimate, according to His own weight and balance, the shekel of the sanctuary :—a sure foundation : no superficial sandy surface ; but a foundation of rock, laid in the depths, firm, immovable, the Rock of Ages. All that is erected on this, partakes of the same lasting character. He that believeth shall not make haste, shall not be ashamed or confounded, shall not be shaken by the storm or tempest. Faith rests on this sure foundation, in contrast with works which rest on the sand. Directly God laid his foundation-stone, which is Jesus Christ, He takes the line and plummet into His own hands, and measures and tests the uprightness of every edifice of man. " Judgment also will I lay to the line, and righteousness to the plummet." He has one, and one only standard, THE RIGHTEOUS ONE. All that comes short of this height of perfection, all that deviates from this tested uprightness, will be tried in judgment. The floods of God's wrath will come : the torrents will descend from above : the hurricane of His fury will beat : and all that is not of Christ, and on Christ, will fall and perish in hopeless confusion. " The hail shall sweep away the refuge of lies ; and the waters shall overflow the hiding-place. When the overflowing scourge shall pass through, then ye shall be trodden down by it." God has promised to shake all things that can be shaken, that we may be assured of the eternal stability of Him, on whom our souls rest—the eternal preciousness of His blood—the sufficient and everlasting righteousness of Him, in whom we are accepted—the solid foundation on which God's everlasting tabernacle rests.

In 1st Peter ii. 4—8, three separate passages of the Old Testament are put together : Isa. xxviii. 16 ; Ps cxviii, 22 ; Isa. viii. 14. " The living stone, elect, precious, laid in Zion :" "the stone disallowed indeed of men, but made the head of the corner :" " and a stone of

stumbling, and a rock of offence, even to them which
stumble at the word."

An allusion having been made, (1st Peter i. 19) to
the precious blood of Christ, as the true redemption-
price, in contrast with silver and gold, as atonement-
money ; the Spirit of God in the apostle seems to have
contemplated Isaiah xxviii. in connection with the vain
conversation, received by tradition from the fathers—
the refuge of lies, and hiding-place of falsehood, of
verse 15. Another allusion to the same chapter occurs
also a little further on. " As new-born babes, desire
the sincere milk of the word." (1st Pet. ii. 2.) " Whom
shall he teach knowledge ? And whom shall he make
to understand doctrine ? Them that are weaned from
the milk, and drawn from the breasts." (Isa, xxviii. 9.)
Again, it appears there is a reason for linking on Isaiah
xxviii. with Isaiah viii. 14, besides the fact of the stone
being spoken of in both places. In chap. xxviii. 13,
the effect upon Israel generally, of the line upon line,
and precept upon precept, concerning Christ, would be
to cause them to go and fall backward, and be broken,
and snared, and taken : as in chap. viii. 14, it had
been declared, that Christ should be for a stone of
stumbling, and for a rock of offence, to both the houses
of Israel; for a gin and for a snare to the inhabitants of
Jerusalem. " And many among them shall stumble and
fall, and be broken, and be snared, and be taken."

It is deeply interesting thus to trace the wonderful
connection of the Scriptures together, and the one per-
vading mind and spirit who indited the whole.

As in the case of the structure built upon sand, the
same worthlessness and instability were stamped, as well
on the building, as on the foundation: so the *living
stones*, built upon *the living Stone*, partake of the value,
preciousness, life, and durability of their foundation.

When the Lord Jesus was on earth, He was openly
refused by the Jewish builders. ("His own received
Him not." " We will not have this man to reign over us."

"Not this man, but Barabbas.") They esteemed Him not : but God raised up this disallowed Stone, and crowned Him with glory and honour; setting Him over the works of His hands; putting all in subjection under His feet; and giving Him to be the head over all things to the Church.

Moreover : Christ crucified was, and is the stumbling-stone to the Jews. Rejected by them when on earth, and still more abhorred by them by reason of His death, He is at this day the rock of offence, the gin and snare, in which they have been snared and taken. They have fallen upon that stone, and been broken.

But not only is it so, as to that nation. Disobedience, or unbelief of the word, (which are synonymous terms,) characterises the masses of Gentiles around us. Christendom occupies much the same place as to the stone, as did the Jewish nation of old. Christ is still disallowed as the sole foundation laid by God. He is not "the preciousness," and the only preciousness, to many that call themselves by His name. His death, the shame and obloquy of His cross, the shedding of His blood as a ransom, are still causes of offence to very many nominal Christians. And in high places in the land, among those who are the builders of the day, the atonement is disallowed; the word of God is impugned ; and refuges of lies, and coverts of falsehood, are erected on all sides. But the storm is not far distant. Soon will the stone fall, and grind to powder those who have thus disallowed Him, God's precious chosen One. Soon will the Gentile image be crushed to atoms under the foot of the King of Kings ; and like the chaff of the summer threshing-floors, driven by the wind, not a vestige will remain of the proud scornful nations of Christendom. The day of visitation is coming, when God will destroy the wisdom of the wise, and bring to nothing the understanding of the prudent : (" Where is the wise? where is the scribe? where is the disputer of this world?")—a day of such an overflowing scourge, that it shall be a vexation, only to understand the report.

One concluding remark, respecting the silver sockets. The goats' hair curtains would exactly reach the silver foundations, in which the boards were fixed. Thus the whole tent of the congregation would proclaim one blessed testimony; viz. that atonement had been made; that a full price had been paid and accepted by God; that a sufficient sin-offering had been slain; and therefore a place of reconciliation, a meeting-place between God and the people had been established; in which He could abide in the midst of them, notwithstanding their waywardness, murmurings, and shortcomings; and to which they might with confidence draw nigh at any time.

The number 12 is remarkably connected with the boards and sockets. There were 48 boards, or four twelves; these stood in 96 sockets, or eight twelves: and each board rested on the atonement-money of 12,000 Israelites.

The four pillars of the vail stood on the remaining four silver sockets; which with the 96, made up the 100.

**The Table of Shewbread**

# THE SILVER TRUMPETS

"The Lord spake unto Moses, saying,

"Make thee two trumpets of silver; of a whole piece shalt thou make them; that thou mayest use them for the calling of the assembly, and for the journeying of the camps.

"And when they shall blow with them, all the assembly shall assemble themselves to thee at the door of the tabernacle of the congregation.

"And if they blow with but one trumpet, then the princes, heads of the thousands of Israel, shall gather themselves unto thee.

"When ye blow an alarm, then the camps that lie on the east parts shall go forward.

"When ye blow an alarm the second time, then the camps that lie on the south side shall take their journey: they shall blow an alarm for their journeys.

"But when the congregation is to be gathered together, ye shall blow, but ye shall not sound an alarm.

"And the sons of Aaron, the priests, shall blow with the trumpets; and they shall be to you for an ordinance for ever throughout your generations.

"And if ye go to war in your land against the enemy that oppresseth you, then ye shall blow an alarm with the trumpets; and ye shall be remembered before the Lord your God, and ye shall be saved from your enemies.

"Also in the day of your gladness, and in your solemn days, and in the beginnings of your months, ye shall blow with the trumpets over your burnt offerings, and over the sacrifices of your peace offerings; that they may be to you for a memorial before your God: I am the Lord your God."—Num. x 1—10

IT may be well to consider this type in connection with what has been said respecting the silver sockets: as the appointment of these trumpets seems to owe its significance to the fact, that they must have been made of silver atonement-money.

It is true, that all the silver paid in half-shekels as ransom-money, was used in forming the hundred sockets, and hooks, and capitals of the court-pillars. But there was an additional numbering, recorded in Num. iii. 40—51, in which the first-born of males of Israel were numbered, amounting to 22,273. For these the Levites were substituted. But the number of the Levites was less by 273 than the first-born of the tribes. God accordingly directed that these 273 first-born Israelites, should be redeemed at the price of five shekels a head, "after the shekel of the sanctuary:—the shekel is 20 gerahs." Here was another source from which silver was derived for the use of Aaron and his sons, in the service of God. How at every turn in the history of this people, the great subject of redemption is made prominent! Type is crowded upon type, expressive of the one great aspect of redemption, viz: *Substitution.*

The life of the Passover-lamb in Egypt was substituted for the life of each family of Israel, gathered in each house, under the shelter of the blood. Again: God claimed Israel's first-born as His, because He had substituted for them, in destruction, the first-born of Egypt.

Every sacrifice on which the hand was laid, betokened substitution. The atonement-money was another aspect of the same truth. The Levites were substituted for the first-born: and lastly, five shekels a-head was a price substituted for the redemption of those, on behalf of whom there were no living Levites to minister before God.

How blessedly all this crowd of types finds its substance in Christ, the Lamb of God, the all-sufficient substitute provided by God.

The two trumpets were to be made of silver, of one piece, that each might give the same sound ; and though that sound was, by doubling it, to be increased in power; yet the note given forth from each trumpet was to be precisely the same, in perfect unison. One clear shrill blast was to rouse the camp, either to assemble themselves together before the tabernacle of the Lord, or to march on their journey. These are first specified (v. 2) as the two great objects for which the trumpets were made : and, as the chapter proceeds, they enlarge into four principal occasions on which these instruments of silver were to be employed.

First : "When they shall blow with them, all the assembly shall assemble themselves to thee at the door of the tabernacle of the congregation. And if they blow with but one trumpet, then the princes, which are the heads of the thousands of Israel, shall gather themselves unto thee." v. 3, 4.

The sound of these silver trumpets was to be the voice to assemble Israel to their king or leader Moses, at the door of the tabernacle. The call was sent forth from in- truments made of the silver redemption-money. They sounded out a cheerful yet solemn note, summoning Israel, as redeemed and numbered for God, to assemble in great congregation in the presence of the Lord; and to hear from the lips of His servant Moses, words of encouragement, direction, or reproof. The very sound that fell upon their ears, reminded them of the fact that they were God's people; redeemed at a price; numbered as His own; delivered from the bondage of Egypt, to be the servants and soldiers of the Most High.

The exhortation in Hebrews x., "not forsaking the assembling of ourselves together," is based on the same truth. Believers individually, having the heart sprinkled from an evil conscience, and personally clean through the precious blood of atonement, are upon that ground, to draw near to God in the holiest ; and next, upon the same ground, to assemble in congregation for worship, prayer, praise, and mutual exhortation. They gather around the High Priest over the house of God, within the vail ; in contrast with Israel, who gathered themselves to Moses at the door of the tabernacle. Let us bear in mind, that we meet not in order to gain access to God, nor to make a way of approach to Him, but because we have been already redeemed, and because the way has been made open into His presence by the death of Christ. The voice of the Great Shepherd calls us together ; the voice that speaks peace and salvation to our souls. Silvery sounds of grace and truth proceed from His lips, poured into them from His heart. He preaches righteousness in the great congregation, and refrains not His lips. And when He sounds at last the great trumpet of redemption, the blessed and mighty blast of which will reach every ransomed ear, He will gather around Him by that sound, the great and glorious company that no man can number, redeemed out of every kindred, and nation, and tongue, at the cost of His precious blood. Then will the great congregation at length be assembled, in the glorious tabernacle not made with hands ; and the eternal song of praise be raised to our God, by the Lord Himself, the chief musician ; and one vast Hallelujah chorus from heaven and earth will echo the joyful sound.

The law was given by Moses, and was accompanied with sounds of terrific majesty. The trumpet waxed louder and louder, and the voice of words was so appalling that the people intreated that the word should be spoken to them no more, and even Moses said, " I exceedingly fear and quake." Here was *truth* proclaimed, apart from *grace;* righteousness apart from mercy. But grace and truth came by Jesus Christ. In Him these two attributes of God marvellously blended. Like the two trumpets of silver which were sounded together, and produced one harmonious note ; so the testimony borne by God's blessed Son, and manifested by Him in His death on the tree, was ever one of mingled grace and truth ; peace and righteousness ; love and holiness ; mercy and judgment.

Secondly : " When ye blow an alarm, then the camps that lie on the east parts shall go forward. When ye blow an alarm the second time, then the camps that lie on the south side shall take their journey : they shall blow an alarm for their journeys. But when the congregation is to be gathered together, ye shall blow, but ye shall not sound an alarm. And the sons of Aaron, the priests, shall blow with the trumpets : and they shall be to you for an ordinance for ever throughout your generations." v. 5—8.

The same sound that summoned Israel into the presence of God, for worship or instruction, also aroused them for the march. The notes given forth by the silver trumpets on both occasions were identical, though they were sounded after a different fashion : for in the case of their journeys, the priests were to blow an alarm. There might be no foe apparently at hand. The path over the desert might seem to be straight-forward and plain enough. Nevertheless, they were always to set out on their fresh march under the sound of an alarm. For the foe was at hand, although they might not know it. The way was difficult and dangerous, although it might appear smooth. Just so is it with the Church of God, and with the individual believer. Every fresh step in the way, every change, is attended with danger and temptation. Satan, the unperceived enemy, hovers about the path of the saint. He lays fresh snares, and digs new pit-falls, at every turn. The soldier of Christ has to march on in careful watchfulness, not ignorant of the devices of the foe, conscious of his own high calling, as a redeemed one of the Lord ; and therefore fearing lest he should sully his spotless garments, or dishonour the great Captain of his salvation.

An allusion to this is apparently made in 1st Peter, i. 17—20. The apostle exhorts the saints, upon two grounds, to pass the time of their sojourning here in fear ; because they could call God their Father, invoking Him to their aid on that account ; and because they had been redeemed, not with corruptible things, as silver and gold, but with the precious blood of Christ. As strangers therefore and pilgrims, he exhorts them to march to the sound of an alarm ; not under fear of wrath or judgment, but in godly fear, reverence for Him whom they could call their Father, and remembering the vast price that had been paid for their redemption.

And so it will ever be. The more we estimate the cost at which we have been ransomed, and the love of Him who spared not His own Son, the more we shall walk carefully and watchfully in the midst of this ensnaring world. The sighs, and groans, and agonies of Christ on the tree—sounds of redemption ; will cause us to walk circumspectly, and with godly fear, even though no danger may seem to be imminent.

Thirdly : " If ye go to war in your land against the enemy that oppresseth you, then ye shall blow an alarm with the trumpets : and ye shall be remembered before the Lord your God, and ye shall be saved from your enemies." v. 9.

There are only two occasions recorded, in which these trumpets of silver were used in war. The first, Num. xxxi. 6, when Israel avenged themselves on the Midianites; a thousand of each tribe being selected to go forth against the foe, accompanied by Phinehas the son of Eleazer the priest, with the holy instruments, and the trumpets *to blow in his hand*.

The other instance is 2nd Chron. xiii. 12. The enemy in this case, was no longer a Midianite host, or a Canaanite nation ; but alas ! it was a portion of Israel opposed to Judah. Abijah the king still preserved the worship of the true God, and set the battle in array against Jeroboam, although the latter numbered an army of double the size. Jeroboam relied on his idols of gold, and the multitude of his host ; Abijah trusted in the presence of the living God, and His priests with sounding trumpets to cry alarm against the foe. Jeroboam was able completely to surround the army of Abijah, so that the battle raged, both in front and in the rear. But in this extremity, they cried unto the Lord, and the priests sounded with the trumpets : and as the men of Judah shouted, it came to pass that God smote Jeroboam, and all Israel, before Judah.

These are instructive scenes. Perils arise both from open adversaries, and from false brethren ; from Satan's hosts, manifestly opposing truth, and from Satan, transformed into an angel of light; and his ministers, as ministers of righteousness. The sound of the silver trumpets was to alarm Israel, when marching in seeming security. The same sound was to alarm God, when Israel was about to be overpowered by the foe.

In like manner, the fact that we are redeemed by the blood of Christ, is ever to be ringing in our ears, to make

us careful and watchful on our journey. And when we
feel the oppression of the enemy; when the rulers of
the darkness of this world attack us in our own land, and
seek to overwhelm and overpower us; we have but to
claim God as our Father, Christ as the Captain of our
Salvation; and let the cry of distress sound in the ears of
the Lord of Hosts, and the victory is surely ours. We
shall be remembered before the Lord our God, and be
saved from our enemies.—" Be strong in the Lord, and in
the power of His might."—" Be strong in the grace
which is in Christ Jesus."—" In all these things we are
more than conquerors, through Him that loved us."—
" Thanks be to God, which giveth us the victory through
our Lord Jesus Christ."

Fourthly : " Also in the days of your gladness, and
in your solemn days, and in the beginnings of your
months, ye shall blow with the trumpets over your burnt
offerings, and over the sacrifices of your peace-offerings,
that they may be to you for a memorial before your God :
I am the Lord your God." v. 10.

The ear of the true Israelite must have been habituated
to the blast of these silver trumpets. He had been called
into the presence of God by them ; He had marched to
their sound in the wilderness ; God's aid had been invoked
through them, to his rescue in the midst of the battle.
Days of joy, and solemn days, when he had to afflict his
soul before the Lord, were ushered in by the same holy
notes : and each fresh period of time, as the month opened
with the new moon, was marked by the like musical
tones falling on his ear. Scarcely a day therefore would be
past, without his thoughts being re-awakened to the fact
that he had been redeemed to God. And as the burnt-
offerings, and peace sacrifices, periodically presented on
God's altar, preserved a constant odour of a sweet savour
before the Lord ; the blowing of these trumpets over
these offerings was intended to remind Israel, that the
value of these sacrifices was theirs ; and to call God's
attention to the blessed fact, that they were accepted as

His people through the shedding of blood, and the substitution of another in their stead.

In like manner, the whole life of a redeemed sinner is to be pervaded by one constant thought, that he is not his own, but belongs to God. A redemption-sound is to be mingled with his hours of joy, or of sorrow. And if he takes note of time in its rapid flight, it should be that he may learn to redeem it, by rendering himself a living sacrifice, holy, and acceptable to the Lord, which is his reasonable service. Is not this truth in type, presented by the beginnings of months marked out in Israel's history, by the blowing of the silver trumpets over the sacrifices.

The expression, "redeeming the time," apparently implies more than merely using the time profitably. It has the thought in it, of *buying back the past* by means of a right use of the present. And is not this ever the way of grace? God would have us profit by past neglect, failures, and sins.

He not only mercifully averts, through the blood of Christ, their sad results in judgment; but through a deeper acquaintance with the value of the cross, gained by the humbling retrospect of the past, He desires that we should be better able to occupy the present moment to His glory. Vain regrets profit nothing. But the believer may profit much by retracing past mistakes and sins, and marking the abundant grace and wisdom, in which God has met every short-coming and folly. Love for Him will be thus increased. He that has had much forgiven will love the more. Mis-spent time may be redeemed by wise and diligent use of precious experiences thus gained. Even as unconverted sinners, we have each passed through our own peculiar training, which if rightly understood, serves to fit us for some especial work for God. What would Paul the apostle have been, had he not previously spent his days as Saul of Tarsus, the persecuting Pharisee?

Surely each believer will have his own peculiar joy in

the work of Christ for himself, as he will have to record his own peculiar history of evil.

May our souls, our lives, be filled with the remembrance of the price that has been paid for us ; and may we be able, in some measure to say with Paul, " The life which I now live in the flesh, I live by the faith of the Son of God, who loved me, and gave Himself for me."

## THE FLOOR OF THE TABERNACLE

THE bare desert formed the floor of the tabernacle ; a singular contrast to the glorious curtains, and golden boards and vessels. To the priests who entered the holy place, and to the High Priest on the day of atonement, who within the vail, sprinkled the blood under the cloud of glory that rested on the mercy-seat, it must have seeemed singularly out of place, that a dwelling, designed for such holy uses, and so resplendent with costliness, beauty, and glory, should have been pitched in the howling wilderness, on the naked ground. But such was God's appointment. The dust of the earth, of which man was made, and to which the sinner, man, was to return—dust, which was the serpent's food—and dust, which betokened death and ruin, formed the floor of God's dwelling-place. This anomalous connection of beauty and barrenness ; of preciousness and worthlessness ; the incorruptible with the perishable ; of glory and vanity ; affords a very striking type of the present dispensation.

The heavens have been opened over our head. We worship and hold converse with God in the highest glory. And yet our members are here upon this earth ; and we walk in the midst of a groaning creation, in a world defaced by sin ; marred by the presence and power of death ; still lying under the curse, and traversed as to its whole length and breadth, by the serpent's path.

The blessed work of Christ, and the mighty power of His resurrection, have as yet accomplished nothing with regard to this lower creation. Redemption, instead of effecting any improvement in things around us, has delivered us *out* of this present evil world; has translated us *out* of the power of Satan, who rules and reigns here, into the kingdom of God's dear Son. The power of Satan, the state of men in general, and the condition of creation itself, remain totally unaffected by the death and resurrection of the Lord Jesus. The devil goes about still as a roaring lion, seeking whom he may devour. He is still the god of this world—the prince of this world—the prince of the power of the air. The whole world lieth in the wicked one; and man's heart has not received one gleam of heavenly light. He remains even in grosser darkness; notwithstanding the wondrous cross and glory of the Lord Jesus Christ. One universal groan reaches the ears of the Lord of Hosts from the whole creation, resulting from the vanity—death—bondage of corruption, to which it is subject. And we ourselves, by reason of the very intercourse with God, into which we have been brought by the blood of Christ, and because of the very hope of glory, which through the Spirit's power we already taste by anticipation, even we ourselves, groan within ourselves, feeling what a wilderness this is through which we are hastening; and eagerly waiting for the time, when these vile bodies shall be made like the glorious body of our risen Lord. No wonder the Lord's people have such strange and mingled experiences. In one sense, they are already raised with Christ : in another, they yet expect the resurrection.

By faith they can say, that even now they are seated in heavenly places in Christ Jesus: and yet they find themselves toiling in the midst of a restless, unprofitable, heartless world; and having to wage a ceaseless warfare with the rulers of darkness. With truth they are able to declare, that they have already died, and that their life is hid with Christ in God: and yet, at the very same time, they have to put to death their members upon the earth, which are full of sin and uncleanness. Already, by the help of the Holy Spirit, (the first-fruit of the land of glory,) they behold a new creation, altogether of God, stretching out, with its unspeakable joys and glories, everywhere around them. Yet still they sojourn in a world where Satan's seat is, and where all is old, and full of decay and corruption. They are even now, created anew in the image of their glorious God: but the old man, with its affections and lusts, is yet present, and has constantly to be resisted. They are not in the flesh, but in the spirit; for the Spirit of Christ dwells in them: but alas! daily and hourly, the flesh continually lusts. Heirs of God, and joint heirs with Christ; but strangers and pilgrims: kings and priests, yet beggars and outcasts: possessing all things, and having nothing: utterly helpless, and yet able to do all things, through Christ that strengthens them: with (as it were) heads in the glory, and feet in the wilderness. Such are the experiences of the people of God, during the present dispensation, whilst the tabernacle of glory is connected with the wilderness-path.

The floor of the tabernacle is only once mentioned, (Num. v. 17,) in connection with that remarkable ordeal to which a wife was to be subjected, if the spirit of jealousy came upon her husband. The priest was commanded to take holy water in an earthen vessel, and to put into it some of the dust that formed the floor of the tabernacle. He then wrote certain fearful curses in a book, and blotted them out with this water, so that it was as it were pervaded with these curses. The suspected wife stood uncovered before God, with the jealousy-offering in her hands, consisting of the tenth part of an ephah of barley-meal, a memorial to bring iniquity to remembrance; and she solemnly pronounced Amen, Amen, to the curses. A handful of the offering was then burnt upon the altar, and the woman drank the

water, which if she was guilty, became bitter within her,
and caused corruption and curse to be made manifest in
her body. The jealous husband taking this course,
freed himself from any participation in her iniquity.
The woman if guilty, alone bore it, and was a curse
among her people.

May not this be looked upon in two aspects ? First,
as a type of Israel, once the wife married to Jehovah,
now suffering under the fearful judgments of His wrath,
the fury of His jealousy, because of their departure in
heart from Him, and because of their guilt in putting to
death His own Son; that death, like the barley meal—
an offering of memorial, calling their iniquity to
remembrance, instead of purging it away :—an evil
and adulterous generation, which though secretly
conscious, to a certain extent, of its own rebellion
against God; has yet boasted itself in the law, and said
Amen, Amen, to the curses pronounced against the very
iniquity which it has committed.

Secondly.—Is not this type to be interpreted also by
*contrast ?* The Husband, instead of clearing Himself
from the iniquity of His wife, by allowing her to drink
the bitter water, has Himself taken the cup, and drained
it to the dregs. God, in the fire of His jealousy, because
of man's departure in heart from Him, mingled a cup of
wrath and indignation, and placed it in the hands of His
own beloved Son. " The cup which my Father hath
given me, shall I not drink it ? " O what a draught
did that cup contain ! holy water, mixed with dust and
curses, God's holy indignation against sin; a hatred and
antipathy to it in every shape, which none but Himself,
the Holy, Holy, Holy, Lord God Almighty could feel
and know, concentrated as it were, in that fearful cup.

Death, the penalty on sin, with all its kingdom of
terrors; and curses pronounced to the full because of a
broken law; these were the ingredients mixed by the
hand of God, and given by Him to His own beloved
Son to drink; in order that we, who have indulged our

sinful lusts, and gratified our self-will, and revelled far off, might escape the holy vengeance due to us as sinners. On the cross, Jesus drank of "the wrath of the Almighty." He was "filled with bitterness, and made drunken with wormwood." "His heart was melted like wax: all His bones were out of joint." The "hot displeasure" of God, as a fire, burned within Him. He was "brought into the dust of death." The Spirit of God, in the Psalms, seems to have selected language, expressive of excruciating bodily suffering, in order to represent to our souls the fearful agony of spirit, which the blessed Lord endured, when Himself bearing our sins in His own body on the tree. He refused the vinegar and gall at the hands of man, when He had tasted it. But He drank "the water of gall," and "the wine of astonishment," from the hands of God. Believers are often too apt to dwell exclusively on the bodily sufferings of our blessed Lord on the cross, instead of contemplating, as far as we are permitted to do, the unspeakable sorrows of Jesus in His soul under the stripes of God, "when it pleased Jehovah to bruise Him; when His soul was made an offering for sin, and He poured out His soul unto death." May we not, with deep reverence, view many passages in the Psalms in this light; and transfer the expressions we find there, respecting sufferings in the bones, the loins, the throat, &c., to the soul and inward mental feelings and untold woes of the blessed Lord; when He tasted death on behalf of the wife of His affections—the Church—rescued out of an adulterous world, and to be presented ere long, to Himself, without spot or blemish, or any such thing.

# THE COURT OF THE TABERNACLE

"And thou shalt make the court of the tabernacle: for the south side southward hangings for the court of fine twined linen of an hundred cubits long for one side.

"And the twenty pillars thereof and their twenty sockets brass; the hooks of the pillars and their fillets silver.

"And likewise for the north side in length hangings of an hundred cubits long, and his twenty pillars and their twenty sockets of brass; the hooks of the pillars and their fillets of silver.

"And for the breadth of the court on the west side shall be hangings of fifty cubits: their pillars ten, and their sockets ten.

"And the breadth of the court on the east side eastward fifty cubits.

"The hangings of one side of the gate shall be fifteen cubits: their pillars three, and their sockets three.

"And on the other side shall be hangings fifteen cubits: their pillars three, and their sockets three.

"And for the gate of the court shall be an hanging of twenty cubits, of blue, and purple, and scarlet, and fine twined linen, wrought with needlework: and their pillars shall be four, and their sockets four.

"All the pillars round about the court shall be filleted with silver; their hooks shall be of silver, and their sockets of brass.

"The length of the court shall be an hundred cubits, and the breadth fifty every where, and the height five cubits of fine twined linen, and their sockets of brass."
Exod. xxvii 9—18

"And he made the court: on the south side southward the hangings of the court fine twined linen, an hundred cubits. Their pillars twenty, and their brazen sockets twenty: the hooks of the pillars and their fillets silver.

"And for the north side the hangings were an hundred cubits, their pillars were twenty, and their sockets of brass twenty; the hooks of the pillars and their fillets of silver.

"And for the west side were hangings of fifty cubits, their pillars ten, and their sockets ten: the hooks of the pillars and their fillets of silver.

"And for the east side eastward fifty cubits. The hangings of the one side of the gate were fifteen cubits; their pillars three, and their sockets three. And for the other side of the court gate, on this hand and that hand, were hangings of fifteen cubits; their pillars three, and their sockets three.

"All the hangings of the court round about were of fine twined linen. And the sockets for the pillars were of brass; the hooks of the pillars and their fillets of silver; and the overlaying of their chapiters of silver; and all the pillars of the court were filleted with silver.

"And the hanging for the gate of the court was needlework, of blue, and purple, and scarlet, and fine twined linen: and twenty cubits was the length, and the height in the breadth was five cubits, answerable to the hangings of the court. And their pillars were four, and their sockets of brass four; their hooks of silver, and the overlaying of their chapiters and their fillets of silver."
Exod. xxxviii 9—19

THE Tabernacle, that is to say, the covered building, stood in the midst of an open space of ground, a hundred cubits long by fifty broad, which was enclosed by a hanging of fine twined linen, and a hanging for the gate, suspended on pillars ; twenty of which stood on the south side, twenty on the north, ten on the west, and ten on the east ; sixty pillars in all.   The Word of God does not state of what these pillars were made. The sockets and capitals alone are mentioned ; the former as being of brass, the latter of silver.   But as in Exod. xxxviii. 24, to the end, (where the quantities of gold, silver, and brass, used in making the tabernacle, are expressed,) no mention is made of either of these three metals as employed in forming the pillars of the court, it may be inferred that they were of shittim-wood.

## THE GATE OF THE COURT

AT the east end of the court, the curtain for the gate hung from four pillars.   This hanging was twenty cubits long ; and as the width of the court was fifty cubits, there were thirty cubits left.   The gate being in the centre, these thirty cubits were divided, fifteen on each side : three pillars, with the hanging of fine twined linen suspended from them, filled up these respective spaces.

The word *Hanging* (mah-sahch) is in the Hebrew, exclusively used for the vail—for the door of the tabernacle—and for the gate of the court.   When connected with the vail, it is often translated *Covering*. Exod. xxxv. 12 ; xxxix. 34 ; xl. 21 ; Num. iv. 5. It is once translated *Curtain*.   " The curtain for the door of the court." Num. iii. 26.   The peculiar use of this word serves to connect together in type, the vail, the door of the tabernacle, and the gate of the court. Each of these hangings covered or hid the interior from

the eyes of one approaching from the outside. Each
had the character of a door : indeed, the word *door* is
once used for the gate of the court. (Num. iii. 26.)
" The curtain for the door of the court." All three
were made of the same materials, arranged in precisely
the same order ; " blue, and purple, and scarlet, and
fine twined linen :" and all three were of the same
dimensions, as regards their area, for, the gate of the
court was twenty cubits long by five high, making a
hundred square cubits. The door-curtain and vail each
occupied a space of ten cubits wide by ten high, or a
hundred square cubits each.

The same truth seems therefore to be embodied in
each of these typical curtains. The same Jesus, God
manifest in the flesh, is pourtrayed in each  There
could be no access to God, of any kind, whether of
comparatively distant worship, or of closest intimacy,
but through the one door, the Lord Jesus. " I am the
door." John x. 7.

The Israelite, who came to the brazen altar with his
sacrifice or gifts, must first pass through the gate of the
court. The priest, that placed incense on the golden
altar within the tabernacle, entered through a second
door-curtain. The high priest, who alone had access
into the holiest, passed through the vail, a third hanging
of the same kind ; and realised the thrice repeated truth
of the only way to God.

Cain was the first who tried another path : and instead
of being able to draw near, his very attempt ended in his
going out from the presence of God, into the land of
banishment. The path, thus at first trodden by only
*one* evil man, has since become a broad way, " the way
of Cain." Thousands follow in his footsteps, and think
to worship and to offer, without passing through the door.

Salvation and worship are inseparably united. The
Samaritan, who had his holy mount Gerizim, and a
liturgy derived by tradition from Jewish sources, though
acknowledging the name of Jehovah, worshipped an

unknown God, as much as the Athenian, who knew not the very name of the true God : for neither the one nor the other knew God's way of salvation.

The Lord Jesus, in John x., seems to have these two thoughts in His mind. Himself the door to God; and the door of salvation. The Pharisees, who had usurped the place of shepherds in the Jewish fold, had cast out one of the true sheep. The Good Shepherd found this outcast one, and spoke to him : and the sheep immediately heard His voice. The Lord then proceeded to speak the parables recorded in John x., respecting the Shepherd and the sheep. He had first proved Himself the Shepherd, by entering in by the door, the way appointed by God. To Him the porter had opened.

It has been suggested, and probably with truth, that the porter, who ushered the Lord Jesus into the fold, was John the Baptist. He had been sent to prepare the way of Jehovah, and stood in a remarkable place, at the end of all the prophets, proclaiming the kingdom of heaven as at hand, and announcing the Lamb of God. The sheep, hearing the Shepherd's voice, followed, and were led by Him out of the fold.

Up to the time of the Lord's death, there had been a people, separated off from the other nations of earth, into a locality chosen by God, and fenced in with a pale of ordinances and commandments; the effect of which was still to preserve them folded off from the rest of mankind. But directly the Lord Jesus had established His title to be the Good Shepherd, by giving His life for the sheep—from that time, no bond of creed or confession, of ordinances or liturgical ceremonies, distinguished the sheep from other men. Jesus Himself became alone the object, the life, and the leader of each individual member of His flock. The badge and safety of the sheep were recognising His voice, and following Him. To draw to Himself, away from every support; to be the one object of the heart's affection; to be known, trusted, loved, followed, and worshipped, was, and is the great purpose of Christ. And so, in this beautiful chapter, He presents Himself as leading them out, and putting them forth, in order that no hedges or barriers might keep them in the right track, but that they might alone be dependent on His voice, and trace His footsteps.

The Lord then speaks of Himself as the door of the sheep; a remarkable expression: not the door of a sheep-fold; but the door of the *sheep*. The door of their life, of their existence as sheep. The door which constituted them sheep; the door to God, the Father and Owner of the sheep. Again the Lord repeats the words, "I am the door," and then adds, "By me if any man enter in, he shall be saved." He gives the general invitation, "if any man." Jew or Gentile, enter into God's presence by Him, salvation is the immediate result. He opens wide the door to the whole world, as we find throughout this Gospel of John.

"Whosoever believeth . . ." iii. 15. "If any man eat . . " vi. 51. "If any man thirst. . . . ." vii. 37. "If any man enter in . . ." x. 9, are all so many intimations of salvation presented in Christ to the world, instead of being narrowed up, as heretofore, to Israel. The brazen serpent; the manna; the smitten rock; and the gate of the court, are all thus offered to any one, be he who he may, Greek or Jew, circumcision or uncircumcision, barbarian, Scythian, bond or free.

"And shall go in and out, and find pasture." The sheep, saved by entering in through Christ and Him crucified, would be safe henceforth in all circumstances; and would find pasture, whether in immediate worship within the tabernacle before the Lord, or whether passing through the wilderness paths of the world. In contrast with Israel of old, who were obliged to go up to Jerusalem, in order to feast in the presence of the Lord; and who, if they wandered from their own land, could not sacrifice, or serve God.

One privilege of a believer now, having life through

Christ, and union with Him, is to find in every circumstance of common life, an occasion for trusting God, and for the exercise of faith, and for blessing to the soul. Pasture now springs up in the wilderness. As the Apostle expresses it, "The life, which I now live in the flesh, I live by the faith of the Son of God, who loved me, and gave Himself for me." The valley of Baca, the dry valley of grief, becomes a well; the rain also fills the pools. Psa. lxxxiv. 6

"I am come, that they might have life, and that they might have it more abundantly." John x. 10. Christ is the door of life; the way, the truth, and the life; eternal life *already* to every one that enters in by Him. Life in all its fulness also in the day of resurrection: in accordance with the words before spoken by the Lord in chap. vi. 40, 54. "This is the will of Him that sent me, that every one which seeth the Son, and believeth on Him, may have everlasting life: and I will raise Him up at the last day. Whoso eateth my flesh, and drinketh my blood, hath eternal life: and I will raise him up at the last day."

"I am the good shepherd. The good shepherd giveth his life for the sheep." chap. x. 11. Again the Lord returns to the fact of His being the Shepherd; but now adds the word *good*, and proves His right to that title by giving His life for the sheep. For them, He would die; He was the Shepherd that was to die. To them, He was the door, by whom they could draw nigh to God; the way of life. The Shepherd and the door are remarkably interchanged.

"I am the good Shepherd, and know my sheep, and am known of mine, like as the Father knoweth me, and as I know the Father: and I lay down my life for the sheep." ver. 14, 15. The Lord Himself was the Lamb of God. He knew the shepherdly care and love of the Father. In like manner as the Father knew Him, He knew His own sheep; and as He knew the Father, His own sheep knew Him.

"And other sheep I have, which are not of this fold. Them also I must bring; and they shall hear my voice; and there shall be one *flock*, and one Shepherd. ver. 16. Our version has inaccurately used the word *fold*, instead of *flock*, in the latter clause of the verse just quoted. There was indeed a Jewish fold: but out of that, the sheep were to be brought: and other Gentile sheep, who had never been of any fold, Jesus would also bring to Himself. Lifted up on the cross, He would draw all men unto Him. Jew and Gentile would lose all characteristics of the flesh, and become sheep alike belonging to one flock of God. Saved by the death of the good Shepherd, and placed under the care of the great Shepherd of the sheep.

There seems therefore, in this discourse of our Lord, to be an intimation that the *door-gate* of the tabernacle-court would be alike open to Gentile as well as Jew. The righteous, whoever they might be, justified in the way of faith, would enter this gate of the Lord, (Ps. cxviii. 20,) this door of faith, opened to the Gentiles.

This Gate of the Court, or hanging, was suspended from four pillars. Being twenty cubits long, ample space would be allowed between each pillar for the admittance of the altar of burnt-offering, which was five cubits in breadth. The curtain for the door of the tabernacle hung upon five pillars : as it was ten cubits wide, the separation between each pillar would be two cubits and a half, which would exactly admit the ark of the testimony.

It is possible that these measurements had reference respectively to these two principal vessels of the court and tabernacle,

In Exod. xxxviii. 18, where the gate of the court is again described, these words are added : "And *the height in the breadth* five cubits, answerable to the hangings of the court." The *height* is here considered *breadth*. This may arise either from the fact that the gate of the

court was so hung, as to make the spaces of entrance
exactly five cubits square, so that the breadth and
height were equal ; or because of the contrast between
the mode of measuring the court-gate, and the mode
adopted in measuring the curtains of the tabernacle. In
the case of the curtains, their height from the ground is
called their length ; whilst their extent from west to
east is called their breadth. This is exactly reversed in
the gate of the court, where the length is its breadth
from south to north, and its breadth its height.

The court itself, with the exception of the gate already
mentioned, was closed by a hanging of fine-twined linen,
five cubits high. As it has been before remarked *fine
linen* seems to be used in Scripture as a type of righteousness—a righteousness equal to all the demands of
God ; enabling him who possesses it to stand in God's
glory : in contrast with sin, by reason of which, all
come short of the glory of God. The Israelite, who
entered through the gate of the court, would be encompassed, shut in, and protected, by this hanging of fine
twined linen. Though in a wilderness, he stood on
holy ground ; and the fine linen by which he was surrounded, shut out from his eye the dreary barren prospect, through which he was wending his way. The
lovely tabernacle of God stood partially revealed to his
gaze. The courts of the Lord's house, overshadowed by
the cloud of glory, were before him. The altar, with
its lamb for the burnt-offering, sent up an odour of a
sweet savour on his behalf. The laver, filled with
water, told him of a fountain, filled with life and purity,
which would cleanse away even the ordinary defilement
contracted whilst passing through a wilderness of death.
He had entered through the gate of the court, the
appointed doorway : within, every object proclaimed
life, peace, righteousness, acceptance, and nearness to
God. Well might the Psalmist say, " How amiable are
thy tabernacles, O Lord of hosts ! My soul longeth,
yea even fainteth for the courts of the Lord : my heart

and my flesh crieth out for the living God." Ps. lxxxiv.
1, 2. Moreover, no deadly foe could enter those precincts. The presence of the living God, manifested over
the ark of His strength, abode there. The hosts of His
people encamped in close and well-ordered ranks all
round; and the court of the tabernacle itself was screened
even from the gaze of an adversary.

Thus this court presented a place of security, of
holiness, and of intercourse with God. Jerusalem on
earth will hereafter afford some such place of refuge for
the nations of the earth. On referring to Rev. xi. 1, 2,
we distinctly learn, that Jerusalem, the holy city, was in
type represented by the court of the temple.

The court of the tabernacle had much the same
analogy as regards the tabernacle itself, as the court of
the temple had with respect to the temple. So that we
may without much fear of mistake, suppose that the
earthly Jerusalem, as it will hereafter be fashioned,
subsequently to the Lord's return, is prefigured by the
court of the tabernacle. It will be a strong city ; its
strength consisting in salvation. " In that day shall this
song be sung in the land of Judah : We have a strong
city ; salvation will God appoint for walls and bulwarks."
The righteous nation will enter in through its gates ;
righteous, because justified by faith in the Lord Jesus ;
the sheep who have entered in by that door. " Open
ye the gates, that the righteous nation, which keepeth
the truth, may enter in." The Rock of ages will manifest Himself there. Living waters will flow from that
city. A fountain will there be opened to the house of
David for sin and uncleanness. It will be the city of
the Great King. God will be known in her palaces for
a refuge. The house of prayer for all nations will
stand there. The uncircumcized and the unclean will
no more enter within those walls. It will be a city of
solemnities. The light of God's glory will stream down
upon it from the heavenly courts above, the dwelling-
place of the risen saints of God ; those mansions of

glory, which Christ is gone to prepare. Blessed time! when Satan shall be bound; and the Lord, the Prince of Peace, will reign gloriously with his church, (the sharer of His throne, and the army of His power,) and will subdue all things under His feet.

The pillars of the court were surmounted with chapiters or capitals of silver, with fillets and hooks of the same precious metal; the fine linen curtain, which enclosed the court, being suspended from these silver hooks. The silver, thus employed, was the remaining portion of the atonement-money. "And of the thousand seven hundred and seventy-five shekels, he made hooks for the pillars, and overlaid their chapiters, and filleted them." Exod. xxxviii. 28.

The fact of the fine linen curtain hanging from silver hooks, fillets, and capitals, which were made of the atonement-money, very significantly directs our thoughts to the inseparable connection between Christ our righteousness, and Christ our redemption.

These two truths have, in systematic theology, been too often severed; so that it has been taught, that we are saved from sin by the death of Jesus; and that we are made righteous by the imputation of His life of obedience.

This virtually depreciates the wondrous cross, and loosens the fine linen hangings of the tabernacle-court from the silver capitals. The truth is, that the justification of a sinner depends alone on the *death* of the blessed Lord Jesus, succeeded by His resurrection, as a necessary consequence of the value of His death.

The one offence of Adam ruined us all. Sin was introduced by him into the world: and death, with all its miseries, entered in consequence. Every child of Adam inherits the complete ruin in spirit, soul, and body, which was the result of his sin. Filthiness of the flesh and spirit, a desperately wicked heart, a carnal mind at enmity with God, together with mortality, and its inseparable attendant, corruption, are the melancholy ills, to which men in the flesh are heirs. One finished righteousness has for ever cancelled all this list of fearful evils, and justified ruined sinners for life and glory. The payment of the true atonement-money, the precious blood, not only cancels every debt which stands against the sinner, but entitles him to be entered in the book of life as a son, and servant of God. In Rom. v. 9, we find *justification* attributed immediately to the blood : and in a subsequent part of the same chapter, it is attributed to one righteousness, v. 18. This verse, ("as by the offence of one, judgment came upon all men to condemnation ; even so, by the righteousness of one, the free gift came upon all men unto justification of life") would be more accurately translated, if "*one offence*" were substituted for "*the offence of one*," and "*one righteousness*" for "*the righteousness of one*." It manifestly exhibits a contrast between *the one* breach of commandment, committed by Adam, and *the one* perfected righteousness accomplished by Christ on the cross. The word translated "righteousness" (dikaioma) see also Rom. viii. 4, is peculiar. It expresses a completed act, a finished righteousness ; and must refer, not to a variety of actions spread over a whole life, but to some deed of perfection, in itself complete, which has made righteousness manifest in every possible sense, in every variety of aspect. Such was the cross of Christ. Faithfulness, obedience, subjection, and dependence upon God, were there perfectly exhibited by the blessed Lord. He trusted, though cast off : He prayed, though unanswered : He loved, though overwhelmed with wrath and judgment. He vindicated the honour, majesty, and truth of God, though himself unprotected, unavenged, and given over to shame and dishonour. He justified the holiness of God at the very time He was bruised by His hand for no iniquity of His own. The two great commandments, "Thou shalt love the Lord thy God with all thy heart, and with all thy soul, and with all thy mind," and "Thou shalt love thy neighbour as thyself," upon which hang all the law and the prophets, had their fulfilment under circumstances of trial, to which no other being has ever been, or could ever be subjected. And the two were so marvellously blended, that they became as it were but one. For the blessed Lord loved man because He loved God. He died to save the sinner, because that sinner was dear to His own heart, being dear to the heart of God. " Thine they were, and Thou gavest them me . . . All mine are thine, and thine are mine."

Adam's offence was the disobedient act of eating the fruit of the forbidden tree. Christ's righteousness was manifested in suffering curse, shame, obloquy, death, on the tree, in obedience to the will of God. He tasted death : His bread was ashes.

The tree of knowledge of good and evil was pleasant to the eyes. It attracted and rivetted the gaze of the woman; and as she looked she forgot the commandment, "Thou shalt not eat thereof." The Lord stedfastly set His face toward the tree of the curse; it was the one object that filled His sight. He beheld it wherever He turned. A groaning creation around called up the cross before Him. The sin, misery, death, and ruin, of every perishing sinner that crossed Him in His path, were so many appeals to His heart, urging Him (may it not be said?) on to Calvary. Every sacrifice; every smoking victim; every flame of fire on the altar; every feast; every sound in the temple; told the same tale; and in type and shadow presented to Him the fearful tree. The bread that He brake ; the ears of corn which afforded a scanty meal to His disciples; the waves that rose and filled the sinking bark in which He sat; all, all had voices to His ear, telling Him of the bruising, the stripes, the smiting, and the judgment to which, each moment as it passed hastened Him on.

The whole world, the heavens above, the earth beneath, the trees, the withering grass, the fading flowers, everything seemed designed to perpetuate to His eye and ear, the one purpose of His entrance into this world

—the Cross : and in humble true hearted obedience to the will of God, He kept the tree in sight.

And who can tell the wondrous appreciation of good and evil realized by the Son of Man, when hanging on the Cross, the holy judgment of God on account of sin, caused Him to sink in deep mire, where there was no standing; and when He confessed the innumerable iniquities of others as His own, estimating to the full the fearful evil of every act of disobedience and insubjection; and feeling the dreadful heavy weight of the wrath of God pressing upon His soul? And what instruction of wisdom was poured into the heart of the Lord ! What a tongue of the learned did He gain from that Cross; that He might speak a word in season to him that was weary!

The Epistle to the Romans, having contrasted the one offence, with the one righteousness; next changes the terms, and proceeds to contrast the disobedience of one, by which many were made sinners, with the obedience of one, by which many were made righteous. Justification, having been previously attributed to the *blood*, is here declared to be the result of Christ's *obedience* That obedience therefore, is His death upon the Cross. If the sin of an ungodly person be blotted out by the blood of Christ, that person must be righteous : there can be no neutral condition. If sin be *not* imputed, righteousness *is* imputed This is very plainly declared in chap. iv. where the blessedness of the man to whom God imputes righteousness, is described by a quotation from Psa. xxxii. which speaks of the blessedness of the man to whom the Lord will not impute sin, because it has been forgiven and covered.

Moreover, righteousness and life are inseparable. The death of Christ can never be severed from His resurrection. He was delivered because of our offences, and raised because of our justification. Sin having been borne, atoned for, put away, purged, by the Lord in His death, the believer is quickened together with Christ,

is accepted in Him, is righteous in Him. "He is the
Lord our Righteousness." "He hath made Him to be sin
for us, that we might be made the righteousness of God
*in* Him."

The type we are considering seems to present some
shadowy outlines of these blessed truths. The wor
shipping Israelite saw that the boards of the tabernacle
owed their stability and sustainment to the fact of a full
atonement-price having been paid: since they were sunk
deep into, and rested firmly on the silver sockets. He
would also perceive, that the fine linen curtain, with
which he was encompassed, hung securely from silver
chapiters, which were part of the same ransom-money.
So the believer stands before God, upon the ground that
he has washed his robes, and made them white in the blood
of the Lamb. He is righteous, because a full atonement
has been made: and he perceives that the new heavens and
the new earth, (the whole of God's glory in the new
creation,) are the result of the complete answer for sin,
which the blessed Lord has made on the cross; and
that heaven itself, the true holy places, into which Christ
the great High Priest has entered, is erected upon the
sure foundation laid in His death.

May not the silver sockets, and silver capitals, also
present unto us Christ, as the foundation-stone, and
head-stone? He is the first and the last. The
beginning and the ending. The socket and the capital.
The Rock of Ages. The Father of eternity, on whom
rest all the everlasting purposes, counsels, and glories of
God. He bears up the pillars of the heavens and
earth. He is crowned with glory and honour. Head
over all things; filling all in all. The commencement
and the completeness of righteousness, holiness, power,
wisdom, and glory.

The size of the court was determined by the length
and breadth of the fine linen hangings. The pillars.
from which these hangings were suspended, must have
stood within the court. Any one therefore, who

approached the tabernacle without entering the gate, could not know upon what the curtains hung. He would see the fine linen, but would not be aware that it hung from hooks and capitals of silver.

This is like the Socinian's gaze at Christ. He to a certain extent, appreciates the righteous character of the Lord Jesus: he may speak of His spotlessness and purity, and may admire the righteous precepts which the Lord has spoken. But he enters not by the door, and therefore perceives not the glory and costliness of the ransom paid on the Cross. He values not the precious blood, and knows not Christ as the Son of God. The perfection of righteousness and obedience, as manifested by the blessed Lord when suffering under the wrath of God, are unknown to this follower of Cain. He sees no beauty in the marred visage and form of the Blessed One when made sin for us. Salvation must ever precede true worship. The Lord Jesus can never be rightly known, till He is known as the Saviour, who has given His flesh and blood, in order that the sinner may eat, and live for ever.

A distant view of the tabernacle and its court would present nothing attractive to the eye. The spectator would only see the top of a long dark coffin-like structure, surrounded by a white linen hanging. The priests, who had entered through the door, were those alone who beheld the wondrous costliness and beauty of the building as viewed from within. And so it must ever be, as it regards our contemplation of Him, to whom this type directs us. A distant view of Christ is ignorance and unbelief. Faith draws near: because faith owns the fact that we, who were once afar off, are made nigh by the blood of Christ.

The vail is rent : the way into the holiest is laid open. The glory of the Lord can now be gazed upon with unveiled face. No bounds, about a mount that might be touched, keep at a distance either the worshipper, or even the ruined sinner. No terrific sounds, or sight of

wrath and judgment, scare away the affrighted beholder
No privileged class are now entitled to wrap up in
mystery the things of God, and to keep far off the
helpless stranger.   The leper full of leprosy, the unclean Gentile dog, the sinner dead in trespasses and sins,
may at once approach the very throne of glory.   He has
but to come, to return : at his first step, he is healed,
cleansed, and fully made meet for the immediate presence
of God.   Christ in all His fulness, Christ in all His
glory, is the gift of God to the lost, far-off sinner.   And
one glance by faith on the Lord Jesus is life, and healing,
and nearness to God.   The saved sinner is not only
loved, and washed in the blood, but made a king and a
priest, and stands as high as any other of the redeemed
family, having but one priest, but one intercessor, the
Lord Jesus Himself.   Superstition, which is another
form of unbelief, talks of holy mysteries of religion, and
appropriates peculiar ceremonies to a consecrated class ;
seeking to shroud in obscurity the bright and glorious
truths, which God has made as manifest as the sun in
the heavens, and as free for all as the very air we
breathe.   It exalts poor wretched sinners, by some
human contrivance, into a place of professed nearness to
God, which others are not supposed to have.   A priestly
or ministerial class, to whom is entrusted by men the
office of dispensing the sacraments, thus in a measure
closes the rent vail, usurping the priestly place, formerly
held by Aaron and his sons, but now for ever abolished ;
practically adopting the words—" Stand by, I am holier
than thou."

All these attempts are, in reality, denials of the full
efficacy of the blood, and the full glory of the resurrection.   Ever since the wondrous cross, a human being is
either in the first Adam, utterly ruined, sinful, dead as
it regards God, and at an unspeakable distance from
Him; or, he is in the last Adam, quickened, raised up,
seated in heavenly places, and thus brought and ever
kept near to God in Christ.   To be one with Christ;

to have Christ as the life ; to eat the flesh and drink
the blood of the Son of Man, and thus to have that life
sustained ; to have Christ as the object of the heart's one
affection, and as the prize ultimately to be reached ; to
contemplate Him, and to have Him dwelling in the heart
by faith ; to abide in Him, and thereby bear much fruit ,
to behold Him, and thus to be changed into His likeness
from glory to glory ; these are the pursuits and privileges
of every child of God : this is the life of a believer.    It
was for this David longed.    " One thing have I desired
of the Lord ; that will I seek after : that I may dwell in
the house of the Lord all the days of my life, to behold
the beauty of the Lord, and to enquire in His temple."
Ps. xxvii. 4.    And again, " How amiable are Thy
tabernacles, O Lord of Hosts ! My soul longeth, yea
even fainteth for the courts of the Lord : my heart and
my flesh crieth out for the living God." Ps. lxxxiv. 1, 2.
And, " O God, thou art my God : early will I seek
thee.    My soul thirsteth for thee, my flesh longeth for
thee, in a dry and thirsty land, where no water is ; to
see thy power and thy glory, so as I have seen thee in
the sanctuary.'" Ps. lxiii. 1, 2.

All difficulties are solved, when the believer enters the
sanctuary, and learns the purposes, and mercy, and love
of God, as therein manifest.    Two Psalms remarkably
declare this.    In the lxxiii., the writer draws a vivid
contrast between the outward prosperity of the ungodly,
and the sorrows and afflictions of the righteous.    He is
stumbled at the seemingly strange and unequal dealings
of God; and is induced, by this survey of mere present
things, and circumstances, almost to regret his own path
of godliness and purity.    But, when he enters the
sanctuary, all is made plain to him.    There, he discerns
the end of the wicked.    He learns to estimate, as a vain
dream, the life of apparent prosperity, which they are
leading.    He also perceives that the path of tribulation,
through which he is passing, is according to the guidance
of God's counsel, and is the sure way to glory: and the

beauty of the Lord so engrosses his soul, that he exclaims—" Whom have I in heaven but thee? and there is none upon earth that I desire beside thee."

In Psalm lxxvii., the same psalmist describes his own feelings of dismay and desolation, because he receives not an immediate response from God to his petitions ; the deliverance he expected does not come. In the sanctuary, however, he learns God's way—His unchangeable course of acting—the eternal purposes of the most High. God's great power to redeem is there displayed. He ever acts upon the same principles, throughout the circumstances of the believer's life. He hath delivered, doth deliver, and will deliver. 2nd Cor. i. 10. And the mighty work of redemption, which He has already displayed in Christ, and which was typified in Israel's deliverance out of Egypt, is the sure pledge that He will ever so deal, in mercy and in power, with His own. If looked at down here, God's way is in the sea, and His path in the great waters. His footsteps are not known. Everything seems to be left in confusion. Satan has his way apparently unchecked : and man cannot understand the mystery of God's dealings. But let the saint get his acquaintance with God, and with the ways of God, from the sanctuary : let him trace the marvellous counsels of wisdom and love, which God has, step by step, unfolded in the gift of His blessed Son : and then let him wait, and patiently expect to see the same skill of wisdom and power, unravelling every tangled intricacy of human life, and bringing to pass His eternal purposes of love and mercy ; so as to lead His people by the right way like a flock, skilfully guided into their rest and everlasting joy.

The Tabernacle must have been pitched on level ground; so that those who walked in its precincts stood secure. An allusion is made to this in Psa. xxvi. David, trusting in the Lord, knew that he should not slide. He loved the habitation of God's house, the place where His honour dwelt. Here he found fellowship and safety. His foot stood in an even place; and in the congregations he blessed the Lord. And so it must ever be. If we walk in the light, as He is in the light, we walk securely. There will be no sliding of the foot: but our feet will be like hinds' feet; and we shall be able to stand firmly on our high places. We shall also have fellowship one with another; true oneness of heart, and communion in the blessed things of peace, joy, and glory, which appertain to us. Moreover, while thus abiding in the holy place, we shall experience the value of the blood as cleansing us from *all* sin As regards all wrath and condemnation, we have been already justified by the blood. But, in proportion as we abide in the secret place of the Most High, we shall discover sins, spots, and defects, of which we were unconscious when out of His presence. The garment which seems to be white, when viewed by the light of a taper, will appear comparatively dark and soiled, when brought into the blaze of sun-light. So it is with the believer. If he be content to pass his time in the busy activities of life, apart from constant intercourse with God, he will not have a tender conscience, or a soul enlightened as to sin, in its defiling and polluting power. He will not perceive the many stains he is daily contracting from the flesh and from the world.

But if he make the dwelling-place of the Most High his habitation, and seek to walk in the light of the glory of God, he will find the unspeakable value of that precious blood, which has not only cleansed, but still maintains its efficacy, and *cleanseth* from all sin, presenting him spotless in the very brightness of God's unveiled light, and enabling him to abide without fear in the presence of the Holy, Holy, Holy, Lord God Almighty.

# PINS AND CORDS

"All the vessels of the tabernacle in all the service thereof, and all the pins thereof, and all the pins of the court, shall be of brass.—Exod. xxvii 19

"And all the pins of the tabernacle, and of the court round about, were of brass.—Exod. xxxviii 20

It will be observed that in the directions given above by the Lord to Moses, cords are not specified, but in Exodus xxxv. 18, where Moses enumerates to the children of Israel, the things that are to be made, he mentions "the pins of the tabernacle, the pins of the court, and *their cords*." Also in Exodus xxxix. 40, when the children of Israel bring that which they had made unto Moses, amongst other things are mentioned, "the hangings of the court, his pillars, and his sockets, and the hanging for the court gate, his *cords, and his pins*."

On turning to Numbers iii. 26, we find committed to the charge of the Sons of Gershon, "the hangings of the court, and the curtain for the door of the court, which is by the tabernacle, and by the altar round about, and *the cords of it* for all the service thereof." The same is again repeated in Numb. iv. 26, with this exception, that instead of "the *cords* of *it*," the expression is "*their cords*." Again, Numb. iii. 37, part of the charge of the Sons of Merari is stated to have been "the pillars of the court round about, and their sockets, and their pins, and their cords." The same is repeated, Numb. iv. 32. From these texts it may be conjectured that there were pins, first for the tabernacle itself. Exod. xxvii. 19.; xxxviii. 20.; xxxv. 18.; xxxviii. 31.

Secondly, for the court. Exod. xxvii. 19.; xxxviii. 20.; xxxv. 18.; xxxviii. 31.

Thirdly, for the court gate. xxxix. 40.

On comparing these texts with Numb. iii. 37, and iv. 32, it will appear that the pins for the court, and for the court gate, were especially connected with the

*135*

pillars, from which the hangings forming the court and the gate were suspended.

The word "*pin*" is elsewhere translated "*nail*," Judges iv. 21, 22.; v. 26, being the tent pin, or iron nail which Jael struck into the temples of Sisera. So also in Isaiah xxxiii. 20.; liv. 2, it is used for the stakes, or pins of a tent.

By means of these pins of brass, the tabernacle and the court were securely fastened to the desert ground; so that no storm, or flood of waters could sweep away this structure, although many of the materials were such as to be easily affected by the wind or rain. May we not be reminded by this type, of the stedfast purpose of Christ, to pursue the path marked out for Him by the Counsels of God, even though that path ended in the storm of judgment, and in the billows of wrath. Neither the fierce attacks of the Tempter, nor the anticipated fearfulness of the death He had to die, turned Him aside from the settled purpose of His heart. "I come to do Thy Will O God." And though He experienced the deep feelings expressed in the 55th Psalm, 4, 5, 6, 8, verses. "My heart is sore pained within me; and the terrors of death are fallen upon me. Fearfulness and trembling are come upon me, and terror hath overwhelmed me. And I said, Oh, that I had wings like a dove, for then would I fly away and be at rest. . . . . . I would hasten my escape from the windy storm, and tempest." Yet He could say, "but I will trust in *thee*." He knew how to cast His burden upon Jehovah, even Him that abideth of old— upon one that shall never suffer the righteous to be moved. His heart was fixed, and God was His exceeding joy.

What a wondrous object of contemplation is the blessed Lord, as revealed to us in the Scriptures of truth. Weak, yet immoveably firm. Himself the Mighty God, yet dependent for every thing on God His Father. Setting His face stedfastly towards Jerusalem

in order to suffer there; and crying out in deep distress,
"O my Father if it be possible let this cup pass from
me! nevertheless not as I will, but as thou wilt."
Upholding all things by the word of His power, even
whilst exclaiming, "I am a worm and no man." Oh!
the wondrous power of that weakness. Oh! the
marvellous victory of that death. Oh! the eternal
stability of Him, laid low in the depths of the grave.

The desert seemingly afforded a shifting foundation
for a tabernacle of glory—but the solid sockets, and
pins of brass, deep set in the ground, made all secure.

The pin, or nail, is elsewhere in the prophets a type
of Christ. "Out of him (Judah) came forth the corner,
out of him the *nail*, out of him the battle bow, out of
him every oppressor together." Zech. x. 4.

Here are manifestly three references to Christ—the
corner, the nail, and the battle bow. The chief corner-
stone, and head-stone of the corner, see Isaiah, Psalms,
and the 1st Epistle of Peter, which Scriptures have
already been referred to in this exposition.

The "nail" firmly securing all God's counsels of
love, mercy, and blessing, and connecting them with
this earth, so that notwithstanding the desolateness and
ruin of such a wilderness, uninterrupted intercourse can
be maintained between believers and the Most High;
and unceasing blessings can flow down from Him
to us.

The Lord Jesus is also prophesied of as *the nail*, in
Isaiah xxii. 20—25. " And it shall come to pass in that
day, that I will call my servant Eliakim the son of
Hilkiah: and I will clothe him with thy robe, and
strengthen him with thy girdle, and I will commit thy
government into his hand: and he shall be a father to
the inhabitants of Jerusalem, and to the house of Judah.
And the key of the house of David will I lay upon his
shoulder; so he shall open, and none shall shut; and
he shall shut, and none shall open. And I will fasten
him as a nail in a sure place; and he shall be for a glo-

rious throne to his father's house. And they shall hang
upon him all the glory of his father's house, the offspring
and the issue, all vessels of small quantity, from the
vessels of cups, even to all the vessels of flagons. In that
day, saith the Lord of hosts, shall the nail that is
fastened in the sure place be removed, and be cut down,
and fall ; and the burden that was upon it shall be cut
off : for the Lord hath spoken it."

Shebna was Hezekiah's treasurer and ruler of his
palace. His great sin, as recorded in this 22nd of Isaiah,
seems to have been an attempt to perpetuate his name,
by marking out for himself a sepulchre near Jerusalem,
(as he that heweth him out a sepulchre on high,) and
graving an habitation for himself in a rock. Like Ab-
salom who sought to hand down his name to posterity
by a pillar that he built. So Shebna made even a place
of death to be a monument for the glory of his own
name. Thus glorying in his shame.

God will not permit any one to boast of death, save
Him that has triumphed over it, even His Son, the Lord
Jesus Christ. A sepulchre hewn out of a rock to gratify
the pride of a worthless sinner, could not be permitted
by God, who foresaw that one, even His own beloved,
would be laid in a similar tomb, having humbled Himself to death, even the death of the cross. Vain man
tries to cover his shame and nakedness with a self-
righteousness of his own devising when living, and even
adorns and decks out his tomb, and builds a massive
mausoleum* as if to make death glorious, and to perpetuate his own name in the very place where God has
marked His judgment upon sin. Shebna's tomb was
also a denial of resurrection ; a resurrection to judgment.

Thus God saw in this treasurer, a man, bent upon
pride and self-exaltation, making death a treasure and

---

* The word mausoleum, is derived from the name of a prince, Mausolus, who
was buried in a tomb so sumptuous and elaborately wrought, that it was accounted
one of the seven wonders of the world. One of God's wonderful works in this
world is His power to *empty* a tomb. One of man's wonderful works is *erecting* a
tomb which shall conceal death, whilst perpetuating a record of it.

an occasion for human glory, instead of reckoning it as
it is in truth, the wages of sin, and a sad evidence of
man's ruin and shame. Isaiah is sent to this treasurer,
and says, " What hast thou here ? And whom has thou
here ?" Two solemn questions : the first, *what* is thine
occupation here ? The second, and who are you that are
thus occupying yourself ? Two questions which might
be well put to all the worldly-minded, who are seeking
to make a lasting name and reputation for themselves
here on earth. Is this the fitting employment for this
" little while," this short span of life ? And who are
those who thus are engrossed in pursuits which can only
end in death and the grave ? Where is their power,
where is their continuance, where is their worthiness ?

The prophet proceeds to sentence this proud self-
willed treasurer to a mighty captivity in a foreign land,
where the Lord would cover him with other garments
than those of glory—garments of shame. And then
the prophecy is given respecting the Lord Jesus, under
the type of Eliakim the son of Hilkiah, who was to
supersede Shebna in the office of treasurer and ruler of
the house. The word " Eliakim" means " my God
shall establish ;" and " Hilkiah," " the portion of Jehovah." Two very significant names, prophetic of the
Lord Jesus ; who having been called as the Lord's
servant, the Lord's portion ; and who having made
Jehovah to be His portion, has been established by God,
set up in resurrection glory, gaining an eternal name and
reputation out of the grave. God has through Him
spoiled principalities and powers, and made a show of
them openly, triumphing over them in the cross.

The prophecy then proceeds, (after a promise of the
robe, girdle, and government to be bestowed on Eliakim,)
in the words quoted of the Lord in Rev. iii. 7. " And
the key of the house of David will I lay upon his
shoulder ; so he shall open and none shall shut, and
he shall shut and none shall open." This key seems
to include the rule of the house of David, and the power

to open the treasures of that house.  And then follows :
" I will fasten him a *nail* in a sure place, and he shall
be for a throne of glory in his father's house."  It will
be observed that the word " *as* a nail," is not in the
original.  Here then again we have the Lord Jesus
spoken of as a nail fastened in a sure place.  And it is
remarkable that the word " *sure*," has the same derivation as the Hebrew word " *amen*."  The Lord Jesus is
the *nail* because He is the *amen*—the holy and the true
—the faithful and true witness—the beginning of the
creation of God.  All " the promises of God in Him
are yea, and in Him amen."  They hang securely dependent on Him like vessels of various capacity, filled
with the wine of joy and blessing.  And on Him also
hangs all the glory of His Father's house, the offspring
and the issue.  The nail driven down into the place of
death, there bruised and made nought him that had
the power of death ; and having this secure foundation,
the nail has become the strength of all God's building.
All rests on Him.  All hangs for support and sustainment on Him.  And He is the beginning of that new
and glorious creation, which shall endure for ever.

In the conclusion of this remarkable prophecy, we
have another nail spoken of, which though " fastened
in a sure place shall be removed, and be cut down and
fall ; and the burden upon it shall be cut off."

Does not this allude to the future destruction of " the
man of sin," " the Antichrist ? "  He will be the nail
securely fastened by Satan's power—he will have all the
rule, government, and treasures of this world, that Satan
can bestow ; and for a time he will prosper, so that his
covenant with death will appear to be firm, and his
agreement with hell will stand.  But the same day that
will make manifest to God's ancient people the Jews,
the Lord Jesus, as a Father and Deliverer to the inhabitants of Jerusalem, and to the house of Judah, and as
a throne of glory to the house of His Father David ; will
be the day in which this masterpiece of Satan's workman-

ship shall be brought to nought ; and the chariots of his glory shall be the shame of his lord's house, "for Jehovah hath spoken it."

It is remarkable that the prophecy in Zechariah quoted above, which alludes to the Lord as " the corner, the nail, and the battle bow," proceeding out of Judah, ends with the words " every oppressor together." Here also there is an apparent allusion to this same antichrist who will combine in himself every species of oppression, and who will be destroyed when, the corner, the nail, and the battle bow of Judah is revealed from heaven as the deliverer of Israel, from the great Pharoah of the earth.

## THE CORDS

SOME of the Cords were the charge and burden of the Merarites. (Num. iii. 37 ; iv. 32.) The rest of the Cords were the charge and burden of the Gershonites. (Num. iii. 26 ; iv. 26.) This is rather a remarkable exception to the arrangement made for the charge and burden of the Tabernacle, its curtains and hangings.

In no other instance did the Merarites and Gershonites carry any similar portions of the Tabernacle, but the distribution of the burdens was in every other case kept quite distinct. It may be that the object of God in thus altering the rule, was to give us a little intimation of a truth important to be remembered, viz., that however varied and different the gifts and occupations of His servants, yet they are members of the one body of Christ. There are mutual interests which link them on together. There are common ties which unite them firmly as one assembly of God's people. There are bands of brotherhood which inseparably bind them in one bundle of life.

This same word " Cords " occurs with reference to the cords of a tent. " Enlarge the place of thy tent,

and let them stretch forth the curtains of thine habitations : spare not, lengthen thy *cords* and strengthen thy
stakes." Isa. liv. 2. "My tent is spoiled, and all my
*cords* are broken ; my children are gone forth of me,
and they are not ; there is none to stretch forth my tent
any more, and to set up my curtains." Jer. x. 20. These
two texts form a beautiful contrast between the past
and present desolation of Israel and Jerusalem ; and the
future prosperity and glory of that city and people after
the Lord's return.

The Tabernacle *cords* were evidently fastened to the
*pins*, like the cords of a tent, and thereby kept the
pillars of the court erect, and also being thrown over
the external coverings of the tabernacle firmly tied
them down, so that they could not be lifted by any
blast of wind from the desert.

It is not stated of what materials they were made.
We gather from Exod. xxxv. 5—19, that they must
have been fashioned of the blue, purple, scarlet, and fine
linen, as these were the only materials which could be
used for such a purpose.

Our salvation rests on two great truths. First, on
the Person of the Saviour Himself, the Son of God, the
Son of Man, whose name is Jesus; and secondly, on
the work He has wrought. These are inseparably
connected together in the word of God, and we cannot
rightly receive the one without the other. The pin
would be no use without the cord connected with it.
The boards of the Tabernacle would not form a dwelling
place, unless the curtains were placed over them. The
ordinary way in which we learn the truth of God is, by
first hearing of the death of the Lord Jesus, and then
contemplating Him, who thus died. Jesus lifted up
upon the tree, attracts us by the cords of a man, the
bands of love. We are drawn to Him away from other
objects, by learning His wondrous grace and love, in
thus placing Himself on the tree of curse for our sakes ;
and then we are led to contemplate the glorious person

who there died. And our wonder and worship grow, as we ponder on the majesty and excellency, the holiness and beauty of Him who suffered for our sakes. The sorrows and love of Him, who loved us and gave Himself for us, are like the cords that bind our hearts to Himself, and that securely fasten the tabernacle of God— Love that endures for ever ; that many waters could not quench ; that floods could not drown. Love that deserves the name of love. Not won by any attractiveness in us : not purchased by any " substance " we could give : any righteousness, any holiness we could bring. Love fixed on us from everlasting, spontaneous, out of the heart of Christ ; and cleaving to us whilst we were yet enemies ; haters of God, despisers of that which was good, and exhibiting nothing but death in trespasses and sins. Sorrows also equalled only by that love, of the same vast unexplored depth.

Though set up from everlasting, and brought forth from all eternity ; and although delighting in God, and God's own delight, yet the delights of the Son of God were also with the sons of men. And wondrously His sympathies, His affections, and His joys, are linked on with creatures here below, who have caused the deep travail of His soul, and yet who will be the fulness of His glory. He will present them faultless in the presence of His glory with exceeding joy.

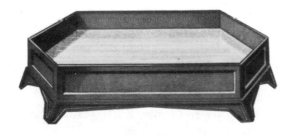

**The Brazen Laver**

Having thus sought to elucidate the beautiful and varied types contained in the tabernacle, it may be well to return to Exodus xxv. which gives the list of the materials for the construction of that building, and its vessels, &c.

"And the Lord spake unto Moses, saying,

"Speak unto the children of Israel, that they bring me an offering: of every man that giveth it willingly with his heart ye shall take my offering.

"And this is the offering which ye shall take of them; gold, and silver, and brass,

"And blue, and purple, and scarlet, and fine linen, and goats' hair,

"And rams' skins dyed red, and badgers' skins, and shittim wood,

"Oil for the light, spices for anointing oil, and for sweet incense,

"Onyx stones, and stones to be set in the ephod, and in the breastplate.

"And let them make me a sanctuary: that I may dwell among them.

"According to all that I shew thee, after the pattern of the tabernacle, and the pattern of all the instruments thereof, even so shall ye make it."—Exod. xxv 1—9

"And Moses spake unto all the congregation of the children of Israel, saying, This is the thing which the Lord commanded, saying,

"Take ye from among you an offering unto the Lord: whosoever is of a willing heart, let him bring it, an offering of the Lord; gold, and silver, and brass,

"And blue, and purple, and scarlet, and fine linen, and goats' hair,

"And rams' skins dyed red, and badgers' skins. and shittim wood,

"And oil for the light, and spices for anointing oil, and for the sweet incense,

'And onyx stones, and stones to be set for the ephod, and for the breastplate."—Exod. xxxv 4—9

THE following is a summary of the supposed typical import of these materials.

*Gold.*—Type of the Divine Glory of the Lord Jesus as Son of God.

*Silver.*—The preciousness of the Lord Jesus as the Ransom for the sinner.

*Brass.*—The power of the Lord Jesus to endure the Cross, because He is God.

*Blue.*—The manifestation of God as love, in the ways and death of Christ.

*Purple.*—The manifestation of the God-man, God manifest in the flesh.

*Scarlet.*—The manifestation of the true dignity and glory of man as seen in the Lord Jesus Christ, the Son of man.

*Fine linen.*—The righteous man exhibiting to the eye of faith " the glory as of the only-begotten of the Father, full of grace and truth."

*Goats' hair.*—The memorial of the death of the Lord Jesus as the offering for sin.

*Rams' skins dyed red.* The outward aspect of Christ as the man of sorrows and acquainted with grief. Born in this world to die.

*Badgers' skins.* The outward aspect of Christ, as having no form nor comeliness to the heart of the natural man.

*Shittim wood.* Translated by the Septuagint, " incorruptible wood." The Lord Jesus, the incorruptible man. " That holy thing," the Son of God.

*Oil for the light.*—The Lord Jesus as the light ; filled with the Spirit.

*Spices for anointing oil.*—The graces of the Spirit in all their fulness manifested by the Christ.

*Spices for sweet incense.*—The fragrant graces of Christ made manifest on the cross, and perpetuated in His intercession.

*Onyx stones, and stones to be set in the ephod and the breastplate.*—The glory and brilliancy of the heavenly one reflected also in His saints.

In these two chapters, ver, 2, 3, and 5, 21, 24 ; also chapter xxxvi. 3, 6, the word " offering," is a peculiar word in the Hebrew ; translated as in the margin, " heave-offering." It occurs again with reference to the silver atonement money, (Exod. xxx. 13, 14, 15,) and it also peculiarly designates the right shoulder of certain sacrifices, therefore called the *heave shoulder.*

The meaning of the word appears to be something lifted on high off the ground. It alludes to the complete separation of the Lord Jesus to God. One who though on the earth, was not of the world ; and who was peculiarly lifted up in separation to God on the cross, and again raised up to the glory of God in resurrection.

These " heave offerings" were to be given with the *heart*, willingly, (Exod. xxv. 2 ; xxxv. 5, 22 ;) not of constraint or necessity, for God loveth the cheerful giver.

Although the tabernacle and its ritual service was connected with the law ; yet as it contained types and figures of Christ, and good things to come, the principles of grace here and there break through the rigidity of commandments.

No true worship can be rendered to God, if the soul be in legal bondage. Neither can God accept the constrained formal obedience of a slavish heart. The willing heart, the free-will offerings, which are the result of a conscience and heart at liberty, are His delight. He is a God who giveth to all liberally, and upbraideth not ; and He expects from His own children the expression of His own character.

The whole life and ways of His beloved Son were expressive of self-devotedness to Him; and a delight in doing His will. And if we would present any acceptable worship or service, we must offer it not only through the Lord Jesus, but in the spirit of the Lord.

" And let them make me a sanctuary, that I may dwell among them." (ver. 8.)

This was the great purpose which God had in view that He might have a holy place in the midst of a people whom He had chosen ; by means of which He might not only occasionally visit them, but *dwell* amongst them. And He has accomplished this blessed purpose through Him to whom the tabernacle pointed. Believers in the Lord Jesus are the temple of God, (1st Cor. iii. 16 ;) they are such corporately as the household of God ; a building fitly framed together, growing into an holy

temple in the Lord—" builded together for an habitation
of God through the Spirit." (Eph. ii. 19—22.) Each
believer also *individually* is a temple of God. " Know
ye not that your body is the temple of the Holy Ghost."
(1st Cor. vi. 19.) These two wondrous facts result
from the Church being the body of Christ, in whom
dwelleth the fulness of the Godhead bodily ; and, our
bodies being the members of Christ.

The tabernacle was to a certain extent the dwelling-
place of the priests. They encamped before it, and ate
the shew-bread in the holy place, and also portions of
the sacrifices in the court of the tabernacle.

One great desire of God is to have us (creatures
though we be of His) in unbroken fellowship with
Himself for ever ; and also that we may have fellowship
with Him. If we would preserve the consciousness of
His presence, we must remember the precept, 2nd Cor.
vi. 14—18 : " Be ye not unequally yoked together with
unbelievers : for what fellowship hath righteousness with
unrighteousness ? and what communion hath light with
darkness ? And what concord hath Christ with Belial ?
or what part hath he that believeth with an infidel ?
And what agreement hath the temple of God with
idols ? for ye are the temple of the living God ; as God
hath said, I will dwell in them and walk in them ; and
I will be their God, and they shall be my people.
Wherefore come out from among them, and be ye
separate, saith the Lord, and touch not the unclean
thing ; and I will receive you, and will be a Father
unto you, and ye shall be my sons and daughters, saith
the Lord Almighty."

Five different words are here used to express every
shade of fellowship. What fellowship hath righteousness and lawlessness ? What communion hath light
towards darkness ? What concord hath Christ towards
Belial ? Or, what part hath the believer with the unbeliever ? And what agreement hath the temple of God
with idols ?

The first word here translated "fellowship,"implies the holding of something together with another. The second word, "communion," seems to involve common interests, resulting from communion in life. The third is well expressed by our word "concord," or agreement in sound and voice with another. The fourth means a share or part in some common object. And the fifth, "agreement," in the way of holding a common sentiment.

The unbeliever is therefore in this passage, considered to be in lawlessness, in darkness, under the sway of Belial, and a worshipper of idols. What a fearful description this is of the worldly-minded unsaved sinner, and yet how true! On the other hand, into what wonderful nearness to God is the believer brought, so as to have common interests ; fellowship in life ; complete concord of heart ; a share in all the rich treasures of glory, and agreement with the thoughts and mind of God.

There are three precepts, (Deut. xxii. 9—11,) which contain very clear directions respecting the conduct and service of the believer. One of these is referred to in the passage in Cor. quoted above.

" Thou shall not sow thy vineyard with divers seeds : lest the fruit of thy seed which thou hast sown, and the fruit of thy vineyard be defiled.

" Thou shall not plow with an ox and an ass together.

" Thou shalt not wear a garment of divers sorts, as of woollen and linen together."

The first of these should regulate our testimony in the church of God. The divers seeds may be very good in their way, and very useful in their proper place. But in the church of God the incorruptible seed of the word alone is to be used. And the servant of God having such a ministry, should follow the example of the apostle Paul, using great plainness of speech, declaring the testimony of God, not with enticing words of man's wisdom, but in demonstration of the spirit and of power.

The object before us, when engaged in the work of the Lord, should be to raise the heart and conscience towards God ; and not the mere pleasing the ear, or gratifying the understanding.

In these days, *mixed seed* is widely scattered ; and it is thought by many Christians that a legitimate way of spreading the truths connected with Christ and the Gospel, is to mix them up with science, literature, fiction, and philosophy. But this, however it may be done with the best motives, is not in agreement with the precept here alluded to ; nor in accordance with the ways of the apostle, who when he came to the most learned and philosophic people in the world, determined not to know any thing among them, save Jesus Christ— Him crucified.

The second precept, "thou shalt not plow with an ox and an ass together," refers to our fellowships. The yoke would rest unevenly upon the ox and ass if they were harnessed together in the plough. One also would retard or pull aside the other. Thus an uneven furrow would be the result, and the work of tillage be imperfectly done.

Any partnership or yoking together the believer with the unbeliever must result in the hindrance of the Lord's work, and in damage to the believer himself. It is impossible for the two to pull together. Their interests, their objects, their desires, their very speech must be different ; and the uneven union must result in the compromise of truth and godliness on the part of the child of God ; by means of which his testimony will be marred, and his own soul will lose much of conscious fellowship with the Father, and with His Son Jesus Christ.

The third commandment, "thou shalt not wear a garment of divers sorts, as of woollen and linen together," refers to the every day habit of the child of God.

In a changeable climate, where cold may follow heat

in rapid succession ; or where the chilly air of night soon dissipates all the warmth of the sun ; it would be very convenient to have a garment, woven of woollen and linen, so as not to be over hot in the day, and to afford sufficient heat at night.

A believer will avoid a good deal of reproach, and escape much contempt if he cleverly adapts himself to the various companies with which he may mingle. A kind of dress, or outward appearance suited to all society.

This " Linsey-woolsey " christianity is certainly comfortable as one passes through the world ; but it suits not the true believer. He should wear his priestly linen garment on all occasions, he should enter no society where he is obliged to conceal it. His life should be Christ. " To me to live is Christ." And no one should be able to question the reality of his faith, or the fact of his being not of the world ; although many may ridicule his folly, or esteem his ways to be those of one not in his right mind.

May the Lord help us all to be more true to Him, and to His Cross. Less conformed to the world, and more manifestly transformed by the renewing of our mind, that we may prove what is that good and acceptable and perfect will of God.

We "are the temple of the living God."

Jesus Christ is in us. Therefore we are exhorted to come out from among unbelievers and to be separate, and not to touch the unclean thing ; then shall we fully know God as our Father, and we shall be living as the sons and daughters of the Lord Almighty.

# THE PRINCIPAL WORKMEN

"And the Lord spake unto Moses, saying,

"See, I have called by name Bezaleel, the son of Uri, the son of Hur, of the tribe of Judah:

"And I have filled him with the spirit of God, in wisdom, and in understanding, and in knowledge, and in all manner of workmanship,

"To devise cunning works, to work in gold, and in silver, and in brass,

"And in cutting of stones, to set them, and in carving of timber, to work in all manner of workmanship.

"And I, behold, I have given with him Aholiab, the son of Ahisamach, of the tribe of Dan: and in the hearts of all that are wise hearted I have put wisdom, that they may make all that I have commanded thee:

"The tabernacle of the congregation, and the ark of the testimony, and the mercy seat that is thereupon, and all the furniture of the tabernacle,

"And the table and his furniture, and the pure candlestick with all his furniture, and the altar of incense,

"And the altar of burnt offering with all his furniture, and the laver and his foot,

"And the cloths of service, and the holy garments for Aaron the priest, and the garments of his sons, to minister in the priest's office,

"And the anointing oil, and sweet incense for the holy place: according to all that I have commanded thee shall they do.— Exod. xxxi 1—11

"And Moses said unto the children of Israel, See, the LORD hath called by name Bezaleel the son of Uri, the son of Hur, of the tribe of Judah;

"And he hath filled him with the spirit of God, in wisdom, in understanding, and in knowledge, and in all manner of workmanship;

"And to devise curious works, to work in gold, and in silver, and in brass,

"And in the cutting of stones, to set them, and in carving of wood, to make any manner of cunning work.

"And he hath put in his heart that he may teach, both he, and Aholiab, the son of Ahisamach, of the tribe of Dan.

"Them hath he filled with wisdom of heart, to work all manner of work, of the engraver, and of the cunning workman, and of the embroiderer, in blue, and in purple, in scarlet, and in fine linen, and of the weaver, even of them that do any work, and of those that devise cunning work.—Exod. xxxv 30—35

THE names of these two Israelites selected by God for the principal work of the tabernacle are very significant.

Bezaleel—means "in the shadow of God."

Uri—light of (the Lord.)

Hur—white, or splendid.

" A shadow," is used in scripture as a figure in various ways. First, the rapidity with which the shadow passes away and leaves no trace behind, is very aptly chosen to represent the rapid decline of life. Job viii. 9. "We are but of yesterday, and know nothing, because our days upon earth are *a shadow*." Psa. cxliv. 4. " Man is like to vanity : his days are *as a shadow* that passeth away." Eccles. vi. 12. " All the days of his (man's) vain life, which he spendeth *as a shadow*". Eccles. viii. 13, " his days which *are as a shadow*." And the Lord of life and glory in His deep expression of weakness on the cross ; cut off in the midst of His days ; exclaims, " My days are like a shadow that declineth." Psa. cii. 11. " I am gone like the shadow when it declineth." Psa. cix. 23.

Secondly, it is used in the sense of defence or protection. Num. xiv. 9, and Eccles. vii. 12, it is translated *defence*. In this sense we find a beautiful allusion to the shadow of the wings of Jehovah. Psa. xvii. 8. " Hide me under the *shadow* of thy wings." Psa. xxxvi. 7. They " put their trust under the *shadow* of thy wings." Psa. lvii. 1. " Yea in the shadow of thy wings will I made my refuge." Psa. lxiii. 7. " Therefore in the shadow of thy wings will I rejoice." The shadow of the Almighty was the safe dwelling-place of Christ. Psa. xci. 1. Jehovah upon His right hand was His shadow of defence. Psa. cxxi. 5.

Thirdly, it is used as a shelter from heat, and a place of refuge and refreshment. Cant. ii. 3. " I sat down under his shadow with great delight." Isa. iv. 6, " for a shadow in the day time from the heat." xxv. 4, and xxxii. 2, " as the shadow of a great rock in a weary land."

In contrast with these we have the expression, "the shadow of death," with its darkness and terrors. Job. x. 21, 22.; xxiv. 17. Psa. xxiii. 4.; cvii. 10. 14, etc.

The name of Bezaleel—in the shadow of God, seems peculiarly to point onwards to the Lord Jesus. He came forth from the Father, and abode in the bosom of God, "the only begotten Son which is in the bosom of the Father." Jehovah was His dwelling-place when on earth; and even on the cross, when He was as it were laying the foundations in death for the temple of God; still He trusted in the Lord, and He knew that He should not be confounded.

The son of Uri.—Light of the Lord. God is Light. His blessed Son is the brightness of His glory, and the express image of His Person—and He is the life, and especially manifested as such, in giving *light* unto men.

The son of Hur.—white, or splendid. Jesus is the spotless one whose white and glistening garments on the holy mount, were emblems of His own white and dazzling purity. Such was the Lord Jesus when here below; the workman selected by God to fashion a dwelling-place for Him, and to make a kingdom of priests unto God and His Father.

Bezaleel was *called* by name
Filled with the spirit of God
In wisdom
In understanding
In knowledge
In all manner of workmanship
And to devise curious work

The blessed Lord says of Himself, " Jehovah hath *called* me from the womb; from the bowels of my mother hath He made mention of my *name*. In the *shadow* of His hand hath He hid me." Isa. xlix 1, 2

The spirit of Jehovah rested upon him
The spirit of wisdom
And understanding
The spirit of counsel

And might.
The spirit of knowledge,
And of the fear of the Lord.

Filled with the spirit of God, the Lord Jesus displayed in His life and ways deep and wondrous blendings of grace and truth; and having learnt obedience by the things which He suffered, He has marvellous skill in dealing with the poor and needy: in seeking and finding the lost: in sympathising with the afflicted and sorrowful, and in succouring the tried and tempted. "With righteousness shall he judge the poor, and reprove with equity for the meek of the earth." "He shall bring forth judgment to the Gentiles. A bruised reed shall He not break, and the smoking flax shall He not quench, He shall bring forth judgment unto truth."

"Thus saith the Lord, in an acceptable time have I heard thee, and in a day of salvation have I helped thee: and I will preserve thee, and give thee for a covenant of the people, to establish the earth, to cause to inherit the desolate heritages. That thou mayest say to the prisoners, go forth; to them that are in darkness, shew yourselves." "The Lord God hath given me the tongue of the learned, that I should know how to speak a word in season to him that is weary." "The spirit of the Lord God is upon me; because the Lord hath anointed me to preach good tidings unto the meek: he hath sent me to bind up the broken hearted, to proclaim liberty to the captives, and the opening of the prison to them that are bound; to proclaim the acceptable year of the Lord, and the day of vengeance of our God; to comfort all that mourn. Isa. xi. 4; xlii. 1, 3; xlix. 8, 9; l. 4; lxi. 1, 2. Such are some of the "curious works" wrought by this servant of the Lord. Himself being the chief object of our worship, wonder and adoration, displaying the glory as of the only begotten of the Father.

The other principal workman engaged in the construction of the Tabernacle was "Aholiab the son of Ahisamach of the tribe of Dan."

Aholiab means, tent of my Father. Again a significant name embracing also the truth, of God revealed as a Father through His blessed Son, in whom dwelt the fulness of the Godhead bodily. It was peculiarly the delight and constant purpose of the Son to manifest the Father. No one else could reveal that name. Philip, though ignorantly, yet rightly expressed a blessed truth when he said " Lord shew us the Father and it sufficeth us." John xiv. 8. He felt that the knowledge of God as the Father was sufficient for everything—rest, peace, quietness, assurance must be the result. Are we able to say it sufficeth us ?—do we find such comfort and confidence through being able to say by the Holy Ghost, " Abba Father," that we lack nothing ? Are our murmuring spirits quieted by this blessed knowledge ? Is restlessness, is discontent at an end ?

What higher word can we utter respecting ourselves than to call God, Father ? What greater love can we taste from God than to know Him as having begotten us to be His children ? " Behold what manner of love the Father hath bestowed on us, that we should be called the Sons of God."

God *commends* His love towards us in telling us that even whilst we were yet sinners Christ died for us— Thus proving to us that His love proceeded from Himself—from His own heart ; and is not any result of attractiveness or obedience in us.

The wondrous *manner* of the love bestowed on us, its vastness is evidenced by the Father calling us His Sons. The *measure* of the love is known only as we estimate the Father's love for His own Son, " thou hast loved them as thou hast loved me." John xvii. 23. The Lord answered Philip, by the words, " have I been so long time with you, and yet hast thou not known ME Philip ? He that hath seen me hath seen the Father, and how sayest thou then shew us the Father. Believest thou not that I am in the Father, and the Father in me." John xiv. 9, 10. Thus the Lord Jesus was not only God manifest in

the flesh ; but He was the full declaration and manifestation of the Father.

*Ahisamach* means, brother of support.

Probably this name primarily refers to the fact that
Aholiab was a fellow helper to Bezaleel in the work
of the Tabernacle.   But is it not worthy of remark
that while we have in Aholiab the name, *Father;* we
have in the name Ahisamach, the word *brother;* and
may there not be in this a little prophetic hint of that
truth contained in Hebrews ii. 9—11, in which we find
the Lord Jesus raised from the suffering of death to a
place of exaltation, where everything is put under His
feet, and in which also it is declared that " He (the Lord
Jesus) who sanctifieth, and they who are sanctified are
all of one, for which cause he is not ashamed to call
them brethren."   He is the dwelling place of God, and
He is the brother of support to His brethren.

These two leading artificers were respectively of the
tribes of Judah and Dan.   Judah being the leading
camp, and Dan the last camp of Israel.   Probably they
were selected from these two tribes, in order that all
Israel might stand representatively included in these men
of the first and last camps.

May there not be also a significance in the names of
the two tribes here selected.   Judah, praise—Dan,
judgment.   The Tabernacle of God is a place for worship
and *praise*, because therein is revealed God's great act of
*judgment* upon sin in the sacrifice of the Lamb of God.

Bezaleel is moreover a type of the Lord Jesus in his
having been instructed by God to teach others. (Exod.
xxxv. 34.)   " The Lord hath put in his heart that he may
teach."   Throughout this beautiful description of those
who wrought in the work of the Tabernacle ; the *heart*
is especially spoken of.   " Wise hearted." Exod. xxviii.
3 ; xxxi. 6 ; xxxv. 10, 25 ; xxxvi. 1, 2, 8.   " Stirred
up in heart." xxxv. 21, 26.   " Willing hearted." xxxv.
22, 29.

God deals especially with the heart and conscience ;

and truth is of little avail, unless it acts not on the head
only, but on the heart's affections. Knowledge puffs
up ; whereas love builds up. The two prayers of the
apostle, Eph. i. and iii. chaps., remarkably deal with the
affections of the children of God. In chap. i. 17, he
prays that " the God of our Lord Jesus Christ the Father
of Glory, may give unto you the spirit of wisdom and
revelation in the knowledge of him ; the eyes of your
*heart* being enlightened ; that ye may know what is the
hope of his calling, and what the riches of the glory of
his inheritance in the saints, and what the exceeding
greatness of his power to usward who believe." We
have in our version, " the eyes of your ' *understanding* '
being enlightened," but the best authorities substitute
" heart" for understanding, and this is in accordance
with the whole tenor of Scripture. The affections have
to be lighted up by the spirit of wisdom and revelation.
We must be " filled with wisdom of heart," in order to
know the three wonderful things presented to us in this
1st chap. of Eph.

1    What is the hope of his calling ?
2    What is the riches of the glory of his inheritance
       in the saints ?
3    What is the exceeding greatness of his power to
       usward who believe ?

" The hope of his calling " embraces the hope of
Christ's coming ; of resurrection ; of seeing Him as He
is ; of seeing face to face ; of knowing as we are known ;
of being like Him ; of being for ever with Him ; of that
fulness of joy which is at God's right hand ; and of those
pleasures which are for evermore.

"The riches of the glory of his inheritance in the
saints" directs our thoughts to the glorious riches which
God has, may we not say, heaped up to Himself in the
saints as His own inheritance. In the Old Testament
we read that Israel was especially the Lord's inheritance.
"Thy people thine inheritance." Deut. ix. 26, 29. " The
Lord's portion is his people: Jacob is the lot of his

inheritance." xxxii. 9. Solomon also in his dedication prayer claims for the people that they are the Lord's people, and His inheritance ; separated from all the people of the earth to that end. 1st Kings, viii. 51, 53. See also Psa. xxviii. 9 ; xxxiii. 12 ; lxxiv. 2 ; lxxviii. 71 ; cvi. 5. In many other passages also of the prophets, the same truth is enunciated. Here in Eph., we have the saints as God's glorious inheritance above, of which perhaps Israel was a faint type below. And surely the eyes of our hearts need to be enlightened in order that we may have some deeper knowledge of the delight which God has and will have in us, as part of His own skilful workmanship, new created in Christ Jesus. And the riches of the glory which He will possess when the Church, the fulness of Him that filleth all in all, shall be raised in union with its blessed Head.

" The exceeding greatness of his' power to usward who believe." The Father of Glory has already wrought this mighty power in Christ, raising Him from the dead, from the very lowest depths of humiliation, and setting Him at His own right hand in the heavenly places, far above all principality, and power, and might, and dominion, and every name that is named, not only in this world, but also in that which is to come. This is a proof and exhibition of the exceeding greatness of His power to usward who believe. And this power already worketh in us, whereby He is able to do exceeding abundantly above all that we ask or think. And by this mighty power He will raise us up eventually into the same glory as the risen Lord, to those same super-heavenly places into which He hath gone, and to be one in manifested union with Him for ever.

The second prayer in this glorious Epistle, is to be "strengthened with might by his spirit in the inner man, in order that Christ may dwell in our hearts by faith.

That we, being rooted and grounded in love, may be able to comprehend with all saints, what is the breadth, and length, and depth and height, and to know the love of Christ which passeth knowledge.

That we might be filled with all the fulness of God."

Surely these deep and high and blessed prayers savour of heart work.    And the blessings which they promise will flow only through the heart's affections and earnest desires stirred up by the Holy Spirit, towards the Father and the Son.

Dimly the Tabernacle with its glorious hangings, its golden vessels : its deeply sunk silver sockets : its lofty capitals : its curiously wrought cherubim of glory upon the mercy-seat : its candlestick of elaborate skilful workmanship : its incense of sweet spices : its fragrant anointing oil : its lamb of sacrifice, all ascending as a sweet savour : its courts : its camp of well arranged hosts numbered in God's book : its cloud of glory, and its pillar of light—dimly indeed, and yet perhaps in measure, this varied assemblage of types may have foreshadowed the objects for which these prayers in the Epistle were offered.    Certainly He that filleth all in all, Christ, who is the first and the last, who is all, and in all, is the great subject of the whole type.

**The Table of Shewbread Partly Covered**

" And the Lord spake unto Moses, saying,

" Speak thou unto the children of Israel, saying, Verily my sabbaths ye shall keep: for it is a sign between me and you throughout your generations; that ye may know that I am the Lord that doth sanctify you.

" Ye shall keep the sabbath therefore: for it is holy unto you: every one that defileth it shall surely be put to death: for whosoever doeth any work therein, that soul shall be cut off from among his people.

" Six days may work be done; but in the seventh is the sabbath of rest, holy to the Lord: whosoever doeth any work in the sabbath day, he shall surely be put to death.

" Wherefore the children of Israel shall keep the sabbath, to observe the sabbath throughout their generations, for a perpetual covenant.

" It is a sign between me and the children of Israel for ever: for in six days the Lord made heaven and earth, and on the seventh day he rested, and was refreshed."—Exod. xxxi 12—17

" And Moses gathered all the congregation of the children of Israel together, and said unto them, These are the words which the Lord hath commanded, that ye should do them,

" Six days shall work be done, but on the seventh day there shall be to you an holy day, a sabbath of rest to the Lord: whosoever doeth work therein shall be put to death.

" Ye shall kindle no fire throughout your habitations upon the sabbath day."—Exod. xxxv 1—3

It will be seen that the Lord *closed* His directions concerning the tabernacle with the commandment respecting the sabbath day. (Exod. xxxi. 12—17.) Moses *commenced* his recapitulation of these directions to the people, with the same commandment about the sabbath. (Exod. xxxv. 1—3.) There is therefore evidently an intimate connection between the truths foreshadowed in the tabernacle, and the rest typified by the sabbath.

We read in Genesis ii. " thus the heavens and the earth were finished, and all the host of them. And

on the seventh day God ended his work which he had
made; and he rested on the seventh day from all his
work which he had made. And God blessed the
seventh day, and sanctified it; because that in it he
had rested from all his work which God created and
made."

Everything had been pronounced by the Creator Himself to be good. No sin, no death, had as yet entered
to mar the works of God's hands. He could rest, and
be refreshed in the contemplation of His own work of
creation; crowned as it was with man, the perfection
and head of it all. Quickly however was this beautiful
scene changed. By the " one man sin entered into the
world, and death by sin." " The whole creation was
made subject to vanity;" and from that time to this,
ceases not to " groan and travail in pain together,"
having been ruined by the entrance of death, and
thereby subjected to the slavery of corruption.

From that time we read no more of God resting.
The first intimation of a *sabbath* for *man* is in Exodus
xvi. where this word occurs for the first time in the
Bible. God had indeed hallowed the *seventh day*, having
Himself rested on it : but it is not called the sabbath,
which means *the rest*, until the *manna* was given to Israel
in the wilderness. And this is in keeping with the truth.
The manna (bread from heaven) was rained down in
profusion for a people stiff-necked and murmuring :
beautiful shadow of " the true bread from heaven,"
" the bread of God," " the bread of life," given in the
riches of God's love to a ruined world ; " of which if
a man eat, he shall live for ever."

In close connection with the manna, came the sabbath.
" It shall come to pass, that on the sixth day they shall
prepare that which they bring in ; and it shall be
twice as much as they gather daily. And it came to
pass, that on the sixth day they gathered twice as much
bread, two omers for one man : and all the rulers of
the congregation came and told Moses. And he said

unto them, this is that which the Lord hath said, To-
morrow is the rest of the holy sabbath unto the Lord.
Six days ye shall gather it ; but on the seventh day,
which is the sabbath, in it there shall be none.  See, for
that the Lord hath given you the sabbath, therefore he
giveth you on the sixth day the bread of two days :
abide ye every man in his place ; let no man go out of
his place on the seventh day.  So the people rested on
the seventh day." Exod. xvi. 5, 22, 23, 26, 29, 30.

God had so provided for Israel in giving them this
strange new bread from heaven, that there was no
necessity for their working in any way on the seventh
day.  Their wants were fully met ; so that they could
cease or rest from any labour or toil.  And here we
have for the first time, man able to rest : " the people
rested on the seventh day."  The first occurrence of the
expression in Scripture since Genesis, chap. ii., where it is
said, " and he (God) rested cn the seventh day."  Is not
this a very significant type of the blessed truth that God
has provided in Christ, the first and only rest that man
can know.  A perfect and eternal sabbath ?

Another peculiar word is employed here for the first
time ; " *the rest* of the holy sabbath ;" and is subsequently used in Scripture in connection with the sabbath
day.  " A sabbath of rest." Exod. xxxi. 15 ; xxxv. 2.
" The day of atonement." Lev. xvi. 31 ; xxiii. 32.
" The day of blowing of trumpets ;" xxiii. 24 ; where
it is translated *sabbath*.   " The feast of tabernacles,"
xxiii. 39 ; where it occurs twice, and is translated
"*sabbath*."  And " the sabbatical year," xxv. 4, 5 ; " a
sabbath of *rest*"—" a year of *rest*."  The word in the
Hebrew is, *shabbah-thohn* ; it may mean *a resting*, a time
or continued act of resting.  It is not unlikely that the
word, Hebrews iv. 9, "there remaineth therefore a rest,
(margin, keeping of a sabbath, a sabbatism,) to the
people of God," is a Greek translation of this Hebrew
word, although it does not occur in the Septuagint.

Israel kept their first, and perhaps their only sab-

batism, in the wilderness of Sin, when the manna was
fresh and pleasant to their taste. Who does not know
the delight, the peace and joy of the first fresh taste of
" the bread of life ?" The rest of soul which Christ
gives to those who labour and are heavy laden ? But,
alas ! how soon is that rest spoiled by the inroads of
Satan and the world ; and by the restlessness of self-
will, pride, and the flesh. If we would retain the rest,
yea, deepen and increase it, we must listen to the Lord's
words, " Take my yoke upon you, and learn of me ;
for I am meek and lowly in heart : and ye shall find
rest unto your souls." Matt. xi. 28, 29. There is a
rest that Christ *gives*, There is a rest we have to
*find*.

In Exod. xvi. 29, it is written, " the Lord hath *given*
you the sabbath, therefore he *giveth* you the bread." We
first, by faith, receive Christ ; the true bread from
heaven, given by God, His Father. We eat His flesh,
the bread which the Son of Man giveth, and rest from
doubt and fear ; from works of our own, and from the
heavy burden of our sins. We experience the joy and
peace of conversion. We cease from our own works,
as God did from His on the seventh day. But soon the
struggle comes, the conflict between flesh and spirit.
Having received rest from Christ as His gift, we have
next to take His yoke upon us. His yoke of love, and
obedience to the Father ; another kind of yoke, an easy
yoke ; another burden, a light burden ; in the place of
the grievous bondage under sin and Satan, and the
heavy load of guilt and misery. And we have to *learn*
of Him, the meek and lowly one in heart, in order that
we may *find* rest to our souls in the midst of temptation
and trial, and difficulties and perplexities in our path.
The meekness and lowliness of Christ were evidenced in
His constant dependence upon God. Never doing His
own will, or pleasing Himself. Never putting forth
His own power, but humbly trusting in, and waiting on
His Father. And His soul was kept in a perfect sab-

bath of rest. Circumstances, however sudden or unex-
pected, never disturbed the serenity of His soul's confidence in God; neither did they cause Him to act
independently of God. He trusted not in any resources
of His own. He was never surprised into an act of
independence, though having almighty power. However
adverse therefore the circumstances, the rest and quiet
assurance of His soul were unbroken. The tempter
might seek to insinuate doubts of His Father's love and
care, but such thoughts found no place in His heart.
He was deaf to such whispers of the enemy. He was
blind as to the circumstances around Him, if those circumstances seemed to militate against the faithful love of God.
Such was His rest all through His pilgrimage below,
till on the cross the billows and waves of judgment, and
the noise of the waterspouts of wrath overwhelmed
Him. And yet even then He trusted, and was delivered.

When the sabbath was connected with the gift of
manna, there was no commandment, but the sabbath
was *given;* and there was no penalty for the breach of
the rest. When the sabbath was subsequently connected with God's work of creation, as in Exod. xx.
8—11; xxxi. 14—17, there was a distinct commandment, and the penalty of *death* was appended to any
breach of it.

This affords a striking contrast, between being under
grace, and under law. Israel before they reached Mount
Sinai were dealt with altogether in the way of grace :
they had come out from Egypt under the shelter of the
passover blood. The power of the almighty hand of
God had been made manifest in their favour, in opening
the depths of the Red Sea, and giving them a passage
through on dry land; whilst their enemies had been
engulphed in its mighty waters. They had murmured
at Marah, and the bitter waters were made sweet. They
had found palm trees and wells ready for them at Elim.
They had murmured in the wilderness of Sin, and the

manna was poured down from heaven in reply. They
murmured again at Rephidim and the smitten rock
yielded its streams of living water. Thus up to their
reaching the mount of fearfulness and judgment, all
God's ways towards them were in unwearied goodness
and mercy.

The 105th Psalm recapitulates these dealings of God
with His people between Egypt and Sinai, and grounds
His ways of grace towards them upon His "remembrance
of His holy promise, and Abraham His servant," v. 42;
and then all the subsequent wilderness journey is omitted,
and the psalm concludes with "he brought forth his people
with joy and his chosen with gladness; and gave them
the lands of the heathen; and they inherited the labour
of the people; that they might observe his statutes and
keep his laws. Hallelujah." v. 42—45. Is there not in
this a prophetic intimation of their entering upon the
land and enjoying it hereafter, on the sure ground of
promise and unlimited grace? When their true sabbath,
their rest shall be connected with the true manna, " the
true Bread," and not with a fiery law, they will enjoy it
in reality, and retain it without fear of ever losing it.

In the Epistle to the Hebrews, chapters iii. and iv.,
*three* rests are spoken of—the rest of Creation; the rest
which Joshua gave; and the rest of God. The two
former have passed away, for in Psa. xcv. 11, God speaks
of another day of rest, although His works of creation
were finished from the foundation of the world; and the
rest which Joshua gave must clearly have been in vain,
for otherwise God would not have spoken by the mouth
of David, of another day, after the people of Israel had
actually been for many years in the land into which
Joshua had brought them. There yet remaineth therefore, a celebration of rest, a full enjoyment of it to the
people of God. An eternal Sabbatism, when they shall
enter into God's own rest, This is yet future. We find
that there is a day of new creation yet to come. " And he
that sat upon the throne said, Behold I make all things

new." Rev. xxi. 5. The old creation with all its groans—
the former things, with their death, sorrow, crying and
pain shall have passed away. A new heaven and a new
earth, will have replaced the present heaven and the
present earth. The holy city, the new Jerusalem, the
Bride, the Lamb's wife, prepared as a bride adorned for
her husband, will be seen in all her eternal freshness,
glory and beauty, coming down from God out of heaven.
The Tabernacle of God will be with men, and He will
dwell with them. The Lord will have reigned the
thousand years, till He shall have put all enemies under
His feet, and God will be all in all.

This is the eternal rest of God. Already it can be
said, " we which have believed do enter into rest." We
have a blessed foretaste of it in the peace of God which
passeth all understanding, and in the victory which God
giveth us through our Lord Jesus Christ. And we shall
begin to keep our Sabbatism at the coming of Christ;
when He will Himself descend with a shout, with the
voice of the Archangel, and with the trump of God, and
when we shall be caught up with the departed saints, all
alike, raised and changed into His likeness, to meet the
Lord in the air. And so shall we ever be with the Lord.

But even during this thousand years resurrection
companionship and reign with Christ, we shall still be
looking for " the new heavens and the new earth," the
new creation in all its completeness and beauty, the
eternal unbroken Sabbatism of God.

The connection of the Sabbath day with the construction of the Tabernacle, may have reference to this rest
that remains, of which the Sabbath connected with the
first creation, was a type.

A contrast may be drawn between the old creation
with the man and the woman, formed at the close of it;
and the new creation, of which the man and the woman
are the commencement. The first Sabbath was broken
(never to be restored) by the entrance in of sin and
death. It stood at the close of the week of God's work.

The closing act of God's creative power being the making the man and the woman.

The putting forth of God's power in new creation is the resurrection of His Son the Lord Jesus Christ, "the last Adam" "the beginning of the creation of God," and "putting all things under His feet," according to Psa. viii. And the next exhibition of God's mighty power in new creation, will be the resurrection of the Church in glory. The new heavens and the new earth will be the closing manifestation of His creative power.

This new creation begins with the rest of a first day, instead of the sabbath of a seventh : and we esteem the *Lord's day* to be *holy*, not because of a legal commandment but upon far higher ground ; because the *name* of the *Lord*, who died for us upon the cross, and who was raised for us from the grave as head over all things to His body the Church, is placed upon it. We celebrate it, because God is able to rest in the completed work of His blessed Son, and has manifested His delight and joy in His beloved, and in the work He has wrought by raising Him from the dead on the first day of the week— Christ is God's rest. We keep the Lord's day, because we can rest from all fear of wrath and judgment, and because we are new creatures in Christ Jesus, quickened together with Him, and seated in heavenly places in Him, washed, cleansed, justified, and shortly to be glorified. And God can rest in us for He sees in us the skilful workmanship of Jesus. New creation work—resurrection work already begun.*

The Sabbath is called "holy"; "a Sabbath to Jehovah"; "a Sabbath of rest—holiness to Jehovah," and "a Sabbath of rest to Jehovah." Exod. xvi. 23, 25 ;

---

* The word, the *Lord's*, (kuriakos) is only used on one other occasion, viz. in 1st Cor. xi. 20, "The *Lord's* Supper." As therefore we rightly observe with peculiar reverence "*the Supper*," because of the name of the Lord attached to it ; so also for the same reason, we have to regard the day called by His name, as belonging in a peculiar way to Himself. A new day, made by Him, and claimed by Him as Lord. The stone which the builders refused, was exalted in resurrection to be the head stone of the corner, upon the day which the Lord hath made. We will rejoice and be glad in it. Psa. cxviii. 22, 24.

xxxi. 15; xxxv. 2.    It was also "holy unto the children
of Israel." Exod. xxxi. 14, and a sign between the Lord
and them. xxxi. 13, 17; and was "a perpetual covenant." xxxi. 16.

We are told in Col. ii. 16, 17, that the Jewish holy
days, the new moons, and the sabbaths, were a shadow
of things to come, but the body is of Christ.    To be in
Christ is to be separated off to God in true holiness.    A
resurrection separation : to be cut off from the body of
the sins of the flesh, and to be risen with Him.    In this
is true rest, for rest must be holiness.    " The wicked
are like the troubled sea when it cannot rest, whose
waters cast up mire and dirt.    There is no peace saith
my God to the wicked." Isa. lvii. 20.

The Sabbath was a sign to Israel.    A token that they
were a people separated off to God, claimed by Himself
in a peculiar way as His creatures ; and for whom He
had prepared a rest in the holy land, provided they kept
His law.    May we not say that the risen Lord Jesus is
a peculiar sign to us ;  an assurance of rest that yet
remains for us.    The first-fruits in resurrection.    A
pledge therefore to us from God that resurrection shall
be our portion, and that we are His peculiar people for
whom He hath reserved an " inheritance, incorruptible
and undefiled, and that fadeth not away."

It will be observed that in Exod. xxxi. 14, " every
one that defileth the Sabbath shall surely be put to death ;
for whosoever doeth any work therein, that soul shall
be cut off from among his people."—v. 15, "whosoever
doeth any work on the Sabbath day, he shall surely be
put to death."    This serves to explain the meaning of
being cut off from his people, a phrase of constant
occurrence under the law.    It is the judgment of death
to be inflicted upon the transgressor.    Four special
occasions may be noted in connection with which this
fearful penalty is threatened.

First—If a man did any work on the Sabbath
Exod. xxxi. 14.

Secondly—If a man did not keep the Passover Num. ix. 13.

Thirdly—If a man eat leavened bread during the feast of unleavened bread. Exod. xii. 15, 19.

Fourthly—If a man did not afflict his soul in the day of atonement. Lev. xxiii. 29.

May *we* not gather some instructive warnings from the non-observance of these four feasts?

First—If Christ be not our true Sabbath; if we are mingling works with that rest of God which He has given, are we not endangering Salvation?

Secondly—If we trust in anything but the shedding of blood, the blood of the true paschal Lamb, for the complete answer to God, on account of sin, and for the complete putting away of His wrath, do we not imperil the soul's safety?

If professing " Christ to be our passover sacrificed for us," we indulge in the sinful lusts of the flesh, the lust of the eye, and the pride of life, are we not eating leavened bread, when we ought to be feeding on Him, the unleavened bread of sincerity and truth? and will not our practice contradict our profession, and prove us to be still of the world, and not of the people of God?

Fourthly—If there be no real affliction of heart, because of sin, when the atonement made by the Lord Jesus in the shedding of His blood, is presented to the soul—but if there be a kind of boastful profession of faith in the doctrines of Salvation, without brokenness of heart because of sin, is not such an one in great peril as to eternal salvation, however well acquainted he may be with doctrinal truth?

The Sabbath therefore having this peculiar place in connection with the Tabernacle appears to intimate to us, that a true rest of soul will be maintained only by our realising the Lord's presence with us, abiding in Him. And that our eternal rest will be attained when we dwell in His presence for ever, in the holy perfection of new creation, on the morning of the resurrection.

# THE FREE GIFTS FOR THE TABERNACLE

"And all the congregation of the children of Israel departed from the presence of Moses.

"And they came, every one whose heart stirred him up, and every one whom his spirit made willing, and they brought the Lord's offering to the work of the tabernacle of the congregation, and for all his service, and for the holy garments.

"And they came, both men and women, as many as were willing hearted, and brought bracelets, and earrings, and rings, and tablets, all jewels of gold: and every man that offered offered an offering of gold unto the Lord.

"And every man, with whom was found blue, and purple, and scarlet, and fine linen, and goats' hair, and red skins of rams, and badgers' skins, brought them.

"Every one that did offer an offering of silver and brass, brought the Lord's offering: and every man, with whom was found shittim wood for any work of the service, brought it.

"And all the women that were wise hearted did spin with their hands, and brought that which they had spun, both of blue, and of purple, and of scarlet, and of fine linen.

"And all the women whose heart stirred them up in wisdom spun goats' hair.

"And the rulers brought onyx stones, and stones to be set, for the ephod, and for the breastplate;

"And spice, and oil for the light, and for the anointing oil, and for the sweet incense,

"The children of Israel brought a willing offering unto the Lord, every man and woman, whose heart made them willing to bring, for all manner of work, which the Lord had commanded to be made by the hand of Moses.—Exod. xxxv 20—29

THE people of Israel responded to the words of the Lord, delivered to them by Moses; and the willing heart was, as it were, stamped upon each gift brought by them for the construction of the tabernacle. The bondage under which law placed them, was for a little while broken through or set aside, by this appeal of the Lord to their hearts. For the tabernacle was a type of Christ, God's free gift, and therefore those who contributed towards it, must show some faint token of the same liberal spirit. The word "willing" is sometimes translated "*free*," 2nd Chron. xxix. 31.; Psa. li. 12. "*Liberal*," Isa. xxxii. 5, 8. Also "*nobles*,"

Numb. xxi. 18.; Psa. lxxxiii. 11. And *"princes"*
1st Sam. ii. 8, etc.  Princely liberality was thus for a
little moment exhibited by that people, of whom the
Lord afterwards complains. " Thou hast not brought
me the small cattle of thy burnt offerings ; neither hast
thou honoured me with thy sacrifices. I have not
caused thee to serve with an offering, nor wearied thee
with incense. Thou hast bought me no sweet cane with
money, neither hast thou filled me with the fat of thy
sacrifices : but thou hast made me to serve with thy sins,
thou hast wearied me with thine iniquities.—Isa. xliii.
23, 24.

It would seem as if the beauty of the type, the costly
gift of God to which it pointed, had suddenly opened
their churlish hearts. Alas ! soon to close again, and
ultimately to reject the very gift itself, which God in
the fulness of His love offered to them.

What a truth this tells us, respecting the way in which
we should seek to please God ! A servile spirit ill befits
one who has tasted of His grace. A covetous heart is
especially an abomination to Him who has not spared
His own Son. Let us only contemplate more deeply,
more truly, the vastness of His gift to us. Let us
learn a little more and more of the heart of God as
shewn in His wondrous love in the gift of Christ, and
we shall acquire a more princely character—more true
nobility of spirit ; and we shall be more ready to yield
ourselves, all we are, and all we have, a willing offering
in His service.

These willing-hearted ones came, both men and
women, and brought first, their gold; " Bracelets,
earrings, rings and tablets, all jewels of Gold." Their
personal ornaments were thus freely given up, as an
heave-offering unto Jehovah. And in this women as
well as men participated; the weak as well as the
strong.

In this respect there is similarity between the *gold*
used in the tabernacle, and the *brass* employed for the

Laver. The brazen mirrors of the women assembling
at the door of the tabernacle of the congregation were
given up by them, for the laver and his foot. Exod.
xxxviii. 8. They preferred to look upon a vessel full
of cleansing water, instead of contemplating their own
beauty in the mirror. Just so a sinner touched by the
grace of God ceases to seek comfort or self-congratula-
tion from his own comeliness; and gladly turns away to
the laver of regeneration, the death of Christ, which
turns his comeliness into corruption, and cleanses him
from the filth of the flesh.

In like manner these Israelitish men and women
preferred the contemplation of the dwelling-place of
God, to personal adornings. They gave up their
jewels of gold (which if worn by themselves would
have attracted the gaze of others to their own persons,)
in order that all eyes and hearts might be set upon the
tabernacle of the Most High.

Are we seeking our adornments from Christ? Are
we gathering glory, comeliness and beauty by gazing
upon Him? Have we the ornament of a meek and
quiet spirit—of priceless value in the sight of God;
because so eminently displayed in His blessed Son?

After specifying that both men and women brought
their jewels of gold it is added, "and every *man* that
offered, an offering of gold unto the Lord." The words
"that offered an offering," are peculiar. It is literally
every man that waved a wave-offering to Jehovah.
The gold is again called a wave-offering. Exod. xxxviii.
24. Thus we have the two words used in this chapter
with reference to the free will offerings of the children
of Israel, "wave-offering," and "heave-offering.'
Two portions of "the peace sacrifice," were respectively
waved and heaved, "the wave breast," and "the
heave shoulder." The action of waving before the
Lord that which was presented to Him seems to denote
the passing it to and fro before His eyes, so that He
may scrutinise every part. Whilst the heaving an

offering would represent lifting it off the earth in separation to Jehovah.

Every man in this instance waved a wave-offering of gold to the Lord, distinct it may be from the jewels also presented. In this action he called attention to the preciousness and purity of the mass of fine gold which he offered. It was the first material presented. It may be because it is the precious metal which in type represents the divine glory of the Lord Jesus. as the Son of God.

We find next, blue, purple, scarlet, fine linen, goats' hair, red skins of rams, and badgers skins brought by *men*. Here all the materials are classed together, which were used for the curtains, hangings, and coverings of the tabernacle. And it is especially said, that " every *man* " who possessed such, brought it. Every manifestation of the Lord Jesus is precious to God, and is an object for our faith to rest upon, and to be occupied with. A man in Christ, will have the word of God richly abiding in him ; his ways will partake of the impress of Christ ; and he will be strong in the grace of the Lord, and in the power of His might. Such an one will be acquainted with all the beauteous displays of God and man, which the Lord hath made manifest. Perhaps those who have advanced a little further than others in the life of faith, have found the Gospels to be both the richest, and deepest study for their hearts ; and by far the most difficult part of Scripture. For without note or comment, they simply pourtray Christ, and leave us to gather, or extract the truth and the blessing from them.

The silver and the brass are next linked together as a " heave-offering."

The brass is in Exod. xxxv. 29, called also a wave-offering.

The silver was derived altogether from the atonement-money. This has already been treated of. It is perhaps here connected with the brass, because there were

sockets made of both metals.  The foundations of
the tabernacle and court, were the result of general
contributions from the whole company of God's people.

The " shittim wood " was also contributed by every
one who happened to have it : and the expression is
added " for any work of the service."  This wood
was used to form the whole framework of the
tabernacle, and the greater part of the holy vessels.
The Lord Jesus as "the Son of Man," has accomplished
God's counsels in redemption.  He has been lifted up
on the cross.  He has been raised to the right hand of
the Throne of glory.  His great "work of service"
has all been accomplished through His having partaken
of flesh and blood.  This truth of His having come
in the flesh is an essential part of the faith of every
believer.

" Every wise hearted woman spun with her hands
the blue and purple, the scarlet and fine linen."  Here
the word " woman " in Hebrew is in the singular
number.  The same word which Adam spoke. Gen. ii.
23, when he said, This is now bone of my bones and
flesh of my flesh : she shall be called woman, (isha)
because she was taken out of man, (ish )

These beautiful colours were handled and spun by
each woman.  May there not be in this a type of the
church, the woman, who delights to trace the beauties
of her Lord, and to handle by faith the word of life,
which describes His loveliness and the perfections of His
character.

" And all the women whose heart stirred them up
in wisdom spun goats' hair."  Here the women are
spoken of collectively in the plural, and they had *a
heart* stirred in wisdom to spin goats' hair.  One heart
led them to this one work.  If it be as before suggested
that the goats' hair for the curtains was derived from
the sin-offerings of the people, or had an allusion
to them ; then we can understand the wisdom of earth
which led the women to this work.

Surely we shall be showing our wisdom of heart, in contemplating Christ " made sin for us," in contrast with all the folly of this world's boasted wisdom, which despises the foolishness of the cross.

The Rulers brought precious stones for the ephod and breastplate. And spices and oil for the light, and for the anointing oil, and for the sweet incense.

The word "ruler" is sometimes translated "captain." Num. chap. ii. throughout ; sometimes " prince." Num. chap. vii. throughout, etc.

They are first mentioned, Exod. xvi. 22, when the double quantity of manna was gathered, to the surprise of these leaders of the congregation.

Thus we find them first interested in the bread from heaven given by God to Israel, and next, bringing those gems on which the names of Israel were to be inscribed, and the oil and perfumes for anointing the tabernacle, and priesthood, and for the daily incense.

In the Church of God, there are those to whom the Lord has given by the Holy Ghost, the gift of rule. Guides of the flock, and whose especial resposibility is to build upon the foundation, that which shall abide the testing day which is coming.

The foundation has already been laid, Jesus Christ. " but let every man take heed how he buildeth thereupon."

Three durable things, gold, silver, precious stones, if built thereupon will abide the fire. Those who lead on, and instruct the Church of God, will build gold, if they seek to raise the hearts and consciences of the Lord's saints to the heavenly standard, Christ. If they act before them " the Apostle and High Priest of their profession," and, bid them as " holy brethren, partakers of the Heavenly calling, consider Him." The Epistle to the Hebrews is full of the glorious display of this gold, and we are exhorted to consider Him, and to consider one another to provoke unto love and to good works.

Building *silver* may mean, seeking to lead the people

of God to follow the ways of divine purity and holiness manifested in the Lord Jesus in all the actions of His grace and love whilst on earth. Perhaps we may call the Gospel by Luke the *Silver* Gospel, and that by John the *Golden* Gospel.

*Precious stones* manifest light in sparkling varied colours as they are turned about. The Epistle to the Ephesians seems to shed the divine lustre of the heavenly calling, and to display the Church as the jewels adorning its glorious Head, the Lord Jesus. This Epistle in its closing exhortations deals with the hearts of the saints, instructing them how to make the highest glories of the heavenly calling shine out in the relationships of this present life. It also exhorts believers to maintain and make manifest the strength and brilliancy of the precious Stone, undimmed by worldliness, and unaffected by the wiles of the devil, or the fiery darts of the wicked one.

To build *precious stones* would be to lead on believers into the truths contained in this Epistle, so that their lives might openly declare their high standing as quickened and raised up together with Christ, not of the world, even as He is not of the world.

On the other hand, we are warned against building wood, hay, stubble.

*Wood* is a very useful material for earth ; but it will not stand the fire. So it is not the ministry of God's builders to be instructing His saints in what may merely fit them for usefulness in earthly things. Many of what are called philanthropic objects, will do very well for the men of this world ; but they will not abide the day that is to try every man's work by fire.

A higher calling is that of the believer. Let the dead bury their dead, but " go thou and preach the kingdom of God," (Luke ix. 59, 60,) was a command of Christ to one, whom He had called to follow Him. Let the dead world care for its own works of death. Our business is to minister life and righteousness, which shall abide for ever.

*Hay* is a degree lower than *wood*, as to its usefulness, and will consume more rapidly in the coming fire. It is dried grass and flowers. It has relics of whatever was fair, but is cut down and withered. There are traces of glory and beauty in the natural man, which cannot fail to remind us of his origin ; but these very tokens of what he once was, are marred by the presence of sin and death

It is not the province of a true servant of God, to cultivate that which seems fair or glorious in the natural man ; but rather to deal with the new man, which " after God is created in righteousness and true holiness." Alas ! much of the literature of the day is an attempt to make the dried grass and flowers of human imagination and invention, a vehicle for the truths of God. A trashy set of religious fictions—or sentimental tales of imagination, are constantly teeming from the press, (fuel only for the fire,) which never can build up the soul of the child of God in its high and heavenly calling.

*Stubble* is fit only for burning—it has not even the fragrance, or the remains of beauty which the *hay* possesses. Have not some of God's own choice servants, (devoted to His work, and loving Him truly,) lent themselves to patronise amusements, such as concerts, and the like, and even popular exhibitions, that must be mere stubble in the sight of God ?

" Every man's work shall be made manifest ; for the day shall declare it, because it shall be revealed by fire ; and the fire shall try every man's work of what sort it is. If any man's work abide which he hath built thereupon, he shall receive a reward. If any man's work shall be burned, he shall suffer loss : but he himself shall be saved ; yet so as by fire." 1st. Cor. iii. 11—15. " *The day*" is an expression with which we are familiar. It refers to the day of our Lord Jesus Christ. 1st Cor. i. 8 ; v. 5 ; 2nd Cor. i. 14, etc., and is contrasted with the darkness of the present night. " The night is far spent, *the day* is at hand." Rom. xiii. 12.

We, as believers in Christ, belong to that day—we are of it—we are children of it. 1st Thes. v. 5, 8. "The day" which we see even now approaching (Heb. x. 25) will commence with the coming of Christ. It will be *a day* of manifestation, when the secrets of all hearts will be revealed. Then each believer raised at the first resurrection in the glory and likeness of Christ, will appear before the tribunal of Christ, and his works in the service of the Lord Jesus will be tested. That which has been like *gold, silver, precious stones*, will abide, and he will receive a reward. That which has been like *wood, hay, stubble*, will pass away for ever, consumed as by fire ; and he will suffer loss, although his individual personal salvation will not be affected thereby.

Lot was as safe as Abraham during the overthrow of Sodom. He escaped from the doomed city with but little else than his life, whilst Abraham could look over the smoking plain with all his own possessions unharmed, surrounding him.

May we be found in that day to have laboured not in vain in the Lord. Taking heed to these warnings of the word of God, lest we be ensnared in this day of expediency by the plausible arguments put forth by men. We live in a time when the rule is, not " what saith the Lord," but " what seems to be most desirable, or most expedient to human judgment or reasoning."

Besides the precious stones, the rulers brought oil for the light and sweet spices for the anointing oil, and for incense.

In the Epistle to the Hebrews, the apostle bids them remember their guides, " who have spoken unto you the word of God, whose faith follow, considering the end of their conversation." xiii. 7. Probably the reference here is to those guides or leaders who had departed to be with Christ. They were to be remembered. A little lower down in the chapter, those guides who were then living are spoken of. " Obey your guides, and submit yourselves, for they watch for your souls as they that

must give account ; that they may do it with joy and not
with grief : for that is unprofitable for you." That is
that they may watch for your souls ; not grieving, but
with joy.

Those leaders who had departed, had left a light of
faith which was to be followed, or imitated. They had
not only *spoken* the word of God, but they had *exhibited*
it in their ways and life, leaving an example to be copied,
the word of God having (as it were) *lived* before the
eyes of the flock.

These Rulers had thus made the light of truth to
shine through the power of the Holy Ghost, and fragrant
graces of the Lord Jesus had been cultivated by them
in their fellowship with the saints. They had " brought
oil for the light and sweet spices."

May there not be somewhat of a contrast between,
" remember your rulers, who have spoken and lived
before you, but who have passed away," and the verse
which follows, " Jesus Christ (is) the same yesterday,
and to day, and for ever." Others, however bright as
examples and earnest as instructors, are gone—Jesus
Christ ever abides. The one author and finisher of faith—
unchangeable in His love, and ceaseless in His living care
of His people.

# THE LIBERAL OFFERINGS

"And Moses called Bezaleel and Aholiab, and every wise hearted man, in whose heart the Lord had put wisdom, even every one whose heart stirred him up to come unto the work to do it:

"And they received of Moses all the offering, which the children of Israel had brought for the work of the service of the sanctuary, to make it withal.  And they brought yet unto him free offerings every morning.

"And all the wise men, that wrought all the work of the sanctuary, came every man from his work which they made;

"And they spake unto Moses, saying, The people bring much more than enough for the service of the work, which the Lord commanded to make.

"And Moses gave commandment, and they caused it to be proclaimed throughout the camp, saying, Let neither man nor woman make any more work for the offering of the sanctuary.  So the people were restrained from bringing.

"For the stuff they had was sufficient for all the work to make it, and too much."—Exod. xxxvi 2—7

WHAT cheerfulness, what devotedness, what liberality was here displayed by the people.  With what a princely open hand they brought their "free offerings" every morning.  Truly the Jacob character had for a little while passed away from them, and they stood forth like the Israel of God.  What a contrast this to the subsequent national sin recorded in Zechariah xi. 12, 13. " And I said unto them, if ye think good, give my price. And if not forbear.  So they weighed for my price, thirty pieces of silver.  And the Lord said unto me, Cast it unto the potter a goodly price that I was prized at of them.  And I took the thirty pieces of silver, and cast them to the potter in the house of the Lord."

In this their early history they lavished their gifts for the construction of a passing type.  Subsequently they prized the reality, the living Jehovah, Emmanuel in the midst of them, at thirty pieces of silver !

In the very house of the Lord itself, adorned with costly stones, lay the thirty pieces of silver ; a witness of the shameful, niggardly price at which they valued God's

most precious gift. Do we not in principle see the same
things around us at the present day? An edifice dedicated to what are so called " religious purposes," is
sumptuously adorned with every kind of human invention and device, to gratify the eye and please the taste.
But if the hearts of many of the liberal givers of the
gold and silver were searched, what would be the value
therein found, of the precious sacrifice, the precious
blood of Christ? Whilst the name of Jehovah Jesus is
in outward profession honoured, is He not in reality
despised and rejected? A form, a ceremony, a type, a
shadow, can be venerated. The flesh can highly esteem
it, because it addresses the senses. But " the Child
born," " the Son given," " the unspeakable gift" of
God, is unknown. Life eternal, salvation, is neglected.
A Cain worship supplants that of the true God. And
under the semblance of religiousness, a desperately
wicked heart secretly despises the precious blood of
Christ.

We have two instances recorded in the Gospels of
the liberal heart. One in Mark xiv. 8, where the
highest commendation perhaps ever given is bestowed by
the Lord upon the woman who brought an alabaster box
of ointment, very precious, and brake it and poured the
contents upon His head. " She hath done what she
could." How few of the Lord's servants reach this
high standard, especially in their manifestation of love for
Him.

The anticipation of His burial called forth this expression of her heart's devotion, which others stigmatised as
wasteful expenditure. She had a glimpse of the wondrous value of that death of deaths which He was to
accomplish ; and she anointed with the costly perfume
the Head which was to be crowned with thorns, and to
be " marred more than any man's."

Oh! that we might follow her example, gathering
from the contemplation of His sorrows on the tree,
increase of our heart's affections ; not counting our lives

dear ; but ready to spend and be spent in His service, " who made Himself poor that we through His poverty might be rich."

> " Love so amazing, so divine,
> Demands my soul, my life, my all."

Another case of rich profusion in giving was that of the poor widow, Mark xii. 41 ; Luke xxi. 1—4. The Lord Jesus was observing how the people cast their offerings into the treasury : many that were rich cast in much.   But the two mites, or one farthing of a certain poor widow, so arrested His attention, that He called to His disciples to mark this great gift.

It was all that she had ; all her living ; and she gave it to God.   Did she expect it would add much to the beauty of the house ?   Or would go far towards some costly ceremonial ?   No ; when the sums were counted over by the treasurer at the close of the day, this farthing was scarcely worth recording in the list of donations.

Men like to head subscription lists with large sums. And the churl is often counted liberal.   God looks at the *heart*, the costly thing in His eyes—" the *heart's* adoration."   The widow in her gift proved her unbounded confidence in God Himself as the giver.   She thus expressed to Him her faith—" precious faith," which the Lord Jesus valued ; for He had humbled Himself so as to be altogether dependent upon His Father.   He was going to enrich God's treasury by giving up Himself, His life, His all, in order to please Him.

We have in 2nd Cor. viii. 1—5, another beautiful example of the grace of God bestowed on the churches of Macedonia.   Opening their hearts, so that " in a great trial of affliction, the abundance of their joy, and their deep poverty, abounded unto the riches of their liberality.   For to their power I bear record, yea, and beyond their power, they were willing of themselves ; praying us with much entreaty, that we would receive

the gift, and take upon us the fellowship of the ministering to the saints. And this they did, not as we
hoped, but first gave their own selves to the Lord, and
to us by the will of God."

Is not this a striking antitype of the liberality above
recorded respecting Israel? All is traced to the grace
of God first bestowed upon these saints and then flowing
out in abundance of joy and riches of liberality. The
"cheerful giver" whom God likes was here displayed,
and the spring of it all must have been their knowledge
of the grace of our Lord Jesus Christ. They first gave
themselves to God.

In Psalm xxii. (that deep psalm of the cross,) the
24th verse might be better translated, "for he hath not
despised nor abhorred the *poverty of the poor one*, neither
hath he hid his face from him : but when he cried unto
him he heard."

What poverty equal to His upon the cross ? What
poverty equal to the poverty of death ? And such a
death ! Forsaken of God ; forsaken of lover and friend.
Nailed in utter weakness to the tree of curse ; so that
the blessed one exclaimed, "I am a worm and no man."
Yet what riches in that death ! What glory, what joy
to God, what abundance of grace ! What treasures of
wisdom and power !

In the case of Israel the people had to be restrained
from bringing, "for the stuff was sufficient, and too
much." But the gold, silver, and brass were reckoned
in definite sums.

"All the gold that was occupied for the work in all
the work of the holy place, even the gold of the offering,
was twenty and nine talents, and seven hundred and
thirty shekels, after the shekel of the sanctuary.

And the silver of them that were numbered of the congregation was an hundred talents, and a thousand seven
hundred and threescore and fifteen shekels, after the
shekel of the sanctuary : a bekah for every man, that is,
half a shekel, after the shekel of the sanctuary, for every

one that went to be numbered, from twenty years old and upward, for six hundred thousand and three thousand and five hundred and fifty men. And of the hundred talents of silver were cast the sockets of the sanctuary, and the sockets of the vail; an hundred sockets of the hundred talents, a talent for a socket. And of the thousand seven hundred seventy and five shekels he made hooks for the pillars, and overlaid their chapiters, and filleted them.

And the brass of the offering was seventy talents, and two thousand and four hundred shekels. And therewith he made the sockets to the door of the tabernacle of the congregation, and the brazen altar, and the brazen grate for it, and all the vessels of the altar, and the sockets of the court round about, and the sockets of the court gate, and all the pins of the tabernacle, and all the pins of the court round about." Exod. xxxviii. 24—31.

When we however regard Him of whom these things were shadows; we have to contrast God's great gift with these comparatively small offerings.

What a depth of truth is contained in the verse, " He that *spared not* His own Son, but delivered Him up for us all." (Rom. viii. 32.)   God's love flowed out unrestrained, unbounded in the gift of Jesus His only begotten Son.  Like a mighty ocean, fathomless, boundless, His love buried every thought of our worthlessness and ingratitude.  Went down beneath our deepest need.  Raised us up to His highest glory.  Overcame every hindrance to our eternal blessing, manifesting itself as it never was seen before, and never can be seen again, in *not sparing* His own Son.

And can this precious gift be estimated ?  The apostle is obliged at the close of one of the chapters in 2nd Cor. where he had been praising *their* liberality, to exclaim, when He contemplated the liberality of God, " thanks be to God for His *unspeakable* gift."

This gift is the measure of God's love to us.  Through

it we are raised to be sons of God. Placed in closer
nearness to Him than any created beings. Loved by
Him as He hath loved His Son. Every doubt, every
uncertainty, every question of heart, should at once be
stilled by the remembrance of this wonderful gift. And
our own affections should be stirred up to worship and
to praise ; and our mouths enlarged to ask what we will,
through the deeper meditation of God's love, in delivering Christ up to death for us.

The gold, silver, and brass, contributed by Israel
were all reckoned in talents and shekels. So highly
did God value these little tokens of their willing hearts,
that He carefully records them, even to the very last
shekel of brass.

He is not unrighteous to forget any work and labour
of love which we show towards His name, in ministering
to the need of His saints. A cup of cold water will
be remembered. But when we seek to count up
His mercies towards us, they are passing knowledge.
" How precious are thy thoughts unto me O God !
How great is the sum of them ! If I should count them,
they are more in number than the sand." Ps. cxxxix.
17, 18.

" Many, O Lord my God, are thy wonderful works
which thou hast done, and thy *thoughts* which are to
us-ward : they cannot be reckoned up in order unto
thee : if I would declare and speak of them, they are
more than can be numbered." Ps. xl. 5. The word
here translated " *thoughts*," may be rendered *devices* ;
it is derived from the same Hebrew root as to "*devise
cunning work*." Surely the skilful devices of God's love
and wisdom towards us, in the gift and work of His
Son, are beyond all calculation. It will take us an
eternity of unbroken rest and blessedness to discover
them. Well might the apostle to the Gentiles rejoice in
having to proclaim "the *unsearchable riches* of Christ."
Eph. iii. 8.

Thus far have we pursued the subject of the Tabernacle. What nas been written should be regarded rather as suggestions for those who read, not as authoritative expositions of the truth.

The succeeding portion will embrace the Priesthood, forming the second division of the subject.

**The Golden Candlestick with Its Lamps and Vessels**
(Uncovered and also Partly Covered)

# THE
# PRIESTHOOD

THE Tabernacle and its vessels, the Priesthood, and the various ministrations connected therewith, form but one subject; although divided for the sake of more distinctly contemplating each portion.

The tabernacle would have been useless without its vessels : and the tabernacle with its vessels, would have been of no service, but for a living family of priests, constantly engaged in various active ministrations within the holy places, and about the various holy vessels.

So closely connected is each part of this subject with the other, that in the directions contained in Exodus, there is no break ; but the command for making the holy garments, and consecrating the priesthood, (Exod. xxviii. and xxix.) comes between the enumeration of some of the holy vessels, and the various parts of the tabernacle. Indeed properly speaking, the 27th chapter should end at verse 19, where "thou shalt command the children of Israel" begins a new subject, viz : directions concerning the oil for the light of the sanctuary. The 28th chapter follows on with the words " and take thou unto thee, etc." and the 29th chapter continues with ordering the sacrifices, etc. for the day of priestly consecration. The 30th again carries on the subject connected with the priesthood, by giving the description of the incense-altar : and the whole closes with the sabbath, at the end of the 31st chapter.

Again ; when all the various parts of the work had been completed, ending with the garments of the priesthood, (chapters xxxvi.—xxxix. verse 31,) the following verse is added : " Thus was all the work of the tabernacle of the tent of the congregation finished; and the children of Israel did according to all that the Lord commanded Moses, so did they." Here, therefore, the priestly garments were considered part of the work of the tabernacle. And if we turn to Heb. viii. we find that "the priests, that offered gifts according to the law, served unto the example and shadow of heavenly things ; as Moses was admonished of God, when he was about to make the tabernacle : for, See, saith he, that thou make all things according to the pattern shewed to thee in the mount." v. 4, 5.

The service of the priests, in offering gifts and sacrifices, is thus connected with the commandments given to Moses in the mount, respecting the making of the tabernacle. The words " See that thou make all things according to the pattern shewed thee in the mount," as recorded in Exodus, were spoken to Moses respecting the holy vessels ; (see Exod. xxv. 40,) but are in Heb. viii. quoted to prove that the priests and their ministrations were examples and shadows of heavenly things. The whole subject is therefore much blended. But as far as possible it is the object of the present exposition, to consider by themselves the Aaronic priesthood, the garments, consecration, and ordinary service.

The High Priest of Israel in His Robes
of Glory and Beauty

**The High Priest of Israel on the
Great Day of Atonement**

# THE PRIESTS

"Take thou unto thee Aaron thy brother, and his sons with him, from among the children of Israel, that he may minister unto me in the priest's office, even Aaron, Nadab and Abihu, Eleazar and Ithamar, Aaron's sons."—Exod. xxviii i

In this direction given to Moses, we may observe how the priestly family is kept distinct from Moses and his descendants : so that neither he himself, nor his sons, have any office of priesthood. This points out a contrast between the priesthood under the law, and that of which Christ is the head. The leadership or kingship of Moses as well as the office of mediator, were in him kept apart from the priesthood, which was confined to Aaron and his sons : and these dignities were thus lodged in different persons. Whereas one object of the Epistle to the Hebrews is to point out the Lord Jesus in resurrection, combining in Himself the various offices and dignities of King, Mediator, Apostle, Surety, Captain, and Shepherd.

The names of Aaron and his sons are significant. Aaron means "very high." He stood supreme, as the high priest ; very high above his own house, as well as exalted above the people : a type thus of the Lord Jesus, whom God has exalted with his right hand, to be a Prince and a Saviour. Acts v. 31. And as it still further to exalt the high priesthood of Jesus above that of Aaron, we have the word "great" added ; so that the Lord is called a *great* high priest. Heb iv. 14.

Aaron's sons have each appropriate names ; Nadab, "willing ;" Abihu, "my Father is He," (that is, God,) Eleazar, "help of God ;" Ithamar, "land of palm." These four words afford a little prophetic intimation of characteristics attaching to the house, of which the Son of God is the Head ; deriving its life from God the Father, and all its power and help from Him ; following in the footsteps also of its blessed Master, in yielding willing and not constrained service to God; and like the palm-trees, lofty in righteousness, and ever bringing forth fruit. Psa. xcii. 12—14. The palm-tree is one of the ornaments of the future temple described by Ezekiel, and was also one of the embellishments of Solomon's temple. It is peculiarly the tree of the desert flourishing where no other could exist; ever marking out to the weary traveller the spot, amidst surrounding desolation, where a grateful shade, and spring of living water, are to be found; and remarkable for longevity and ceaseless fruitfulness. Thus it was an apt emblem of the heavenly priesthood.

The wording of the first verse is remarkable: "Take unto thee Aaron, and his sons with him, that *he* may minister." Aaron and his sons formed but one ministry in the priest's office: and Aaron could not exercise his service, unless his sons were taken with him. Is there not in this, an intimation of the union in priesthood of Christ and his house; and that one great object of his priesthood is, that He may minister to God respecting his house?

**The Ark and Mercy Seat**

# THE GARMENTS FOR GLORY & BEAUTY

"And thou shalt make holy garments for Aaron thy brother for glory and for beauty.

"And thou shalt speak unto all that are wise hearted, whom I have filled with the spirit of wisdom, that they may make Aaron's garments to consecrate him, that he may minister unto me in the priest's office.

"And these are the garments which they shall make; a breastplate, and an ephod, and a robe, and a broidered coat, a mitre, and a girdle: and they shall make holy garments for Aaron thy brother, and his sons, that he may minister unto me in the priest's office."—Exod. xxviii 2—4

THE garments for glory and beauty are next directed to be made, that Aaron might be consecrated, in order to minister in the priest's office. Thus Aaron was fitted, by reason of his garments, for this holy office. They dignified his person, covering him with a glory and beauty, which in himself he possessed not. To all this, the priesthood of the Lord stands out in bright and blessed contrast. The dignity and glory which are His, and which were His from everlasting as the Son, magnify the office which He holds. His life of obedience, and his death upon the tree, making Him manifest as the only begotten of the Father, full of grace and truth, proved Him to be worthy of the highest exaltation at the right hand of God ; and that He had the heart of a priest, and of a good shepherd, who would care to the uttermost for the sheep of God. The office added dignity to Aaron : whereas Christ dignifies the office.

It may be well here to point out some of the contrasts drawn in the word of God, between the priesthood of Aaron and that of Christ. Aaron was *called* to be priest whilst living amongst men. The Lord Jesus was called by resurrection from among the dead to be a high priest. The fact of resurrection, when God said to Him, " Thou art my Son, this day have I begotten thee," constituted Him high priest ; for sonship is the great element of the heavenly priesthood. Indeed the whole Epistle to the Hebrews, turns upon that especial

name of the Lord Jesus, " the Son." All the beauty
and glory of the Gospel is connected with that name.
It is the name which the Lord holds because He is
God ; and therefore when a believer is baptised, he is
baptised into the name of the Father, and of the Son,
and of the Holy Ghost ; the names forming but one
name of the Godhead.

The love of God in the gift of Christ all turns upon
that wondrous truth, that He was and is the only-
begotten Son of God ; not because made of a woman ;
not because made flesh ; but because of His eternal
relationship of wondrous divine existence, to the Father;
incomprehensible indeed to us, as is the whole mystery
of the Sonship ; (for none knoweth the Son, but the
Father;) but received by faith.   The love of God in the
gift of Christ depends upon this great truth.   It was
not a love which merely caused the incarnation of the
Word, and thereby established a new relation of
Sonship, which had not previously existed.   Had this
been the case, it would not have been true that God
*sent*, or *gave*, his only begotten Son.   He could not
give, or send, a Son whom He possessed not.   Neither
did any fresh love spring up in the heart of the Father
towards the Word made flesh.   No new affection of
Father towards Son commenced, when the blessed Lord
was born of the Virgin.   But that eternal love towards
His Only-Begotten, the ever existing One in the bosom
of the Father—that love which God had reposed in
Him who was ever the Son, the brightness of His
glory, and the express image of His person—that love
manifested itself towards poor ruined fallen creatures ;
so that God has proved, in the gift of Jesus, that He
has loved us, worms of the dust as we are, as He loves
Him, the only begotten One in His bosom.   It is also
said that by Him, the Son, " the brightness of his
glory, and the express image of his person, " God
made the worlds. Heb. i.   (In our translation of the
2nd verse, " *his* Son " is substituted for " *the* Son.")

The same truth is expressed, Col. i. 15—17, "Who is the image of the invisible God, the first-born of every creature. For by him were all things created, that are in heaven, and that are in earth, visible and invisible; whether they be thrones, or dominions, or principalities, or powers ; all things were created by him, and for him. And he is before all things ; and by him all things consist." Here the Lord Jesus is declared pre-eminent, because *born* before all creation ; proved by His creating all things. All fulness dwells in Him ; fulness of Sonship ; fulness of every glory.

Again : the Lord Jesus is addressed by the Father as God, because He is THE SON. " Unto the Son, he saith : Thy throne, O God, is for ever and ever . . and, Thou, Lord, in the beginning hast laid the foundation of the earth, and the heavens are the works of thy hands. They shall perish ; but thou remainest: they all shall wax old as doth a garment ; and as a vesture shalt thou fold them up, and they shall be changed. But thou art *the same*; and thy years shall not fail." Heb. i. 8—12. To the Son, He saith, Thou art *the same*. Thus, incarnation did not create Sonship ; but, *the Son* was the same from everlasting, is the same now, and shall be for ever.

The Son of God was indeed *manifested* in incarnation : (1st John iii. 8.) and the *love of God* was *manifested* towards us, because God sent His only begotten Son into the world, that we might live through Him. And we have seen, and do testify, that the Father *sent the Son* to be the Saviour of the world. (iv. 9, 14.)

The revelation of the Father could only be made by the Son. He declared Him. " He that hath seen me, hath seen the Father." And the truth of the pre-existence of the Father would be destroyed, were there a doubt as to the eternity of the Son, *as Son*. In one remarkable text, He is called " the Son of the Father,"—" Grace be with you, mercy and peace, from God the Father, and from the Lord Jesus Christ, the Son of the Father." 2nd John 3.

And the truth of the eternity of the Sonship is really

the doctrine of Christ : as it is written, " He that *abideth* in the doctrine of Christ, he hath both the Father and the Son." v. 9.   The Lord Jesus is the only begotten Son of God, in His divine eternal relationship to God the Father.   When born of the virgin, the name " Son of God" was again given to Him :—" that holy thing, which shall be born of thee, shall be called the Son of God."   And again, when raised from the dead, God said unto Him, " Thou art my Son : this day have I begotten thee."   It is to be observed in the 2nd Psalm, that two words are employed in the original ; the one a Hebrew, the other a Chaldee word for Son.   " Thou art my Son :" *Ben* is Hebrew.   " Kiss the Son :" *Bar* is Chaldee.   Is not this change made, because the proclamation of the Son, to be worshipped and obeyed, is given to the Babylonish kingdoms of the world, which are described in the image, and the four beasts of Daniel ; the princes whereof crucified the Lord of glory ?

Again : this truth of the eternal Godhead of the Son, as the only begotten of the Father, is intimately bound up with the presence and power of the Holy Ghost in the believer.   " The Holy Spirit is called the Spirit of His Son;" and as such, He teaches us to cry, "Abba, Father;" to use the same words, as the Lord Jesus Himself could use; to know the same love, as the Son Himself knows ; not the love of God to a mere creature ; but the love wherewith God loved His Son from everlasting ; a love which chose us in Christ, before the foundation of the world ; which predestinated us, to be conformed to the image of His Son ; and which we shall taste to the full, when that which is in part shall be done away, and that which is perfect shall come.   God sent His own Son in the likeness of sinful flesh ; in our likeness ; having predestinated us to be conformed to His likeness.

The Holy Ghost, the spirit of sonship, beareth witness with our spirit, that we are the children of God ; and if children, then heirs ; the inheritance is ours, because we are sons, as the inheritance is Christ's because He is the

Son : according to Heb. i. 4, where it is said, "He hath *inherited* a more excellent name" than angels ; not received it for the first time by incarnation ; for then it would not be inherited.

Many more texts might be quoted, to establish this leading truth of the Gospel : but these may be sufficient. God grant that no child of His, may through carnal reasoning, or the self-will of the flesh, lose in any degree fellowship with the Father, and with His Son Jesus Christ ; through not holding the eternal Sonship of Christ, as declared in the Word of God.

But to return to the contrast between Aaron and Christ. Aaron was taken from among men, Heb. v. 1. He differed in no respect from the men, for whom he was ordained to offer gifts and sacrifices. He was compassed with infirmity, like they were, and therefore as much needed to offer for his own sins, as for those of others. (v. 3.)

Christ, on the other hand, was not taken from among men. He was raised from the dead, the Son of God. No infirmity ever clave to Him. No trace of sin, or mortality (the result of sin) attached to Him. He was born that holy thing, the Son of God. He was raised from the dead, by the decree, " Thou art my Son."— called of God, a high priest for ever, after the order of Melchizedek ; called up in resurrection, glory, and power.

The High Priest, under the law, had compassion on the ignorant, and on them that were out of the way, because he was conscious of infirmities in himself. The very fact of being himself a sinner, was one qualification for that priesthood.

The Lord Jesus, through His life of sorrow and temptation, was perfected for priesthood. He is able to sympathise, because He has been tempted in all points like as we are, yet without sin. He suffered, being tempted ; and is therefore able to succour them that are tempted. The dreadful whisperings of the enemy, which He was called to endure, filled his soul with holy abhorrence, and taught Him to feel pity for us, who are subject to the assaults of that fearful foe, and who, alas ! too often yield a response in our hearts to his evil suggestions.

The dreadful death under curse, the full wages of sin, which ever presented itself in anticipation to the heart of the Lord, cast a sorrowful shade over His holy devoted life; and in humble obedience and submission to the will of God, He pursued his pathway to the cross, where at length He tasted the reality of that which no anticipation could equal ; and was heard, by being raised from the dead, the great High Priest of His people.

His life was a life of learning obedience by the things which He suffered ; in contrast with the life of a mere human priest, who, if he learned anything, was constantly discovering disobedience and sin, even though lifted up into a high place, and thereby exempted from much of the suffering around him.

The priests of the house of Levi were made without an oath ; and in consequence, some of them were cut off from the priesthood, as in the case of Nadab and Abihu, and Eli's line.

The Lord Jesus was made priest with an oath ; " the Lord sware, and will not repent :" the unchangeableness of God's word and oath established the Lord Jesus as the surety of a better covenant. The priesthood, under the law, passed on from father to son. But this One, the Lord Jesus, because He continueth ever, hath an unchangeable priesthood ; that is, one that is not transferred, or, passed not on. The Aaronic priests were sons of Levi : our Lord sprang out of Judah, the kingly line. Aaron was, in many respects, as to the ministrations he fulfilled, a shadow of Christ. But Christ himself arose after the similitude of Melchizedek. This is doubly interesting : for Melchizedek himself is presented to us in Scripture without any pedigree ; " without father, without mother, without descent, having neither beginning of days, nor end of life ;" and in these respects, made like unto the Son of God. Thus, before the incarnation of the Son, Melchizedek is presented, a type of Him, as to his eternal Godhead *as the Son* ; the only human being in the Bible, who has the aspect of divinity cast around him, in order that he may represent the Son. Some have imagined, that Melchizedek was Christ himself. But it is clear, from this passage, and from the other already quoted, that he was only a type of the Son of God ; and that the words " without father, without mother, &c.," allude to his sudden appearance, as narrated in Genesis, where no parentage is recorded, and no time of his birth or death, and no mention is made of his age. Thus Melchizedek was made like unto the Son of God ; and Christ arose, a Priest like Melchizedek. There is a double reflection.

Aaron was made a priest, after the law of a carnal commandment ; that is a commandment, which had reference to his origin in the flesh from the tribe of Levi. Whereas Christ became High Priest after the power of an endless life ; the glorious eternal power of resurrection. Life received out of death, and making manifest His victory over death, constituted Him the great High Priest.

These appear to be some of the leading features of contrast between the priesthood under the law, and the priesthood of Christ. Other particulars will, from time to time, present themselves to our notice, as we pursue this deeply interesting subject.

Let us now proceed with Exodus xxviii 4.

" These are the garments which they shall make ; a breastplate, and an ephod, and a robe, and a broidered coat, and a mitre, and a girdle." Without these, Aaron could not be priest : they form a sevenfold completeness ; and typify the various powers, responsibilities, and qualities, connected with that office. Again : Aaron's sons are associated with him in the directions given—"and they shall make holy garments for Aaron thy brother, and his sons :" and the sentence which has been before commented on, is repeated ;—" that *he* may minister unto me in the priest's office."

# THE EPHOD

"And they shall take gold, and blue, and purple, and scarlet, and fine linen.

"And they shall make the ephod of gold, of blue, and of purple, of scarlet, and fine twined linen, with cunning work.—Exod. xxviii 5, 6

"And of the blue, and purple, and scarlet, they made cloths of service, to do service in the holy place, and made the holy garments for Aaron; as the Lord commanded Moses.

"And he made the ephod of gold, blue, and purple, and scarlet, and fine twined linen.—Exod. xxxix 1, 2

THE two materials here specified, are gold, and fine twined linen; the others—blue, purple, and scarlet— are colours, emblazoned upon the fine twined linen, and everywhere interlaced by the gold. The mode in which this was done, is described in chap. xxxix. iii. "And they did beat the gold into thin plates, and cut it into wires, to work it in the blue, and in the purple, and in the scarlet, and in the fine linen, with cunning work." Thus, the strength and glory of the gold was intimately blended with every part of the ephod, and gave firmness, as well as brilliancy, to the whole fabric. In other respects, the texture was the same as that of the vail. The word *change* is only used in Scripture respecting ourselves as sinners, and as having mortal corruptible bodies. "We shall all be changed." "The dead shall be raised incorruptible, and we shall be changed," whether sleeping or alive at the coming of the Lord. The word here used is the same as in Heb. i, with reference to Creation: "as a vesture shalt thou fold them (the earth and the heavens) up, and they shall be *changed*." Another word is used, Phil. iii. 21, "who shall change (or, transform) our body of humiliation; that it may be fashioned like unto his glorious body." Resurrection, to the blessed Lord, was no such change. "Thou art *the same*," was the word spoken to Him by God, when on the cross. He is the same, whether yesterday in humiliation, or to-day in glory; the same, eternally. And yet, He was crucified through weakness, and His days on earth are spoken of as "the days of *His flesh*;" words which are not applicable to Him any more. Whilst on earth He partook of flesh and blood in order to die. In resurrection, He has a body of glory. It was impossible that He could be holden of death ; and He cannot again return to it. Raised in *power* ; declared to be the Son of God *with power*, according to the Spirit of holiness, by the resurrection from the dead. Almighty strength, and divine majesty, are now manifested in Him, (in contrast with His days of weakness,) faintly typified by the wire of solid gold, which everywhere pervaded the ephod of the high priest.

There is still the same fulness of the love of God, in Him now, and pourtrayed by the heavenly blue, as He manifested when on earth. The royal dignity of the Son of David, the princely heart of munificence, mercy, and justice, abide in Him, now that He is seated upon the throne of the majesty in the heavens :—Scarlet as well as blue, are colours of the ephod. The purple also—the new and wondrous colour, which combines in itself both the blue and the scarlet—was curiously wrought in this priestly garment ; a colour denoting that great mystery, so inseparably connected with all contemplation of the ways, thoughts, and words of Jesus; viz : that He did combine the wisdom, love, holiness, and power of God, with every true feeling, affection, and sympathy, proper to man. All these glories and beauties were inwrought in a vesture of fine twined linen. The righteous One, who had manifested unsullied purity and unblemished spotlessness on earth, has been raised up, the Son of Man, in glory; because of His perfect obedience, and the delight which He had in accomplishing the will of God.

Having before more fully entered upon the subject of the colours, this notice of them may be deemed sufficient.

# THE EPHOD GIRDLE

"It shall have the two shoulderpieces thereof joined at the two edges thereof; and so it shall be joined together.

"And the curious girdle of the ephod, which is upon it, shall be of the same, according to the work thereof; even of gold, of blue, and purple, and scarlet, and fine twined linen.— Exod. xxviii 7, 8

"They made shoulderpieces for it, to couple it together; by the two edges was it coupled together.

"And the curious girdle of his ephod, that was upon it, was of the same, according to the work thereof; of gold, blue, and purple, and scarlet, and fine twined linen; as the Lord commanded Moses.— Exod. xxxix 4, 5

THE Ephod seems to have been made of two pieces, joined together at the shoulders, and bound to the person of the high priest by a girdle or belt.

The word translated "curious girdle," is not that usually employed for "girdle;" indeed there is no idea of girding connected with it at all. It is solely used to express this part of the ephod, and is a Hebrew word expressing a curious device or embroidery. It seems to have been a *belt*, to bind the ephod to the high priest, rather than a girdle to strengthen the loins. In Exodus xxix. 5, (and gird him with the curious girdle of the ephod,) and Lev. viii. 7, (and bound it unto him therewith,) the expression literally is "and ephodized him with it:" the object apparently being to convey the thought, that this curious belt so connected the ephod with the person who wore it, as to impart to him the virtues it contained. In Lev. viii. 7, the word "and he *girded* him with the curious belt" is the only occasion where the ordinary word *gird* is connected with this belt

# THE ONYX-STONES, OUCHES, AND CHAINS

" And thou shalt take two onyx stones, and grave on them the names of the children of Israel :

" Six of their names on one stone, and the other six names of the rest on the other stone, according to their birth.

" With the work of an engraver in stone, like the engravings of a signet, shalt thou engrave the two stones with the names of the children of Israel : thou shalt make them to be set in ouches of gold.

" And thou shalt put the two stones upon the shoulders of the ephod for stones of memorial unto the children of Israel : and Aaron shall bear their names before the Lord upon his two shoulders for a memorial.

" And thou shalt make ouches of gold ;

" And two chains of pure gold at the ends ; of wreathen work shalt thou make them, and fasten the wreathen chains to the ouches. —Exod. xxviii 9—14

" And they wrought onyx-stones inclosed in ouches of gold, graven, as signets are graven, with the names of the children of Israel.

" And he put them on the shoulders of the ephod, that they should be stones for a memorial to the children of Israel ; as the Lord commanded Moses."—Exod. xxxix 6, 7

THE onyx-stones are especially mentioned in the list of things commanded to be brought, Exod. xxv. 7. " Onyx-stones, and stones to be set in the ephod, and in the breastplate." They were engraved with the names of the children of Israel, according to their *birth;* six on each stone. They were enclosed in ouches, or settings of gold :—for the word translated *ouches* is derived from a Hebrew verb, " to set." Exod. xxviii. 20. " They shall be *set* in gold." These onyx-stones in their settings were fastened upon the shoulder-pieces of the ephod, so as to rest upon the shoulders of the high priest. " And thou shalt put the two stones upon the shoulders of the ephod, for stones of memorial unto the children of Israel : and Aaron shall bear their names before the Lord, upon his two shoulders, for a memorial."

The Hebrew word, translated *onyx*, is derived by Robertson (Clav : Pent :) from an unused root, signifying "to shine with the lustre of fire." It was evidently a very precious stone. (See Job xxviii. 16, "the *precious* onyx ;") and not the onyx of modern times, which is neither precious nor brilliant.

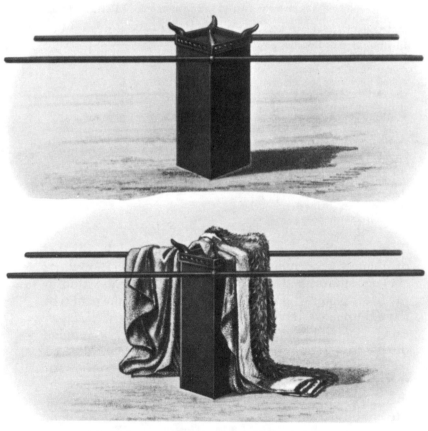

**The Altar of Incense**
(Uncovered and Partly Covered)

# THE BREASTPLATE

" And thou shalt make the breastplate of judgment with cunning work ; after the work of the ephod thou shalt make it ; of gold, of blue, and of purple, and of scarlet, and of fine twined linen, shalt thou make it.

" Foursquare it shall be being doubled ; a span shall be the length thereof, and a span shall be the breadth thereof.

" And thou shalt set in it settings of stones, even four rows of stones : the first row shall be a sardius, a topaz, and a carbuncle : this shall be the first row.

" And the second row shall be an emerald, a sapphire, and a diamond.

" And the third row a ligure, an agate, and an amethyst.

" And the fourth row a beryl, and an onyx, and a jaspar : they shall be set in gold in their inclosings.

" And the stones shall be with the names of the children of Israel, twelve, according to their names, like the engravings of a signet ; every one with his name shall they be according to the twelve tribes.

" And thou shalt make upon the breastplate chains at the ends of wreathen work of pure gold.

" And thou shalt make upon the breastplate two rings of gold, and shalt put the two rings on the two ends of the breastplate.

" And thou shalt put the two wreathen chains of gold in the two rings which are on the ends of the breastplate.

" And the other two ends of the two wreathen chains thou

" And he made the breastplate of cunning work, like the work of the ephod ; of gold, blue, and purple, and scarlet, and fine twined linen.

" It was foursquare ; they made the breastplate double : a span was the length thereof, and a span the breadth thereof, being doubled.

" And they set in it four rows of stones : the first row was a sardius, a topaz, and a carbuncle : this was the first row.

" And the second row, an emerald, a sapphire, and a diamond.

" And the third row, a ligure, an agate, and an amethyst.

" And the fourth row, a beryl, an onyx, and a jasper : they were enclosed in ouches of gold in their inclosings.

" And the stones were according to the names of the children of Israel, twelve, according to their names, like the engravings of a signet, every one with his name, according to the twelve tribes.

" And they made upon the breastplate chains at the ends, of wreathen work of pure gold.

" And they made two ouches of gold, and two gold rings ; and put the two rings in the two ends of the breastplate.

" And they put the two wreathen chains of gold in the two rings on the ends of the breastplate.

" And the two ends of the two wreathen chains they fastened in the two ouches, and put them on the shoulderpieces of the ephod, before it.

shalt fasten in the two ouches, and put them on the shoulder-pieces of the ephod before it.

"And thou shalt make two rings of gold, and thou shalt put them upon the two ends of the breastplate in the border thereof, which is in the side of the ephod inward.

"And two other rings of gold thou shalt make, and shalt put them on the two sides of the ephod underneath, toward the forepart thereof, over against the other coupling thereof, above the curious girdle of the ephod.

"And they shall bind the breastplate by the rings thereof unto the rings of the ephod with a lace of blue, that it may be above the curious girdle of the ephod, and that the breastplate be not loosed from the ephod.

"And Aaron shall bear the names of the children of Israel in the breastplate of judgment upon his heart, when he goeth in unto the holy place, for a memorial before the Lord continually."
—Exod. xxviii 15—29

"And they made two rings of gold, and put them on the two ends of the breastplate, upon the border of it, which was on the side of the ephod inward.

"And they made two other golden rings, and put them on the two sides of the ephod underneath, toward the forepart of it, over against the other coupling thereof, above the curious girdle of the ephod.

"And they did bind the breastplate by his rings unto the rings of the ephod with a lace of blue, that it might be above the curious girdle of the ephod, and that the breastplate might not be loosed from the ephod: as the Lord commanded Moses."—Exod. xxxix 8—21

THE word translated "breastplate" is supposed by Gesenius to mean "ornament." It is solely used to express this part of the high priest's dress, and occurs nowhere else in Scripture. The Septuagint translates it by the Greek word *logeion*, or oracle. It was made of the same materials as the ephod ; was doubled, so as to form a kind of bag, and had four rows of precious stones set in it, three in each row ; each stone engraved with the name of one of the children of Israel.

Into this breastplate, so doubled, were put " the urim and the thummim." Two rings of gold were placed inwards, at the bottom of the breastplate : and two golden rings were attached to the ephod, just above the curious belt : so that the breastplate was bound to the

ephod by a lace of blue, coupling these rings. Two
wreathen chains of gold were fastened to the ouches,
in which the onyx-stones were set ; and were also
fastened, at their other ends, to two rings at the top of
the breastplate. Thus, the ephod, onyx-stones, and
breastplate, were all linked together in one.

It may here be observed, that the translation " at
the ends," (xxviii. 14, 22, and xxxix. 15,) should,
according to Gesenius, be rendered "twisted work,"
like the twisting of a rope : and the passage will read
thus : " Two chains of pure gold, twisted wreathen-
work shalt thou make them."

Let us now seek the interpretation of this portion of
the high priest's dress. The ephod, with its shoulder-
stones and breastplate, formed peculiarly the *prophetic*
dress of the high priest. By means of it, he learned the
counsel of God, and was able thus to declare what
course the people should take, or what events were
about to happen. Properly speaking, this should have
been done before the ark and mercy-seat. Thus we
find Saul, accompanied by Ahiah the Lord's priest in
Shiloh wearing an ephod, commands the ark to be
brought, that he may ascertain the meaning of the
tumult among the Philistines. But, instead of waiting
to receive any response from God, he binds Israel with
a curse and enters into the battle. (1st Sam. xiv. 3, 18.)
Abiathar, the only surviving priest of the line of Eli,
fled to David with the ephod in his hand, having escaped
the slaughter at Nob. David ascertained by this means,
the purpose of the men of Keilah to deliver him up to
Saul. (1st Sam. xxiii. 6.) Again, in the affair at Ziklag,
David consulted the Lord through Abiathar and the
ephod ; and obtained a favourable answer. (1st Sam.
xxx. 7, 8.) On a subsequent occasion, we read of
David enquiring of the Lord, and obtaining answers,
(2nd Sam. ii. 1 :) and although in this instance, the
priest and ephod are not mentioned, yet judging from
the previous instances, it is probable that the same mode

of enquiry was adopted. In these cases, the *ark* was not with David ; but only the priest and ephod.

Israel stood doubly represented by the high priest in the presence of God. On the brilliant stones that rested on his shoulders, their names were engraved *according to their birth.*

| *On the onyx on the left shoulder* | *On the onyx on the right shoulder* |
|---|---|
| Gad | Reuben |
| Asher | Simeon |
| Issachar | Levi |
| Zebulun | Judah |
| Joseph | Dan |
| Benjamin | Naphtali |

The stones on the *breastplate* however, were arranged in four rows of three ; and the names were engraven on them, *according to the tribes.*

*The first row*

| Carbuncle | Topaz | Sardius |
|---|---|---|
| Zebulun | Issachar | Judah |

*The second row*

| Diamond | Sapphire | Emerald |
|---|---|---|
| Gad | Simeon | Reuben |

*The third row*

| Amethyst | Agate | Ligure |
|---|---|---|
| Benjamin | Manasseh | Ephraim |

*The fourth row*

| Jasper | Onyx | Beryl |
|---|---|---|
| Naphtali | Asher | Dan |

As the Hebrew language is written from right to left, the stones, with their inscribed names, would probably be arranged as here set forth. This is the order of the tribes, as they were arranged in their camp, and in the march.

Does not this twofold arrangement of Israel, according to birth, and according to tribes, point out to us the two aspects in which we stand as believers before God, presented in our great High Priest, the Lord Jesus? If looked at in the onyx-stones, there was no difference between one of the children of Israel and another. They were alike children of the same father, and each was presented in the same glory and beauty. No order of precedence was adopted : no conduct evinced by any, altered the arrangement. Reuben might prove unstable as water : and yet he was first in one of the stones. Benjamin and Joseph might be especial favourites : yet they were last. In point of fact, each of the two stones gave forth its glowing brilliancy equally to each of the six names inscribed thereon.

Thus it is with all the Israel of God. If viewed with reference to their birth of God, there can be no difference. One is as precious and glorious as another. The infinite cost of the blood of Christ has been paid alike for each and all. Each has indissoluble union with the risen Lord, in life and glory. Each has been loved with an everlasting love, and chosen from everlasting in Him. And the Lord, as the great High Priest, bears up each alike in the perfection of His own glory before God. The shepherd, when he had found the lost sheep, laid it on his shoulders, rejoicing, and bore it thus in safety to his home. The Great Shepherd of the sheep will not cease to bear on His shoulders the weakest of the flock, until He at last places it in the mansion of rest and joy, which He is gone to prepare. When the resurrection-morning comes every one of the redeemed will be like Christ, and will be manifested then in the same beauty and glory, in which now he is representatively upheld, on the shoulder of the great High Priest before God.

God has predestinated those whom He foreknew to be conformed to the image of His Son : and as seen in Christ—the First-born among many brethren—they are even now, not only justified, but glorified. A whole family, whether in heaven or on earth, yet named of the Father of our Lord Jesus Christ, children and therefore heirs of God, and joint-heirs with Christ.

But the children of Israel were represented in an entirely *different* order, and after a different manner, on the *breastplate* of the high priest. Each *there* had his own peculiar precious stone, and his own peculiar place. Judah was the head of the first row : and Dan took the lead in the last. The gorgeous colour of the ruby shone out from one : the soft refreshing green of the emerald was visible in another : the brilliant light of the diamond flashed out from a third : and the heavenly azure of the sapphire was displayed in a fourth. Thus, each had his own peculiar glory and beauty : each differed from, without rivalling the other : and each filled his appointed place in the order of God. There was unity, combined with diversity. God is able to create variety, without that variety involving inferiority And so it is with the individuals that compose the Church of God. Each reflects Christ : and yet Christ is seen in each, with a peculiar beauty and glory, into which another does not intrude. Each has his place also in the body : a responsibility to exhibit Christ in that very place, which belongs to himself and not to another ; for which he alone is fitted, and without which the symmetry of the body would not be complete, and its beauty would be defective. Moreover, the individual glory of the saint above will probably have a close connection with the place which he has occupied in the body below ; a connection, which would inevitably be broken, were it not for the unwearied love and faithfulness of the great High Priest.

With respect to the precious stones but little is known. There have been many laboured attempts made by learned men, to discover the real names of these gems ; but with the exception of four or five, most biblical critics acknowledge the subject to be involved in obscurity.

## THE SARDIUS (Heb. Odem.)

THIS was evidently a stone of a *red* colour. And it is interesting to observe, that the same three letters of the Hebrew compose the word *Adam*—the name given by God to the man and the woman, (Gen. v. 2,) including them both in this one appellative : the man and the woman together forming the one Adam. One of the titles now of the Lord Jesus, is the last Adam, the life-giving Spirit, in whom all, who shall ever live, are seen in the purpose of God, and in due time will be manifested as His fulness ; the woman forming the completeness of the man. The name of *Judah* (praise) was inscribed on this stone ; praise, worship, glory to God, being one of the leading objects, which He has in view in that great mystery, Christ and the Church.

The *red* colour seems also to be significant, in this first jewel of the breastplate : for it is the colour of wine, (Prov. xxiii. 31 ;) it is also the colour of blood. (2nd Kings iii. 22 ; Isa. lxiii. 2.) Judah was to be the object of praise, according to the blessing of Jacob, (Gen. xlix. 8,) and also would be filled with praise, because filled with joy. His land was to be a land of vineyards ; and in the beautiful passage from the last words of Israel, we have a very striking typical prophecy respecting the use of the vine and the pressed grape, by this tribe of praise :—" Binding his foal unto the vine, and his ass's colt unto the choice vine, he washed his garments in wine, and his clothes in the blood of grapes. His eyes shall be red with wine ; and his teeth white with milk." (Ver. 11, 12.) The most common actions in life were thus to be linked on with the vine ; and so far from desecrating the choice vine by using it for ordinary purposes, even the ass's colt was to be bound to it.

Does not this foreshadow the daily, hourly responsibility of the believer, to do all things in the name of the Lord Jesus, giving thanks ?    A great temptation of the adversary is, to try and divide the life of a child of God into two distinct portions, one a kind of secular, and the other a religious life.    So that on appointed days, seasons, or hours, Christ is sought, and confessed, and worshipped : and the Bible becomes the book perused, and the subject of meditation.    But except at these times, Christ is neglected ; His name is studiously concealed ; and the ordinary business of life is conducted, it may be with strict propriety and integrity, but not with reference to the precepts of the word of God, or to His glory.    Not so however, when praise and worship are the great pursuits of the believer ; when he realizes his princely calling and standing, as one of that royal line, of whom the Lord Jesus is the Head ; and one of that priestly house, over which He is the High Priest.

Judah also washed his garments in wine, and his clothes in the blood of grapes.    The vine was used and referred to in all his ordinary pursuits in the field.    The blood of the grape was employed for cleansing his clothes and garments.    The every-day clothes were thus purged, as well as the robes of state and glory. So again the believer finds the daily need of that precious blood, which cleanseth us from all sin : which removes the defilements arising from contact with an evil world without, and from an evil heart within ; and which preserves unspotted our priestly robes of purity, so that we have access at all times into the presence of God.

But more than this :—" His eyes shall be red with wine, and his teeth white with milk." He drank so deep of this joyous cup, that his very countenance betokened the effects of it. Alas, how little do men say

of believers now, " These men are full of new wine ! "
How little do our countenances display the fact that we
have been taking large draughts of the cup of salvation !
How seldom is the Christian found so exhilarated by
the joy of Christ as to be deemed by the world an
enthusiast, a madman, unfit for the ambitions and pursuits so eagerly followed all around !  " The children
of this world are, in their generation, wiser than the
children of light."  They set before themselves wealth,
fame, or pleasure, as the steady object of their pursuit.
They toil unceasingly after these vanities.  They drink
intoxicating draughts incessantly, and determine that
to-morrow shall be as this day, and much more
abundant.

These drunkards of Ephraim, whose glorious beauty
is a fading flower, are numerous.  But we rarely greet
the servant of the Lord, with his mouth full of praise,
and his heart full of joy ; captivated by that one blessed
object, Jesus Christ, and Him crucified ; determining
to know nothing else ; and able to say in truth—
" To me, to live is Christ."  Where the eyes are red
with this heavenly wine, the teeth are sure to be white
with the milk of the Word.  Instead of the adder's
poison being under the lips, these rejoicing saints of
God, will like new-born babes, drink that unmixed
nourishment so largely, that it flows out at the mouth ;
and the testimony will go forth for Jesus, which may
indeed be despised by the wise and prudent amongst
men, but will be mighty, through the power of God, for
blessing and salvation to the needy and thirsty around.

The red glorious colour of the Sardius seems
to be well connected with the name of Judah.  The
Lord Jesus Himself is the first to utter praise to God as
the result of His baptism of blood.  " In the midst of
the church will I praise thee."  And as we contemplate
Him, and taste of His joy, so do we yield to God
thanksgiving, and shine forth with something of the
beauty of this first stone of the breastplate.

# THE TOPAZ    (Heb. Pitdah.)

Most writers agree, that this is the gem known in modern days as the topaz, a precious stone of a rich yellow lustre. The derivation of the Hebrew word seems doubtful. On this stone was engraven the name *Issachar;* the meaning of which is learned from Gen. xxx. 18, "hath given hire, or recompense." This word carries us back to Gen. xv. 1. Abram had fought a great battle against the four confederate kings, had rescued Lot, and had retaken all the spoil. That wonderful personage Melchizedek, had met and blessed him ; and Abram had lifted up his hand to Jehovah, the most high God, the possessor of heaven and earth, that he would not take from a thread even to a shoe-latchet of the captured booty, lest the king of Sodom should be able to say, he had made Abram rich. It was after these things, that the word of the Lord came to him in a vision, saying, "Fear not Abram : I am thy shield, and thy exceeding great *reward.*" The word *reward* is the same as is found in the name Issachar. God is Himself the reward and the rewarder of faith. His glory is the defence and portion of those who obey with the obedience of faith. The father of the faithful would not touch even the spoils he himself had taken from the enemy ; lest in the slightest degree, he should seem to be indebted to the King of Sodom. It had been in the strength of God, trusting in Him, that he had gained the victory : and he would receive his recompense only from God. And large indeed was the recompense. "*I* am thine exceeding great reward."

The Lord Jesus Himself is the true Issachar, as He is the true Judah. He trusted in God, and has been delivered ; having finished the work which God gave Him to do, and glorified His name on the earth. He has received His reward, for which He prayed, John xvii. 5. "And now, O Father, glorify Thou me, with

*212*

thine own self, with the glory which I had with thee before the world was." Having been obedient unto death, even the death of the cross, God has highly exalted Him, and given Him the name which is above every name.

Twice it is recorded by the prophet Isaiah, "Behold, his *reward* is with him." Isa. xl. 10, and lxii. 11. And in this reward, the Church of God partakes. "The glory which Thou gavest me, I have given them."

To this the Apostle presses forward, as he says, "that I may win Christ, and be found in him." Like Abram of old, the apostle despises wealth, honours, fame, and (what is far more ensnaring) his own self-righteousness; counts all things but loss, suffers the loss of all things, and counts them but dung compared with the glory and beauty of Christ, his prize; his crown of righteousness; his crown of life; his crown of glory; his aim; his goal; his exceeding great reward.

It is said of Issachar: "Issachar is a strong ass, couching down between two burdens. And he saw that rest was good, and the land that it was pleasant; and bowed his shoulder to bear, and became a servant unto tribute." (Gen. xlix. 14, 15.)

Instead of "between two burdens," this is translated by Mr. H. Craik, "between the cattle-pens." Robertson translates it, "between two hearth-stones." In either case, the idea sought to be conveyed seems to be this : that Issachar, anticipating the goodness of the rest, and pleasantness of the land, (the rest, like that which the beast of burden experiences after the day's toil, when he stretches himself at ease in the home of his master,) resolved, for the sake of this reward, to bow his shoulder to bear, and become subject to servitude Something in accordance with this is the exhortation (in Heb. iii and iv.) Israel despised the pleasant land, and also questioned their ability to enter and possess it, because they disbelieved God's promise, and God's help. " Their carcases therefore fell in the wilderness."

God has set before us His own rest. Let us therefore labour to enter into His rest; let us view the pleasant land, the inheritance incorruptible, undefiled, and that fadeth not away. Let us contemplate the rest, and see how good it is; and let us labour on in faith, assured that God, by the mighty hand of our great Captain of Salvation, Jesus, will bring us safely in and give us that fulness of joy, and those pleasures for evermore which are at His right hand.

## THE CARBUNCLE　(Heb. Bareketh)

This word is evidently derived from a Hebrew root, often used for *lightning;* and also translated *glittering;* and designates a stone of a flashing redness. Upon it, *Zebulun* was engraved. If we turn to Gen. xxx. 20, Leah says, on the birth of this child, "God hath endued me with a good dowry: now will my husband dwell with me, because I have borne him six sons:" and she called his name Zebulun (dwelling.)

Jacob thus prophesies respecting Zebulun:—"Zebulun shall dwell at the haven of the sea; and he shall be for an haven of ships; and his border shall be unto Zidon." Gen. xlix. 13. And Moses blesses the tribe as follows, coupling them with Issachar:—"Rejoice, Zebulun, in thy going out; and Issachar, in thy tents. They shall call the people unto the mountain; there, they shall offer sacrifices of righteousness: for they shall suck of the abundance of the seas, and of treasures hid in the sand." Deut. xxxiii. 18, 19. Thus Zebulun, whilst possessing a permanent habitation, was to afford a place of safety for ships, was to go out in order to call peoples to the mount Zion, where sacrifices of righteousness were to be offered. Probably their sucking of the abundance of the seas, and treasures hid in the sand, is an allusion

also to their missionary efforts, spread ovei all the
earth, when nations will be induced to bring their glory
and honour to Jerusalem, and she shall suck the milk
of the Gentiles, and the breast of kings.

On the breastplate of the high priest, Zebulun shot
forth with lightning splendour ; combining the two
thoughts of our dwelling in the presence of God, and
therefore shining out to give light to others.

This precious stone, with its engraved title, proclaims
to us the truth, that our great High Priest is ever
watchful to bear us on His heart, so that we may abide
under the shadow of the Almighty. He ever dwelt in the
secret place of the Most High, the only Begotten in the
bosom of the Father. He knows the blessed security,
peace, and joy of that place of rest, that safe abode. For a
season He tasted on the cross, the anguish of being cast
out and forsaken, whilst the heavy billows of God's wrath
obscured for a while, the light of that countenance, in
which He loved to dwell. He took that place oi
unutterable woe, in order that, as the great Shepherd
of the sheep, He might enable us to say, "I shall dwell
in the house of the Lord for ever." And surely from
our place of rest, we can look out in safety upon the
fearful floods that overwhelmed Him ; upon the billows
and waves that passed over Him : and we have to be
ambassadors to a lost world ; to seek to lead them to
that same meek and lowly One, who can give them rest;
and that they may offer sacrifices of righteousness, and
rejoice in the presence of the Lord.


## THE EMERALD (Heb. Nophech)

The second row commenced with the Emerald. It is
doubtful if this stone be here intended. In Ezek. xxviii.
13, the margin translates it, Chrysoprase. Robertson
derives it from an Arabic root, signifying, to transmit,

or pervade. On this stone the name of Reuben was inscribed.

Upon the birth of her first-born, Leah exclaimed, "Surely the Lord hath *looked upon* my affliction;" and accordingly she called his name Reuben, "See a Son." This child—looked upon by Jacob as his might, the beginning of his strength, the excellency of dignity, and the excellency of power—proved unstable as water; in fact, manifested only to a greater degree, the instability of his father. But this name has been engraved upon a precious stone. A name transferred from unstable flesh, to a stone of durable lustre, and well-proved strength. God has proclaimed the great fact of the gift of a Son. "Unto us a Child is born : unto us a Son is given :" a Son who is the brightness of His glory, and the express image of His person ; His first-born; His only begotten; His wisdom and power ; the beginning of His strength ; pre-eminent in dignity ; pre-eminent in power ; a tried stone.

Reuben, unstable as water, retained not the pre-eminence. The SON in all things has the pre-eminence, (Col. i. 18,) and we have looked upon Him ; we have seen His glory, the glory as of the only-begotten of the Father, full of grace and truth. God has looked on our affliction, and has bidden us *see a Son* : and we have obeyed His blessed command. And now, as we behold His face as in a glass, we are changed into His likeness from glory to glory, as by the Spirit of the Lord. And Jesus, the great High Priest, presents us each to God in His own likeness—"not ashamed to call us brethren"— and calls on the Father to *see a Son* in each of us that believe on His name ; and will present us in a little while, faultless in the presence of His glory with exceeding joy. "Behold, what manner of love the Father has bestowed on us, that we should be called the Sons of God ! Already are we the Sons of God, and it hath not yet been manifested what we shall be : but, when He shall be manifested, we shall be like Him; for we shall see Him as He is." Wondrous glory! wondrous exaltation! and yet in no other way, could God in His wisdom declare His marvellous love to us. In no other way could He prove the infinite value of His gift of His own Son, and the unspeakable preciousness of His blood.

However poor, feeble, weak, and failing we may be here on earth, shewing forth but little, alas! of the beauty and glory of Christ; manifesting but feeble traces of our likeness to Him who is the Son of God; yet in the sanctuary above, how different does the saint appear! There he is presented in the fulness of Jesus: there he shines forth in the beauty of God's Beloved: and in a little while, each believer will bear the unclouded image of Him who created him. And the Lord Himself, the first-born amongst many brethren, will call the attention of the world to the glory of His risen Church, exclaiming—" Behold, I and the children which God hath given me." The men of the true Reuben will not be few. (Deut. xxxiii. 6.)

## THE SAPPHIRE (Heb. Sappeer)

The English word Sapphire is evidently taken from the Hebrew Sappeer; or from the Greek, which has the same sound. And the gem, known in modern times as the sapphire, is probably the same. The Hebrew word is derived from a verb signifying, to scratch or polish, and hence to write, and to number.

This precious stone, with its pure deep blue, formed the pavement under the feet of the God of Israel, as seen by the elders in Exod. xxiv. 10. And the throne of glory, gazed on by Ezekiel, (i. 26; and x. 1,) had the appearance of a sapphire stone.

The Bride in her wonderful portraiture of her Beloved, speaks of his hands as gold rings set with the beryl: his belly as bright ivory overlaid with sapphires.

(Cant. v. 14.)    Here the word translated *belly*, is in most other passages more correctly rendered *bowels;* and is once called *heart*. Psa. xl. 8.    " I delight to do thy will, O my God : yea, thy law is within my heart."    The inward seat of the affections is thus expressed.    A similar use of the same figure is often found in the New Testament, as, for instance, " I long after you in the bowels of Christ." Phil. i. 8.    " If there be any bowels and mercies." ii. 1.    "Put on bowels of mercies, kindness, meekness." Col. iii. 12.    " Shutteth up his bowels of compassion." 1st John iii. 17.    There is yet one more allusion to the Sapphire, which may be quoted. Lam. iv. 7. "Her Nazarites were purer than snow, they were whiter than milk; they were more ruddy in body than rubies ; their polishing was of sapphire."    The word here translated *polishing*, would rather seem to have reference to the entire separation of the Nazarites from all defilement of the world.    It is no where else translated *polishing ;* but the verb from which it is derived means, " to cut off, or divide :" and in the description of the future division of the land of Israel, the same word is rendered " the separate place." Ezek. xli. and xlii.

This precious stone of the breast-plate displayed the same heavenly colour which stood first in the vail and in the ephod—*the blue*.    This is the body of heaven in its clearness :  for God dwells there, and God is love. The throne of glory, as seen by the prophet, exhibits this celestial colour ; for it is the throne of grace.

Love fills the heart of the Bridegroom, like precious sapphire gems.    Love was the costly grace which He manifested, when upon the cross, the eye of God searched the inwards of that blessed victim.    And those who would be Nazarites, separated off to God in their walk, and following the blessed footsteps of the Nazarene, must have that heavenly grace, as the power of their separation. Their polishing must be as sapphires.

The name of Simeon was aptly inscribed on this most precious stone.    The Lord had *looked upon* the affliction of the wife, and had given her Reuben. He had *heard* that she was hated, and given her the second son, whom she called Simeon, "*hearing*." So subsequently in the history of Israel, the Lord recalls these two names of the two first children, and says, "I have surely *seen* the affliction of my people which are in Egypt, and I have *heard* their cry." Exod. iii. 7. Acts vii. 34. Their misery stirred up the bowels of His compassion, and in full unmerited grace He came down to deliver them. Weakness, oppression, wretchedness, hard bondage— to be hated and despised—these are the attractions that win the compassion and pitifulness of God. He hears the cry of the desolate. Psalm cvii. is from beginning to end, a Simeon history—God always hearing the cry of the distressed ; but alas ! man always forgetting the gracious hand of Him that has helped.—God's help a common occurrence ; man's praise in return for His goodness, a rare sound.

And whilst God's ear is attentive to our cry—whilst one of His attributes is, that *He hears* ; we have also to hear Him ; to have the ear always open to a ceaseless sound of love and mercy. Love, that is shewn us even in correction and rebuke ; love, that has not spared His own Son, and which withholds nothing that can be given *with* His Son. Our great High Priest is able to present on His heart, the jewel inscribed with Simeon's name ; because His ear was opened to hear and learn two great lessons from God. First, His ear was wakened morning by morning, that He might have the tongue of the learned, so as to speak a word in season to him that is weary. And also His ear was opened, so that He turned not back, but gave His back to the smiters, and His cheeks to them that plucked off the hair. He hid not His face from shame and spitting. Isa. l. Wonderful instruction this, involving the knowledge, not only of the deep counsels of God, but of God Himself. The lips of the blessed Lord were open to pour forth grace, but He was dumb as a sheep before his shearers. He knew when to be silent and when to speak ; for He ever waited on God. And now as our High Priest, He hearkens for us, and presents us as listeners to the voice of God. O may we have more of this grace of Christ, to bow the ear to wisdom : then shall we regard discretion, and our lips will keep knowledge.

## THE DIAMOND (Heb. Yah-ghalohm)

It is not certain that the Hebrew word, here translated Diamond, means that precious stone, although its derivation would seem to imply that a very hard stone is intended. Robertson, in his Clav : Pent : derives the Hebrew word from a root signifying "to break in pieces, or bruise ;" implying therefore, that this stone is one which breaks or scratches all others—as is the case with the diamond.

The name of the tribe Gad was engraved on this stone. A question has been raised as to the meaning of this word, some interpreting it, according to our version, " a troop." Others think that it means " good fortune;" but from the passage, Gen. xlix. 19, it seems evident from the Hebrew, that the signification, troop, or multitude, is the correct one. There seems also to be a very appropriate connexion between the three names on the stones of the second row of the breast-plate ; " see a son : hearing : a troop." God manifests His own blessed Son : His voice is heard : and a multitude is gathered to Him. The Lord's own words, in John x. are in accordance with these truths : " My sheep hear my voice : other sheep I have, which are not of this fold ; them also I must bring, and they shall hear my voice ; and there shall be one flock, and one shepherd."

There may in this type be an allusion to the vast company of the redeemed, both Jews and Gentiles, all borne, as one united body, on the heart of the great High

Priest. A countless multitude, that no man can number, and yet presented in perfect unity of glory and perfection to God ; and preserved so, notwithstanding all disunity and separation here below. In Rev. xix, we behold the great Captain of salvation placing Himself at the head of the armies in heaven—the mighty hosts of the redeemed, and coming forth with them, conquering and to conquer ; all having been alike washed in His precious blood, and having been alike sustained by His ceaseless intercession. There may be also some connexion between the hard and indestructible character of the stone, here translated " diamond," and the name engraved on it : the invincible power, and eternal security of the troop whose names are deeply engraven on the heart of the Lord Jesus. God has engraven the graving thereof : and they will be more than conquerors, through Him who hath loved them.

Jacob's prophetic blessing, respecting this tribe is, " Gad—a troop shall attack him : but he shall drive them back at the last." (Gen. xlix. 19.) And Moses speaks as follows :

" Blessed be he who enlargeth Gad :
He dwelleth as a lion,
And teareth the arm, and the crown of the head.
And he saw that the first-fruits were his ;
For there, in the portion assigned by the law-giver,
he was securely located :
And he went forth, as leading the people,
To execute the justice of Jehovah,
And His judgments with Israel."

Although in both these passages, we have special prophetic declarations concerning Israel in the latter days, yet we cannot but be struck with the analogy which they present, respecting the present and future history of the people of God. Attacked by hosts of enemies, and yet overcoming at last. Daily enlarged and increased in numbers by Him who shall see of the travail of His soul, and shall be satisfied. To enjoy in a little while, the portion assigned them by their great

Law-giver, in the heavenly inheritance, incorruptible and undefiled, and which fadeth not away. Thus entering upon the first fruits of resurrection-glory, in union with Him who is the first-fruits of them that sleep, and executing hereafter the judgments of Jehovah : for, " do ye not know that the saints shall judge the world?" "Know ye not that we shall judge angels ?" 1st Cor. vi. 2. 3.

## THE LIGURE (HEB. LEH-SHAM)

INTERPRETERS are quite at a loss respecting this stone. Ephraim was engraved upon it. This name of Joseph's second son has that remarkable dual termination, which is also found in other words in Hebrew, (such as heaven, Jerusalem, etc.,) and seems to express double fruit or double increase. Joseph found the land of affliction to be the land where God made him fruitful. He had been cast into a pit by his brethren—sold as a slave— imprisoned—his feet hurt with fetters—he was laid in iron. Thus peculiarly had Egypt been to him a land of affliction. But he had been raised suddenly from a prison to a throne. And in the midst of the years of plentifulness, (so that the corn could not be measured for its abundance,) the Lord had given him two sons, Manasseh and Ephraim ; the latter of whom he called by this expressive name of "fruitfulness," in thankfulness to God for the wondrous way in which He had turned the place of his deepest trial into one of blessing and fruit-bearing.

In this beautiful type, we read the story of the Cross. Believers are the blessing that God has given to Christ in the land of His affliction. The corn of wheat has fallen into the ground ; and having died, it has brought forth much fruit : and the Lord Jesus can say, from the throne of His glory, " Behold, I and the children whom God hath given me." The almond-rod cut off, and laid up in death before the Lord, has been found in the morning, covered with fruit, blossoms, and buds.

In like manner, the great High Priest has ordained that His people should go and bring forth fruit, that His Father may be glorified.

The true Vine, the fruitful bough by the well, produces clusters of rich fruit to God, by means of the life-giving sap, with which it invigorates and fertilizes its branches : and fruitfulness will be found generally to be produced in the members of Christ through affliction and tribulation.

The Father also as the Husbandman, cleanses the branches in order that righteousness, which is the peaceable fruit, may be yielded to His glory. We have received out of the fulness of Christ, and grace corresponding to every grace that is in Him. And may that one cluster—"the fruit of the Spirit—love, joy, peace, long suffering, gentleness, goodness, faith, meekness, temperance"—be abundantly borne by each of the ten thousands of the spiritual Ephraim. It is comforting to the soul to know that our great High Priest sustains all of us before God as fruitful branches : and though there may be apparently but little progress made—and though the difficulties and temptations are great—still every child of God will be found to the praise and honour and glory of Him, in the day of manifestation which is fast approaching. " Ye have not chosen me ; but I have chosen you, and ordained you, that ye should go and bring forth fruit, and that your fruit should remain." John xv. 16.


## THE AGATE (HEB. SHVOO)

THIS stone, like the preceding is unknown. It occurs only in the two passages in Exodus where the stones of the breastplate are enumerated. The name of Joseph's elder son Manasseh was engraved upon it. The meaning of this word is "forgetfulness." "And Joseph called the name of the first-born, Manasseh; for God, said he, hath made me forget all my toil, and all my father's house." Gen. xli. 51. The order in which the names of his two sons occurs, is reversed in the arrangement of the tribes, because in Jacob's blessing, the younger, Ephraim, was preferred before the elder, Manasseh. But in Christian experience, forgetfulness must precede fruitfulness. Joseph very emphatically declares that it was God who enabled him to forget two things—all his toil, and all his father's house.

The power to cast off the remembrance of the past, so that it shall not intrude in the way of stirring up either murmurings or vain regrets, must come from God. He alone also, can give deliverance from old habits and associations, so that the believer may be able to walk at liberty, both from the bondage of his own evil nature, and from all alliances with the world. It is the power of the Cross alone that can accomplish this. By it the Apostle was able to say, he had been crucified to the world, and the world to him. He could speak also of another crucifixion, viz : that he, Saul of Tarsus, the man in the flesh, had been crucified with Christ; so that he no longer was alive, as in the flesh; he was blotted out from the land of the living in the reckoning of God. Saul the persecutor, the Pharisee, the religious self-righteous man, was gone; and he lived again, not as of the old creation, but Christ lived in him. Though he had a life still in the flesh, which he lived by the faith of the Son of God, who loved him, and gave Himself for him; yet he himself was not in the flesh, but in the Spirit. By that same cross of Christ he was able also to forget the things that were behind. His toil after salvation—his rigid observances under law—things that formerly had been gain to him—all these he could count but loss;

and remembering them no more, he pressed on to win Christ.

Death is the true land of forgetfulness : and it is our happy privilege, as believers, to reckon ourselves to have died ; to count that God Himself has forgotten us as lost sinners, blotted out of the book of His remembrance, in the death of His Beloved Son ; and to know that we are in Christ raised from the dead, that we may bring forth fruit unto God.

Manasseh (forgetfulness) thus precedes Ephraim (fruitfulness.) But not only did Joseph, by the help of God, forget all his toil, but all his father's house. Not indeed that his affection was one whit the less towards them : his heart was still full of love for his brethren ; and his father was ever preserved with filial affection and reverence in his memory. But he had no wish to return again into those scenes and circumstances from which God had delivered him. He had no lingering regrets after the earthly fellowships in which his mere natural heart had been once engaged. He yearned after his kindred with a true heavenly longing for their eternal welfare. And God gave him wondrous skill so to deal with the hearts and consciences of his brethren, when the time came, that they truly felt their sin, and had their thoughts directed towards God.

Abraham was the first who was thus called to forget his country, kindred, and father's house : and he, and the patriarchs Isaac and Jacob turned not back again towards the country from which they came out. If they had been mindful of it, they might have had opportunity to have returned. But their hearts were so occupied with the better heavenly country, to which by faith they looked forward, that the former things dwelt not in their memories.

Lot's wife affords a solemn warning to the contrary.

In Psalm xlv. 10, the bride is exhorted to forget her own people, and her father's house, and thus to become more attractive to the King. But, in order to do so, she must first hearken and consider. Her ear must be filled with His voice, and she must consider His comeliness and perfection.

God has placed before us one object of attraction—the Son of Man lifted up on the cross, and exalted to the throne: and in order to have the true Manasseh character, we must fill our eyes and hearts with Him: and then shall we be able to count as dung all other things, and to close our eyes and ears, like dead men, to the world around us; having our hearts filled with the melody of His voice, and by faith already standing in the midst of a new creation, where " old things have passed away, and all things have become new, and all things are of God."


## THE AMETHYST (Heb. Agh-lah-mah)

Most commentators agree that the stone, known at present as the amethyst, is here designated by the Hebrew word. The Oriental amethyst is a stone of great hardness and beauty, of a fine violet or purple colour.

There is something very affecting in the history of the birth of Benjamin. His mother, Rachel, the favourite wife of Jacob, had envied her sister, Leah, and in the bitterness of her spirit had said to her husband, " Give me children, *or else I die.*" And Jacob's anger was kindled against Rachel : and he said, " Am I in God's stead, who hath withheld from thee the fruit of the womb?" (Gen. xxx.) This was a mournful expression of hers, sadly fulfilled in the very gift she so much coveted. And when God afterwards remembered Rachel, and hearkened to her, and opened her womb, so that she conceived and bare a son, she called his name

Joseph, saying—the Lord shall add to me another son.
The very name she gave to her eldest was thus prophetic as to the birth of another ; though she little
thought of the sorrow which would accompany this
second gift ; and that God had hearkened to her, when
she said—" Give me children, or else I die."

An instructive lesson this for us. If God were to
grant in all cases our petitions, would it not be to our
grief and hurt, instead of conducing to our real happiness and blessing ? We know not what to pray for as
we ought : and therefore in wondrous love God has
given us His Holy Spirit, who makes intercession for us
with groanings which cannot be uttered, and who ever
intercedes according to God : so that we cannot fail of
receiving the mercies and blessings we really need.

There is also another truth expressed in Romans viii.
which should greatly strengthen our faith. " He that
spared not His own Son, but delivered him up for us
all, how shall He not with Him also freely give us all
things ?" Compared with this wondrous gift, all other
gifts are small. This unspeakable gift cost the heart's
affections of the giver. God had to bruise His Beloved ; to offer up His Only-Begotten : therefore He
can freely give everything else. He spared not His
own Son. How is it then, that we possess not all
things ? How is it, that many of our requests are not
answered ? Because God will only give such things as
He can bestow *with Him*—with Christ. Any gift that
will not consort, that will not harmonize, that cannot be
held in fellowship with that one great proof of His love
—the gift of Jesus—He will in mercy withhold.

Israel, in self-willed eagerness, demanded a king.
God yielded to their request and gave one in His anger,
of this very tribe of Benjamin : and Saul became a sore
scourge to that people. The results of some of his
ways, spreading desolation and death, continued even
after he himself had been cut off : as in the case of the
Gibeonites. (2nd Sam. xxi.) Thus God may in judg-

ment give, or in mercy withhold the answers to our requests.

It may be, that Jacob was wrong in leaving Bethel. God had bidden him *dwell* there. (Gen. xxxv. 1.) The death of Deborah, Rebekah's nurse, and the consequent weeping, may have rendered the place distasteful to him, though it was the house of God. He journeyed thence, and met with a deeper sorrow : for his favourite wife Rachel died in giving birth to her second son ; calling his name, as she expired, Ben-oni, or " Son of my sorrow." Instead of his being the son of her hope and earnest desire, he was thus the occasion of her sorrow in death.

But Jacob's faith rose above these circumstances of deep affliction, and he called him Benjamin, son of his right hand ; giving thus to his youngest the pre-eminence, as if he had been his eldest ; and as it were, anticipating the great enigma, propounded afterwards by Samson :— " Out of the eater came forth meat, and out of the strong came forth sweetness." Obtaining an object of affection, and strength, and power to himself out of sorrow and death.

Is there not a significant type in this, of the glorious strength that God has manifested in the resurrection of the Son of His right hand ? What power and might were displayed when He raised Him from the dead, and set Him at His own right hand, far above all principality and power, and might and dominion !

We have many places in Scripture where the right hand of the Lord is mentioned. Glorious in power, dashing in pieces the enemy, (Exod. xv. 6,)—saving, (Psa. xvii. 7, and xx. 6,)—upholding, (Psa. xviii. 35, and lxiii. 8,)—full of righteousness, (Psa. xlviii. 10 ; Isa. xli. 10,)—purchasing, (Psa. lxxviii. 54,)—planting, (Psa. lxxx. 15.) In this psalm the Lord Jesus is especially designated as the Man of God's right hand : and in v. 15 He is spoken of as the Branch ; or, as it might be better translated, *Son*, whom Thou hast made

strong for Thyself : and in v. 17, the Son of Man,
whom Thou hast made strong for Thyself. High,
(Psa. lxxxix. 13.) Victorious, (Psa. xcviii. 1.) Exalted,
and doing valiantly. (Psa. cxviii. 15, 16.)

In all these passages, is there not a distinct allusion to
the Son of God Himself ? Christ, who is the power as
well as the wisdom of God ; by whom all the counsels
of the Most High have been and will be accomplished.
Whose name is above every name : and who is the
righteousness of God to the believer. It is to be observed also, that this youngest son of Jacob was the
only one upon whom his father bestowed a name. In
this he stands out as a type of Him, to whom God has
given a name that is above every name.

But there is, in this name, borne upon the breastplate of the high priest, a type also of that wondrous
company, the Church, made up of sons of God ; who,
in union with Christ, will manifest the strength and
power of God's right hand, in the glory that shall be
revealed. Who, even now, shew to principalities and
powers the grace and manifold wisdom of God ; in
whom the exceeding greatness of God's mighty power
works ; even that same glorious power that raised Christ
from the dead, and set Him at the right hand of the
Majesty on high.

Our great High Priest upholds His saints in this
wondrous lofty standing before God. According to that
glory and power, in which they will be manifested
hereafter, so already are they beheld and sustained upon
the heart of the High Priest in the holiest.


## BERYL (Heb. Tarshish)

THE name of this stone in the Hebrew, is precisely the
same as that of the place Tarshish ; and it is supposed
to be derived from a root, signifying "to break or subdue.'

The hands of the bridegroom, in the Song of Solomon, are compared to gold rings set with the beryl. The chariot wheels of swiftness and power, terrible for their size, and rolling in unswerving majesty in every direction connected with the Cherubim of glory, in Ezek. i. 16, and x. 9, are described as of the colour of the beryl. These uses of the beryl in the passages quoted, seem to indicate that it is a stone emblematic of mighty subduing power; and the name of Dan, or judgment, was engraved on it.

This began the fourth and last row of the stones on the breast-plate. Praise stood at the commencement; Judgment headed the three last tribes of the camp :— judgment which was to extend in two directions. For Dan was to judge his people. He was also to be as a lion's whelp, leaping on the prey from Bashan. Gen. xlix. 16 ; Deut. xxxiii. 22.

A double judgment is also committed to the children of God : a present exercise of discipline within the house of God : ("Do not ye judge them that are within?" 1st Cor. v. 12) and a future place of authority and rule. ("Know ye not, that the saints shall judge the world ? . . . Know ye not, that we shall judge angels." 1st. Cor. vi. 2, 3.) This first exercise of internal judgment is grounded on the fact of all being brethren under the one Lordship of Christ ; and it is therefore the exercise of brotherly supervision, according to the mind of the Lord as Head of the church, expressed in His Word. Where Dan is spoken of as judging his people, it is " as one of the tribes of Israel ;" not as exalted above them, or set over them, but one amongst them.

But, with regard to the future, the saints will judge the world, by reason of their kingly standing. " To him that overcometh, and keepeth my works unto the end, to him will I give power over the nations : and he shall rule them with a rod of iron ; as the vessels of a potter shall they be broken to shivers ; even as I received of my Father." Rev. ii. 26, 27. " To him that overcometh will I grant to sit with me in my throne : even as I also overcame, and am set down with my Father in His throne." Rev. iii. 2 1. What a sudden leap, as of a lion's whelp, will that be, when the Lord Himself, as the Judge, comes forth with the armies of heaven, the assembled saints, gathered round Him as joint executors of His judgments, and surprises in a moment this slumbering world, with the sudden outpouring of His vengeance. Rev. xix. 14 ; 2nd Thes. i. 7, 8. In Rev. v. the Church seems to be in symbol presented in two aspects ; as the throned elders, and the living creatures. As elders, admitted into the counsel of God. Robed in white, and therefore priests unto Him. Seated on thrones, and thus kings, holding authority to rule and judge. Crowned as conquerors, who have fought and overcome ; who have run, and have obtained the prize. In the symbols or the living creatures, we behold executive power delegated to them, to accomplish in " the world to come," the counsels of God. Thus are the saints seen in vision, as seated on thrones of judgment, ruling under the King ot Kings and Lord of Lords.

But if our place hereafter, as the saints of God, is to judge the world ; and if it be a responsibility already resting on us collectively, to exercise vigilant yet gracious judgment within the body ; does not also the name of Dan, or Judge, attach to us individually ? Are we not to exercise a rigid and constant self-judgment, in order that we may the better be able to help and exhort our brethren around us ? In 1st Cor. xi., the saints are directed to judge themselves, and to examine themselves. The result of this must always be the discovery of our own shortcomings, infirmities, and corruption : which necessarily tends to cast us again upon the grace of God ; upon the precious blood of Christ, and upon His living intercession. We shall be humbled by every fresh review of our own helplessness and sinfulness ; and then the remembrance of Him will be true and blessed. We shall discern with increased reality the Lord's body, eat

His flesh and drink His blood by faith, so as to be
strengthened, as well as comforted and refreshed. Is
not every exercise of conscience, which ends in self-
abasement, a result of the constant work of our great
High Priest, who upholds us on His breast before God ;
and who, by the Holy Spirit, through the Word, keeps
the heart alive and awake to a sense of its own weakness
and unworthiness, and to a constant feeling of dependence
on Himself.

## ONYX (HEB. SHOH-HAM)

RESPECTING this stone it has been before observed that
the Hebrew root from which the name is supposed to
be derived, signifies "a flashing forth of splendour."
The names of all the sons of Jacob were inscribed on
the two onyx-stones, placed upon the shoulders of the
High Priest.

Asher was engraven on this onyx-stone of the breastplate. There may be some significance in this : for
Asher means *blessedness*. The blessednesses implied in
all the various names of Jacob's sons were combined in
this one complete blessedness graven on this precious
onyx-stone. The word translated *blessed* or *happy*, in the
Psalms, and in a few other places, is a remarkable one
in the Hebrew : for it is the plural of this word Asher.
For instance, in the 1st Psalm, "Blessed is the man"
. . . ." might be literally translated, "The *blessednesses* of the man . . . ." And in the xxxii. Psalm,
"Blessed is he whose transgression is forgiven." "The
*blessednesses* of him whose transgression is forgiven."
Leah when she gave this name to her adopted son, (for
he was the child of Zilpah her bond-maid) exclaimed—
"In my blessedness, or happiness ; for the daughters
will call me blessed : and she called his name, Blessed:"
thus recording in the name of Asher, her own happiness,

and the report respecting herself, that would be spread by others.

Is there not a similar expression of joy from the lips of the Virgin, when she in that beautiful song of praise, magnifies the Lord, and rejoices in God her Saviour, because He had regarded the low estate of His handmaiden : " for, behold, from henceforth all generations shall call me blessed." Elizabeth also pronounces this same word *(makarios,)* the Sept. word for Asher " Blessed is she that believed : for there shall be a performance of those things which were told her from the Lord." Luke i. 48, 45.

If we trace the blessedness pronounced in the Psalms and Proverbs, we shall find many of the blessings connected with the names of the children of Israel on the breastplate. Thus, there is the *Judah* blessing, in Psa. lxxxiv. ; the blessing of constantly abiding in the house of the Lord, and still *praising* Him : and in Psa. lxxxix. 15, Blessed is the people that know the joyful sound of redemption. Mercy and truth going before the face of Jehovah ; justice and judgment being the habitation of His throne. Mercy to pardon in the way of truth ; justice to forgive, because of judgment already executed upon the Lamb of God. " They shall walk, O Lord, in the light of Thy countenance. In Thy name shall they rejoice all the day ; and in Thy righteousness shall they be exalted. For Thou art the glory of their strength : and in Thy favour our horn shall be exalted. For Jehovah is our shield : and the Holy One of Israel is our King."

*Issachar : Hire or Reward,* as the blessing of service. " Blessed is every one that feareth the Lord ; that walketh in His ways. For thou shalt eat the labour of thine hands : happy shalt thou be, and it shall be well with thee." Psa. cxxviii. 1, 2.

*Zebulon : Dwelling.*—" Blessed is the man whom Thou choosest, and causest to approach unto Thee, that he may *dwell* in thy courts : we shall be satisfied with

the goodness of thy house, even of thy holy temple."
Psa. lxv. 4.

*Reuben: See a Son.*—"I will declare the decree : the
Lord hath said unto me, Thou art my Son · this day nave
I begotten Thee . . . . Blessed are all they that
trust in Him" Psa. ii. 7, 12. "Blessed is the man that
maketh Jehovah his trust." Psa. xl. 4. "Blessed is he
that considereth the poor." Psa. xli. 1 Is not the Lord
Jesus, the Son of God, here contemplated as the poor one?

*Simeon, Hearing.*—"Blessed is the man that *heareth*
me, watching daily at my gates, waiting at the posts of
my doors." Prov. viii. 34. "Blessed is the man whom
thou chastenest, O Lord, and teachest him out of thy
law, that thou mayest give him rest from the days of
adversity." Psa. xciv. 12, 13.

*Gad, a Troop.*—"Blessed is the man that feareth the
Lord ; that delighteth greatly in his commandments.
His seed shall be mighty upon earth : the generation
of the upright shall be blessed." Psa. cxii. 1, 2.
"Blessed* is the man that hath his quiver full of them :
they shall not be ashamed ; but they shall speak with
the enemies in the gate." Psa. cxxvii. 5.

*Ephraim, Fruitfulness.*—"Blessed is the man that
walketh not in the counsel of the ungodly, nor standeth
in the way of sinners, nor sitteth in the seat of the scornful. But his delight is in the law of the Lord : and in
his law doth he meditate day and night. And he shall
be like a tree planted by the rivers of water, that bringeth
forth his fruit in his season : his leaf also shall not wither,
and whatsoever he doeth shall prosper." Psa. i. 1—3.

This Ephraim blessing primarily belongs only to the
Lord Himself, the true fruitful One, from whom all
others derive their fruit. The blessed Jesus is the only
one who has never walked in the counsel of the
ungodly, stood in the way of sinners, or sat in the seat
of the scornful : and of Him alone can it be said,

---

* "Blessed" is the same word as is translated "Happy" in our version.

" *Whatsoever* he doeth it shall prosper." But if we
abide in Him, we also may bear much fruit. We may
realize the blessing of Jeremiah, xvii 7," Blessed is the
man that trusteth in the Lord, and whose hope the Lord
is. For he shall be as a tree planted by the waters,
and that spreadeth out her roots by the river, and shall
not see when heat cometh, but her leaf shall be green ;
and shall not be careful in the year of drought, neither
shall cease from yielding fruit." " Those that be
planted in the house of the Lord, shall flourish in the
courts of our God. They shall still bring forth fruit
in old age : they shall be fat and flourishing." Psa. xcii.
13, 14.

*Manasseh*, *Forgetfulness.*—Although we cannot directly
appropriate to ourselves the blessing of Psalm i. yet
we have the same word " blessed " bestowed on us in
Psa. xxxii. the blessing of righteousness reckoned to us
without works, even the blessing of God, being able to
say—" Thy sins and thine iniquities will I remember
no more."—His power to forget and forgive. " Blessed
is he whose transgression is forgiven, whose sin is
covered : blessed is the man unto whom the Lord
imputeth not iniquity, and in whose spirit there is no
guile."

What a wondrous mercy it is, that after having
wearied God with our iniquities, and after having made
Him to serve with our sins, He should draw the veil of
oblivion over the past, and for His own sake declare—
" I, even I, am he that blotteth out thy transgressions,
and will not remember thy sins." Isa. xliii. 25.

*Benjamin*, *Son of the right hand.*—All blessing be
ascribed to the Son of God's right hand : all glory,
power, might, and strength, are His. " Worthy is the
Lamb that was slain to receive power, and riches, and
wisdom, and strength, and honour, and glory, and
blessing. Blessing, and honour, and glory, and power
be unto him that sitteth upon the throne, and unto
the Lamb for ever and ever." Rev. v. 12, 13.

And we, being heirs of God and joint-heirs with Christ, shall inherit the blessing obtained for us by the mighty power of God's own Son in conquering death, and him that had the power of death, that is the devil ; and ascending on high ; raised far above all principality and power, Head over all things to the church.

*Dan, Judging.*—"Blessed are they that keep judgment, and he that doeth righteousness at all times." Psa. cvi. 3. The blessing of being able to discriminate between darkness and light, to separate the precious from the vile, as well as of enforcing the will of God, and governing righteously, belongs to Dan ; and appertains to the Lord's people who listen to His voice, and seek to walk in His ways.

*Naphtali* is the last tribe, and will be alluded to shortly.

In Deut. xxxiii. 24, Moses concludes his blessing very appropriately with *Asher*. " Let Asher be blessed with (or rather, in his) children : let him be acceptable to his brethren : and let him dip his foot in oil." A threefold prosperity. Blessed through his children ; the faithfulness and love of those whom he had begotten, reflecting back blessings on their parent. His presence and counsel received with favour by his brethren ; and his foot, or path, constantly enriched with fatness.

The believer, who serves in the gospel of the grace of God, would desire this blessing, that he may say of those whom he has begotten in the gospel, what the Apostle says to the Thessalonians : " For what is our hope, or joy, or crown of rejoicing ? Are not even ye in the presence of our Lord Jesus Christ at his coming ? For ye are our glory and joy." 1st Thes. ii. 19, 20 ; and of the Philippians : " My brethren dearly beloved and longed for ; my joy and crown." Phil. iv. 1. The Apostle John also expresses himself in similar language : " I have no greater joy than to hear that my children walk in truth." 3rd John 4.

The Lord Himself takes the pre-eminence in this

Asher blessing, when standing in the midst of His saints, He points to Himself and to those around Him, redeemed by His blood, saying, Behold I and the children whom God hath given me. Heb. ii. 13.

" Let him be acceptable to his brethren."

This blessing also Paul desired when he said, "Receive us : we have wronged no man. . . . 2nd Cor. vii. 2. Indeed, his epistles to the Corinthians and Galatians breathe out his earnest desire that he might be welcomed to their hearts, and might stand amongst them as a brother as well as teacher, accepted by them.

" Let him dip his foot in oil." This seems to apply more to the individual walk of the believer; so following the Lord, that he may find the fatness which His paths drop : for "all the paths of the Lord are mercy and truth to such as keep his covenant and his testimonies." Psa. xxv. 10. The feet, shod with the preparation of the gospel of peace, will surely be as if dipped in oil; carrying the riches of grace wherever they tread, and beautiful upon the mountains, because bringing from a far-off heavenly country, good tidings, publishing peace." Isa. lii. 7.

" Thy shoes shall be iron and brass : and as thy days, so shall thy strength be." Deut. xxxiii. 25. Some translators have altered the word " shoes " into "bars," supposing the metaphor to refer to the bolts and bars upon a door. But our translation would seem more in accordance with the truth contained in the whole passage, and is preserved by Robertson (Clav. Pent.) although he notices the other renderings.

There is a beautiful contrast between the shoes armed with iron and brass, and the foot dipped in oil; the latter, the gracious walk of the believer; the former, the destructive power which he will receive hereafter over the enemies of God.

We find the Lord Himself occupying these two positions. Grace and truth came by Him. The Son of Man came not to destroy men's lives, but to save

them. And yet when presented as hereafter to be
revealed, He is seen with the feet of fine brass, as if
they burned in a furnace. He will rule with a sceptre
of iron, and dash his foes in pieces like a potter's vessel.
The feet also of His saints will be as if shod with iron
and brass; for the God of peace shall bruise Satan
under their feet shortly. Rom. xvi. 20.

It is seldom that we have the latter part of this verse,
Deut. xxxiii. 25, correctly quoted. The ordinary way
is as if it were written, As thy day is, so shall thy
strength be. Whereas our translation reads, "As thy
days, thy strength." And if we retain this translation,
it gives quite a different meaning from the ordinary
application of the passage; which is generally understood
to imply, that according to the necessity in which a
believer may find himself through trials or difficulties,
according to the day of temptation; so strength will be
ministered to him from the Lord. A very blessed and
indisputable truth; but not declared in this passage
of Scripture, which does not contemplate a time of
weakness or trial, but one of triumph, happiness, and
prosperity.

If we retain the word *strength*, the meaning would
seem to be, As thy days of age are prolonged, thy
strength and vigour will increase instead of diminishing;
contrary to the course of nature, when ordinarily with
old age comes infirmity. But the word translated
strength, is by able biblical critics believed to mean
*rest*, or *affluence*. And this would appear exactly to
accord with the beautiful passage, (Prov. iii.) where, in
v. 13, the word *asher* occurs, or the happinesses,
blessednesses of the man that findeth wisdom; and
amongst other blessings, length of days is in her right
hand, and in her left hand, riches and honour—riches
and honour commensurate with length of days. "As
thy days, thy rest, or affluence."

In the conclusion of the blessing, the word *asher*
again occurs: "Happy (or blessed) art thou, O Israel:

who is like unto thee ? O people saved by Jehovah !
the shield of thy help, and who is the sword of thy
excellency. Thine enemies also shall yield thee feigned
submission, and thou shalt tread upon their high places."

A glorious prospect thus awaits that people, when
their Jehovah, the Lord of hosts, shall come and rescue
and save them. Already these blessings are ours as
belonging to the Israel of God—a people saved by
Jehovah Jesus, the shield of our help, and who is also
the glorious weapon of our might ; who makes us in all
things to be more than conquerors, and gives us a
resurrection victory in the midst of our circumstances
here, to end in the triumph of resurrection at His return.

At the end of the 8th of Romans we have the shield
as well as the sword : "If God be for us, who can be
against us?" If Jehovah be our shield, who can assault
us ? and again : "In all these things we are more than
conquerors, through him that loved us." He that hath
loved us, and given Himself for us, is the sword of our
excellency ; causing us not only to be conquerors, but
more than conquerors ; to take the spoil as well as gain
the victory.

We may close these allusions to the name of Asher
with the priestly blessing. Num. vi. 24—27.

"The Lord bless thee, and keep thee.

The Lord make his face shine on thee, and be
gracious to thee.

The Lord lift up his countenance upon thee, and
give thee peace.

And they shall put my name upon the children of
Israel, and I will bless them."

## JASPER (Heb. Jahsh-peh)

It is probable that some variety of the jasper,
displaying various brilliant hues, but with which we are
at present unacquainted, was used for this twelfth stone

of the breastplate.   Upon it the name of Naphtali was
engraven.   The Hebrew, translated in our version
" wrestling," is derived from a word meaning to twist :
and is supposed, by some, to have a different signification from that given in our translation.   It is not the
same as that in Gen. xxxii. where the angel of God
wrestled with Jacob.   Nevertheless, on comparing the
passages, we shall find that the word *prevailed* is the
same in all these places.   It may be that Rachel, in
giving the name Naphtali to the son of her maid Bilhah,
meant to imply that she had, through " strivings of
God," prevailed, so that a child was born.   So that
there is a prophetic allusion to the subsequent wrestling
of the angel with Jacob, on which occasion the name of
Israel was bestowed.

Let us now turn to that very instructive chapter
Gen. xxxii.   Jacob had, at God's command, left Padan
Aram (Gen. xxxi. 3,) to return to the land of his
fathers.   He had seen God's remarkable interference on
his behalf when pursued by Laban ; and now, still more
to reassure him, the angels of God met him ; so that he
said, " This is God's host ;" and called the name of the
place Mahanaim, or " two  camps :"  probably with
reference to the hosts of God forming one camp, and
his own company another.   Although thus surrounded
with the hosts of God; and  himself and his company
forming one of God's encampments, yet his heart trem-
bled ; and he sent messengers to Esau with a servile
salutation ; and in the folly of human expediency, even
announced to his brother, the freebooter, the fact of
his being possessed of abundance of flocks and herds.
Wise as he thought himself in the flesh, he is taken in
his own craftiness; for the messengers return announcing
the approach of Esau with a large company of armed
men.   Jacob had by his very message, stirred up the
cupidity of his marauding brother.   Dismayed at the
result of his own folly, he next divided his company
into two bands, hoping that the one might escape if the

other were smitten: strangely forgetting the two camps, which a little before, had been presented to him by God. Having thus made his own arrangements, he pours out his heart in deep and blessed prayer and self-abasement before God, entreating His help and deliverance. But no sooner has he risen from his knees, than again he practises a fresh expedient, hoping to appease his brother Esau by a present, which he selects and spreads out to the best advantage. And having thus counselled to the best of his ability how to meet this emergency in his own wisdom, he sent his family over the brook, remaining himself in solitude, in perplexity, and doubtless almost in despair.

In all this we see the strange mixture of unbelief, craft, expediency, and servility of the flesh; and yet, a measure of faith and dependence on God, such as we often discover in ourselves ; one moment seeking the aid of the Lord, at another devising plans of our own.

"Jacob was left alone, and there wrestled a man with him until the breaking of the day." It is here to be observed that the man wrestled with Jacob, and Jacob had power, through the strength of his flesh to withstand the wrestlings against him, of this messenger from God. "And when he saw that he prevailed not against him, he touched the hollow of Jacob's thigh, and the hollow of Jacob's thigh was out of joint." An instructive lesson this ; teaching us that the flesh cannot be subjected, but must be withered and crushed; for "the carnal mind is enmity against God ; and is not subject to the law of God, neither indeed can be."

Jacob's power of opposition was now gone. He could no longer be an antagonist to the mighty wrestler ; he had lost all the strength of nature ; he was crippled and withered as to the very sinews of his power. But with the loss of natural ability to withstand God, he gained a new power to prevail with God. He hung on in helplessness, upon the neck of him whom he had before withstood

" And he (the angel) said, Let me go ; for the day breaketh. And he said, I will not let thee go, except thou bless me. And he said unto him, What is thy name ? And he said, Jacob. And he said, Thy name shall be called no more Jacob, but Israel ; for as a prince hast thou power with God and with men, and hast prevailed."

On reference to the passage in Hosea xii. 3, 4. we learn what this power with God was. He wept and made supplication. Weakness, weeping, and entreaty, are irresistible with God. As the Apostle truly says, " When I am weak, then I am strong." This is the way to deal with Jehovah after a princely fashion : for His own beloved Son, " in the days of his flesh, offered up prayers and supplications with strong crying and tears, and was heard, in that he feared." The weakness of the cross was a mighty appeal to the heart of God ; and the glory of resurrection is His reply to the strong crying and tears of His beloved Son. He has prevailed, and has the name of Israel ; prince with God and with men.

Naphtali surely instructs us in this double lesson, how God has wrestled against our flesh, and overcome it by putting it to death and withering up all its strength ; the old man having been crucified with Christ : and how we prevail with God, and therefore with men, by lowly heart-broken dependence on Him, compelled by our very helplessness to cleave to Him, to take hold of His strength in order to make peace with Him.

It is to be observed that the sardine is the first, and the jasper the last stone of the breastplate ; and in the Revelation iv. 3, " He that sat upon the throne was to look upon like a jaspar and a sardine stone." There seems to be some typical connexion between these two symbols. If the names of Judah and Naphtali were, as it is believed, engraven on these two stones, then the manifested glory which shines forth from God upon His throne, is the result of the great wrestlings of His heart in the gift of His blessed Son. The work of the new creation is not like that of the old, accomplished by the breath of His mouth, but by the travail of the soul of Jesus. The work of salvation is a difficult work, engrossing the love, wisdom, power, and skill of God : the righteous are with difficulty saved.

The varied lustres of the jasper may be taken to typify all the diversified and accumulated resources of God, employed in the great work of new creation. The sardine stone, with Judah, " praise" inscribed upon it, may also have been selected to pourtray the glory of the enthroned Jehovah, because He inhabits the praises of Israel, and those praises ascend to Him by reason of His mercy, wisdom, and power in their redemption, having provided the Lamb for their salvation.

In the blessing of Jacob, Naphtali is thus recorded : " Naphtali is a hind let loose: he giveth goodly words." Gen. xlix. 21. May there not be an allusion to this in that wondrous psalm of the Cross, the xxii, which is headed, " To the chief musician upon Aijeleth Shahar, or the hind of the morning." It is a psalm in which the deep wrestlings of the soul of Christ are expressed, the pains of the travail of His soul. But suddenly it changes from the deep tones of woe to the joyful song of deliverance. In the midst of the 21st verse, resurrection deliverance comes in : " Thou hast heard me from the horns of the unicorns."

The morning without clouds breaks : the hind is let loose, and bounds away to the high places, giving goodly words, or words of fairness and pleasantness. " I will declare thy name unto my brethren ; in the midst of the church will I sing praise unto Thee."

The hind is also used in Scripture as an emblem of gentleness and love. Thus, in the Song of Solomon : " I charge ye, O ye daughters of Jerusalem, by the roes and by the hinds of the field, that ye stir not up, nor awake my love till he (she) please." ii. 7, and iii. 5. The allusion here is to the gentleness of the hind, which is easily scared. Again, Prov. v 19., "Let her be unto thee as the loving hind." Here the hind is used as a symbol of affection.

The feet of the hind enable it to stand securely upon the summit of lofty crags, out of the reach of danger, and lifted above the snares and pitfalls of the world below. "He maketh my feet like hinds' feet, and setteth me upon my high places." 2nd Sam. xxii. 34. Psa. xviii. 33. "The Lord God is my strength : and he will make my feet like hinds' feet, and he will make me to walk upon mine high places." Hab. iii. 19.

He that is the Lion of the tribe of Judah, is also like the gentle loving hind of Naphtali. On the morning of His resurrection, when God had loosed the pains of death, and He, the Lord of life and glory was bounding up to the highest heavens ; still, as the gentle loving hind, He stayed on His path to comfort the heart of Mary, and to give her that blessed message to His brethren, "I am ascending to my Father, and your Father; and to my God, and your God." The goodly words were given by this Hind of the morning. And He has made *our* feet like hinds' feet ; we are raised up together with Him ; and we have to stand upon the high places, to which we as believers have thus been exalted ; and not to let Satan cast us down from our excellency. We have, as of Naphtali, to wrestle, not against flesh and blood, but against principalities, against powers, against the rulers of the darkness of this world, against spirits or wickedness in the heavenly (or high) places. Eph. vi. 12. But Jehovah God is our strength. His great Priest has known the power of the enemy, and has conquered ; and He will enable us to overcome and maintain our stand on high. He will uphold us in our wrestlings against the foe, by bringing to our remembrance His throes of anguish on the tree, and by clothing us with His strength. Let us therefore maintain our resurrection standing. Let us stand fast in the liberty with which Christ has made us free ; not

entangled by any yoke of bondage as regards works,
or rites, or ceremonies, as if anything could be added to
the perfect justification of the blood. Neither let us
give way to the seductions of the god of this world, who
would fain ensnare us with its vanities and ambitions, its
honours and its wealth, who would bring a dark veil of
coldness and deadness over our hearts, hiding from our
eyes the glory of our heavenly calling, alienating our
hearts and affections from the Lord, seeking to set them
upon things on the earth. Let us be "satisfied with
the favour of the Lord, and be full of the blessing of
Jehovah." Deut. xxxiii. 23.

Having endeavoured to connect the precious stones
on the breastplate with the names of the tribes, and to
seek their typical import ; let us now turn to the further
description of the high priest's dress, contained in
Exod. xxviii. 22—25. "Thou shalt make upon the
breastplate chains at the ends of wreathen work of pure
gold. And thou shalt make upon the breastplate two
rings of gold, and shalt put the two rings in the two
ends of the breastplate. And thou shalt put the two
wreathen chains of gold in the two rings, which are in
the ends of the breastplate. And the other two ends of
the two wreathen chains thou shalt fasten in the two
ouches, and put them on the shoulder-pieces of the
ephod before it."

The object of these two chains was to fasten the
breastplate so securely to the settings, in which the
onyx-stones were enclosed in the shoulder-pieces of the
ephod, that by no possibility could they be separated.

The chains were wreathen and twisted like a rope ;
for both words are employed : wreathen, interwoven,
or intertwined.

The same word is used, Judg. xv. 13, 14 ; and xvi.
11, 12 ; also Psa. ii. 3, for cords or ropes. Ezek. xix.
11, and xxxi. 3, 5, thick boughs or branches. Hosea
xi. 4, bands of love. "Twisted work" is Gesenius'
translation of the Hebrew word, which our version

gives, " at the ends." Exod. xxviii. 14 ; and xxxix. 15.
Thus he would translate the passages : " And two
chains of pure gold, wreathen, thou shalt make them
twisted work." The object in adding the word "*twisted*"
to " *wreathen*" appears to imply a combination of skill
and strength ; and that the breastplate might be indis-
solubly connected with the shoulder-stones. Every
movement of the high priest's shoulders would affect
the breastplate : and every beat of his heart which
agitated the breastplate would be conveyed, by means of
the wreathen chains, to the covering of the shoulders.

There is a beautiful significance in this, reminding us
how the mighty power of the arm of the Lord is intimately linked on with the tenderness of His heart of
love. No action of His strength is disconnected from
His counsels of mercy and grace towards His saints.
He makes all things work together for good to them
that love Him. His arm and His heart are combined
incessantly in sustaining them in their high calling. He
is able to keep them from falling, and to present them
faultless before the presence of His glory with exceeding joy. They shall never perish ; neither shall any
pluck them out of the Shepherd's hand : and who shall
separate them from His love ?

Every stone is set in solid gold ; and rings of gold, and
chains of gold, firmly knit together the jewels upon
the shoulder and the heart. It is by His divine glory
and power, of which the gold is a faint emblem, that
the Lord upholds in unceasing brilliancy, each member
of His body, in union with Himself ; maintaining all
in their place of strength upon His *shoulders*, as children
of God. And notwithstanding their waywardness and
frequent acts of disobedience, preserving them upon His
*heart*, as the servants and soldiers of the Most High.

In the Song of Solomon, the bride alludes to these
two positions, in which she desires to be maintained by
her Beloved. " Set me as a signet upon thine heart, as
a signet upon thine arm." Let my name be graven deep

in thine heart, where love is strong as death ; which
many waters have not quenched ; which the floods of
Almighty wrath have not drowned. And let my name
be also graven in the place of thy power ; that I may
be upheld from sin and folly, and give thee no cause
for jealousy. That I may not be like the adulterers and
adulteresses, who seek the friendship of the world. We
are exhorted to be strong in the grace which is in Christ
Jesus ; to remember our place in His affections. To
" be strong in the Lord, and in the power of His
might ;" to keep in mind the strength of His almighty
arm.

There is a very blessed connection between the
breastplate and shoulder-pieces of the *high priest*, and
the wave-breast and heave-shoulder of the *peace-sacrifice*.
These portions of that offering were peculiarly given by
a statute of the Lord to Aaron and his sons. " The
wave-breast and the heave-shoulder, have I taken of the
children of Israel, from off the sacrifices of their peace-
offerings, and have given them unto Aaron the priest,
and unto his sons, by a statute for ever, from among the
children of Israel." Lev. vii. 34, and x. 15 ; Num.
xviii. 18.

The breast was waved to and fro before God. It
called the attention of the Most High to its intrinsic
purity and spotlessness. Also, like the waving of the
hand when one friend salutes another—it silently proclaimed *peace*. The heave-shoulder was the right
shoulder ; and as its name implies, was lifted off the
earth towards Jehovah. These portions of the sacrifice
were given to Aaron for food, to sustain him in his
priestly service, and to strengthen him for his duties on
behalf of the people Israel. Our great High Priest
having, as the peace-sacrifice, presented Himself without
spot to God, and made reconciliation for the sins of
the people, now bears, engraven on His very heart,
the names of those for whom He suffered. He proved
Himself worthy of the charge committed to Him, by

His deep love in giving His life for them. He has borne their names in judgment through the deep billows of God's wrath : therefore He bears their names in glory, and keeps them with unwearied love and diligence until He shall present them unto Himself, a glorious church, not having spot or wrinkle, or any such thing, but holy, and without blemish.

The strength also of His shoulder has been proved . for He has been lifted up on the tree, bearing the heavy burden of all our guilt, misery, and sin : and He has borne it away for ever. That same shoulder of Almighty power now upholds in glory the names of God's children, and will bear them on until He shall present them faultless in the presence of His glory with exceeding joy. Ephes. v. 25, tells us of the wave-breast, of the peace-sacrifice, and consequently, of the heart of the great High Priest. " Christ loved the church, and gave Himself for it." 1st Pet. ii. 24. " Who, his own self, bare our sins in his own body on the tree," fulfils the heave-shoulder : and Jude 24 presents the same shoulder of power, preserving the saints onward, faultless to the end.


## THE MEMORIAL

Exod. xxviii. 12. " And thou shalt put the two stones upon the shoulders of the ephod, for stones of memorial unto the children of Israel : and Aaron shall bear their names before the Lord upon his two shoulders for a memorial." xxxix. 7. " And he put them (the onyx-stones) on the shoulders of the ephod, that they should be stones for a memorial to the children of Israel, as the Lord commanded." xxviii. 29. " And Aaron shall bear the names of the children of Israel in the breastplate of judgment upon his heart, when he goeth in unto the holy place, for a memorial before the Lord continually."

Israel had one feast, to which this word "memorial" was peculiarly attached—the feast of the passover. " This day shall be unto you for a memorial : and ye shall keep it a feast to the Lord throughout your generations : ye shall keep it a feast by an ordinance for ever." Exod. xii. 14, and xiii 9. They had therefore two constant reasons for remembering the Lord—their deliverance from judgment and bondage in Egypt, by the blood of the paschal lamb ; and their acceptance in the brilliancy and glory of precious stones before the Lord, on the shoulders of the high priest, where their names were engraved according to their birth ; children of Israel ; of him who as prince with God and with men, had power, and had prevailed.

There are two memorials to us, as believers, which should be constantly kept in remembrance—our redemption through the precious blood of the Lamb—redemption not only from wrath, but from this present evil world—and our standing before God as His children, upheld in His presence, in all the glory and beauty of His Son.

The names of the children of Israel, on the shoulder-stones and on the breastplate, were also borne as a memorial *before the Lord*. Aaron could not enter the holy place without reminding Jehovah of the love and perfection in which Israel stood accepted before Him. The sevenfold light of the candlestick in the holy place, and the light of God's glory from between the Cherubim, over the mercy-seat, in the holy of holies, caused the precious stones to send forth their brilliancy and various beautiful tints, so as to attract the eyes of the Lord of Hosts. In like manner, we have a constant memorial before Him, in our great High Priest, who presents us, in the fulness of His love and power, bright with His own glory ; spotless in His own holiness ; righteous, because He is our righteousness ; and strong, for He is our strength ; emblazoned on the heart of love, and on the shoulders of power ; shining forth with

His own glory and beauty, as jewels adorning Him, from whom alone all our lustre and perfection spring.

*Continually.* This word is especially connected with the *shew-bread*, Exod. xxv. 30. "Thou shalt set upon the table shew-bread before me alway, or continually." Lev. xxiv. 8 ; Numb. iv. 7.

With the *candlestick :* "to cause the lamp to burn always, or continually." Exod. xxvii. 20 ; Lev. xxiv. 2, 3, 4.

With the *incense,* " a perpetual, or continual incense before the Lord." Exod. xxx. 8.

With the *burnt-offering* and the *fire* on the altar. Exod. xxix. 38, 42 ; Lev. vi. 13 ; Numb. xxviii. 3, 6.

With the *meat-offering.* Lev. vi. 20 ; Numb. iv. 16.

With the *golden plate* on the forehead of the high priest. Exod. xxviii. 38.

It tells us of the ceaseless presence of Christ before God for us. That He ever liveth to make intercession for us. That the efficacy of His sacrifice is perpetual ; and that we, as believers, are ever presented in the fulness of His glory before God. Complete in Him. Accepted in the Beloved. His priestly ministrations on behalf of His people never fail. With unwearied faithfulness He continues with them and for them to the end of the world.

# THE URIM AND THE THUMMIM

"And thou shalt put in the breast-plate of judgment the Urim and the Thummim: and they shall be upon Aaron's heart when he goeth in before the Lord: and Aaron shall bear the judgment of the children of Israel upon his heart continually." Exod. xxviii 30

The breastplate was made of the same materials as the ephod: and it was doubled or folded, so as to form a bag, into which the Urim and the Thummim were put. As to the Urim and the Thummim, whether they were precious stones bearing those significant names, or what they were, no one is able at present to decide. Urim means *Lights*, being the plural of the word very commonly used for Light. Thummim, *Perfections*. In the Septuagint these two words are translated by *delosis* and *aletheia* (Manifestation and Truth.) These mysterious contents of the breastplate seem to direct our thoughts to the heart of the Lord Jesus, as containing all lights and perfections, all grace and truth, all mercies and righteousness. In Him was *light:* and He manifested forth that light; He declared the Father. He is the light of the glory of God: all fulness of light dwells in Him. The Septuagint translation, *Manifestation*, is not an inappropriate expression, though it is rather a paraphrase than a translation.

We are told, in Ephesians, v. 13, "Whatsoever doth make manifest is light." The high priest, with the Urim in his breast-plate, became the channel by which God made manifest His counsels. The Lord Jesus, as the great High Priest, makes known the counsels and purposes of God. He is light; and in Him is no darkness at all; so that the mind and will of God can be perfectly revealed to Him, and can by Him be communicated to His saints. He is the brightness or shining forth of God's glory, the irradiation of God.

The Thummim also, or all perfections of truth and holiness, dwell in Him. Light and truth, love and

holiness, grace and righteousness are inseparable.
Sometimes we find the Urim mentioned without the
Thummim. Num. xxvii. 21. The Lord, speaking to
Moses of Joshua, says, " He shall stand before Eleazer
the priest, who shall ask counsel for him after the judg-
ment of *Urim*, before Jehovah." In 1st Sam. xxviii. 6,
it is said of Saul, that " when he enquired of Jehovah,
Jehovah answered him not, neither by dreams, nor by
Urim, nor by prophets."

From these two passages it is clear that by means of
the Urim, or lights, in the breastplate of the high priest,
the counsel, judgment, and prophetic guidance of Jehovah
were revealed. In James i. 17, God is called the Father
of lights, from whom every good gift and every perfect
gift cometh down, and with whom is no variableness,
neither shadow of turning. Here we have God as the
Father of Urim, or lights ; and He is also Thummim,
or perfections ; for with Him is no variableness,
not the *shade* of a turn. " He is the Rock ; His work
is perfect ; for all His ways are judgment : a God of
truth, and without iniquity, just and right is He." Deut.
xxxii. 4. "His *way* is also perfect." Psa. xviii. 30. His
great High Priest, the Son, makes manifest the heart
and works and ways of the Father ; and through Him,
every good gift and every perfect gift comes down to us
from above, from the Father of lights. It may here be
observed, that the word translated " without blemish,"
with reference to the passover-lamb, and the sacrifices in
Leviticus and Numbers, is the same as is also translated
" perfect," in fact, very similar to the word Thummim.
The Lord Jesus first manifested Himself as the unblemished Lamb of God ; and now He is the holy, harmless,
undefiled High Priest, full of all "lights and perfections,"
and revealing " *the Father of lights*," (James i. 17,) " *the
Father of mercies*," (2nd Cor. i. 3,) " *the Father of glory*,"
(Eph. i. 17,) and " *the Father of spirits*," (Heb. xii. 9.)

In three other passages, the Urim and Thummim are
mentioned together. Deut. xxxiii. 8 ; Ezra ii. 63 ; and

Neh. vii. 65. "Urim" is also translated "fire" and "fires." Isa. xxiv. 15; xxxi. 9; xliv. 16; xlvii. 14; l. 11; Ezek. v. 2.

In the vision of the Son of Man, (Rev. i. 12—16,) the eyes of the High Priest, in the midst of the seven golden candlesticks, were as a flame of fire. The lights and perfections of God searched into the ways of the seven churches; and the Priest of the Most High could say, as He addressed each separately, "I know thy works," and could give a word of encouragement or of rebuke, according as it was needed. "Holiness becometh thine house, O Lord, for ever." Psa. xciii. 5. And thus the Priest of that house marks every thing that defiles, and raises His warning voice against the delusions of His saints, in order that He may restore them to fellowship with the Father and the Son; and that they may worship the Lord in the beauty of holiness. "The Father seeketh such to worship Him."

Aaron was to bear the names of the children of Israel in the breastplate of judgment upon his heart for a memorial before the Lord continually. The Urim and Thummim also, placed in the breastplate of judgment, were to be upon Aaron's heart, that he might bear the judgment of the children of Israel upon his heart before the Lord continually. Exod. xxviii. 29, 30.

Thus the *names* and the *judgment* of Israel were always on the heart of the high priest when he appeared before the Lord. Their names, indelibly engraved on precious stones, shone out in beauty and glory before Jehovah. Not one was wanting; not one inferior to another; but each flashed out with his own peculiar lustre and colour, and each retained his own place in the firm setting of gold. The Lord Jesus, in anticipation of His cross, rendered up an account to God of those sheep committed to His care. "While I was with them in the world, I kept them in Thy name: those whom Thou gavest me I have kept; and none of them is lost, but the son of perdition, that the scripture might be fulfilled." John

xvii. 12. One indeed was missing from the twelve ; one, of whom the Lord had previously said, " He is a devil," (John vi. 70) and " not clean " (John xiii. 10, 11.) But even this did not account for his being lost. The true reason is here given : " that the scripture might be fulfilled." Now *that same blessed Lord* upholds firmly and deeply engraven on His heart, every child of God ; so that we may boldly say, who shall separate us from the love of Christ ? And He sustains each believer in the peculiar value and preciousness attaching to each in the estimate of God ; so that when the jewels are made up, not one shall be wanting ; but each shall retain eternally his own place in the heart of Christ, and in the glory of God. This seems to be represented by the *names* of the children of Israel being borne on the breast-plate of judgment, on the heart of the high priest, before the Lord. Besides this, the *judgment* of the children of Israel was borne upon his heart. And this judgment was expressed by the Urim and Thummim placed in the breastplate. In the *former* case there was an individual presentation of each name in glory and beauty. In this instance, there is a collective estimate of the whole assembly, as sustained in lights and perfections upon the heart of the high priest. In like manner, it is said of the Church as a whole, that Christ has " loved it, and given Himself for it, that He might sanctify and cleanse it with the washing of water by the word, that He might present it to Himself, a glorious church, not having spot, or wrinkle, or any such thing, but that it should be holy and without blemish." Eph. v. 25—27. He sustains it to this end, in a unity of lights and perfections on his heart before God ; and He bears each individual, so that He shall present *each* also faultless in the presence of His glory with exceeding joy. God's judgment respecting the Church is, that it stands in the lights and perfections of Christ, accepted in the Beloved. The sentence is pronounced already—a verdict of full eternal approval : and the day will soon come, when altogether we shall be like Christ; for we shall see Him as He is. God commends His love towards us, in that, while we were yet sinners, Christ died for us. Rom. v. 8. He bids us behold what manner of love He has bestowed on us, even that we should be called the sons of God: (1st John iii. 1) and the extent of His love is measured by that wondrous word of Christ—" Thou hast loved them, as thou hast loved me." John xvii. 23. And the glory of the redeemed Church will be according to the manner and measure of this unspeakable love, of which the High Priest is even now the witness.

This ephod of glory and beauty, with its onyx-stones upon the shoulders, linked on with the breastplate of judgment, presented three memorials of Israel before the Lord. The onyx-stones upon the shoulders bore their names before the Lord according to their birth; a memorial of the strength and power with which they were upheld in the presence of Jehovah. Exod. xxviii. 12. And these stones were also stones of memorial unto the children of Israel themselves. They were to remember the power and glory with which they had been by birth connected. Every one with his name, according to the twelve tribes, graven on his own precious stone on the breastplate, was borne upon the heart of the high priest, when he went into the holy place. And the Urim and the Thummim, put in the breastplate of judgment, expressed God's judgment of the children of Israel also upon the heart of the high priest.

In the Septuagint, the breastplate is called *Logeion* or Oracle; since, by means of it, the high priest obtained oracular responses from God. Are we not instructed (amongst other things) in this truth? viz : that all the counsels of God are only to be learned through the Lord Jesus, the High Priest; and that all the purposes of God are closely connected with His own people, the Church of the present dispensation, and the Israel of the future. So that even the history of the world, and of the various nations and individuals inhabiting it, is inseparably connected with the glory of Christ in union with His saints, and His future reign with them over the earth.

The famine in Egypt was the occasion for Joseph's exaltation, and for bringing his brethren down into that country. And in the Lord's parable, (Luke xv.) the famine in the distant land was one of the means which God used to make the wanderer think of his father's home. All things are by Christ and for Christ; and He is Head over all things to the Church.

## THE ROBE OF THE EPHOD

"And thou shalt make the robe of the ephod all ot blue.

"And there shall be an hole in the top of it, in the midst thereof: it shall have a binding of woven work round about the hole of it, as it were the hole of an habergeon, that it be not rent."—Exod. xxviii 31, 32

"And he made the robe of the ephod of woven work, all of blue.

"And there was an hole in the midst of the robe, as the hole of an habergeon, with a band round about the hole, that it should not rend.—Exod. xxxix 22, 23

THIS is the first occurrence of this word *robe* in the Bible. The Hebrew word is subsequently translated *robe*, 1st Sam. xxiv. 4; 1st Chron. xv. 27; Job xxix. 14; Ezek. xxvi. 16, in all which cases it specifies a garment worn by a king or prince. It is also translated *mantle*, 1st Sam. xv. 27; Ezra ix. 3, 5; Job i. 20, and ii. 12; Psa. cix. 29; and *cloak*, Isa. lix. 17.

From all these uses of the word it may be inferred, that the robe of the ephod was a garment of special dignity; a robe of office; and which gave also a *princely* character to the high priest. No material is specified, but the colour only, *blue*: and it was the work of a weaver.

It is remarkable, in Psalm xlv., how the garments of the king are described as if made of sweet perfumes;

as here the garment of the high priest is made only of colour. In our version the word *smell* is in italics. " All thy garments . . . . . of myrrh, aloes, and cassia," is the literal translation. Thus colour and sweet odour are the very materials of the priestly and kingly robes.

It was the work of a weaver ; Bezaleel and Aholiab having been filled with wisdom of heart to execute this fabric. (Exod. xxxv. 30, 35.) This robe embodied the colour of the heavens ; it was all of blue. It seems to have typified the especial glory of the true High Priest, whose name is *Prince of Peace ; the Lord of Peace ;* and who wears His princely robes as King of Righteousness, and King of Peace, upon the ground of having made full, perfect, and eternal peace through the blood of His cross. God, known as love, is the God of peace : and He has brought again from the dead our Lord Jesus, that Great Shepherd of the sheep, through the blood of the everlasting covenant. That title, " *the Great Shepherd of the sheep*," seems to sum up in one name the whole of the priesthood of Christ, as described in the Epistle to the Hebrews. He is the Great Shepherd ; for He is King as well as Priest. He has royal power ; a royal heart : royal glory ; and His dominions are righteousness and peace ; and He is the Shepherd, having proved His love and care for the sheep, in laying down His life for them ; and all His priestly service on their behalf is conducted with the heart of a good Shepherd, who loves His own, and whose own the sheep are.

This is, therefore, a princely, priestly, shepherd robe. It displays the love of God as seen in the gift of His Son, and as manifested by the Son Himself, in laying down His life, and so making peace. It was a robe which covered the high priest from head to foot, and showed the great object of his priesthood, namely, to maintain, on the behalf of His own, that peace with God which He had procured at the cost of His own blood, and which the God of peace had sealed and established, by raising Him from the dead through the blood of the everlasting covenant—a covenant, of which the main term is, " I will forgive their iniquity, and I will remember their sin no more :" a covenant which is ever new, and therefore cannot vanish away, but is everlasting ; and of which the King of Righteousness and King of Peace is the Mediator.

This robe was all of one piece, woven from the top throughout : and a provision was made, by means of a binding of woven work round about the hole in the top of it, that it should not rend or be rent. And so strong was this band, that the hole is likened to the hole of an habergeon, or breastplate of armour. Is not this very significant of the unchanging love of Christ ? and therefore of the firm and eternal peace obtained and maintained by Him for us ; so that nothing can interfere to mar or disturb it. Strong, like a coat of mail, no power of evil can rend this princely robe. Christ Himself is our peace : and through His death God has made peace in His high places. And though our sins of ingratitude, failings, and wanderings here below are numberless, still unbroken peace is preserved above by our faithful High Priest.

This part of the high priest's dress is called " the robe or the ephod." We may consider the ephod as representing the names " Wonderful, Counsellor :" for, it was curiously wrought ; and it was the garment whereby God's counsel was ascertained and made known. So this robe marked out its wearer to be the " Prince of peace:" and the Lord Jesus as the Counsellor, is especially Prince of Peace, because all the counsels and purposes of God have, as their object, perfect reconciliation and peace. He is "the God of peace, who shall bruise Satan under our feet shortly," by the power of Him whom He raised from the dead, through the blood of the everlasting covenant, to be the Great Shepherd of the sheep. And, having made peace through the blood of His cross, the counsel of the Father is, by Him to reconcile all things unto Himself, whether they be things in earth, or things in heaven, (Col. i. 20.)

The Lord Jesus is a throned Priest, wearing robes of priesthood and royalty combined. He bears the glory; " He shall sit and rule upon His throne ; and He shall be a priest upon His throne ; and the counsel of peace shall be between them both," (Zech. vi. 13 :) that is, the counsel of peace between the King and the Priest ; so that He wields the kingly sceptre of rule and judgment, with a priestly heart and purpose of mercy and peace. And this will be manifested in the future reign of the Prince of Peace, as it is already revealed to believers. There is a comforting and beautiful benediction (2nd Thes. iii. 16.) " Now the Lord of peace Himself give you peace always, by all means. The Lord be with you all." *The Lord of peace Himself*—He who alone, as true King of Salem, King of peace, has the power of giving peace—has the rule of peace—*Himself*, that blessed word, which tells us of all the perfection and glory of His person—*give you peace always*, at all times, on all occasions, in all circumstances, in all scenes ; *by all means ;* making the very attacks of the enemy end in peace ; making the very temptations, weaknesses, and worthlessness of the flesh tend to establish peace in the heart ; making sorrows and trials which seem to be most adverse, yet to result in most perfect peace. Surely this is His princely power. This tells us how He is invested by the God of love and peace with all glory and strength, so as to confirm and fill our hearts with peace unto the end.

The first priestly word spoken by the Lord to His assembled disciples after His resurrection was, " Peace be with you." And his own peace, ("my peace,") He has given and left with us. And what must that peace be ? The assurance of being that delight and joy of God ; the perfect confidence that God is well pleased in all He has wrought ; and the power to look forward to all the attacks of Satan, and yet to see them all ending in His own glory, and in the subjugation of all things to God. Such must be the peace which the Lord has, and which He has bestowed. Do we realize it ? Do we believe that God delights in us as His children ? Once enemies ; now reconciled to Him by the death of Christ, and to be presented to Him holy, and unblameable, and unreproveable in His sight.

Have we such firm rest in the Lord, and in all that He has done, that we have joy and peace in believing, and are assured that God rests in us, because He rests in Christ ? And can we look at Satan's power, and the world's opposition ; can we contemplate even our own failure, and that of the Church of God all round us · and yet with peace of soul, look forward to the final closing scene, when the Lord Himself shall come, and all things shall be found to have worked together for good, and to have accomplished the purposes of God ?

**The Ark and Mercy Seat Partly Covered**

# THE GOLDEN BELLS AND POMEGRANATES

"And beneath, upon the hem of it, thou shalt make pomegranates of blue, and of purple, and of scarlet, round about the hem thereof; and bells of gold between them round about: a golden bell and a pomegranate, a golden bell and a pomegranate, upon the hem of the robe round about. And it shall be upon Aaron to minister; and his sound shall be heard when he goeth in unto the holy place before the Lord, and when he cometh out, that he die not."—Exod. xxviii 33—35

"And they made, upon the hems of the robe, pomegranates of blue, and purple, and scarlet, twined. And they made bells of pure gold, and put the bells between the pomegranates upon the hem of the robe, round about between the pomegranates; a bell and a pomegranate, a bell and a pomegranate, round about the hem of the robe to minister in, as the Lord commanded Moses."
—Exod. xxxix 24—26

IT will be remarked that, in Exod. xxxix. 24, the word *hems* in the plural is used. It should have been in the plural throughout ; viz. Exod. xxviii. 33, twice ; and xxxix. 25, 26. It is elsewhere translated *skirts*, Jer. xiii. 22, 26 ; Nah. iii. 5 ; Lam. i. 9. In Isa. vi. 1, it is translated *train*. The margin reads there also *skirts*. Manifestly therefore, the flowing skirts of the robe are hereby intended. Around them were placed pomegranates of three colours, blue, purple, scarlet, intertwined, (" fine twined linen" is not in the original,) and alternating with each pomegranate was a bell of pure gold. The only adornings of this heavenly robe were fruits gathered from the earth. The high priest thus proclaimed on his entrance into the holiest, that he had come from the world below, from whence some of the very ornaments of his garments had been obtained. Pomegranates are especially mentioned as fruits of the Holy Land

The spies brought of the pomegranates, Num. xiii. 23. The good land into which the Lord brought them, was a "land of vines and fig trees and pomegranates, a land of oil-olive and honey." Deut. viii. 8. No such fruits as these were found in Egypt. Indeed it is remarkable that the children of Israel, when their hearts turned back to that land of bondage, spoke only of melons, cucumbers, leeks, onions, and garlick ; the two former being fruits borne close to the earth ; and the latter, roots of the earth. May there not be something significant in this ? The dainties of Egypt, and its savoury food are procured from low earthly sources ; while the fruits of the land are lifted off the ground, and ripen in the fresh air and sunshine of heaven.

There seems to be a connexion between the vine and the pomegranate ; as the flourishing of the former, and the budding of the latter, are mentioned together in the Song of Solomon, vi. 11, and vii. 12. Also the juice of the pomegranate and spiced wine are mingled together in Cant. viii. 2. These are the pleasant fruits in which the beloved delights. And the only ornaments on the skirts of the high priest's robe were these rich embroideries, in the various beautifully blended colours of the blue, purple, and scarlet. The fruit of the Spirit—"love, joy, peace, long-suffering, gentleness, goodness, faith, meekness, temperance," (Gal. v. 22.) forms one beautifully connected cluster, like a cluster of grapes. Observe, they are not said to be *fruits* of the Spirit, but *fruit ;* because each of these graces is dependent on, and connected with the others. And if one is present, all are there ; for we have received out of Christ's fulness, and grace corresponding to grace in Him. It should be our endeavour therefore, that the whole cluster should appear ; each grape, as it were, in due proportion. The Father is the husbandman, and He is glorified if we bear much fruit. And He exercises His discipline in order that righteousness, which is the true peaceable fruit, may abound.

There seems to be, therefore, a fitting connexion between the robe of the Prince of peace, and the peaceable fruit adorning its hem. In a sinner's justification, righteousness is the ground of peace, but in the justified person righteousness, as a *fruit*, springs from the soil of peace. James iii. 18. And the Lord Jesus having made peace, and rooted us in love, can rightly expect from His saints, fruit to the glory of God.

The contrast between the words *fruit* and *works* is very instructive. Works may be the result of a legal servile spirit. They may be exacted through fear, or be aimed at in order to gratify a self-righteous and self-complacent conscience. But fruit is the spontaneous manifestation of life within, the outpouring of a heart at peace with God, the evidence of new creation, and the presence and power of the Holy Spirit.

Between each two pomegranates there was a golden bell. The golden sound was connected with the rich juicy fruit. And as the high priest approached the holy place, his steps sent forth a heavenly melody; and when he returned again from the immediate presence of the glory into the camp, his retiring footsteps still rang out an unearthly sound.

There seems to have been much misapprehension, in the minds of some, as to the meaning of this type. Commentators have explained it to signify that the high priest was still living when he went to make atonement, so that the people outside might be made aware of the fact, by the sound of the bells. But this is contrary altogether to the words of the text, and to the facts of the case.

The words are : " His sound shall be heard when he goeth in unto the holy place before the Lord, and when he cometh out, that he die not :" (or, lest he should die :) not in order that the people might know that he was not dead. In fact, when the high priest went in with the blood on the great day of atonement, he was not attired in his robes of glory and beauty, and consequently had no bells on his robe. It was the blood on that occasion which protected him, and uttered (we may say) a sound to God : for the blood of sprinkling speaks better things than that of Abel. Heb. xii. 24. The high priest, in this his official dress, drew nigh to God on behalf of his people ; a wayward, stiff-necked, and often rebellious and murmuring people. He came from a camp where sounds of strife, contention, and ambition filled the air. But he must bear none of these sounds of earth and flesh into the sanctuary. God must hear the approach of one towards Him announced by heavenly sounds sent forth by his footsteps, although he came from the midst of such a din of worldliness and confusion. His walk therefore, though surrounded by these scenes, must be a heavenly walk : and his thoughts and intercessions concerning that people must be respecting their fruitfulness to God, and not to have regard to earthly ambitions, emulations, or glory and prosperity in the world.

Thus Aaron was provided with these golden bells, which necessarily sent forth a divine and tuneful sound, lest he should die.

Again, his retiring footsteps, away from the immediate presence of God back into the camp, were to speak the same truth; he must return into the ordinary occupations of life, still making his footsteps known, as from heaven. His feet must be thus beautiful, because sending forth as he stepped, sounds of heavenly holiness and peace. And though amidst the boisterous hum of human life, to the natural ear these golden bells might seem to give forth but a feeble melody, yet they uttered a still small voice which would reach the listening ear, and would arrest the true hearted worshipper, and turn his thoughts in holiness and faith towards God.

Does not this give us a faint type of our great High Priest ? His whole occupation for us in the sanctuary is concerning our walk and fruit-bearing towards God. No mere human thoughts intrude into His heart respecting us. His desire is not for our prosperity in worldly things ; for our advancement in earthly

greatness ; or for our success in the things of this life ;
but that whilst abiding in the world, we may be kept
from the evil of it, and may glorify the Father in
bearing much fruit.

We behold Him also in another scene, walking in
the midst of the golden candlesticks, as the high priest
of old might have walked in the midst of Israel's camps.
And in this vision of the Revelation, the Son of Man is
clothed with this priestly robe of blue. For, in the
Greek of the Revelation, it is called *podeerees*—a
garment down to the foot—which is the name given to
the robe of the ephod in the Septuagint, Exod. xxviii. 31.
Here the ephod, with its shoulder-pieces and breastplate,
was laid aside ; for the Son of man was not occupying
His priestly office Godward on behalf of His people.
But He is described as coming forth from God, and
walking in the midst of the churches to scrutinize their
ways, and to give rebukes, warnings, and promises.

He is, as it were, come out of the holiest, and still
sends forth the holy golden sound, while investigating
the ways of His saints. And though He has to reprove,
still the blue robe of heavenly grace and peace, is bound
around Him with the girdle of gold, to fasten it securely;
so that no failures which He might witness in His saints,
should have power to unloose His love towards them ;
but His heart of constant unwavering affection, beats
towards them beneath the breasts of consolations ; and
His divine love for them strengthens Him, as it were,
for this trying scrutinizing service.

Is there not a remarkable suitability in the Lord Jesus
being thus represented as attired in the blue robe of the
Prince of peace, while He walks in the midst of the
golden candlesticks, and looks with eyes of searching
holiness into their ways, saying : " I know thy works ? "

# THE MITRE

"And thou shalt make the mitre of fine linen."—Exod. xxviii 39

"And a mitre of fine linen."—Exod. xxxix 28

THE Hebrew word *Mitznepheth*, here translated Mitre, is used exclusively for the head-dress of the high priest, except in one passage, Ezek. xxi. 26. It is derived from a verb signifying "to roll, or wind round;" possibly intimating that the high priest's mitre was wound round his head, like a tiara.

There is another word kindred to this, *Tzaneeph*, translated Diadem. Job. xxix. 14.; Isa. lxii. 3.—Hoods, Isa. iii. 23.—and Mitre, Zech. iii. 5. But this word probably means a band or fillet; which was an emblem of royalty in the East ; and in Zech. iii. 5. there may be an intimation of the change of the priestly order from that of Aaron to that of Melchizedek. Joshua, the high priest, is first represented standing in priestly garments, which are filthy. These garments are removed from him ; his iniquity passes away ; he is clothed with other garments; and a fair diadem is placed on his head. A kingly as well as priestly dignity is conferred on him.

The different purposes mentioned in scripture, for which the head was covered, appear at first sight somewhat contradictory : but these may be reconciled, if we take into account the various *ways* in which this was done. For instance, 2nd Sam. xv. 30., "David went up by the ascent of mount Olivet, and wept as he went up, and had his head covered ; and he went barefoot ; and all the people that was with him covered every man his head ; and they went up, weeping as they went up." —Esther vi. 12., "Haman hasted to his house, mourning, and having his head covered."—Jer. xiv. iii., "They were ashamed and confounded, and covered their heads." In these cases, probably a mantle or sackcloth was thrown over the head covering the usual head-dress,

and to some extent enveloping the person. This was
done as a token of self-humiliation, grief, and shame.
In modern days, the hood worn as an outward sign of
mourning, may have been borrowed from this ancient
custom. On the other hand, to have the head *uncovered*,
that is deprived of its ordinary dress, was also an
expression of shame and dishonour. The leper was
commanded to have his head bare. Lev. xiii. 45. And
in Ezek. xxiv. 17, the prophet is ordered to bind the tire
of his head upon him, and not to shew any signs of
mourning. Also, upon the death of Nadab and Abihu,
(Lev. x. 6) Aaron, Eleazer, and Ithamar are forbidden
to uncover their heads ; and (Lev. xxi. 10) the high
priest is not allowed to uncover his head, although shame
and dishonour fall upon him through the sin of his
daughter.—The beautiful captive (Deut. xxi. 12) was to
shave her head, and bewail her father and mother.
*Baldness* was a sign of dishonour ; Jer. xlvii. 5, and
xlviii. 37 ; Ezek. vii. 18.

In the New Testament, the woman is directed to cover
her head, 1st Cor. xi. 3—10, because "the head of the
woman is the man ;" whereas the man is to be uncovered,
because he is the image and glory of God. In the
assemblies therefore of the people of God, the woman,
standing as a representative of the Church in subjection
to Christ, covers her head. ; the man, being a type of
Christ Himself as the Head of the Church, *uncovers* his
head.

This seems to prove that the mitre, covering the head
of the high priest, was a type of his being subject to God,
and that he was always supposed to be standing in the
presence of God. He was never to lose sight of this
glorious calling ; but his life was to be spent in the
tabernacle of the Most High, ready to accomplish God's
commands, and submissive to His will. The white fine
linen of which it was made, is an emblem of that
righteousness and purity, which must be manifested in
one who stands in the presence of God on behalf of others.

The Ancient of days (Dan. vii. 9) is represented in vision, as having a garment white as snow, and the hair of his head like the pure wool. Wisdom and righteousness are manifested by Him who sits on the throne of judgment.

In Rev. i. 14, the Son of Man, in the midst of the golden candlesticks, scrutinizing their works in the exercise of His priestly office, is thus seen by John: " His head and his hairs were white like wool, as white as snow." Here again, the snow-white head and hairs betoken purity, righteousness, and wisdom.

It is written also, " The hoary head is a crown of glory, if it be found in the way of righteousness." (Prov. xvi. 31) and " The beauty of old men is the grey (or hoary) head." Prov. xx. 29.

The Lord Jesus, the great High Priest, is the Everlasting Father ; or, as it perhaps might be rendered, " the Father of eternity." He is the wisdom as well as the power of God. He is Wisdom, as described in Prov. viii. " Counsel is mine, and sound wisdom : I am understanding ; I have strength. Jehovah possessed me in the beginning of his way, before his works of old. I was set up from everlasting ; from the beginning ; or ever the earth was : when there were no depths, I was brought forth ; when there were no fountains abounding with water. Before the mountains were settled, before the hills was I brought forth." (Verse 14, and 22—25.)

In Micah also, the ruler in Israel is one whose goings forth have been from of old, from everlasting. (Mic. v. 2.)

Our High Priest, the Son of God, has the wisdom of eternity. He has manifested the wisdom of God in creation. He is the wisdom of God, and power of God, in redemption. And he exercises in perfect righteousness, and in entire subjection, all this wisdom and power on behalf of the saints of the Most High. May not this mitre of the high priest have some typical allusion to these glories of Christ ?

It has been before observed, that the only other occurrence of this word Mitre, in the Bible, except in

connexion with Israel's high priest, is in Ezck. xxi. 25—
27. " And thou, profane wicked prince of Israel, whose
day is come, when iniquity shall have an end, thus saith
the Lord Jehovah, Remove the *diadem*, and take off
the crown ; this shall not be the same ; exalt him that is
low, and abase him that is high. I will overturn,
overturn, overturn it ; and it shall be no more, until he
come, whose right it is ; and I will give it him." The
word here rendered *diadem* is really *mitre*. This remarkable prophecy seems to point onward to a " profane and
wicked prince of Israel," who will arise, and who will
wear not only the crown of royalty, but the mitre of
priesthood ; in fact, who will arrogantly and blasphemously assume both regal and priestly power, in Satanic
mockery of the true priest and king, the Lord Jesus.
The Antichrist, " whose coming is after the working of
Satan, in all power and signs and wonders of falsehood,
and in all deceit of unrighteousness for them that perish :
because they received not the love of the truth, that they
might be saved." 2nd Thes. ii. 9, 10. Also 1st John
ii. 18, 22—In his day, iniquity rises to its height ; and
therefore it will have an end : and He will come, whose
right it is ; or, as it might be translated, " to whom the
judgment is committed," and God will give it Him. For,
he that is low shall be exalted, and he that is high shall
be abased. The King of righteousness, and King of
peace, the Priest of the most high God, will come, and
take to Himself His great power, and reign, and destroy
this profane wicked prince. God will exalt thus openly
Him who has been as low down even as to the death of
the cross, and will abase down to hell the arrogant man
of sin, and all his followers.

This prophecy clearly shews that the Antichrist will
assume a headship in religion, as well as a throne of
royal power over the nations of the Roman earth, and
that he will be prince of Israel, professing to be even
their god.

What a solemn thought it is, that this age closes with

Satan's subtle imitation of the Christ of God, whom the world will receive, and to whom the princes of this world will yield allegiance ! Men receive not the love of the truth, that they might be saved : and therefore, God will send them strong delusion, that they should believe THE lie.

## THE GOLDEN PLATE

" And thou shalt make a plate of pure gold, and grave upon it, like the engravings of a signet, HOLINESS TO THE LORD.

" And thou shalt put it on a blue lace, that it may be upon the mitre ; upon the forefront of the mitre it shall be.

" And it shall be upon Aaron's forehead, that Aaron may bear the iniquity of the holy things which the children of Israel shall hallow in all their holy gifts; and it shall be always upon his forehead, that they may be accepted before the Lord."—Exod, xxviii 36—38

" And they made the plate of the holy crown of pure gold, and wrote upon it a writing, like to the engravings of a signet, HOLI-NESS TO THE LORD.

" And they tied unto it a lace of blue, to fasten it on high upon the mitre; as the Lord commanded Moses."—Exod. xxxix 30, 31

THIS golden plate is described before the mitre, (see chap. xxviii. 39) the object of the mitre being, to enable the high priest to wear this plate of gold before the Lord.

The word *plate* (Tzeetz) is elsewhere, with but one exception, translated *flower*. For instance, Psa. ciii. 15, 16, " As for man, his days are as grass : as a *flower* of the field, so he flourisheth. For the wind passeth over it, and it is gone ; and the place thereof shall know it no more."—Isa. xxviii. 1, 4, " Whose glorious beauty is a fading *flower*,"—Isa. xl. 6, 7, 8, " All flesh is grass, and all the goodliness thereof as the *flower* of the field. The grass withereth, the *flower* fadeth."

May not this word have been chosen to direct our thoughts to the contrast between the beautiful, though fading flower of the field, to which man in his glory is likened, and the imperishable glory of the flower of gold, borne on the forehead of the high priest, with its holy inscription ? Deeply engraved on this golden plate, like the engravings of a signet, was the writing, HOLINESS TO JEHOVAH. One short expressive sentence, indelibly fixed upon the forehead of the high priest, without which he could not appear in the presence of the Lord, on behalf of Israel.

What a volume of truth does this little sentence contain ! How expressive of Him, who alone has title to bear it, the true Priest ! A life of holy separation to God, ending in the Nazarite separation of the cross, made manifest the fitness of God's blessed Son, to be the priest for ever. God has exalted Him, because of His deep and holy self-humiliation, in first emptying Himself, taking upon Himself the form of a servant, and in being made in the likeness of men ; next, in humbling Himself, and becoming obedient unto death ; and lastly, to such a death, even the death of the cross :—a wondrous threefold humiliation. Throughout this lowly course, Holiness to Jehovah was the ruling purpose of His mind.

The forehead is especially that portion of the human countenance on which is depicted the purpose, will, and mind. Impudence and self-will are marked there. Jer. iii. 3, "Thou hast a whore's *forehead.*"—Ezek. iii. 7, "All the house of Israel are impudent (margin, stiff of *forehead.*) and hard-hearted."—Isa. xlviii. 4, "I knew that thou art obstinate, and thy neck as an iron sinew, and thy *brow* brass." Stern resolution, also, in a *good* cause, is expressed by the forehead.—Ezek. iii. 8. 9, "I have made thy *forehead* strong against their foreheads . . . . . As an adament, harder than flint, have I made thy *forehead.*"—Isa. l. 7, "The Lord Jehovah will help me : therefore shall I not be confounded : therefore have I set my face like a flint, and I know that I shall not be ashamed."

The worst species of leprosy, as described in Lev

xiii. 42, 44, was when that fearful plague made its appearance in the *forehead*. "He is a leprous man ; he is unclean; the priest shall pronounce him *utterly* unclean; the plague is in his head." The self-will of our evil hearts exhibits itself in two ways ; in the indulgence of the lusts of the flesh ; and in the insubjection of the mind and reason to the word of God. Leprosy of the forehead is of the latter character, of which we perceive abundant traces at the present day. Men seem to think that their minds, as well as their lips, are their own : "Who is Lord over us ?" Psa. xii. 4. And thus, speculations of every kind are indulged at the expense of the word of God, though under the pretence of maintaining, defending, or explaining it. And the children of God themselves give heed to these things, and read, admire, and praise them. Death is openly declared to have existed prior to the fall of man. This world is said to be a creation out of pre-existent creations : and men have even gone so far as to write about a pre-adamite man  The deluge also, is openly declared to have been so slight and partial, that no traces of it remain. The marvel is, that God's saints should for a moment, allow their minds to indulge in these unhallowed triflings with His truth.

But the Word of God is powerless against these speculations. What with the oppositions of science falsely so called, on the one hand, and superstitious indulgence of human traditions and fancies on the other ; truth is well nigh fallen in the street. "Yea, truth faileth ; and he that departeth from evil maketh himself a prey," (margin : is accounted mad.) Isa. lix. 14, 15. Yes, the time is come, when those who will cleave to the Bible, and nothing else, must be content to take the place of fools in the estimation of men around them ; or to be accounted mad, as the prophet says ; and to wait for the coming of the Lord, when the secrets of all hearts will be revealed, when "the wisdom of this world, and of the princes of this world, will come to nought." " Cease ye from man, whose breath is in his nostrils : for wherein is he to be accounted of ?" " The Lord alone shall be exalted in that day."

One remarkable case of leprosy in the forehead, is recorded in 2nd Chron. xxvi. Uzziah, king of Judah, sought the Lord and prospered, as long as he was under the instruction of Zechariah, who had understanding in the visions of God. He was a man also of simple tastes, loving husbandry ; of much power and skill in invention ; and a philanthropist. He fortified Jerusalem ; built towers in the desert ; digged many wells. Moreover, he had a powerful army, and his name spread abroad : for he was marvellously helped till he was strong. But when he was strong, his heart was lifted up to his destruction. He shewed his self-will in transgressing against the word of God : for he went into the temple of the Lord to burn incense on the altar of incense. He thus arrogated to himself the place of priesthood, though God had not called him. The high priest, Azariah, with a company of priests of the Lord, valiant men, withstood the king, and said : " It appertaineth not to thee, Uzziah, to burn incense unto the Lord, but to the priests, the sons of Aaron, that are consecrated to burn incense : go out of the sanctuary, for thou hast trespassed : neither shall it be for thine honour from the Lord God. Then Uzziah was wroth, and had a censer in his hand to burn incense : and while he was wroth with the priests, the leprosy even rose up in his forehead before the priests in the house of the Lord, from beside the incense-altar. And Azariah the chief priest, and all the priests, looked upon him ; and behold, he was leprous in his forehead ; and they thrust him out from thence ; yea, himself hasted to go out, because the Lord had smitten him. And Uzziah the king was a leper unto the day of his death, and dwelt in a several house, a leper : for he was cut off from the house of the Lord."

This history of God's sudden judgment upon the

king stands out remarkably in the midst of the history of the kings of Judah ; a solemn warning against all self-willed perversions of the truth of God. Idolatries had been practised ; and yet those kings who sanctioned or led the way in such evil courses, had not been smitten. But here was a man who had more light and truth, and whom God had greatly prospered. The very mercies and blessings he had received from the Lord, raised his pride ; and his heart was lifted up to his destruction, so that he committed a fearful religious error ; something of the same character as that which had been manifested before in Korah.

God had appointed an ordered priesthood of His own selection : and what right had any one, however exalted, to interfere with that order, or to usurp its holy offices ?

God has also His own order of priesthood at this time, of which the Lord Jesus, the great High Priest, is the head. The priesthood is a family loved of Christ ; washed from their sins by Him in His own blood ; anointed with the Holy Spirit ; and separated off to God from the world, in the power of eternal life, in resurrection ; a risen company, quickened together with Christ, raised up together with Him ; including all true believers. How the leprosy of arrogant self-will and pride, shews itself in those who usurp the place of nearness to God as His priests, when they have not been washed from their sins, and have not the gift of the Holy Ghost bestowed upon them ! Surely this is a leprosy of the very worst character ; a leprosy of the forehead ; a grievous sin in the sight of God, because it is a consecration of the very filthiness of human self-will ; an attempt to make pride and assumption a holy thing ; a pretence of the flesh, as if God could be deceived.

We are naturally prone to weigh and measure sins by certain conventional standards. Immoral practices of the flesh are openly stigmatized : natural conscience can appreciate their evil. On the other hand, self-indulgence of the mind is little, if at all, condemned. Men account those comparatively blameless who take upon themselves the conducting of all kinds of religious observances towards God, although they be, in His sight, still dead in trespasses and sins.

" Satan is transformed into an angel of light ;" and no marvel therefore, that his devices take the form of religious devotedness, or of approving the Scriptures, all the time that he is insidiously attempting to undermine them.

May we be preserved from in any way countenancing such leprosy of the forehead : and having such great and precious promises as are given to us by God in His Word, may we " cleanse ourselves from all filthiness of the flesh and spirit, perfecting holiness in the fear of God." (2nd Cor. vii. 1.)

The inscription, HOLINESS TO JEHOVAH, upon the golden plate, affords us a beautiful type of the truth legibly written on the forehead of our great High Priest, in contrast with the constant spots of leprous defilement which God sees in our holy things. The Lord Jesus, a little while before His death, in His last prayer amidst His disciples, said : " For their sakes I sanctify myself, that they also might be sanctified through the truth." Holiness to the Lord expresses that great truth which the Cross manifested. There the Lord Jesus sanctified Himself to God, a sacrifice wholly presented to Jehovah And again, in resurrection, " holiness to the Lord" is declared in the High Priest. It is written, (Heb. vii.) " Such an high priest became us, holy, harmless, undefiled, separate from sinners, and made higher than the heavens." A wonderful way of speaking of the High Priest, with reference to ourselves. It is not here said that we *needed* such an high priest ; but that such an one *became* us. What must be the height of glory and holiness into which we shall be raised, since such is the High Priest whom God has chosen to be our representative and head !

This sentence was indelibly engraved, " like the engravings of a signet " or a seal, on the plate of gold. It is also called " a writing." It was the stamp of Jehovah's name upon the forehead of the high priest, claiming him as His own ; as one peculiarly separated off in holiness to Himself. In like manner we read in Rev. vii. 2—4, of an angel sealing the servants of God in their foreheads with the seal of the living God ; and in chap. xiv. 1, we read of a company standing with the Lamb on Mount Sion, " having His Father's name *written* in their foreheads." Here again this remarkable type is used. God selects, out of a multitude given over to destruction, a company for Himself. Also in Rev. xxii 4, where the servants of God are described in the heavenly city, it is said, " they shall see his face, and his name shall be in their foreheads." What a contrast this, to the fearful judgment upon those who have not the seal of God in their foreheads, but who bear the mark of the beast instead. Rev. xiii. 16, and xx. 4.

The days are approaching when men will be manifestly ranged on one side or the other. Their very countenances will proclaim whether they belong to God and the Lamb, or to Satan and Antichrist. No half-measures will be allowed ; but men will be compelled definitely to make their choice, and to be numbered either for God unto eternal life, or for the man of sin unto eternal perdition.

Although the Aaronic priesthood did not combine in its order, king and priest together, yet there seems to be in the garments, prophetic indications of a time when such would be the case. Thus we have the word *robe* given to one portion of the dress ; and the mitre, with its golden plate bound round it by a lace of blue, formed a very near approach to the attire of royalty in some of the eastern monarchs. The *mitre* is translated *diadem*. Ezek. xxi. 26. In the latin translation by Montanus, it is called *cidaris*, which was the royal bonnet worn by the kings of **Persia**, encircled by a blue ribband called the diadem.*

This ribband may be observed round the head of George III. on some of our coins. In Rev. xii. 3, the Dragon is represented as having seven diadems upon his seven heads ; and in chap. xiii. 1, the beast has ten diadems upon his ten horns. Here evidently these diadems are emblems of royalties. And in chap. xix. 12, the Lord is represented as coming forth, having many diadems, He being King of kings.

The other Greek word used for crown *(Stephanos)* properly refers to the crown that was bestowed upon a conqueror as a reward of victory, or which was given to the successful competitor in the ancient contests for strength or swiftness. In this sense it is commonly used in the New Testament. Thus we have the crowns of " life," " righteousness," and " glory."

This golden plate has the word *crown* attached to it : " the plate of the holy crown." Exod. xxxix. 30, Lev. viii. 9, and in Exod. xxix. 6, it is designated as " the holy crown," including the golden plate and the blue lace. The Hebrew word for crown, here employed, is *nezer*, found also 2nd Sam. i. 10, (Saul's royal crown,) 2nd Kings. xi. 12, and 2nd Chron. xxiii. 11, (the royal crown placed upon the head of Jehoash when he was proclaimed king.) Psa. lxxxix. 39, and cxxxii. 18, where also the crown royal is manifestly intended. It is a remarkable word, because throughout Num. vi., it is translated *Nazariteship*, *Consecration*, and *Separation*, and is thus beautifully applicable to the golden plate upon the forehead of the high priest, whose true royalty consisted in being separated off in holiness to Jehovah.

The Lord Jesus, because He preserved throughout

---

* The diadem originally means the blue and white band worn by the Asiatic monarchs round the tiara. Subsequently, the diadem was a broad white band, fastened round the head, and tied in a bow behind, adopted by other nations as an ensign of sovereignty. Thus, in works of art, the diadem indicates a regal station, like the crown of modern times." (Rich's Companion.)

His life, and when made sin, and in death, His holy Nazariteship to God, has been raised the High Priest and King for ever, after the order of Melchizedek. The same Psalm, cx., which speaks of Him as David's Lord, who is to rule in kingly power hereafter in the midst of His enemies, smiting through kings in the day of His wrath, and wounding the *head* over many countries, (the wilful king, the Antichrist.)—the same Psalm also declares Him the Priest, made so by God's oath.

Surely "holiness to the Lord" is true royal dignity and glory. Where that truth is inscribed upon the forehead, there will be no servile subjection to sin or Satan. There will not be the yielding to self, or the indulging of a will contrary to that of the Lord. Neither will there be any cringing to man, but complete unswerving devotedness of heart and mind to Him whose name is "holy," the unchangeable I AM, with whom is no variableness, neither shadow of turning. Would that we might follow more closely the ways of our great High Priest, perfecting holiness in the fear of the Lord!

The holy crown was fastened "*on high*" upon the mitre, (Exod. xxxix. 31) and was *always* to be on Aaron's forehead, (Exod. xxviii. 38) that he might "bear the iniquity of the holy things, which the children of Israel should hallow in all their holy gifts, that they might be accepted before the Lord." The eye of Jehovah was to fall first upon this holy plate, with its deep inscription ; therefore it was to be borne on high. The high priest, also, must never be without it : but, as continually as the lamb was presented on the altar for a burnt-offering ; and as the shew-bread stood perpetually in the presence of God ; and the seven-branched candlestick shed forth its constant light in the sanctuary ; and lastly, as the incense constantly ascended in a fragrant cloud from the golden altar ; so the living high priest always presented himself to Jehovah, in holy devoted separateness, as the representative of the people. He was to bear the iniquity of their holy things ; that is especially of the holy gifts, which the children of Israel might give to the Lord.

In his representative character, Aaron clothed with " garments for glory and beauty," was to bear the names of the children of Israel before the Lord upon his two shoulders for a memorial. He was also to bear their names in the breastplate upon his breast, for a memorial before the Lord.

He was to bear the *judgment* of the children of Israel upon his heart before the Lord.

And he was to bear the iniquity of their holy things.

Thus the shoulders of his strength, the heart of his affections, and the forehead of his mind and counsel, were all employed on behalf of the people, for whom he ministered before the Lord.

We may, by means of this type, be enabled to distinguish between the sacrifice bearing sin in the way of wrath, and the priest bearing the iniquity of an already saved people. When the question of judgment upon sin was involved, nothing could expiate but the shedding of blood ; for, without shedding of blood there is no remission. But, after sinners are perfectly saved as regards deliverance from wrath, and have forgiveness of sins, they stand before God in an entirely new relation. They are children, saints, priests, kings, and worshippers. In their very best services however, sin still cleaves to that which they do. Even the gifts they sanctify to God are tainted with their own iniquity. It is on this account that they need a High Priest, to stand in His presence, presenting to the Lord the very contrast of what they are ; holy, where they are unholy ; righteous, though they be sinful ; pure, though they be defiled ;—a High Priest, who is also the propitiation ; and whose intercession of perpetual fragrance sustains them in continual acceptance, and carries on their salvation to the very end. It is with reference to this truth that we read,

"This One (the Lord Jesus,) because He continueth ever, hath an unchangeable priesthood. Wherefore He is able to save them to the uttermost, (to the very end,) that come unto God by Him ; seeing He ever liveth to make intercession for them." Heb. vii. 24, 25. And again : "If any man sin, we have an Advocate with the Father, Jesus Christ the righteous : and He is the propitiation for our sins." 1st John ii. 1, 2. And in Rom. v. 9, 10, "Much more then, being now justified by His blood, we shall be saved from wrath through Him. For if, when we were enemies, we were reconciled to God by the death of His Son, much more, being reconciled, we shall be saved by His life:" (or rather, *in* His life.) Justification is stated to have been accomplished by His blood ; *now* accomplished. But there is another salvation also intimated, to which the words "much more" are attached. Having been already justified by His blood, much more then shall we be saved from wrath through Him. This evidently has reference to the Lord Jesus as the High Priest, saving to the end those that come unto God by Him. Again, we have another "much more" in the following verse. Whilst enemies, having been reconciled to God by the death of His Son ; much more, we shall be saved in His life. For, the Lord Jesus is not only our living representative before God, and ever living to make intercession ; but we, as reconciled persons, have a salvation in union with Him. He is our life : and there is an indissoluble life-existence between the believer and Christ.

Aaron could only present "Holiness to Jehovah" engraved upon the holy crown, on his forehead. Christ *is* Holiness to Jehovah. Aaron stood only on behalf of Israel, before the Lord. Christ not only stands on behalf of His people, but they are united to Him in His life. We are members of His body, of His flesh, and of His bones.

What a remarkable connexion : "*Iniquity* of *holy* things !" Could we ever have conceived that two such words could be united ? Yet so it is. Our very best gifts to God are defiled by the iniquity of the giver Our purest worship is mingled with infirmity and sin. Our most devoted acts are tainted with self-pleasing, pride, and complacency. What a merciful provision has been made for us in this living Christ ; who even now appears in the presence of God for us, and through whom we can draw near with boldness, and present gifts and sacrifices acceptable to the Father.

## THE EMBROIDERED COAT

"And thou shalt embroider the coat of fine linen."—Exod. xxviii 39

"And they made coats of fine linen."—Exod. xxxix 27

THE portion of the High Priest's dress called the coat, was more properly a tunic ; the Hebrew and Greek words being very similar. It was the innermost garment worn by the high priest, being placed first upon him after he was washed. Lev. viii. 7. It seems to be derived from a verb meaning " to cover, or hide." It is called a broidered coat. Exod. xxviii. 4, and in the 39th verse of the same chap., " thou shalt *embroider* the coat. When made it is said to be of *woven* work. (xxxix. 27.)

The word embroider (shahvatz) only occurs once more. Exod. xxviii. 20, " they (the precious stones) *shall be set* in gold." In 2nd Sam. i. 9, the same word in the Hebrew is translated " *anguish* is come upon me: " the margin however reads " my coat of mail, or my embroidered coat hindereth me."

Ouches, or settings (Exod. xxviii. 11, 13, 14, 25 ; also xxxix. 13, 16) is derived from the same word as embroider. Psa. xlv. 13, the king's daughter is represented as having a clothing " of *wrought* gold." Here " wrought " is again the same word. Judging from the various uses of the word which we have above, it may be concluded that the fine linen coat was interwoven, like net, or chequer work, so as to present, what in modern days we should call, a *damask* appearance, combining weaving with a species of embroidery. " *Fine twined linen* " was used for the door curtain ; the vail ; the ten curtains ; the court of the tabernacle ; the gate of the court ; the high priest's ephod ; the curious girdle of the ephod ; and the breastplate.

" Fine linen," without the word " twined," was employed in making the mitre and broidered coat of the high priest : and the coats and bonnets of the priests. It is difficult to say why this variation occurs. The word " *twined*" would imply that the fine linen was twisted into a strand of many threads, before it was worked into the curtains and garments. It may be in order to give it more strength.

The blue robe, and gorgeous ephod, with its cluster of brilliant precious stones on the shoulders and breastplate, would entirely conceal from the eye of an observer this fine linen coat. Beneath therefore the splendid dress of the high priest there was a more humble attire of pure white, though it was still a " garment for glory and beauty." The outer garments were distinctly of a representative character : that is, they bore the names of Israel before the Lord. And also, the pomegranates around the hem of the robe, had relation to that people as bearing fruit to God. But in this under tunic there was no apparent connexion with that people. It was rather the personal clothing of the high priest ; manifesting him, beneath all his official glory as one who could minister before the Lord in a perfect righteousness of his own. A glory and beauty no less costly and precious than was displayed by the other garments, though to the eye of sense not so striking in appearance.

In fact, the high priest could not have worn his magnificent apparel unless he could previously exhibit a spotless purity, diversified in every possible way like the embroidered fine linen coat.

The Lord Jesus, in the days of His flesh, passed through an ordeal of temptation and suffering, throughout which He evinced His complete fitness to be the great High Priest in resurrection, shewing forth a righteousness and holiness, as well as grace, sympathy and tenderness which proved Him perfectly suited for the high dignity and responsibility to which God called Him by an oath, " thou art a Priest for ever after the order of Melchisedek." " King of righteousness," first, by reason of His own intrinsic righteousness. " King of peace," next, because able to introduce perfect peace into His dominions.

This coat is the same word as we find in Gen. iii. 21, " unto Adam also and his wife did the Lord God make *coats* of skins, and clothed them." Disobedience had made them sinners, and naked to their shame. They had invented a mode of concealing that shame from one another, and it answered their purpose well for a time, until the voice of the Lord God was heard in the garden.

Man's ingenuity was thus first developed through sin. His inventive faculty shewed itself in devising a way by means of which he hid his own shame from the eyes of his fellow, and pacified a disquieted conscience.

Cain was the next to exhibit still further this remarkable power of invention, fostering his pride in the very act of worshipping God. He began by what may be called *religious* inventions ; and when they failed turned his attention to others of an entirely worldly kind. He and his family were the great architects, agriculturists, artificers, and musicians of the antidiluvian world, as well as founders of a self-righteous religious system.

The aprons of fig leaves which gave self-complacency to the man and woman after the fall, proved of no avail when God manifested His presence in the garden. Fertile in expedients, our first parents next sought

amongst the trees of the garden a hiding place from th
presence of the Lord, and Adam confessed that his
nakedness had made him fear, although he had before
attempted to conceal that nakedness, and had for a time
effectually done so, so far as Eve and himself were
concerned.

The religious garments which men devise to hide their
nature of sin and shame, become mere " spiders' webs"
when the presence of God is realized. " The covering
is narrower than that he can wrap himself in it."
" They weave the spider's web." " Their webs shall
not become garments, neither shall they cover themselves
with their works." Isa. xxviii. 20, lix. 5, 6.

After that wonderful interview between the Lord
God and fallen man, and after Adam had shown an
entirely new intelligence, the intelligence of faith, by
calling his wife's name Eve, (life) because she was the
mother of all living, " unto Adam also and his wife did
the Lord God make coats of skins and clothed them."

These coats were for clothing as well as to hide their
shame. They were not their own ; not of their own
invention, but *made* by Jehovah from skin taken off
some slain victim, and *placed* by His hand upon the
man and woman who needed them.

It may be here observed that "*skin*" is in the original
in the singular number, and not plural as in our version,
apparently to make the type more significant ; *one* victim
supplying the whole covering. Also the Hebrew word
translated skin, is derived from a root, signifying to be
naked. The victim was made naked, stripped of its
skin, that a covering might be provided for the naked
ones. What a type of Him who went into the shame
and nakedness of death, that we through His obedience
might be made righteous.

The high priest's coat of fine linen, woven in a
beautifully embroidered pattern, may appropriately
represent the righteous servant, " By his knowledge
shall my righteous servant justify many, for he shall

bear their iniquities." Isa. liii. 11. God's righteous
Servant has borne our iniquities, and in that death upon
the cross has made His obedience, His righteousness
manifest to the full. He now therefore justifies us by
His blood. He has washed us from our sins in His
own blood. This justification becomes ours in the
way of faith, " by his knowledge," that is, " by the
knowledge of him " through faith.

Because He justifies us by having borne our iniquities,
He is our advocate with the Father. One who
completely identifies Himself with us and maintains our
cause, notwithstanding our sin and failure Jesus Christ
the *righteous*, personally spotless in righteousness and
holiness ; and at the same time, the propitiation for our
sins. A representative who can appear for us before
God, on the ground of His own perfect obedience and
purity; and who can present for us the "precious blood
which cleanseth us from all sin," the efficiency of which
is daily and hourly perpetuated, preserving us in perfect
cleanness in the presence of the Father, as His children,
kings, and priests.

How the blessed Lord was vindicated as the
righteous man at the very moment of His condemnation.
Judas was obliged to confess to the chief priests and
elders, that he had sinned and betrayed innocent blood.
The pieces of silver which he returned were silent
witnesses to this truth. Matt. xxvii. 4.

Pilate thrice repeated the words, " I find no fault in
Him," and declared that He was a righteous person.
John xviii. 38. xix. 4, 6. Matt. xxvii. 24.

The wife of Pilate sent to beg he would have nothing
to do with that righteous man. Matt. xxvii. 19.

Herod also could discover no evil in the ways of
Jesus. Luke xxiii. 15.

On the cross, a malefactor condemned himself whilst
he vindicated Christ, "this man hath done nothing
amiss." Luke xxiii. 41.

And the Gentile Centurion was the first after the

Lord had given up the Ghost, to glorify God, by proclaiming the truth, " certainly this was a righteous man." Luke xxiii. 47.

Three times in the Acts is the Lord called the Righteous One. Peter in preaching to the Jews, says : " Ye denied the holy one, and the *Just*," (or righteous one,) iii.14.

Stephen, in his last address, tells them " that their fathers had slain them who shewed before of the coming of the *Just* One." vii. 52.

And Paul in relating the facts connected with his conversion, repeats the words of Ananias to him. " The God of our fathers hath chosen thee, that thou shouldest know his will, and see that *Just One*, and shouldest hear the voice of his mouth." xxii. 14.  God has vindicated His Son by raising Him to His own right hand of power and glory ; and the Holy Ghost come down from heaven is witness of the exaltation of Jesus, and of the guilt of the world in putting Him to death.

The world is condemned under a threefold sentence ; and the Holy Spirit is by His presence here, an evidence of its solemn judgment.

In John xvi. 7—11, the Lord Jesus promises to His disciples, after His departure, to send the Comforter : " And when he is come, he will reprove the world of sin, and of righteousness, and of judgment." That is, the presence of the Comforter here, abiding with God's people, would of itself be the sentence of conviction of the world.  Not that he would convict the souls of all men in the world, of sin.  The Lord was not speaking of this action of the Holy Spirit upon the heart and conscience of the sinner ; but of the solemn fact, that the personal presence of the Comforter with the children of God, would be the condemnation of the world as in God's sight.  First, on the ground of sin, " because they believe not on me."  The fact of Christ's absence, and the result of that absence, the presence of the Holy Spirit here, proves that the world was guilty of the deepest sin, viz. unbelief of Him.

This is the crowning sin of all others. If the world had believed, had known and owned Him, its princes would not have slain Him. But they manifested their complete ignorance and unbelief by killing the Lord of glory ; and under the guilt of this sin the world lies. The Spirit of God having come, sent by the crucified and risen Christ, is the conviction of the world upon this ground.

Secondly, " of righteousness, because I go to my Father, and ye see me no more." God and the world are fearfully at issue upon the question of righteousness. And the question has been brought to a definite point by the death of Christ. The world has slain Him as a malefactor, hanged Him upon a tree with thieves : preferred an abominable criminal, guilty of robbery, sedition, and murder, to the Son of God. But God has raised the same rejected and despised Christ to the throne of His glory, and counted Him worthy of sitting at the right hand of His Majesty in the heavens.

What a solemn difference thus exists upon the question of righteousness, between the world and God. Why is Jesus gone to the Father ? Why do His people see Him no more ? Why has the Holy Spirit come ? Because He has been murdered and slain ; rejected and disowned ; scourged, spit upon, stripped naked, and crucified. He has been dealt with thus, as an un- righteous one by the world. God has received Him as the righteous one to glory. And the people of God have the Holy Spirit as the Comforter, because of Christ's rejection, and His exaltation to the highest heavens.

Lastly, " of judgment, because the prince of this world is judged."

Three times in the Gospel of John is the title " prince of this world" given to Satan by the Lord Jesus.

" Now is the judgment of this world ; now shall the prince of this world be cast out." xii. 31.

This the Lord spoke in contemplation of His Cross. His being lifted up upon the tree, was at the same time the judgment of the world, the dethronement of its Prince as to the final result, and offered a new source of attraction, powerful enough to draw unto Himself away from the allurements of the world, and the seductions of Satan.

" Hereafter I will not talk much with you, for the prince of this world cometh and hath nothing in me." xiv. 30. The Lord's converse with His disciples was about to cease, for He was to meet and resist unto blood the closing fierce attacks of the adversary. But that prince would find nothing in Christ of which he could obtain one moment's possession. No shaft of the tempter could lodge in that bosom of purity. No temptation would have any response from that Righteous One. The prince of this world had no possession of any kind in Christ. For the first and last time he found a Man, proof against every inlet to sin, every suggestion of evil. One of whom it could be said, " Jehovah is well pleased for His righteousness' sake." And though the serpent was permitted to bruise the heel of the woman's seed, in that very act he hurled down destruction upon himself. The cross of Christ, and its inseparable result, resurrection, was the judgment of the prince of this world.

The coming of the Holy Spirit from the throne of glory, to which God had exalted His Son, is the evidence that this is a judged world, because Satan its prince has been vanquished, made nought of, and judged. Thus we live in a place already sentenced. The blood of the Lamb has redeemed us out of it to God : and we must look away to another region, to another country for righteousness and holiness. " Delivered out of the power of darkness, and translated into the kingdom of God's dear Son," our life, our hopes, our affections, and our fellowships are above. Christ is there, God's righteous servant, our Great High Priest, " who of God is made unto us wisdom, and righteousness, and sanctification, and redemption."

# THE GIRDLE

" A broidered coat, a mitre, and a girdle.

"And thou shalt make the girdle of needlework."—Exod. xxviii 4, 39

" And a girdle of fine twined linen, and blue, and purple, and scarlet needlework,"—Ex. xxxix 29

IT has been before observed, that " the curious girdle of the ephod" was not a girdle in the ordinary sense of the word, (*see page* 200.) The true girdle, *(avneht,)* is here described. The Hebrew word is exclusively used for this inner girdle, and that of the high priest on the day of atonement, and for the girdles of the priests ; except in one other instance, Isa. xxii. 21, where Eliakim is to be clothed with Shebna's robe, (coat,) and strengthened with his *girdle.*

The use in this passage of the two parts of the priestly dress, *coat*, and *girdle*, may intimate, that the treasurer and ruler of David's house stood in a kind of priestly capacity : and may afford another instance of the frequent incidental allusions in Scripture to the future glory of the Lord Jesus ; who will combine with His office of Priest, that of King, Lord, Treasurer, Governor, and Ruler.

This girdle was made of the same materials as those of the vail ; but the order of their arrangement was that of the innermost curtains of the tabernacle, viz. " fine linen, blue, purple, scarlet."

The fine linen, type of righteousness comes first, answering to that beautiful passage in Isaiah xi. 5. " Righteousness shall be the girdle of his loins, and faithfulness, the girdle of his reins." Righteousness and faithfulness which the Lord Jesus has made perfectly manifest, and proved to the utmost in His death upon the cross. Faithfulness is the same word as truth.

The object of the girdle was to strengthen the loins for service. And the high priest, beneath his outward

garments of majesty, glory, brilliancy, and power, still
preserved his place, as the girded righteous servant of
the Lord. So the Lord Jesus upon the throne of glory,
having all power in heaven and in earth, and with the
name above every name, yet delights to maintain His
place as God's servant, fulfilling the Father's counsels,
and accomplishing His will in the salvation and ultimate
perfection of those that are His.

We have in John xiii. a striking illustration of our
blessed Lord's holy service; deeply instructive to us in
two ways; first, as teaching us what His present occupations are in our behalf, and next, as giving us an
example which we have to follow, if we would taste of
His happiness and joy.

The chapter opens with these words : "Now before
the feast of the passover, when Jesus knew that his hour
was come, that he should depart out of this world unto
the Father, having loved his own which were in the
world, he loved them unto the end."

The cross was thus before Him, that strange pathway of sorrow by which He was to depart out of this
world unto the Father. The joy was before Him of
being with the Father; but His love, unshaken by the
fearful prospect of woe, or by the joyous hope of unspeakable rest and gladness, abode firm in His bosom
towards His own. "He loved them unto the end."
Faithfulness of true affection for them, and true devotedness to God, was the girdle of His loins.

"And supper being ended, the devil having now put
into the heart of Judas Iscariot, Simon's son, to betray
him ;

Jesus knowing that the Father had given all things
into his hands, and that he was come from God, and
went to God ;

He riseth from supper,
And laid aside his garments ;
And took a towel,
And girded himself.

After that he poureth water into a basin,
And began to wash the disciples' feet,
And to wipe them with the towel wherewith he was
girded."

The supper which afforded emblems of His broken
body and shed blood, was still before them. The devil
had now full mastery of the heart of Judas. Thus in
*figure* the Cross was passed. Satan had accomplished
his purpose. Jesus took His stand as one who had
gained the victory. He knew that the Father had given
all things into His hands. All power in heaven and
earth was His. He had come from God, and He was
going to God. " He had come forth from the Father
and had come into the world ; again, He was about to
leave the world and to return to the Father."—John
xvi. 28.

Here is the true power for lowly service. The consciousness of a height of glory and exaltation beyond
all mere human reach ; and the knowledge that God is
the strength, as well as the object of all service.

We have next a picture of the perfection of service,
a seven-fold action of the Lord.

" He riseth from supper." He ceases to rest in the
interchange only of thought and feeling in fellowship
with " His own." He stands as one who has a work
to accomplish.

" And laid aside his garments." He divests Himself
of any robe of dignity that might impede his lowly and
active ministry.

" And took a towel," or linen cloth. The girdle of
righteousness ; the righteousness of true obedience to
God.

" And girded himself." Thus standing before His
disciples and before His Father as the true servant .
delighting in His Father's will, and rejoicing in His
purpose to bless others.

" After that he poureth water into a basin." The
words " after that" may be significant. The first part
of this wonderful scene may be typical of the deep

and blessed service of Christ on the cross, whereby He provided that cleansing which should not only purge the sinner so as to make a full atonement for him and justify him, but should also cleanse him and keep him clean on to the end of his course. The precious blood, in the shedding of which there is remission of sins, and which cleanseth us from all sin.

" And began to wash the disciples' feet." They sat whilst the Lord stooped to wash even their feet. He bent down to their need, that He might cleanse away every stain of defilement which they had unavoidably contracted, in passing through a world of sin and death. A priestly ministration this of the Lord in glory: keeping us from falling, upholding us by His living intercession. Daily and hourly cleansing us from ten thousand contacts with evil, of which we are not conscious, that He may finally present us faultless in the presence of His glory with exceeding joy.

" And to wipe them with the towel wherewith he was girded." Using the spotless girdle to wipe off all remaining traces of defilement, so as to complete the cleansing. In this action two thoughts are embodied. The cleansing power of the blood itself, and the application of it by the living High Priest, who though exalted in glory, still ministers to us in humble, lowly service.

It may here be remarked that the Lord uses two words subsequently, in answer to Peter. " He that is washed, needeth not save to wash his feet." That is, he who has been once completely washed all over, only needs afterwards to have his feet washed, but is clean every whit.

The first words, " he that is *washed*," is the same as that in Rev. i. 5. " Unto him that loved us and *washed* us from our sins in his own blood." Expressing the complete priestly cleansing, which the sinner first receives, making him at once clean for God. The subsequent cleansing having reference to his conduct and his ways, rather than to his person

" So after he had washed their feet, and had taken
his garments, and was set down again, he said unto
them, know ye what I have done to you ? Ye call me
Master and Lord : and ye say well ; for so I am. If I
then, your Lord and Master, have washed your feet,
ye also ought to wash one another's feet ; for I have
given you an example, that ye should do as I have done
to you. Verily, verily, I say unto you, the servant is not
greater than his lord ; neither he that is sent, greater
than he that sent him. If ye know these things happy
are ye if ye do them." The question often occurs, how
should this precept and example of our Lord and Master
be carried out ? One way in which we may wash
one another's feet is by prayer and intercession for one
another : especially where we know that the world
and Satan are presenting snares and temptations, which
may turn the feet aside into paths of defilement. " Looking diligently lest any man fail of the grace of God :
lest any root of bitterness springing up trouble you, and
thereby many be defiled." Heb. xii. 15.

Another mode of fulfilling this direction of the Lord
is by seeking to deliver any of the Lord's people, that
may be ensnared, from the entanglements into which they
may have fallen. But the example of the Lord must
be accurately followed, when we attempt to deal with the
failures of our brethren. Many have been fastened more
firmly in that which is evil, through the proud and un-
gracious way in which they have been dealt with.
Herein therefore this beautiful action of Christ is of
great value. He divested Himself of all seeming
superiority, though He was truly " Lord and Master."
He stooped to the feet of those He washed. He did
it calmly, gently, and effectually ; and failed not to
*wipe* the feet after He had washed them. In all this
we have a pattern of meekness, grace, and compassion,
which we should do well to imitate.

In John xvii, Jesus takes the place by anticipation
beyond the Cross. He speaks of His having glorified the

Father on the earth, and having finished the work given Him to do. And says, " now I am no more in the world ;" looking back to the time as passed when He was with His disciples in the world. This wonderful chapter especially reveals to us, the subjects of deepest interest to the heart of Christ, and of constant intercession between Him and the Father. It opens to us the holiest, and tells us what the converse is there between the Son and the Father ; the High Priest, and God. We find the Lord still keeping His place as the righteous servant, rendering an account of His work, and asking to be glorified, in order that He may pursue the same object for which He came down to die, viz. to glorify the Father, " Glorify thy Son that thy Son also may glorify thee." He closes His prayer with the words, " I have declared unto them thy name and will declare it, that the love wherewith thou hast loved me, may be in them and I in them." He serves us still in making known to our souls the unspeakable value of the name, Father. And through the revelation of that name instructing our hearts in the Father's love towards *us,* as towards His own blessed Son.

The fine linen coat, and girdle of needlework, were as much garments for glory and beauty, as the gorgeous ephod with its breastplate of precious stones. Who shall estimate the glory and beauty of the Lord, as God's servant, who has glorified Him on earth and glorifies Him still ? The glory and beauty of spotless righteousness and obedience, manifested to the full here below in every scene and circumstance of human life : perfected in the suffering of the cross in death, and now perpetuated for ever in the holiest above.

# THE GARMENTS FOR AARON'S SONS

"And for Aaron's sons thou shalt make coats. And thou shalt make for them girdles, and bonnets shalt thou make for them for glory and for beauty."—Exod. xxviii 40

"And they made coats of fine linen of woven work for Aaron and for his sons.

"And goodly bonnets of fine linen."—Exod. xxxix 27, 28

THE Garments for glory and beauty with which the sons of Aaron were clothed, consisted of coats, girdles, and bonnets of fine twined linen. There was no ornament or embroidery : no gold or brilliant colours. They were arrayed in pure white garments.

Aaron, as the high priest, appeared in the presence of the Lord in a representative character, personating we may say, the whole nation Israel, and upholding it in the glory and beauty required by God ; bearing the names of the tribes on his shoulders and breastplate, graven on precious stones. His sons the priests stood in no such official dignity, but had access into the holy place and ministered at the altar, on behalf of the people, not as representing them, but rather as leaders of their worship, and instructors of them in the holy things of God. They were types of one aspect of the church of God—the heavenly priesthood. In the Revelation, the four and twenty elders have a priestly standing; they form the heavenly council, being elders, and therefore also judges. They are seated on *thrones*, because kings. They are clothed in white raiment, as priests, and they have on their heads crowns of gold, that is, victor's crowns, or chaplets. Chap. iv. 4.

The countless multitude are also seen clothed with white robes ; a priestly company serving day and night in the heavenly temple. Chap. vii. 9. The Lamb's wife is seen arrayed in fine linen clean and white : for the fine linen is the *righteousness* of saints. Chap. xix. 8.

We have white raiment also alluded to in Rev. iii. 4, 18 ; and in vi. 11.

Thus the priestly dress of fine linen, and the garments of unsullied whiteness represent the same thing—spotless righteousness. The standing of the believer in Christ before God ; not having his own righteousnesses, but the righteousness which is of God by faith.

There is an interesting passage in Isaiah lxi. 10, " I will greatly rejoice in the Lord, my soul shall be joyful in my God ; for he hath clothed me with the garments of salvation, he hath covered me with the robe of right-eousness, as a bridegroom decketh himself with orna-ments, and as a bride adorneth herself with her jewels."

It will be observed from the margin that this might be translated, "as a bridegroom decketh himself as a priest with ornaments," and the word for ornaments is the same as that used Exod. xxxix. 28, " *goodly* bonnets." The garments of salvation, the robe of righteousness, are like the bridegroom's priestly glory ; and like the bride's adornments. May not this passage in Isaiah have been in the mind of the Spirit of God, when inditing that portion of Rev. xix. 8, referred to above.

The bridal ornaments are the priestly robes of fine linen. Christ our righteousness. The Church will shine forth in His spotless white and glistening raiment, clean and bright, clothed with Christ.

We are exhorted Rom. xiii. 14, to " *put on* the Lord Jesus Christ," and in Gal. iii. 27, it is said, " as many of you as have been baptized into Christ have *put on* Christ."

As believers in Jesus we have already put on Christ. He is our spotless robe of righteousness. But we have also to remember the exhortation to be constantly putting on the Lord Jesus Christ. Our conduct and walk should correspond with our real standing before God, and our way to aim at this is by setting the Lord alway before us, and seeking to walk in His steps ; remembering ever to connect our thoughts and meditations of Him with His death upon the cross ; for thereby we shall get the strength we need, at the same time, that we have before us the perfect example.

In this respect the Lord's people often fail and are discouraged : they very properly look at the Lord Jesus as the pattern of what they should be in their Christian course, but they fail to realize the power required in order to follow Him. This arises from their not eating His flesh and drinking His blood whilst they gaze on Him.

We shall find many beautiful illustrations of this truth in the Epistles. Paul, when he says, " the life which I now live in the flesh I live by the faith of the Son of God," immediately adds, " who loved me, and gave himself for me," proving that all his strength was derived from this remembrance of the love of Christ, manifested in His death. Both the Epistles to the Corinthians are filled with direct or incidental allusions to the death of Christ. They are Epistles containing many rebukes, and much practical exhortation. When the apostle Peter puts before those to whom he wrote, the exceedingly difficult grace of bearing patiently sufferings wrongly inflicted, he presents Christ as an example, and adds " who his own self bare our sins in his own body on the tree—by whose stripes ye were healed."


# GIRDLES

"And thou shalt make for them girdles." Exod. xxviii 40

WE have no mention of these girdles as subsequently made in Exod. xxxix. But Moses is directed to gird Aaron and his sons with girdles. Exod. xxix. 9. And he does so as related in Lev. viii. 13. We have allusions in the New Testament to the girdle, both as a portion of the believer's armour, and as a part of his ordinary garments.

"Wherefore take unto you the whole armour of God,

that ye may be able to withstand in the evil day, and having done all to stand. Stand therefore having your loins girt about with truth, and having on the breastplate of righteousness, and your feet shod with the preparation of the gospel of peace ; above all taking the shield of faith, wherewith ye shall be able to quench all the fiery darts of the wicked. And take the helmet of salvation, and the sword of the spirit, which is the word of God." Eph. vi. 13—17.

This Epistle which begins with the perfect rest, and blessing of believers in Christ, ("blessed with all spiritual blessings in heavenly places in Christ:" "raised up together, and made to sit together in heavenly places in Christ Jesus." i. 3, ii. 6.) closes with a description of the most severe struggle and conflict, to which we are continually exposed. It tells us we are seated, and afterwards bids us "*stand*." It assures us of an inheritance obtained in Christ, but exhorts us to wrestle against enemies usurping possession of the place of our inheritance. It extends the sphere of conflict from the world to the highest heavens ; and whilst telling us of the exceeding greatness of God's power towards us, and in us, according to the working of the might of His power which he wrought in Christ when He raised Him from the dead, at the same time encourages us to be strong in the Lord and in the power of His might. This is ever the order of the Epistles. Our full blessings with all their stability and irreversible security in Christ are first declared ; and then follow exhortations to realize and use them, and to live in the power of them. God ever declares the victory won before He sends us into the conflict. We must by faith realize our perfect rest and peace and security, before we attempt to stand in conflict with the foe. We fight *from* rest and victory, instead of *for* them.

In this Scripture we are told to put on the whole armour of God, that we may be able to stand against the wiles of the devil ; to wrestle against the vast

principalities and powers of wicked spirits, rulers of the
darkness of this world; and to quench all the fiery darts
of the wicked one. A wonderful combination of evil
spirits with deceits, dark delusions, and fiery weapons
arrayed against us. Little do we comprehend the
vastness of the struggle, and alas! slow are we often to
perceive the snares and guileful devices laid for us.
We need to take unto us, and to put on the whole
armour of God, that we may " withstand " and
" stand." Twice we are exhorted to " *stand*," for we
have no ground to gain; we have only to hold our own.
God has raised us up in Christ to the loftiest height of
glory—we cannot attain a higher place, for there is none.
All we have to do is to maintain our footing firm in the
super-heavenly places. The armour for offence and
defence has been provided by God, and the strength
alone is His.

It is to be observed that the Girdle is mentioned *first*.
" Girded about as to your loins with truth."

And the sword is mentioned last ; "the sword of the
Spirit which is the word of God." The girdle and
sword must be closely connected together, and all the rest
of the armour seems, as it were, to be included within
these two pieces. Truth is unchangeable, eternal; it can
never alter or vary with time or circumstances. It is
fixed like the everlasting hills. It is the word of God.
It is Christ. The whole strength of the warrior to
stand and wrestle depends upon the close fitting of this
firm girdle. If his loins be weak, and not knit firmly
by this sinew of strength, Satan will soon cast him down
from his excellency, and he would then cease to stand
in his high calling, and would probably sink into some
darkness of the world's delusions : ensnared either by
its vanities and glittering honours, or its learned
speculations of so called wisdom. Truth, that is,
the word of God, all that centres in Christ and
proceeds from Him, is our only support and our only
weapon ; our girdle and our sword.

The Girdle is also an important part of the ordinary garments of the believer, as a priest and servant.

In Luke xii. 35, 36, the Lord exhorts His disciples to be ready for His return. " Let your loins be girded about, and your lights burning ; and ye yourselves like unto men that wait for their Lord."

They are to have the true attitude of expectancy, which can only be maintained by constant activity in service, and letting the light of truth shine out. The hope of the Lord's return will not really abide in the heart, unless we keep our loins girded as engaged in our Master's work, and let our light shine out before men. An inactive believer is sure to become a worldly minded one, and he will begin to eat and drink with the drunken. He will have companionship with the men of the world, whose intoxicating pursuits of avarice, ambition, and pleasure, deaden their hearts and consciences to all the truth of God. "*Occupy* till I come," is another precept of Jesus of the same kind, as "let your loins be girded." The light also must not be hidden. The bed and the bushel are two snares to the *believer*. Men indeed do not put the candle under either ; for the children of this world are in their generation wiser than the children of light. Indolence and supineness, of which the bed is an emblem, enervate many of those who ought to let their light shine brightly ; whilst the active and engrossing pursuits of life, legitimate in their way, trade and commerce, of which the bushel is a " resemblance." Zech. v. 6, alas ! too often bury out of sight the manifestation of the life and light of the believer.

We find another exhortation 1st Peter i. 13, "Wherefore gird up the loins of your mind, be sober, and hope to the end for the grace which is to be brought unto you at the revelation of Jesus Christ." Here believers are especially addressed as strangers and pilgrims on their journey through a foreign country into their own land, where an inheritance incorruptible and undefiled, and that fadeth not away is reserved for them.

Two subjects of an all engrossing nature are presented to them. Subjects which the very prophets who spoke of them understood not, though they enquired and searched diligently, and which the angels of glory desire to look into : " the *sufferings* of Christ, and the *glories* after these." If we would press on as strangers and pilgrims, we must gird up the loins of our mind, to the constant contemplation of the great Salvation, which comprises these two subjects.

A man who allows his garments to be loose, and who girds not up his loins, will make but little progress on his journey. We must therefore gather in our loose floating thoughts and wandering imaginations, and learn to fix more continually our minds and understandings upon the death, resurrection, and coming of Jesus, and the great truths connected therewith, if we would pursue our path with less distraction. The girded priest and pilgrim must also be sober. The Lord gave a precept to Aaron and his sons, not to drink wine or strong drink when officiating in the Tabernacle. Lev. x. 9. The pilgrim also will walk unsteadily if he indulge himself in intoxicating draughts. We live in a world especially given up at the present time to drunkenness of all kinds. Men are hurrying on their projects with a determination of purpose, an eagerness of mind which prove that they have drunk largely of Babylon's golden cup of abominations. What with science, commerce, exhibitions, politics, wars, commotions, men have no time for considerations respecting eternity. The god of this world has filled up with consummate skill every moment of human existence ; and all hurry with railroad velocity, along the broad road that leads to destruction. In the midst of this scene the girded servant of the Lord must be sober, and hope on to the end, assuredly knowing that grace will be brought to him, (even the glory itself, for glory is grace,) at the revelation of Jesus Christ. 1st Peter i. 13. The revelation of that hidden One whom the world has rejected, and of whom it is willingly ignorant.

In the Revelation, the Son of Man, as seen in visions by John, was "girt about the paps with a golden girdle." The object of this girdle seems not to have been to strengthen Him who wore it for priestly service of judgment, but rather to bind the robe of blue—the robe of heavenly love and peace firmly around His heart, so that in the midst of searching words of reproof and warning, mercies might be poured forth from breasts of consolations.

In Rev. xv. 6, the seven angels having the seven plagues, are seen coming out of the temple clothed in pure and white linen, their breasts girded with golden girdles.

Here again the girdle is not upon the loins, the emblem probably being, that the heart of the angels to whom the vials of wrath were entrusted, needed to be strengthened for their terrible work of judgment. The fine linen, expressive of righteousness was therefore firmly girt with gold around their breasts.

## THE BONNETS

"And bonnets shalt thou make for them, for glory and for beauty.—Exod. xxviii 40

"And goodly bonnets of fine linen.—Exod. xxxix 28

THE word *(migbahgohth)* translated "bonnets" only occurs four times, and is exclusively used for the head dress of the priests. It is derived from a verb signifying "elevation," often used for a hill. They apparently differed from the mitre of the high priest, in the fact that they were *bound* round the heads of the priests, which is never said of the mitre.

And *put* (margin *bind*) the bonnets on them. Exod. xxix. 9.

And *put* (margin *bound*) bonnets upon them. Lev. viii. 13.

They were probably rolls of fine linen, folded like a turban round the head. The word translated " goodly," (Exod. xxxix. 28,) is worthy of notice. It is rendered " *bonnets.*" Isa. iii. 20, ; Ezek. xliv. 18, ; " *tire of the head.*" Ezek. xxiv. 17, 23, ; " *beauty.*" Isa. lxi. 3. ; " *Ornaments.*" Isa. lxi. 10, and is derived from a verb, signifying " to beautify, or glorify."

These head dresses were therefore for exaltation, for ornament, and for glory and beauty.

It has been before remarked that the covering of the head betokened subjection, and the recognition of being in the presence of a superior. The Jews to this day, always keep their heads covered in the synagogue ; and even in private, when a strict Jew opens the Bible he covers his head. A priestly standing is one of constant subjection to the revealed will of God ; and of abiding consciousness of His presence. And this is true dignity. God has raised us up in perfect righteousness, complete in Christ, ever to abide before Him ; His kings and priests. And in this height of elevation, we walk in the liberty of Christ, holding Him only as our Head, subject to Him in all things, and " not the servants of man." The righteousness of faith—the obedience of faith, instead of the self-will of the flesh, and the unsubject mind, is the truly priestly clothing from head to foot. Being made free from sin we are servants of righteousness, servants of God. Rom. vi. 18, 22. Our blessed occupation is during this night of the world's darkness, to stand in the house of the Lord to praise His name. Psa. cxxxiv. 1 ; cxxxv. 1—3.

These head-tires of white are said to be goodly or ornamental. There was nothing of display to attract the common gaze, but like the adorning recommended for Christian women, (1st Pet. iii. 4, 5,) they were types of the meek and quiet spirit which in the sight of God is of great price. Like the holy women of old who trusted in God, and thus adorned themselves, in subjection to their own husbands.

There is a " glory and beauty " in spotless righteousness which may be little accounted of by men, but which enables us to approach God with confidence, and fits us for His Holy presence. Such was in type the dress of Aaron's sons the priests. Psa. cxxxii. 9.

## THE LINEN BREECHES

"And thou shalt make them linen breeches to cover their nakedness; from the loins even unto the thighs they shall reach :

"And they shall be upon Aaron, and upon his sons, when they come in unto the tabernacle of the congregation, or when they come near unto the altar to minister in the holy place ; that they bear not iniquity, and die : it shall be a statute for ever unto him and his seed after him."—Exod. xxviii 42, 43

"And linen breeches of fine twined linen."—Exod. xxxix 28

A REMARKABLE exception here occurs ; a difficulty is also presented, respecting the materials of which this article of priestly dress was made. In Exod. xxviii. 42, the word *linen* is used; but in the Hebrew " *bad* " is employed to express this, and not " *shehsh*." This last is the word used in all other instances, and denotes the only material of the kind said to be brought by the people ; the word is usually translated *fine linen*. This is not all : for in Exod. xxxix. 28, both words occur, which may be translated " and the breeches the linen (*bad*) ; fine linen twined (*shehsh-mash*)". It may be, two sorts of linen were woven together.

In the other places where these vestments are mentioned they are only called "breeches of linen" (*bad.*) Lev. vi. 10 ; xvi. 4. The garments for gloiy and beauty apparently close at Exod. xxviii. 40, and they seem to be the only garments needed for the consecration of the priests : see v. 41, and Lev. viii. 7, 9, 13. But when officiating in certain service, Aaron and his sons had to put on the linen breeches. "When they came in unto the tabernacle of the congregation, or when they came near unto the altar to minister in the holy place, (v. 43.) That is, when they came into the covered building, or when they ministered at the *incense* altar, which is the altar in the holy place. It is probable therefore, that in all ordinary ministrations at the altar of burnt-offering, they were not worn. The two ceremonies recorded Lev. vi. 10 ; and xvi. 4, being exceptions and peculiar.

The first result of the entrance of sin was to discover to man his own nakedness. The feeling of shame, a guilty feeling crept over his soul : and his attention was immediately directed to some mode of quieting his conscience in this respect, that he might appear unabashed in the presence of his fellow. No thought of his fall as regarded God, or of his inability to stand in His presence, occurred to him. And so it is to this day. The great object which men propose to themselves is to quiet their own consciences, and to stand well with their neighbours. To this end they invent a religion. As soon as we have to do with God, the conscience is convicted, and the guilt and shame which before were quieted, spring up within, and nothing can still the restless uneasiness of the heart. We become aware that all things are naked and opened to the eyes of Him with whom we have to do. The soul in vain attempts concealment. The still small voice of God sounds within, and drags the culprit out to stand before Him.

It is here that a righteousness not our own becomes unspeakably precious to the soul. A covering that both blots out all sin, and for ever clothes the sinner with spotless purity ; which conceals from the searching eye of God all iniquity, and in so doing completely justifies the sinner before Him. Psa. xxxii. 1, 2.

The sinner not only needs, for the sake of his peace, to know that his innumerable transgressions are forgiven, but also, that the sin and iniquity of his evil heart, his evil nature, his corrupt self, is gone for ever from the sight and remembrance of God. The nakedness of the flesh must be obliterated, otherwise there can be no confidence of access to God's presence— there can be no true-hearted service rendered to Him.

These last mentioned garments of the priests directly shadow this truth. They were " to cover the flesh of their nakedness," and to reach " from the loins to the thighs." The whole strength of nature was thus to be concealed ; that strength of evil which would be manifested in the walk of the sinner, and which would oppose God with all its energy, as in the case of Jacob with whom the angel wrestled.

This part of the dress was especially required when the priests entered the more immediate presence of God. They would know more of their own iniquity in proportion as they drew near unto Him. And He provided that covering in order that they might not *bear* their iniquity and die. There seems to be here a beautiful allusion to the truth, so often expressed in the Word of God, viz., that the righteousness of God by faith is justification through the blood. If sin be covered from the eye of Jehovah, He sees perfect righteousness. If the priest could hide his nakedness, " the nakedness of the flesh" from God, he would no longer bear his own iniquity and die. And how can this be accomplished ? Isaiah liii. reveals the way. God's righteous servant justifies many through faith in Him, by having borne their iniquities.

This is one of those eternal statutes, an irreversible decree of the Lord which cannot be evaded. Whoever draws nigh to God, must previously have had his guilt and ruin buried out of sight.

In connection with this type, another precept of the Lord may be noticed. " An altar of earth thou shalt make unto me, and shalt sacrifice thereon thy burnt offerings, and thy peace offerings, thy sheep and thine oxen : in all places where I record my name I will come unto thee, and I will bless thee. And if thou wilt make me an altar of stone, thou shalt not build it of hewn stone : for if thou lift thy tool upon it, thou hast polluted it. Neither shalt thou go up by steps unto mine altar, that thy nakedness be not discovered thereon." Exod. xx. 24—26.

We have here three directions respecting altars which might be erected in certain cases.

If God were to record His name in some peculiar place, an altar might be erected there for burnt-offerings and peace-offerings ; but it must be of earth. This commandment necessitated that the name of Jehovah must first be known and trusted, before sacrifice could be presented to Him. He must have displayed His own power and mercy, so as to record His name, and then the Israelite was at liberty to perpetuate his remembrance of that name, by offerings of sheep and oxen upon an altar of earth.

The altar was not to be the object. In idolatrous worship, the shape and costly materials of which the altar is composed especially engross the thoughts of the worshipper, and it becomes the attractive object. But the name of Jehovah was that which the Israelite had to remember. And earth ready on the spot was to be used for building up a sacrificial place.

Are we not here taught, to lay no stress upon the imposing ceremonials, with which men seek to please the eye and gratify the imagination in religious observances? " Worship in spirit and in truth" is what God requires; and the very absence of pomp and fleshly dignity, will conduce to lowliness of heart and self-abasement, and will at least help towards reality in drawing nigh to God. The altar of earth was a lowly thing, and stood out in contrast with the high places, selected by the heathen nations of Canaan, for their places of worship. Calvary was a place of no esteem. The Cross had no attractiveness for the eye, and He who hung on it had " no beauty that we should desire Him."

If the Israelite made an altar of stone he was not to build it of hewn stone. The rough unhewn stones around him were to be taken ; and no shapeliness to please the natural eye was to be attempted. " To lift up a tool" upon it would pollute it. Here again the same truth is recorded with additions. The Cross of shame, and woe, and curse has in modern days been turned into an ornamental device. It is stamped in gold ; emblazoned in colours ; and worn as an ornament of female dress. Truly it is polluted by being thus handled by human fancy !

We have two kinds of religion running in powerful streams around us ; a Cross without a Christ ; and, a Christ without a Cross.

In the first case the mere emblem is cherished and portrayed in every variety of form ; whilst the living Christ, who died, is not trusted. The emblems of His flesh and blood it may be, reverenced : His flesh and blood in reality not eaten and drunk. Outward adornments of holy things carefully and elaborately wrought. Vestments, and buildings, and altars, studied with deep interest, formed after patterns recovered out of by-gone days of darkness and idolatry ; whilst the true priests washed in the precious blood of the Lamb are almost unknown. The building of " living stones" in union with " the living stone," is disregarded ; and the tree of curse, and He who hung on it, are in reality despised.

In the latter, a Christ without a Cross, a wide-spread taint of Socinianism pervades vast numbers of the religious publications of the day. Christ is presented as an *example* to the unbeliever, instead of being exalted as a Saviour through the blood of His Cross. Mankind is supposed to have been raised in the scale of existence by the Son of God having become man. A kind of regeneration of the human race is preached through "the Word having been made flesh," and the sinner is directed to cultivate his own better thoughts and feelings, and to aim at a kind of mystical abstraction of soul, instead of being pointed to the Son of Man lifted up upon the tree. What is all this but trampling under foot the blood of Christ?

"Steps" were not to be made to God's altar. It was to stand on the level ground, upon the dust of the earth, so that any one might approach it immediately, without having to advance higher and higher to reach it. Beautiful type this, of the universal aspect of the Cross of Christ, presented by God to the whole needy world. No priest stands between the sinner and God to intercede for him, or to help him in his approach, for he needs none. In his ungodliness, his sins, his uncleanness, degraded, lost, undone, a prey of Satan, and steeped in iniquity, he may at once accept the gift of God's love, His blessed Son. Neither has he to advance step by step in reformation or improvement, before he may venture to draw near to the sacrifice God has provided. Every attempt Godward, every step higher, is only a further discovery of the nakedness of the flesh. Every outward amendment, as a plea for the mercy of God is a fresh exposure of the uncleanness and evil of the heart. It is a slander on the death of Christ; it impugns the love and mercy of God. He has fully calculated the sinner's corruption and sin, and He has provided according to that divine calculation, a sufficiency in the blood of the Lamb to meet every necessity; to blot out all iniquity, and to give everlasting righteousness.

If we would see our nakedness in all its evil, God has laid it bare in the death of His Son; and that same death clothes us for ever, and fits us for His glory. A sinner is either far off from God in the distance of utter condemnation ; or, he is made nigh by the blood of Christ. There are no steps of approach or improvement. There can be no interval between death and life : between lost and found.

This concludes the priestly garments for glory and beauty. There were other garments which will be hereafter noticed, mentioned in Leviticus.

When all the work of the tabernacle was finished it was brought to Moses.

"Thus was all the work of the tabernacle of the tent of the congregation finished : and the children of Israel did according to all that the Lord commanded Moses, so did they.

"And they brought the tabernacle unto Moses, the tent, and all his furniture, his taches, his boards, his bars, and his pillars, and his sockets,

"And the covering of rams' skins dyed red, and the covering of badgers' skins, and the vail of the covering,

"The ark of the testimony, and the staves thereof, and the mercy seat,

"The table, and all the vessels thereof, and the shewbread,

"The pure candlestick, with the lamps thereof, even with the lamps to be set in order, and all the vessels thereof, and the oil for light,

"And the golden altar, and the anointing oil, and the sweet incense, and the hanging for the tabernacle door,

"The brazen altar, and his gate of brass, his staves, and all his vessels, the laver and his foot,

"The hangings of the court, his pillars, and his sockets, and the hanging for the court gate, his cords, and his pins, and all the vessels of the service of the tabernacle, for the tent of the congregation,

"The cloths of service to do service in the holy place, and the holy garments for Aaron the priest, and his sons' garments, to minister in the priest's office.

"According to all that the Lord commanded Moses, so the children of Israel made all the work.

"And Moses did look upon all the work, and, behold, they had done it as the Lord had commanded, even so had they done it : and Moses blessed them."—Exod. xxix 32—43

THE enumeration of the things thus made, is divided out into seven portions, as may be perceived on looking down the verses : connecting those together which begin with the word " and." For instance, verses 33 and 34 are the first portions, viz, the tabernacle and vail.

Verse 35, the second, the ark and mercy seat.

Verse 36, the third, the table of shewbread and its vessels.

Verses 37 and 38, the fourth, including the candle-stick, the golden altar of incense, the anointing oil, and the tabernacle door.

Verse 39, the fifth, the brazen altar and the laver.

Verse 40, the sixth, the court of the tabernacle.

Verse 41, the seventh, the cloths of service, and the priests' garments.

There is in this enumeration a classing together of certain things which are more intimately connected, and which it is interesting to contemplate. The vail is classed with the tabernacle itself : because it divided the building into two distinct parts or rooms, and it is called the vail of the covering because it covered or hid the ark and mercy-seat, and holy of holies. (Allusion has been before made to this in the exposition of the vail.)

The candlestick, golden altar, anointing oil, and sweet incense, are classed together, because there was a close connection between them. Incense was burned upon the altar when the lamps were dressed and lighted. One constituent also of the anointing oil, was the same kind of oil as that for the light. Light, fragrance of Christ's work, and the graces of the Holy Spirit, are closely connected together. The hanging of the taber-nacle door was also classed with these, because, by means of that door, the way of access was provided to these vessels of priestly service.*

The brazen altar and laver are connected, for no ministry could take place at the former, unless the priests had washed their hands and feet at the latter. It is to be observed also, that all the vessels of service were presented to Moses, ready for use. The mercy-seat was brought with the ark and staves. The shewbread was presented with the table. Oil for light with the candlestick, and sweet incense with the golden altar.

This betokens an understanding of the objects for which these various holy vessels were made. We should

---

* In the work on "The Holy Vessels," this subject is fully treated, together with the connection of the different Vessels of the Tabernacle one with the other,

do well to imitate this by seeking to know more of the various blessed occupations of our High Priest in the presence of God for us.

This is the only chapter in the Bible where it is recorded of a people, that they finished and did all that the Lord commanded. This is thrice repeated.

"The children of Israel did according to all that the Lord commanded Moses, so did they."

"According to all that the Lord commanded Moses, so the children of Israel made all the work."

"They had done it as the Lord had commanded, even so had they done it." Exod. xxxix. 32, 42, 43.

What a high commendation is this! Where shall we find a people who have followed this example? Can it be said of the Church of God—according to all that the Lord has commanded, so have they done. Have we attended as minutely to His directions, as this people followed accurately the commandments of the Lord given to them by Moses. His word to us, is, "If ye love me keep my commandments." Alas! we seem to think we may dispense with this little precept, or vary that appointment as we think fit. We hear of "non-essentials," and "things that are immaterial." Sometimes even the question is asked, "what does it signify?"

Could the Lord have placed this thrice repeated commendation of the children of Israel, at the close of this book of Exodus, if they had felt at liberty to omit some little "border" of a holy vessel—some "pin" or "cord;" or if they had thought the golden altar too plain, and had added ornaments to it: or the dress of the priests too common, and had embroidered it with more costly materials? If God's directions were enough for *them*, and they kept within His commandments, adding nothing to them, and omitting none of them; ought we not to consider that His words in the New Testament are sufficient for *our* instruction and guidance, in all matters of Gospel truth, worship, and service? Would it not be well for us to confine ourselves within the limits of His holy word, and also to hold all the truths it contains ?

We have moreover an infallible interpreter ever present with us, and dwelling in us ; the Spirit of truth, the Holy Ghost ; so that we are without excuse if we abide by human traditions, instead of cleaving to the word of God ; or if we willingly remain in ignorance of what that word declares.

The blessing of Moses rested on the people, when he saw how they had carried out to the letter the will of God. The blessing of a greater than Moses will abundantly rest on us, if we diligently give ourselves, first to ascertain the mind of God as revealed in His word ; and next, seek to the utmost of our power by the help of the Holy Spirit, to carry out the mind and will of God. As we do His will we shall still know more of His teaching. Our path will become more and more the path of the righteous, of the obedient ones, shining more and more unto the perfect day. And we shall find our prayers more fully answered, and our hearts more full of joy. And our fellowship with the Father and with His Son, Jesus Christ, and with one another will be more complete and uninterrupted. "If ye abide in me, and my words abide in you, ye shall ask what ye will and it shall be done unto you." John xv. 7. "If a man love me, he will keep my words : and my Father will love him, and we will come unto him, and make our abode with him." xiv. 23.

# THE REARING UP OF THE TABERNACLE

"And the Lord spake unto Moses, saying,

"On the first day of the first month shalt thou set up the tabernacle of the tent of the congregation.

"And thou shalt put therein the ark of the testimony, and cover the ark with the vail.

"And thou shalt bring in the table, and set in order the things that are to be set in order upon it; and thou shalt bring in the candlestick, and light the lamps thereof.

"And thou shalt set the altar of gold for the incense before the ark of the testimony, and put the hanging of the door to the tabernacle.

"And thou shalt set the altar of the burnt offering before the door of the tabernacle of the tent of the congregation.

"And thou shalt set the laver between the tent of the congregation and the altar, and shalt put water therein.

"And thou shalt set up the court round about, and hang up the hanging at the court gate.

"And thou shalt take the anointing oil, and anoint the tabernacle, and all that is therein, and shalt hallow it, and all the vessels thereof: and it shall be holy.

"And thou shalt anoint the altar of the burnt offering, and all nis vessels, and sanctify the altar: and it shall be an altar most holy.

"And thou shalt anoint the laver and his foot, and sanctify it.

"And thou shalt bring Aaron and his sons unto the door of the tabernacle of the congregation, and wash them with water.

"And it came to pass in the first month in the second year, on the first day of the month, that the tabernacle was reared up.

"And Moses reared up the tabernacle, and fastened his sockets, and set up the boards thereof, and put in the bars thereof, and reared up his pillars.

"And he spread abroad the tent over the tabernacle, and put the covering of the tent above upon it; as the Lord commanded Moses.

"And he took and put the testimony into the ark, and set the staves on the ark, and put the mercy seat above upon the ark:

"And he brought the ark into the tabernacle, and set up the vail of the covering, and covered the ark of the testimony; as the Lord commanded Moses.

"And he put the table in the tent of the congregation, upon the side of the tabernacle northward, without the vail.

"And he set the bread in order upon it before the Lord; as the Lord commanded Moses.

"And he put the candlestick in the tent of the congregation, over against the table, on the side of the tabernacle southward.

"And he lighted the lamps before the Lord; as the Lord commanded Moses.

"And he put the golden altar in the tent of the congregation before the vail:

"And he burnt sweet incense thereon; as the Lord commanded Moses.

"And he set up the hanging at the door of the tabernacle.

"And he put the altar of burnt offering by the door of the taber-

The Tabernacle with Its Coverings Rolled Back

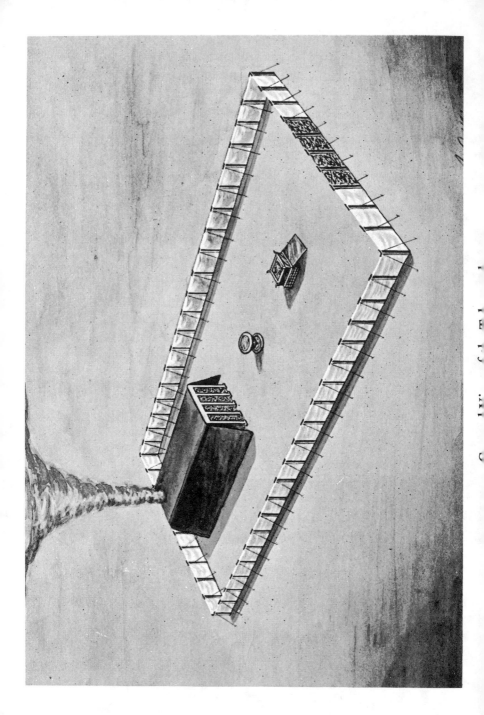

"And thou shalt put upon Aaron the holy garments, and anoint him, and sanctify him; that he may minister unto me in the priest's office.

"And thou shalt bring his sons, and clothe them with coats:

"And thou shalt anoint them, as thou didst anoint their father, that they may minister unto me in the priest's office: for their anointing shall surely be an everlasting priesthood throughout their generations.

"Thus did Moses: according to all that the Lord commanded him, so did he."—Exod. xl 1—16

nacle of the tent of the congregation, and offered upon it the burnt offering and the meat offering; as the Lord commanded Moses.

"And he set the laver between the tent of the congregation and the altar, and put water there, to wash withal.

"And Moses and Aaron and his sons washed their hands and their feet thereat:

"When they went into the tent of the congregation, and when they came near unto the altar, they washed; as the Lord commanded Moses.

"And he reared up the court round about the tabernacle and the altar, and set up the hanging of the court gate. So Moses finished the work."—Exod. xl 17—33

A NEW order of time was instituted by God when Israel was delivered from wrath and from Egypt, through the blood of the paschal Lamb. "And the Lord spake unto Moses and Aaron in the land of Egypt, saying, This month shall be unto you the beginning of months, it shall be the first month of the year to you." Exod. xii. 1, 2. For the first time also was that people nationally contemplated, and constituted an assembly or congregation, (v. 6,) and accounted the hosts of the Lord. v. 41.

The name Israel was then given to them, (v. 15,) and they were reckoned in houses and families. v. 3, 21, 27. Thus they dated their existence as a people from the ordinance of the passover, and their first year commenced.

The months had run out during their sojourn in the wilderness, and now their second year of national existence was celebrated by the erection of the Tabernacle. God selected the desert for this glorious building. He could not dwell in the midst of them in Egypt; but as strangers and pilgrims, redeemed by the blood of the Lamb to Himself, separated off from that land of darkness and of death, He could take up His abode in the midst of them.  He could dwell among them and walk among them, and be their God  They were His people.  A striking type this of God in reality dwelling in the midst of His church, because they are a people redeemed to Him by the blood of the true paschal Lamb.  " Not of the world even as Christ is not of the world."

As the people had completed *their* part of the work according to the minute commands of God ; so Moses did " according to all the Lord commanded *him*, so did he."  And seven times is that short emphatic sentence repeated " as the Lord commanded Moses.  Exod. xl. 19, 21, 23, 25, 27, 29, 32.  The tabernacle was made, reared up, filled with its appointed vessels, and set in order for use according to the exact requirements of God.  No pin was wanting, no addition to the perfect work was attempted.  And the same word " finished," (so Moses finished the work, v. 33,) is emphatically used, as when God had completed His work of creation.  " Thus the heavens and the earth were *finished :* and in the seventh day God *ended* His work which He had made."  Gen. ii. 1, 2.  His creation work was ended on the seventh day.  This work of the Tabernacle was finished on the *first* day.  A type of the great redemption work of Christ, which was completed on the day of His resurrection, the first day of the week.

# THE CLOUD

" Then a cloud covered the tent of the congregation, and the glory
of the Lord filled the tabernacle.

" And Moses was not able to enter into the tent of the congregation,
because the cloud abode thereon, and the glory of the Lord filled the
tabernacle.

" And when the cloud was taken up from over the tabernacle, the
children of Israel went onward in all their journeys :

" But if the cloud were not taken up, then they journeyed not till
the day that it was taken up.

" For the cloud of the Lord was upon the tabernacle by day, and fire
was on it by night, in the sight of all the house of Israel, throughout
all their journeys."—Exod. xl 34—38

THE first mention of the Cloud occurs in Exod. xiii
20—22. " And they took their journey from Succoth,
and encamped in Etham, in the edge of the wilderness.
And the Lord went before them by day in a pillar of a
cloud, to lead them the way ; and by night in a pillar of
fire, to give them light ; to go by day and night : He
took not away the pillar of the cloud by day, nor the
pillar of fire by night, from before the people."

The Israelites had fairly left Egypt, having journeyed
from Succoth, *(booths,)* and encamped in the edge of the
wilderness. The Lord now manifested His presence as
their Leader, going before them by day, in the pillar of
a cloud, and by night, in the pillar of fire. The first
guidance of this cloud was indeed a strange one : for,
instead of leading them far away into the wilderness out
of the reach of their enemies, it turned down by the
west coast of the Red Sea, and led them into a defile,
where they were shut in by the sea, in their front, and
mountains on each side, so that Pharoah said, " they are
entangled in the land." They seemed to offer him an
easy prey ; and he pursued them with all his host.

The cloud having thus brought them into a place of
difficulty, next varied its position. " And the angel of
God, which went before the camp of Israel, removed
and went behind them ; and the pillar of the cloud went

*317*

from before their face, and stood behind them. And it came between the camp of the Egyptians and the camp of Israel; and it was a cloud and darkness to them, but it gave light by night to these : so that the one came not near the other all the night." Exod. xiv. 19, 20. The cloud became their defence, protecting them from the approach of the enemy. It also lighted up a path between walls of deep and dark waters, opened for them through the sea, by the almighty power of God.

Pharaoh urged on by the blinding power of Satan, pursued them into the sea. " And it came to pass, that in the morning watch the Lord looked unto the host of the Egyptians through the pillar of fire and of the cloud, and troubled the host of the Egyptians, and took off their chariot wheels, that they drave them heavily : so that the Egyptians said, Let us flee from the face of Israel; for the Lord fighteth for them against the Egyptians." ver. 24, 25.

Thus was that mighty host of Egypt taken in its own craftiness. The swift chariots of their strength became the hindrance to their escape ; and when the morning dawned, and Moses at the command of God, stretched forth his hand over the sea, the sea returned to its strength, and overwhelmed in its mighty waters all the host of Pharaoh : " There remained not so much as one of them."

The next record of the cloud is in Exod. xvi. 10. The whole congregation murmured because they saw no provision of bread to supply their need. They had become accustomed to the presence of the cloud after a month's journeyings. That which at first doubtless astonished and comforted them, (the manifested presence of God going before them,) had become an ordinary thing, and they turned their murmurings against Moses and Aaron, declaring that *they* had brought them into the wilderness, to kill the whole assembly with hunger.

The Lord answers these bitter complaints of unbelief

by a promise of fulness of bread. "And Moses and
Aaron said unto the children of Israel, At even then ye
shall know that the Lord hath brought you out of the
land of Egypt. And in the morning then ye shall see
the glory of the Lord," (ver. 6, 7.)

The quails were to cover the camp in the evening,
and the manna was to witness to the glory of the Lord
in the morning. In confirmation of this, Moses spake
unto Aaron, "Say unto all the congregation of the
children of Israel, Come near before the Lord : for he
hath heard your murmurings. And it came to pass, as
Aaron spake unto the whole congregation of the
children of Israel, that they looked towards the wilderness, and, behold, the glory of the Lord appeared in
the cloud," (ver. 9, 10.)

Here were two remarkable displays of the glory
of Jehovah. A manifestation of that glory in the
morning, in the vast provision of bread from heaven,
strewed upon "the face of the wilderness." A display
also of His glory in the bright shining cloud, appearing
before them in the same wilderness. Two very significant types to us. First, the gift of the bread of life ;
a resurrection gift : to communicate life eternal, and
then to sustain it. Jesus, "the true bread from heaven,"
our wilderness food. Secondly, the constant companionship of God with us through our wilderness journey,
notwithstanding the murmurings of our unbelieving
hearts.

After the fearful sin of the golden calf "Moses took
the tent, and pitched it without the camp, afar off from
the camp, and called it the tent of the congregation, and
it came to pass that every one which sought the Lord
went out unto the tent of the congregation which was
without the camp. And it came to pass when Moses
went into the tent, that all the people rose up and stood
every man at his tent door, and looked after Moses until
he was gone into the tent. And it came to pass, as
Moses entered into the tent, the cloudy pillar descended,

and stood at the tent door, and talked with Moses. And all the people saw the cloudy pillar stand at the tent door : and all the people rose up and worshipped, every man in his tent door." Exod. xxxiii. 7—10.

It will be observed that throughout this passage the word " tabernacle " does not occur in the original. In fact the tabernacle had not yet been constructed.

Moses took a *tent* (probably that in which he was accustomed to assemble the elders of the people for their instruction) and pitched it afar off without the camp, giving it the name subsequently used for the tabernacle, that is, " the tent of the congregation." God sanctioned this act of His servant by descending to the tent door in the pillar of the cloud, and thence talking with Moses.

The camp had become a leprous unclean place by reason of the worship of the golden calf, and every one that sought the Lord, had to go out afar off from it.

Israel's dwelling place in the wilderness had become very much what the professing church is now. Moses had gone up into the mount, and the people having lost sight of the man to whom they had attributed their deliverance out of Egypt, were in dismay because they saw no leader who could go before them through the wilderness. Their eyes were blinded by unbelief, so that they saw not the pillar of the cloud, and they remembered not the mighty power of Jehovah, who had wrought their deliverance. The flesh can only trust in man, " and make flesh its arm." It cannot confide in the living God.

Aaron, actuated it may be by fear, yielded to their request, and made a molten calf of gold, and fashioned it with a graving tool, and they said "These be thy gods O Israel which brought thee up out of the land of Egypt. And Aaron built an altar before it, and made proclamation, and said, Tomorrow is a feast to Jehovah."

How could nominal Christianity exist if it were not sustained by an ordered worldly priesthood, with a worldly sanctuary and ceremonials ? It bears the name

of Christ, just as the worship of the golden calf bore
the name of Jehovah, but it is the flesh's substitute for
faith. It addresses the senses, or deals with the imagination, but heart and conscience are neglected.

It is remarkable in this history that the people called
themselves by the one name of Israel, just as the mass
of unbelievers claim to be Christians.

" And they rose up early on the morrow, and offered
burnt offerings, and brought peace offerings ; and the
people sat down to eat and to drink, and rose up to play."
The Spirit of God quotes the latter part of this verse
in 1st Cor. x. 7, as an exhortation to us, " neither be
ye idolators as were some of them ; as it is written, the
people sat down to eat and drink, and rose up to play."

We are not so much warned against the grossness of
idolatry as displayed in the worship of a golden calf, and
as it may still be seen in the Popery and Puseyism
around us. It requires but little spiritual sensitiveness
to recoil from such barefaced abominations. But, we
are exhorted not to follow the worldly practices which
inseparably accompany all false religion ; viz., sitting
down to eat and drink, and rising up to play.

When the people of Israel mixed the name of their true
God with an idol, they settled down in the wilderness,
turning it into a very Egypt, or Sodom ; making it a
place of revelry and amusement. And so, in proportion
as the Church of God ceases to walk by faith, and to
trust in the unseen presence of an absent Lord, and to wait
for His return, she will settle down at ease in the world;
she will make that, which should be a desert, a place of
rest and enjoyment; and she will " begin to eat and drink
with the drunken," saying in her heart, " my Lord
delayeth His coming."

" Dearly beloved, I beseech you as strangers and
pilgrims abstain from fleshly lusts, which war against
the soul." 1st Peter ii. 11. " Little children, keep
yourselves from idols." 1st John v. 21.

Moses, who had been up with the Lord during this

scene of profanation, discerned at once the polluted state of the camp ; and pitched the tent for a meeting place with God afar off ; and all the true worshippers resorted thither, where the Lord manifested His presence in the pillar of the cloud.

Thus early in Israel's history, the place of little esteem in the eyes of men, became that of true fellowship with God.

Subsequently the death of the Lord Jesus outside the gate of Jerusalem, proclaimed the same truth in a still more emphatic way ; and the apostle exhorts us to " go forth unto Jesus, without the camp, bearing his reproach, for here have we no continuing city, but we seek one to come." The Cross of Christ has put an end to all religion of mere form and ceremony. Even that which was originally handed down from God by Moses, has become a system of weak and beggarly elements, classed by the apostle Paul with idolatry, (Gal. iv. 8—10) and true-hearted believers separating themselves from the religions of the day, have to follow their Lord, bearing His reproach ; seeking a city that is to come, daily realizing that they are strangers here ; and instead of conforming to the world and its respectable religious ceremonies, they are to " assemble themselves together, exhorting one another, and so much the more as they see the day approaching."

Moses, after having conversed with God face to face, turned again into the Camp. He was able to re-enter the place of profanation without contracting defilement, because he had the power and presence of God with him. " But his servant Joshua, a young man, departed not out of the tabernacle." (tent.)

This is an important hint to those who are young in faith, not to venture into worldly scenes, or into mixed religious associations, lest they become ensnared, and be not able to stand. Like Joshua they should abide in the presence of the Lord, even though it involve separation from much that is attractive and enticing.

Moses in his pleading with God on this occasion makes three requests, of all importance. Three petitions which it will be well for us to have constantly in our hearts.

" Shew me now thy way ;" " If thy presence go not with me, carry us not up hence ;" and, " I beseech thee shew me thy glory."

God's way is in the sanctuary, (Psa. lxxvii. 13) there the blood of the Lamb speaks in a voice of peace and reconciliation. There the holiness of God is made known by His judgment upon sin, in the cross of His beloved Son. God's way is a way of holiness and righteousness ; and if we would pursue His path, we must avoid all ways into which we cannot carry the remembrance of the cross. We must shun all companionships from which the name of Jesus is excluded. A way, without the power to testify to the precious blood of Christ, cannot be God's way.

If we know His way, we are then sure of His presence. He will go with us. And what is life worth, if God be not with us ? Where can the soul find rest ? How can peace of mind be preserved, but by abiding in the secret place of the Most High—and how can we prosper, or triumph, or bear fruit, unless we are habitually in the presence of God ? Moses knew that if God went with them they would be truly a separated people from all the people upon the face of the earth. The way and presence of God will ever preserve us from contacts with the world around us.

Emboldened by God's ready response to his requests, Moses made a third petition, " I beseech thee shew me thy glory." "And the Lord said, I will make all my goodness pass before thee." So the Lord provided for Moses a place by Him that he might stand upon *the rock*, and be put in a cleft of the rock, and be covered with His hand.

Accordingly Moses went up into Mount Sinai in the morning, and then the Lord descended in the cloud and stood with him and passed by before him, and proclaimed "Jehovah, Jehovah God, merciful and gracious, long-suffering, and abundant in goodness and truth, keeping mercy for thousands, forgiving iniquity and transgression and sin, and that will by no means clear the guilty; visiting the iniquity of the fathers upon the children, and upon the children's children, unto the third, and to the fourth generation."

Thus from this cloud of glory the Lord made all His goodness pass before Moses and proclaimed His name. The name by which He was to be known throughout all the hosts of Israel, and which He would make manifest in all His dealings with them. Blessed as this revelation of God was, yet it only gave a distant view of His glory. It remained for "the only begotten of the Father" to declare His name fully. The blessed Lord in the very act of revealing God in all the height and depth of His boundless love, and wisdom and grace, through His death, provided at the same time a way of approach to God; whereby with confidence we may draw near, and know His unveiled glory, and abide in His holy presence without fear.

God has provided for us the "Rock of Ages," He has hidden us in a cleft of that rock : He has sheltered us by His hand. But He has done more than give us a distant or passing view of Himself. We have *seen* the Father, we have *known* the Father. John xiv. 7—9.

When the Tabernacle was set up as described in Exod. xl., then the cloud covered the tent of the congregation, and the glory of the Lord filled the Tabernacle. This is repeated twice, verses 34, 35. It is interesting to observe that the two names are here given "the tent of the congregation," and "the tabernacle." The former designating this building as the tent of assembly for the people, Israel ; the latter as the dwelling place of God.

A striking similarity occurs between this setting up of the Tabernacle, and the subsequent consecration of the

Temple. " And it came to pass, when the priests were come out of the holy place, that the cloud filled the house of the Lord, so that the priests could not stand to minister because of the cloud : for the glory of the Lord had filled the house of the Lord." 1st Kings viii. 10, 11 ; see also 2nd Chron. v. 13, 14. In both instances a dwelling place had been erected according to the precise directions given by God. Neither man's thought, or taste, or imagination had been consulted. But the Lord had given the complete pattern, and Moses with the workmen under him, and Solomon with those employed by him, had to the letter, fulfilled the commands of God. May we not say that *implicit obedience* was the peculiar characteristic stamped upon each building, and upon every part.

There is however, a difference between the two consecrations. In the case of the tabernacle it is simply related that Moses finished the work, then a cloud covered the tent of the congregation. The lamps had been lighted, the incense was burning in the holy place, the burnt-offering was sending up its sweet savour from the brazen altar ; the tabernacle, and its vessels, were standing complete and in full use, before the Lord ; when thus He manifested His presence and glory, in approval of the faithful way in which His requirements had been carried out ; and according to His promise, " there I will meet with the children of Israel, and the tabernacle shall be sanctified by my glory. And I will sanctify the tabernacle of the congregation, and the altar : I will sanctify also both Aaron and his sons, to minister to me in the priest's office. And I will dwell among the children of Israel, and will be their God. And they shall know that I am the Lord their God, that brought them forth out of the land of Egypt, that I may dwell among them : I am the Lord their God." Exod. xxix. 43—46.

This was a dwelling place for the Lord in the midst of His people, during their wilderness journey, and

during their season of warfare and conflict in the land
before it was subdued, so that a reign of peace might
begin under Solomon.

We find in the Epistle to the Hebrews the tabernacle
alone mentioned as a type, and no direct reference to
the temple; because we are strangers and pilgrims,
pressing on, towards our glorious city of habitation
whose maker and builder is God; and we have at the
same time conflict with wicked spirits in heavenly places,
seeking to hinder us from keeping possession of our
own inheritance above, into which we have already
been introduced in Christ; and where by faith we
stand.

When the temple was dedicated, the ark had entered
its final rest; for the staves which bore it on the journey
were removed from their rings. Countless victims from
the altar sent up their sweet savour towards God, and
one sound of trumpet, music, and song, burst forth
from priests and Levites, " praising the Lord for he
is good for his mercy endureth for ever." It was a
scene typical of the future glory, when the resurrection
shout, blended with the trumpet's sound from heaven
and rolling on " as the voice of many waters and as the
voice of mighty thunderings," combined with harp and
song, will sound forth the great eternal truth, that God
is good, that His mercy endureth for ever.

In both instances the cloud of glory so filled the
place that all human ministry was suspended. Moses
was not able to enter the tabernacle; indeed he had
finished his work—the great object was accomplished,
God was there. The priests could not stand to minister
in the temple, for the great end of their priesthood was
accomplished, the glory of God filled the house.

" And on the day that the tabernacle was reared up
the cloud covered the tabernacle, namely the tent of the
testimony: and at even there was upon the tabernacle
as it were the appearance of fire, until the morning. So
it was alway: the cloud covered it by day, and the

appearance of fire by night. And when the cloud was taken up from the tabernacle, then after that the children of Israel journeyed : and in the place where the cloud abode, there the children of Israel pitched their tents. At the commandment of the Lord the children of Israel journeyed, and at the commandment of the Lord they pitched : as long as the cloud abode upon the tabernacle they rested in their tents. And when the cloud tarried long upon the tabernacle many days, then the children of Israel kept the charge of the Lord, and journeyed not. And so it was, when the cloud was a few days upon the tabernacle ; according to the commandment of the Lord they abode in their tents, and according to the commandment of the Lord they journeyed. And so it was, when the cloud abode from even unto the morning, and that the cloud was taken up in the morning, then they journeyed : whether it was by day or by night that the cloud was taken up, they journeyed. Or whether it were two days, or a month, or a year, that the cloud tarried upon the tabernacle, remaining thereon, the children of Israel abode in their tents, and journeyed not : but when it was taken up, they journeyed. At the commandment of the Lord they rested in the tents, and at the commandment of the Lord they journeyed : they kept the charge of the Lord, at the commandment of the Lord by the hand of Moses." Numb. ix. 15—23.

In this passage we have a very full account of the cloud. And seven times do the words " at the commandment of the Lord" occur in connection with this manifestation of His presence. " At the commandment of the Lord the children of Israel journeyed." (Verses 18, 20, 23.) " At the commandment of the Lord," they pitched, abode in their tents, rested in their tents. (Verses 18, 20, 23.) " At the commandment of the Lord they kept the charge of the Lord." (Ver. 23.)

The moving of the cloud was " the commandment of the Lord" for their journeying. The resting of the cloud was " the commandment of the Lord" for pitching their tents. The prolonged tarrying of the cloud upon the tabernacle, was " the commandment of the Lord" for them to keep the charge of the Lord.

Throughout this passage, the word translated *commandment*, is literally " *mouth*."

The cloud was God's mode of declaring to them His will ; and they had to watch its movements in order to ascertain that will.

We have no external beacon to direct us, as to our journeys through this world. But we have that which is far better, the in-dwelling of the Holy Spirit. Far better, because God does not deal with us now as slaves, bidding us go hither and thither without our having any fellowship with Him or His purposes. He deals with us as children, having given us the spirit of Sonship whereby we cry, " Abba, Father." He would have us seek to know His mind and will in every fresh change that we propose. In this respect the Word must first be consulted that we may ascertain whether the counsel of our hearts is in any way opposed to the smallest injunctions of Christ. If so, it is plain that we have not the guidance of God for our undertaking.

On the other hand, there are many changes in our place of service, or in our circumstances of life, which may have in them no decided evil as contrary to the direct word of God ; but which must be yet submitted to Him in prayerful and patient waiting, that we may have His guidance.

In these things we are very ignorant of the leadings of the Holy Spirit. He has been so long grieved by us, and our faith is so weak, that we are but little conscious of His blessed directing power. Doubtless where there is confession of our low estate, and a true desire to ascertain the will of God, He will make known that will, either by a direct intimation upon our souls, or by so ordering circumstances round us, that we shall be able to perceive it.

We have to learn from Israel's history, to move at a moment's notice. The cloud was often an inconvenient interruption to their will. By night or day they had to journey. Scarcely had they pitched their tents, when again the signal might be given for another journey onward. The place they were in might seem most convenient; and yet they might have to remove to a spot just the contrary. God gave no account of His purposes. The cloud seemed to be an expression of the words " I will."

Are we content to be guided by God, when that guidance crosses our self-will and our purposes? Do we really believe that He knows best? And are our utterances true, when we ask for His leading, and when we profess to desire to know His will?

When the cloud tarried long, Israel was not to be listless or impatient. They had always a definite work and service to accomplish, expressed by the words, " to keep the charge of the Lord."

So the believer has always a service for God, and an important one, though his daily life may have but little variety. He has to contemplate Christ. He has to keep his heart with all diligence. He has to remember his fellow saints in prayer. He has to learn what "the patience of hope" means; and what is expressed by those words, " I waited patiently for the Lord." And how they may be combined with the concluding paragraph of the same Psalm, " make no tarrying O my God." xl. 1. 17.

Many a saint of God has to endure long the monotony of a couch of weakness and sickness, laid aside from active service, and perhaps deprived of much power of thought; but to such the church of God owes much They are sustaining the hands of many servants of the Lord by prayers night and day. Their faith and patience are a bright testimony for Jesus; and the sick chamber is often a meeting place for many of the Lord's people.

"The fruit of the spirit, love, joy, peace, long-suffering, gentleness, goodness, faith, meekness, temperance," may be all abundantly borne to the glory of God, by those who are quite excluded from the activities of the Christian life. Very precious, and alas! comparatively rare, is such fruit.

" The pillar of the cloud by day," became " a pillar of fire by night." It was to give light in the night ; "by night in a pillar of fire to give them light." Exod. xiii. 21.

" It gave light by night to these." (Israel) xiv. 20. " Fire to give light in the night." Psa. cv. 39. " The pillar of fire by night, to shew them light." Neh. ix. 19.

Thus light streamed from the tabernacle all over the camp. The darkness was no darkness to them. " The night was light about them." Psa. cxxxix. 11.

A very significant type of the church of God, who not only have the Lord Jesus as their light, but who are "light in the Lord." God has brought us out of darkness into His marvellous light. And we are no longer "of the night, nor of darkness," but "children of light and of the day." Although it is night all around, yet the true light shineth upon God's children, and that light makes manifest what is true and what is false.

A wonderful message has been declared to us, that " God is light, and in him is no darkness at all." He can allow of no compromise with evil. Ways of crookedness and expediency, which we find sometimes practised by saints in the Old Testament times, cannot be permitted now, since this message has been delivered to us, that God is light. A message confirmed by the solemn judgment upon sin, manifested in the cross of Christ.

" If we say we have fellowship with him, and walk in darkness, we lie and do not the truth." We may make strong assertions respecting our intercourse with God, but if we walk in darkness, our assertions are mere falsehood.

The truth has to be "done" —lived— and we shall

shew by our ways whether we have communion with God. "But if we walk in the light as he is in the light, we have fellowship one with another, and the blood of Jesus Christ his Son cleanseth us from all sin."

One great evidence of walking in the light is, that we have fellowship one with another. Fellowship, not with a restricted company, not merely with those who think precisely as we do, but with *one another*. The words "one another" have a wide sense—they include all saints ; and we may fairly estimate our communion with the Father and the Son, by our capacity for fellowship with the Lord's people. We shall also more constantly realize the cleansing power of the precious blood as we walk in the light with God, and as intercourse with one another causes the evil of our hearts, the sectarian spirit of the flesh to rise up within our bosoms ; discovering of what spirit we naturally are, and necessarily casting us upon the value of that blood, which not only has cleansed, but *cleanseth* us from all sin.

The pillar was not only a light to the whole camp, but gave light in the way. "Thou leddest them in the night by a pillar of fire, to give them light in the way wherein they should go." "The pillar of fire by night, to shew them light, and the way wherein they should go." Neh. ix. 12, 19. Our path may sometimes be very obscure, and then the danger is, that we seek by our own wisdom and efforts to throw light upon it. Oftentimes also the believer mistakes the *providences* of God, for the guidance of God. Moses is an instructive example to us in this respect. By a remarkable series of events, he was made to pass the first forty years of his life in Pharaoh's court ; brought up as the son of Pharaoh's daughter. Carnal reasoning would have suggested, "continue where you are, God has placed you in your present circumstances, and you may be very useful in your place of honour and authority, both in easing the burdens of the children of Israel, and in instructing the learned in Egypt in the knowledge of the true God." But he judged otherwise. Light from the Lord told him that the reproach of Christ was to be preferred to the treasures of Egypt. Making one bold decided step, he identified himself with an oppressed, despised people. Setting aside all the advantages in which from his infancy he had been remarkably placed by the providence of God, he took the path of faith, and became for many years a wanderer far off from his brethren, whom it was his desire to serve.

On the other hand Abraham, in his early history exhibits to us the opposite of this. Having been led into the land of promise by the guidance of God ; and having implicity trusted Him for a length of time ; when famine came he went down into Egypt, not consulting the Lord as to his course, but induced by the fact that there was plenty in that country, whilst there was scarcity in the land where he was.

The results of this false step clave to him for many years ; Hagar the Egyptian slave was brought from thence.

Should we not be able to discern the guidance of God ; should the pillar by night be for some reason hidden from our sight, it is an intimation to us that we are to be still. " Who is among you that feareth the Lord, that obeyeth the voice of his servant, that walketh in darkness, and. hath no light ? let him trust in the name of the Lord, and stay upon his God." Isa. l. 10. We are to exercise *faith* in our God ; to trust in Him, and stay or lean upon Him. Perhaps there is no more difficult or trying exercise of faith, than patiently to wait for the help and guidance of the Lord, when circumstances are difficult and dark. The flesh prone to be either restless or sluggish, would tempt one to activity when the Lord says, " wait ;" and to indolence when He says, "act."

" Behold, all ye that kindle a fire, that compass yourselves about with sparks ; walk in the light of your fire, and in the sparks that ye have kindled. This shall ye have of mine hand, ye shall lie down in sorrow. Ver. 11.

The Lord preserve us from walking in the false light of our carnal wisdom, and from compassing ourselves about with sparks of human reason and expediency.

The word of God, and the Spirit of God, will be our infallible guides, if we truly submit ourselves and our own will to them. "Thy word is a lamp unto my feet, and a light unto my path." That word which first gave light by its entrance into the soul through the power of the Holy Ghost, will continue to shed its light upon the path all our journey through.

"Light is *sown* for the righteous." The "incorruptible seed" of the word is scattered by the hand of God all along our way ; and the more faithfully we follow the guidance of that word, the more will our path be that of the just, shining more and more unto the perfect day.

Another use of the cloud was to be a covering or shelter for Israel during the day. The first allusion to this is in Num. x. 34, "And the cloud of the Lord was upon them by day, when they went out of the camp." In this instance the cloud seems to have been displaced. Moses sought to induce Hobab to accompany the children of Israel in their journeys ; and on his refusal, repeated his request upon the ground that they were to encamp in the wilderness, and that he might be to them instead of eyes. The Lord could not permit this. No human wisdom or experience could be allowed to supplant the direct guidance of God. Accordingly we find that the Lord Himself took the lead, (if we may so express it, in person,) for the ark of the covenant of the Lord went before them. The cloud thus superseded by the ark, spread itself over them by day, when they went out of the camp on the march. An allusion to this is again made, Num. xiv. 14. "Thy cloud standeth over them," and Psa. cv. 39, "He spread a cloud for a covering." If we are under the guidance of God, we are also under

His protection and shelter. "The Lord is thy keeper. The Lord is thy shade upon thy right hand. The sun shall not smite thee by day, nor the moon by night. The Lord shall preserve thy going out and thy coming in from this time forth, and even for evermore." Psa. cxxi. 5, 6, 8.

The cloud on ordinary occasions, searched out a fitting place for a temporary rest in the wilderness, where they might pitch their tents. Deut. i. 33, "Who went in the way before you to search you out a place to pitch your tents in, in fire by night, to shew you by what way ye should go, and in a cloud by day."

The shepherd care of God was beautifully manifested in the movements of the cloud. That favourite Psalm the 23rd, is a short but full description of the Lord's watchful care of His people. It speaks for the most part in the *present tense*.

Jehovah is my Shepherd.

He maketh me to lie down in green pastures.

He leadeth me beside the still waters.

He restoreth my soul.

He leadeth me in the paths of righteousness for His name's sake.

Thou art with me.

Thy rod and thy staff they comfort me.

Thou preparest a table before me in the presence of mine enemies.

Thou anointest my head with oil,

My cup runneth over.

The green pastures and still waters are places of encampment, where the believer finds rest, food, and refreshment.

The paths of righteousness are the wilderness journeyings.

In the very presence of enemies the table is prepared for strengthening the soul for conflict.

The head is enriched with oil, and the countenance thus made to shine, though the path be rugged, and

The cup of joy brims over, although the way be full of sorrow and trial.

The only *futures* of the psalm are—first, an absolute negative—

I shall *not* want.

Secondly.—Should even the path lie in the valley of the shadow of death,

I will fear *no* evil.

Thirdly.—An absolute certainty of goodness and mercy following all the days of one's life, and the closing future, with its sure eternity of glory,

I will dwell in the house of the Lord for evei.

The only place for " goodness and mercy" in the pathway of the believer, is *behind* him ; for the Shep-herd is in *front* to lead—*at hand* to restore—and *with* him, as on the right hand and on the left, to dispel even the fear of evil.

Thus goodness and mercy close up the rear, pre-venting any failings and faults of the past from overtaking the child of God ; obliterating the heel-prints of past iniquities, and pursuing him so as to hasten his entrance into the house of the Lord.

The pillar of cloud and of fire by day and by night, seem to have somewhat symbolized this shepherd care of the Lord.

It was a guide, a defence, a shelter, a light, a place of intercourse with God, from whence He spoke, and from whence He manifested His power and His glory.

This token of the presence of Jehovah reappeared after a lapse of ages, upon the Mount of Transfiguration. Israel's Lord was there. Their departed leader, Moses, was summoned from the grave ; and one of their choicest prophets, Elijah, was brought from the glory, as His attendants upon the holy mount.

It was a scene depicting, and anticipative of the Lord's coming, when the dead saints will be raised and the living ones changed, represented by Moses and Elijah, types of each company. The bright cloud of glory received them, and the disciples, (Peter, James, and John,) feared, when they saw them enter the cloud.

The cloud will again appear upon the earth during the future reign of the Lord Jesus. This is foretold in Isa. iv. 4, 5. A remnant of the people of Israel will be spared in Jerusalem after they have passed through the fearful oppression of the man of sin, the wilful king, and that remnant will be all holy. They will look upon Him whom they have pierced, and mourn.

Jerusalem will be established, and will become the city of the great King. " And the Lord will create upon every dwelling place of Mount Zion, and upon her assemblies, a cloud and smoke by day, and the shining of a flaming fire by night : for upon all the glory shall be a defence."

Israel's wanderings of unbelief will then all be at an end, and the presence of the cloud will make manifest that the former loving kindness and tender mercies of God, have never utterly forsaken them. They will then be reminded of their early history, and of the unchangeableness of Jehovah, for "His gifts and calling are without repentance."

Having endeavoured to trace out the type of the Tabernacle, and the priestly garments, and to cite some of the Scriptures wherein allusions are made to this wide subject, we have to turn back again, and contemplate the consecration of the Priesthood, directed in Exodus xxix., and accomplished in Lev. viii. and ix.

The Book of Exodus closes with the rearing up of the Tabernacle, with which the consecration of the priesthood was intimately connected. See Exod. xl. 9—15. The subject is however interrupted by directions given from the Tabernacle by Jehovah, respecting the various sacrifices, occupying the seven first chapters of the book of Leviticus, and then we have Aaron and his sons fully installed into the office of Priests. As if God would have our thoughts more occupied with the sacrifices, than with the priests who had to conduct them.

# THE CONSECRATION OF THE PRIESTS

"And this is the thing that thou shalt do unto them to hallow them, to minister unto me in the priest's office: Take one young bullock, and two rams without blemish,

"And unleavened bread, and cakes unleavened tempered with oil, and wafers unleavened anointed with oil: of wheaten flour shalt thou make them.

"And thou shalt put them into one basket, and bring them in the basket, with the bullock and the two rams.

"And Aaron and his sons thou shalt bring unto the door of the tabernacle of the congregation, and shalt wash them with water.

"And thou shalt take the garments, and put upon Aaron the coat, and the robe of the ephod, and the ephod, and the breastplate, and gird him with the curious girdle of the ephod:

"And thou shalt put the mitre upon his head, and put the holy crown upon the mitre."—Exod. xxix 1—6

"And the Lord spake unto Moses. saying,

"Take Aaron and his sons with him, and the garments, and the anointing oil, and a bullock for the sin offering, and two rams, and a basket of unleavened bread ;

"And gather thou all the congregation together unto the door of the tabernacle of the congregation.

"And Moses did as the Lord commanded him ; and the assembly was gathered together unto the door of the tabernacle of the congregation.

"And Moses said unto the congregation, This is the thing which the Lord commanded to be done.

"And Moses brought Aaron and his sons, and washed them with water.

"And he put upon him the coat, and girded him with the girdle, and clothed him with the robe, and put the ephod upon him, and he girded him with the curious girdle of the ephod, and bound it unto him therewith.

"And he put the breastplate upon him: also he put in the breastplate the Urim and the Thummim.

"And he put the mitre. upon his head ; also upon the mitre, even upon his forefront, did he put the golden plate, the holy crown ; as the Lord commanded Moses."—Lev. viii 1—9

It is interesting to observe that seven different things were necessary for the consecration of the priests.

Aaron and his sons were to be
*Taken,*
*Brought,*
*Washed,*
*Clothed,*
*Anointed,*
*Their hands filled,*
*And they were to be sanctified.*

" *Taken.*" " Take thou unto thee Aaron thy brother, and his sons with him, from among the children of Israel." Exod. xxviii. 1. " Take Aaron and his sons with him." Lev. viii. 2. Allusion is probably made to this in Heb. v. 1, " every high priest taken from among men."

Aaron was thus " called of God " unto the priesthood. He did not take this honour unto himself, or assume it out of his own fancy or self-will. " So also Christ glorified not himself to be made an high priest." Heb. v. 5. He was God's servant, His *elect* in whom His soul delighted. He was the *called* of Jehovah. " I the Lord have called thee in righteousness." " The Lord hath called me from the womb." Isa. xlii. 1, 6 ; xlix. 1. And finally God raised him from the dead, saying unto Him, " thou art my Son, this day have I begotten thee "— and, " thou art a priest for ever after the order of Melchizedeck "—thus taking Him from among the dead, and giving Him His call in resurrection, " called of God an high priest after the order of Melchizedeck." Heb. v. 10.

What was true of Aaron was also true of his sons ; they were also " taken," or called unto the priesthood. And the Lord severely judged the sin of Korah, when he endeavoured to assume the priesthood, although he had apparently a nearer title to it than any of the other tribes, seeing he was of Levi.

And what is true of Christ as the High Priest is also true of all His priestly house—They are called of God. " We know that all things work together for good to them that love God, to them who are the called according to his purpose. For whom he did foreknow, he also did predestinate to be conformed to the image of his Son, that he might be the firstborn among many brethren. Moreover whom he did predestinate, them he also called." Rom. viii. 28—30. " Holy brethren, partakers of the heavenly calling, consider the apostle and high priest of our profession Christ Jesus." Heb. iii. 1.

Sonship afresh declared in resurrection was joined with God's oath calling the Lord Jesus to be a Priest. So also, Christ's own house of priests are children of God, " *of one* " with Him that sanctifieth them, so that He is not ashamed to call them brethren. Of one life, of one Father, of one resurrection ; of one family with Him who is the Head. If the Lord so judged the sin of Korah for attempting to intrude upon the earthly priesthood, what will be His solemn sentence against those who assume to be of the heavenly priesthood, taking their authority from mere human appointment, but who are still of the world, unconverted lost sinners—ignorant of God and of Christ, and leading into the ditch the blind, having their own eyes darkened.

" *Brought.*" " Aaron and his sons, thou shalt *bring* unto the door of the tabernacle of the congregation." " Moses *brought* Aaron and his sons." Exod. xxix. 4 ; xl. 12 ; Lev. viii. 6. Having been selected from the rest of Israel, and from the tribe of Levi, Aaron and his sons were brought before the Lord, to the door of the tabernacle of the congregation, where already the assembly was gathered together. The whole ceremony of their consecration was conducted in the presence of the Lord, and in the presence of the people, The objects for which they were sanctified as priests, were twofold first, that they might be brought near to God, and secondly, that they might use the access which was given to them, for the benefit and blessing of the people

The Lord Jesus was brought again from the dead as the great shepherd of the sheep, and the High Priest of

His people. "He is now in the presence of God for us."
"He ever liveth to make intercession for us." His
interests, His affections, His intercourse with God, are
all in full ceaseless exercise on behalf of His own. His
thoughts, His heart are with us here.

Ourselves being priests brought nigh to God, children
of God, and of the household of Christ, we should have
our interests, our affections occupied in the work and
service of God on behalf of His saints. There is now
no assembly distinct from the priestly house ; but all
who compose the assembly of God are kings and priests
alike. In this respect therefore, there is a contrast
between the scene in Lev. viii, where, Aaron and his
sons, were distinct from the congregation ; and the church
of God, which is composed of the saints of the Most
High, all alike loved by the Father, and by Christ—
all alike washed in His precious blood—all children of
God, and " kings and priests unto His God and Father."

Resurrection is, we may say, the new standing which
God has given all that are His. It is a calling above
the heavens, super-heavenly. The believer begins his
existence as raised from among the dead—receiving a
life in union with the risen Christ, " quickened together
with him," brought nigh to God in Christ Jesus, by the
blood of Christ ; partaker of a super-heavenly calling,
which has left the flesh and the world, and death, far,
far behind ; separated off for ever to God in Christ ; a
calling of which Christ Himself in glory is the pattern ;
a profession of which He is the apostle, instructing the
saints in all its blessings and glories; and of which He is
the High Priest, ministering the power of such a
wondrous calling, and sustaining the believer unceasingly
in its height and glory.

" *Washed.*" " And shall wash them with water."
" And washed them with water." Exod. xxix. 4 ; xl.
12 ; Lev. viii. 6. This was the only time when Aaron
and his sons were washed by another with water. Other
washings they had constantly to observe, such as washing

their hands and feet, but on this occasion they were washed all over. It is very interesting to remark here, that although in the Hebrew the same word *(rah-ghatz)* is used for both bathing or washing the whole of the body in water, and for washing the hands and feet ; yet, in the Septuagint two words are employed ; the one *(louo)* for the washing the whole body : (Exod. xxix. 4 ; xl. 12 ; Lev. viii. 6) and the word *(nipzo,* in later Greek *nipto,)* for the washing the hands and feet. Exod. xxx. 18, 19, 20, 21 ; xl. 30, 31, 32.

The use of the two words appears to be kept very distinct in John xiii. where the Lord employs them both. When he speaks of washing the disciples' feet, He uses the word " *nipto ;*" but when He alludes to their having been altogether washed from their sins, and being personally clean, He uses the word " *louo.*" John xiii. 10 ; " he that is washed " *louo* " (or that has been perfectly washed all over,) needeth not save to wash his feet, " *nipto,*" but is clean every whit ; and ye are clean but not all." They were all personally clean except Judas, for they had all in truth believed on the Lord Jesus, with the exception of that false professor—and subsequently when he was gone out, the Lord could say of them all, without an exception, " ye are clean." John xv. 3. So the believer at the present time has been once for all washed, and is clean. But he contracts daily defilements, which need to be washed off through the constant intercession of Christ, and ceaseless cleansing power of the blood   although he never again has to be rewashed all over, but is every whit clean, and made meet for the inheritance of the saints in light.

This washing of the priests is evidently a figure of the complete cleansing, through which the sinner passes when he is saved, the washing of regeneration. It is the blood of Christ applied to the person by the Lord Himself, through the word, and by the instrumentality of the Holy Spirit. Thus in Rev. i. 5, it is said, "Unto Him that loveth us and washed us from our sins in his own blood." Here the precious blood is the bath in which we have been washed from our sins, by the Lord Jesus. In Eph. v. 25, 26, it is written, " Christ loved the church and gave himself for it, that he might sanctify and cleanse it by the washing of water by the word." In this passage, the same word is employed for *washing* as that in Titus iii. 5, " the washing of regeneration." The word of God is here designated as the bath of water in which the church is cleansed : the Scriptures of truth revealing the death of Christ, and when received by faith, cleansing the sinner, and being also the incorruptible seed of life.

In John iii. the Lord Jesus says to Nicodemus, " Except a man be born of water and of the Spirit, he cannot enter into the kingdom of God." Here the new birth is effected by that which cleanses, and by the power of the Holy Ghost. The blood of Christ revealed in the Word of God and applied by the power of the Holy Ghost, regenerates the soul. Subsequently in the same chapter the Lord explains the mystery, by stating that the Son of Man must be lifted up upon the cross, and that whosoever believeth in Him should not perish, but have eternal life. Christ crucified, gazed upon by faith, becomes thus the source of life to the sinner perishing in his sins.

In 1st Cor. vi. 9—11, the apostle describes a variety of fearful uncleannesses and sins, which shut out those that commit them from the kingdom of God ; and then adds, " Such were some of you : but ye are washed, but ye are sanctified, but ye are justified in the name of the Lord Jesus, and by the Spirit of our God." In this beautiful passage we have the threefold condition of the saved sinner : washed, made holy, and made righteous ; and all through the power of the name of Christ, applied by the Spirit of God. The consecration of priests which we are considering presents also three aspects of the work of Christ.

They were washed, Lev. viii. 6 ; they were sanctified,

**v.** 30 : and clothed with the linen garments, v, 13, emblems of righteousness.

The most direct reference to this washing is in Heb. x. 22. " Let us draw near with a true heart, in full assurance of faith, having our hearts sprinkled from an evil conscience, and our bodies washed with pure water."

In this chapter the sinner is through the one offering of Christ, for ever sanctified and perfected for priesthood. A striking contrast is instituted between the outward sprinkling of the blood upon the persons and garments of the priests in Leviticus, and the inward sprinkling of the blood by the Spirit of God, upon the hearts of believers ; cleansing them not only from sin, but from an evil conscience, which would otherwise keep them at a distance from God. Their bodies also are said to be washed with pure water, like the priests in Lev. viii. The word " pure" being added in order to distinguish the cleansing water of the New Testament from the mere typical water of the Old Testament.

The precious blood of Christ, the true Laver of regeneration, not only cleanses, so as to free us from wrath and judgment, but makes us altogether personally clean, in order that we may with confidence draw near to God. Ours is not a mere salvation from sins, and the penalty due to them ; but it is a salvation of our whole persons ; so that our bodies are the Lord's, and we are redeemed *to God* by the blood. It is this perfect fitness to stand in the presence of God which is here represented by the bodies washed with pure water. All distance between ourselves and the Most High has been abolished ; we are made nigh by the blood of Christ, and it is our responsibility to know and use this nearness of approach, in the full assurance of faith.

" *Clothed.*" Aaron and his sons were all washed together. In this perhaps there was a shadow of the resurrection of Christ and the Church, accomplished in the sight of God at the same time. Aaron was however

"*clothed*" separately and before his sons. Exod. xxix.
5, 6; xl, 13; Lev. viii. 7—9.

It is interesting to observe the order in which the
garments were placed upon Aaron by Moses. The
words in the Hebrew also are varied. First, he put
upon him, (or literally, gave to him,) the coat. This is
the embroidered coat described in Exod. xxviii. 39, and
already referred to in page 281 of this work.

Next, " he girded him with the girdle." The girdle
of needle-work. Exod xxviii. 39; and xxxix. 29,
(page 289) these were the two innermost garments.
Then " he clothed him with the robe," " the robe of
the ephod," Exod. xxviii. 31—35, (page 256 :) and
put the ephod upon him, (literally gave to him, the
ephod;) and girded him with the curious girdle of the
ephod—or, the ephod-belt—and bound it unto him
therewith : (literally ephodized him therewith.) Exod.
xxviii. 6—8. (pages 198, 200.)

And he put the breastplate upon him, (literally placed;)
also he put in (or gave to) the breastplate the Urim and
the Thummim. Exod. xxviii. 15—30, (page 203.)

And he put (or placed) the mitre upon his head :
also upon the mitre upon his forehead did he put
(placed) the golden plate, the holy crown. Exod. xxviii.
36, 38. (page 266.)

Thus Aaron was fully clothed in the garments for
glory and beauty : and here is marked the first division
of the chapter we are considering, by the words, " *as
the Lord commanded Moses*."

This seems again to be an intimation of the separate
glorious standing of the High Priest in his representative
capacity on behalf of others ; and may also dimly intimate the fact of the Lord Jesus, being raised as the
Great High Priest for His people, previous to their
being actually raised, as they will be at His second
coming. Before that great day of manifestation arrives,
we already by faith see Jesus at the right hand of God,
" crowned with glory and honour.'

# THE ANOINTING OIL

"Moreover the Lord spake unto Moses, saying,

"Take thou also unto thee principal spices, of pure myrrh five hundred, and of sweet cinnamon half so much, two hundred and fifty, and of sweet calamus two hundred and fifty,

"And of cassia five hundred, after the shekel of the sanctuary, and of olive oil an hin:

"And thou shalt make it an oil of holy ointment, an ointment compound after the art of the apothecary: it shall be an holy anointing oil.

"And thou shalt anoint the tabernacle of the congregation therewith, and the ark of the testimony,

"And the table and all his vessels, and the candlestick and his vessels, and the altar of incense,

"And the altar of burnt offering with all his vessels, and the laver and his foot.

"And thou shalt sanctify them, that they may be most holy: whatsoever toucheth them shall be holy.

"And thou shalt anoint Aaron and his sons, and consecrate them that they may minister unto me in the priest's office.

"And thou shalt speak unto the children of Israel, saying, This shall be an holy anointing oil unto me throughout your generations.

"Upon man's flesh shall it not be poured neither shall ye make any other like it, after the composition of it: it is holy, and it shall be holy unto you.

"Whosoever compoundeth any like it, or whosoever putteth any of it upon a stranger, shall even be cut off from his people."—Exod. xxx 22—33

A HIN of olive oil mingled with four spices formed this fragrant compound.

Of myrrh there was five hundred.

Of cinnamon two hundred and fifty

Of calamus two hundred and fifty.

And of cassia five hundred.

Thus the two middle spices added together equalled in weight the first, the myrrh ; and the last, the cassia ; the four forming three weights of five hundred.

*Myrrh.*—Myrrh has the word "*pure*" attached to it. This word (*drohr*, Heb.) is always translated wherever it elsewhere occurs, "*liberty.*"

"Proclaim *liberty* throughout the land unto all the

345

inhabitants thereof : it shall be a jubilee unto you ; and ye shall return every man unto his possession, and ye shall return every man unto his family." Lev. xxv. 10.

" The Spirit of the Lord God is upon me ; because the Lord hath anointed me to preach glad tidings unto the meek ; he hath sent me to bind up the broken-hearted, to proclaim *liberty* to the captives, and the opening of the prison to them that are bound." Isa. lxi. 1.

Proclaim *liberty*. Jer. xxxiv. 8, 15, 17.

The year of *liberty*. Ezek. xlvi. 17.

Another word translated " *sweet smelling*," Cant. v. 5, 13, is connected with *myrrh*. (The margin has it, *passing*, or, running about.) Both words, "*pure*," and " *sweet smelling*," may have reference to the myrrh flowing out spontaneously, or freely from the plant.

In Canticles v. 5, the hands and fingers of the Bride are represented as dropping with *myrrh* upon the handles of the Lock when she rose to open to her beloved. And in the 13th verse the lips of the Bridegroom are likened unto " lilies dropping sweet smelling *myrrh*."

The full fragrance of this spice is descriptive of the beloved Himself. " A bundle of *myrrh* is my well-beloved unto me." Cant. i. 13. And " all his garments are of *myrrh*, and aloes, and cassia." Psa. xlv. 8.

Amongst the plants of the enclosed garden, descriptive of the Bride, are " *myrrh* and aloes, with all principal spices." Cant. iv. 14. And the Bridegroom in chap. v. 1, enters His garden, and says, " I have gathered my *myrrh* with my spice." She is herself represented at the conclusion of her wilderness journey, "like pillars of smoke, perfumed with *myrrh* and frankincense, with all powders of the merchant." Cant. iii. 6.

The mountains of *myrrh*, and the hill of frankincense, are the safe and pleasant places of retreat to which the Bridegroom invites the Bride, until the day break and the shadows flee away ; in contrast with the lion's dens, and mountains of the leopards.

The adulterous woman, type of the seducing world

around us, professes also to use this perfume. " I have perfumed my bed with *myrrh*, aloes, and cinnamon." Prov. vii. 17.

This spice was probably bitter to the taste, as its Hebrew derivative implies. An oil was extracted from it, which was used for purification. Esther ii. 12.

" *Sweet cinnamon*," properly cinnamon of spice, or aromatic cinnamon, occurs again, Cant. iv. 14, another of the plants of the enclosed garden—the Spouse ; and Proverbs vii. 17, where it is connected with myrrh and aloes, as a perfume for the bed

"*Sweet Calamus*," or cane of spice, or aromatic cane This word " calamus," is translated

*Stalk.*—Gen. xli. 5, 22.

*Branch*, of the candlestick.—Exod. xxv. 31, 32, 33, 35, 36, etc.

*Reed.*—1st Kings xiv. 15 ; 2nd Kings xviii. 21, etc.

*Sweet Cane.*—Isa. xliii. 24 ; Jer. vi. 20.

*Balance.*—Isa. xlvi. 6.

And *a measuring reed*, or rod.—Ezek. xl. 3, etc.

This is also another of the plants of the enclosed garden. Cant. iv. 14.

"*Cassia*."—This word only occurs once more in the Scripture. Ezek. xxvii. 19. Its origin is doubtful, but if the derivation suggested by Robertson be correct, it springs from a root which signifies "to cleave," and also "to stoop" and "bow down."

These spices gave their fragrance to the oil with which Aaron was anointed.

The fragrant graces of the Holy Spirit seem to be typified by this holy perfume.

In Isa. xi. 1—3, we have a prophecy respecting the Lord Jesus ; as a rod springing from the stem of Jesse; a branch out of his roots ; referring to His being of the seed of David, as born into this world ; and it is said, " The Spirit of the Lord shall rest upon him ;

The spirit of wisdom and understanding,
The spirit of counsel and might,

The spirit of knowledge and of the fear of the Lord, and shall make him of quick understanding (or *scent* or *smell*) in the fear of the Lord."

Possibly the anointing oil may have some typical reference to the Holy Spirit, thus resting on Him. It is remarkable that the way in which these graces of the Spirit are arranged in Isaiah, has some analogy to the proportions of the spices in the anointing oil. There were five hundred of Myrrh which would answer to the "Spirit of wisdom and understanding." There were two hundred and fifty of Cinnamon, and two hundred and fifty of Calamus, which would correspond with "the spirit of counsel and might," each in equal proportions. The spirit of "wisdom and understanding" being represented by one spice, because there is a close connection between wisdom and understanding, one could hardly exist without the other; whereas there is a considerable difference between "counsel" and "might," which is expressed by the two distinct spices "cinnamon" and "calamus:" the two together making another five hundred in weight. The "spirit of knowledge and of the fear of the Lord" being represented lastly by the five hundred of "Cassia"; one spice only; for all true knowledge is embodied in the "fear of the Lord." Without the fear of the Lord man is a fool. If he reverence not God, and believe not in His word, he is like the beasts that perish; or rather he is more brutish than the ox or ass. For "the ox knoweth his owner, and the ass his master's crib;" but a man ignorant of God, does not know; he is a fool, saying in his heart, "there is no God."

The words of wisdom and understanding dropped freely from the lips of the blessed Lord when he was on earth, like sweet smelling myrrh from the lips of the bridegroom. When questioned by the high priest as to His doctrine, Jesus answered, "I spake openly to the world; I ever taught in the synagogue, and in the temple, whither the Jews always resort; and in secret

have I said nothing." John xviii. 20. His words were
spirit and life. His tongue was the tongue of the wise,
using knowledge aright, and giving health to sin-sick
souls. His lips dispersed knowledge, and His mouth
was instructed by His heart. The law which proceeded
out of His mouth was a fountain of life, to cause men
to depart from the snares of death. Prov. xii. 18;
xiii. 14; xv. 2, 7; xvi. 23.

Grace proceeding from a heart of love, was poured
into His lips. Psa. xlv. 2.

In like manner should the hands and fingers of the
Bride drop with wisdom like myrrh, from handling the
word of life, instead of touching that unclean thing the
world. And out of the heart's affections should flow
living waters to a thirsty world around, through the
power and help of that same blessed Spirit received
from the anointed Head.

The spirit of counsel rested also upon Christ; and
His name is Counsellor. He understood completely
the purposes of God, and undertook nothing without
duly taking counsel with the Most High. The
testimonies of the Lord were especially His counsellors.
Psa. cxix. 24. And he blessed the Lord for giving
him counsel. Psa. xvi. 7. When upon the tree His
utterances of woe and anguish were the Spirit's utterances
in the prophetic psalms. And when suffering from
the thirst of death, His desire was still to magnify the
word of God; and knowing that all things had been
accomplished, and that one only Scripture remained to
be fulfilled, said, "I thirst." And when he had
received the last proof of human scorn and hatred,
had tasted the vinegar placed upon the bitter hyssop,
He uttered that most memorable and blessed sentence,
"it is finished." The counsels of God were accomplished, not a jot or tittle had fallen to the ground;
and He who was filled with the spirit of counsel,
bowed His head and gave up the Ghost. What
**fragrance** of unspeakable value there was in those

words and in that act.   What a sweet full perfume of richest obedience, rose up to God from that tree of curse.

The spirit of *power* also abode upon Him.   Power to help the weak ; to comfort the sorrowing ; to bear the afflictions of the afflicted ; to bear our griefs and carry our sorrows.   Power to save instead of to destroy. Might, used in the perfection of grace and lowliness, to bind up the broken hearted ; to proclaim liberty to the captive, and the opening of the prison to them that are bound.

The spirit of knowledge and of the fear of the Lord, made Him of quick perception in the fear of the Lord, so that His judgments were correct, were righteous.

The fear of the Lord that is wisdom. Job. xxviii. 28.

The fear of the Lord is the beginning of wisdom. Psa. cxi. 10.

The fear of the Lord is the beginning of wisdom. Prov. ix. 10.

The fear of the Lord is the instruction of wisdom. Prov. xv. 33.

The fear of the Lord is the beginning of knowledge. Prov. i. 7.

The fear of the Lord is clean. Psa. xix. 9.

The fear of the Lord is to hate evil. Prov. viii. 13.

The fear of the Lord is a fountain of life. Prov xiv. 27.

The fear of the Lord (is) to life. Prov. xix. 23.

The fear of the Lord prolongeth days. Prov. x. 27.

In the fear of the Lord is strong confidence. Prov. xiv. 26.

And now that the Lord is in the glory exalted, and dwelling on high, the same spirit rests upon Him ; and He will come forth in a little while, and " will fill Zion with judgment and righteousness, and wisdom and knowledge shall be the stability of thy times, and strength of salvation : the fear of the Lord is his treasure." Isa. xxxiii. 5, 6.

The spices of which the anointing oil was made, are called "*principal*," standing at the head of the most esteemed perfumes. The oil was to be skilfully mingled with them ; a holy ointment ; an ointment compound after the art of the apothecary ; a holy anointing oil. The fragrance of the spices was to be evenly diffused through the whole hin of oil olive, so that no one perfume took precedence above another ; but the oil sent forth the fragrance of all alike.

A beautiful type this of the graces of the Holy Spirit, which were all displayed in the Lord Jesus, without one interfering with, or suppressing another ; ever sending up to God a perfection of fragrance.

This holy anointing oil was not to be " poured upon man's flesh." It was poured on Aaron's *head* after the mitre and holy crown had been placed on him. Although the Aaronic priesthood was in reality a priesthood in the flesh, for Aaron was " taken from among men," yet there seems to be an intimation of another priesthood given in this precept, which was not to be in the flesh, but in resurrection.

Flesh, human flesh, is sinful and corrupt. There can be no congeniality between it and the graces of the Holy Spirit. The flesh must ever lust against the spirit, they cannot agree together. And as the word of God says, " Ye are not in the flesh, but in the spirit, if so be that the spirit of God dwell in you." In the flesh there dwelleth no good thing.

No one therefore can have the Holy Spirit, unless he be born of the spirit, a new creature in Christ Jesus.

Another precept connected with the holy anointing oil was, that no imitation was to be made of it, " neither shall ye make any other like it, after the composition of it : it is holy, and it shall be holy unto you. Whosoever compoundeth any like it, shall be cut off from his people."

There is an assumption at the present day, of a power to convey the Holy Spirit by virtue of a mere human

appointment.   There is also a danger amongst the
children of God themselves, of assuming to be guided
by and acting under the power and direction of the
Holy Spirit, when they are only indulging their own
self-will or self-conceit.   In both cases the Holy Spirit
is greatly dishonoured.   To suppose on the one hand,
that He is handed down through a channel of
unconverted sinners, so as to be bestowed by the
laying on of the hands of one who happens to have
an official standing in the nominal church, by reason
of some political favour, is surely greatly to outrage the
holiness and Godhead of the blesssed Spirit.   On the
other hand, where such superstitious sinful practices
are rightly disowned, believers should be careful not
to grieve that Holy Spirit by imitations of His power
and grace ; and not profess to be prompted or led by
Him, unless their habitual lowly walk, and study of
and acquaintance with the word of God, give them a
warrant for believing that they truly have the teaching
and help of the Spirit of truth and holiness.   The
Spirit of God will not be found to teach or lead a
believer when he is meeting in an assembly of God's
children, unless that believer is habitually under the
guidance and instruction of the same spirit in his
ordinary life, in his own house, and in his daily
occupations.   Not only does the Spirit divide to every
man in the church of God, severally as He will, gifts
for the edification of the body ; but those upon whom
He bestows such gifts, need to study the word of God,
and to cultivate the conscious presence and help of the
Spirit Himself, if they would use them to the profit
of others.

   Is there not also a danger of a false spirituality—
—refinement—imagination—sentiment—a danger from
the habit of contrasting spirit with that which is material ?
True spirituality is always essentially connected with
*Truth.*   It was " in the power of the Spirit," that the
Lord uttered the truth, (Luke iv. 25—27,) which so

enraged the men of Nazareth. Mysticism may pass for
spirituality.

This holy anointing oil was not to be put upon a
*stranger*. In this precept we have an intimation that no
unconverted person, ought on any account to be allowed
to take any part in the service or worship of God. He
does not belong to God's people. He is not of the
house—the Church of God—he is not one of the
family of whom God is the Father. He is a stranger ;
and until he is washed from his sins in the blood of
Christ, and is a child of God by faith in Christ Jesus,
he can have no part or lot in any thing connected with
the true worship of God. They that worship Him
*must* worship Him in Spirit and in truth. An unconverted person is without Christ, and he is therefore an
*alien* from the commonwealth of Israel, and a stranger
from the covenants of promise, having no hope, and
without God in the world. Eph. ii. 12.

" *Anointed*." Moses took this " anointing oil, and
anointed the tabernacle, and all that was therein, and
sanctified them. And he sprinkled thereof upon the
altar seven times, and anointed the altar and all his
vessels, both the laver and his foot, to sanctify them."
Lev. viii. 10, 11 ; see also Exod. xxx. 26—29; xl. 9—11.

The vessels of the sanctuary represent various offices
of priesthood, which the Lord now sustains on behalf
of His people. The same Eternal Spirit by which He
offered Himself as the sacrifice without spot to God,
(Heb. ix. 14,) is still the power of His service in " the
tabernacle not made with hands, eternal in the heavens."

In Acts i. 2, we find that the Lord Jesus after His
resurrection, was still speaking through the Holy Ghost ;
" Until the day in which he was taken up, after that he
through the Holy Ghost had given commandments to
the apostles whom he had chosen."

Moses next poured of the anointing oil upon Aaron's
head, and anointed him to sanctify him. Lev. viii. 12.
It is to be observed that the oil was not *poured* upon

Aaron's sons, but upon Aaron's head *alone*. Thus Aaron stood clothed in garments for glory and beauty, and anointed, previous to the clothing of his sons. In fact, he was the only *anointed one* of the house : the word "*anointed*" being in Exod. xxix. 7, and Lev. viii. 12, confined to Aaron, a type of the Messiah, the Christ, the Anointed One. The anointing of Aaron's sons was included in the anointing of Aaron himself. " And thou shalt anoint Aaron and his sons." Exod. xxx. 30. " Of the anointing of Aaron and of the anointing of his sons." Lev. vii. 35.

A passage in Exod. xl. 15, seems to contradict this. " And thou shalt anoint them, (Aaron's sons,) as thou didst anoint their father ; that they may minister unto me in the priest's office : for their anointing shall surely be an everlasting priesthood throughout their generations." But this text looks onward apparently to the succession of the sons of Aaron, who were to execute the office of high priest after his death.

In Numbers iii. 3, we have another passage which speaks of Aaron's sons as anointed. " These are the names of the sons of Aaron, the priests which were anointed, whom he consecrated to minister in the priest's office." Here also the anointing of Aaron seems to have been considered the anointing of his sons. So remarkably is this thought carried on, that when Aaron was about to die, Moses stripped off his garments and put them upon Eleazer his son. Numb. xx. 23—28. But we do not read of Eleazer having been anointed. It is as if the anointing of his father was perpetuated unto himself. The anointing oil was indeed *sprinkled* upon Aaron's sons, to which reference will subsequently be made ; but this is kept quite distinct from the *pouring* of the oil upon Aaron himself.

The Lord Jesus was the Christ, the Anointed One from His birth. He was also anointed with the Holy Spirit at His baptism, for service. Thus in the synagogue at Nazareth, where He seems to have commenced

His testimony after His baptism in Jordan, and the descent of the Holy Ghost upon Him, He opened the book of the prophet Isaiah, and found the place where it was written, " The Spirit of the Lord is upon me, because he hath anointed me to preach the Gospel to the poor." Luke iv. 18 ; Isa. lxi. 1. Also Peter in his discourse to Cornelius and his house, refers to this anointing; " How God anointed Jesus of Nazareth with the Holy Ghost and with power." Acts x. 38. Again in resurrection He was anointed with the Holy Ghost, Priest, and King according to Psalm ii. " Yet have I set (margin anointed) my King upon my holy hill of Zion," ver. 6. That same psalm speaks of the kings of the earth and their rulers taking counsel together against Jehovah, and against His Christ. Peter quotes the psalm, Acts iv. 25, 26, and adds, " For of a truth against thy holy Child Jesus, whom thou hast *anointed*, both Herod, and Pontius Pilate, with the Gentiles, and the people of Israel, were gathered together." And continues his prayer as if the same company were still in league against the same Christ. " And now Lord behold their threatenings ; and grant unto thy servants, that with all boldness they may speak thy word, by stretching forth thine hand to heal ; and that signs and wonders may be done by the name of thy holy Child Jesus." Ver 29, 30.

In Psa. xlv. where the Lord is especially represented as the King in resurrection, His anointing is alluded to as a reward of His righteous service. " Thou lovest righteousness and hatest wickedness, therefore God thy God hath anointed thee with the oil of gladness above thy fellows," ver. 7 ; Heb. i. 9. In Acts ii. 30, 31, Peter speaking of the resurrection of the Lord, foretold by David in the Psalms, says, therefore he, (David,) " being a prophet, and knowing that God had sworn with an oath to him that of the fruit of his loins according to the flesh, he would raise up *Christ* to sit on his throne ; he, seeing this before, spoke of the resurrection of Christ."

**And** adds a little further on, " God hath made this same Jesus, whom ye have crucified, both Lord and *Christ*," ver. 36.

The holy anointing oil was *poured* upon the head of Aaron, being poured upon the mitre which covered his head. This is again referred to in Lev. xxi. 10—12. " He that is high priest *among his brethren* upon whose head the anointing oil was *poured*—the crown of the anointing oil of his God is upon him."

The Lord Jesus is also the High Priest *among His brethren;* allusion to which is made in Heb. ii. 11: " For both he that sanctifieth, and they who are sanctified are all of one ; for which cause he is not ashamed to call them brethren ; saying, I will declare thy name unto my brethren ; in the midst of the Church will I sing praise unto thee." He stands as the Anointed One, the Christ, in the midst of His brethren, the Church. And He will be the leader of their praises in glory when the morning of the resurrection comes, and He presents them individually faultless before the presence of His glory with exceeding joy ; presenting the Church to Himself, " a glorious Church not having spot or wrinkle, or any such thing, but holy and without blemish." Jude 24 ; Eph. v. 27.

This anointing oil is spoken of as the *crown* of the anointing oil of his God, (Lev. xxi. 12 ;) or, may it not rather be translated without the " of"—the crown, (that is) the oil, the anointing (oil) of his God : the anointing oil of his God, being the crown ; communicating to him a priestly, and a kind of regal dignity. An allusion being here made by anticipation to the royal priesthood, of which Melchizedek was the true type, and of which Christ Himself is the true commencement

Oil was *poured* \* upon the head of the high priest, and upon the head of the king. 1st Sam. x. 1 ; 2nd Kings ix. 3, 6. It is worthy of remark that Saul

---

\* In our translation of Lev. xiv. 18, it would seem as if oil were *poured* upon the head of the leper; but the word used here is not in the Heb. pour, but *give;* " he shall give upon the head of him that is to be cleansed."

was anointed captain. 1st Sam. ix. 16 ; x. 1. Subsequently Samuel alluding to this anointing, speaks of it as anointing for kingship. xv. 1, 17.

David was thrice anointed. He was anointed to God as His king in the midst of his brethren. 1st Sam. xvi. 3, 13 ; 2nd Sam. xii. 7. He was anointed king by the men of Judah, over the house of Judah. 2nd Sam. ii. 4, 7. He was lastly anointed king over Israel, by the elders of Israel. 2nd Sam. v. 3, 17.

Thus David was especially anointed *to God*. And a similar expression occurs again only with respect to Solomon, who was twice anointed ; first, by Zadoc the priest and Nathan the prophet, 1st Kings i. 34, 39, 45 ; and the second time anointed king *unto the Lord.* 1st Chron. xxix. 22.

The Lord Jesus has made us *kings* and priests *unto* God and His Father. Rev. i. 6. And He is Himself especially God's King — " My King "—" His Christ." Psa. ii 6 ; ii. 2 ; xviii. 50.

It has been before observed that the word " anointed" is confined in Exod. xxix. 7, and Lev. viii. to Aaron the high priest, and is not used in reference to his sons. So the Heavenly Priesthood, of which Christ is the head, receive the anointing of the Spirit by virtue of their union with the risen Christ. His body, the Church, was formed of Him in death and resurrection ; as Eve was fashioned by God's hands out of Adam while he was in a deep sleep, which the Lord God had caused to fall upon him. The remarkable expression is used in Gen. ii. 22, with reference to this—" And the rib which the Lord God had taken from man, *builded* he a woman, and brought her unto the man."

The very rib itself God builded a woman. It is not said " out of," or " of " the rib. Neither did God breathe any breath of life into the woman, as He is said to have done with respect to the man. But the life of the woman was part of the life which the man had already received from God. God " brought her unto

the man, and Adam said this is now bone of my bones,
and flesh of my flesh. She shall be called woman
(isha, or female man,) because she was taken out of
man" (ish.)   A beautiful type this of the church,
which is Christ's body; fashioned out of His death,
springing up in union with Him in resurrection,
composed of members of His body, of His flesh, and
of His bones, partaker of life in union with and derived
from Him.   God's gift to Christ, to be presented
faultless before the presence of His glory, on the
morning of the resurrection.

This body is now in the process of being formed,
"in continuance fashioned," the members having been
all written in the book of God, and having been all
seen in union with Christ when He was raised from
the dead, and curiously wrought in the lowest parts
of the earth.

Allusion is made to this in Eph. iv. 9, where the
Lord is spoken of as having ascended up on high, and
giving gifts unto men—His ascension being the result
of His having descended first into the lower parts of
the earth.   This expression "lower parts of the earth,"
(katotera,) Eph. iv. 9, seems to be taken from the
Greek of the 139th Psalm, (Sept. cxxxviii. 15,) where
we have the words "*lowest* parts of the earth."
(*tois katotato.*)

The Lord Jesus being raised up from the dead, and
exalted by the right hand of God, and having received
of the Father the promise of the Holy Ghost, shed
forth that blessed spirit upon His disciples, thereby
giving gifts which should fit them for their various
places in the body; knitting them together in the unity
of the Spirit, that they might grow up into Him in all
things which is the head even Christ.

We have this type of the anointing of Aaron
alluded to in Psa. cxxxiii, "Behold how good and how
pleasant it is for brethren to dwell together in unity.
It is like the precious ointment upon the head, that ran

down upon the beard, even Aaron's beard, that went down to the skirts of his garments."

The good oil is spoken of as first upon the head, then descending upon the beard, and finally upon the skirts of Aaron's garments. The word which we translate " skirts," is properly " *mouth* " in the singular number. It is nowhere else in Scripture translated skirts, but on two other occasions when connected with dress it is rendered " hole," and " collar." It is the " hole " in the top of the blue robe of the Ephod, around which a band was placed that it be not rent. Exod. xxviii. 32.; xxxix. 23. In Job xxx. 18, the same word is rendered " *collar* of my coat. Two entirely different Hebrew words are used for " *skirts*."

From this it has been surmised, that the allusion is to the holy anointing oil descending from Aaron's beard, upon the hole of the blue robe of the Ephod, which was very close to the breastplate ; and that the type thus employed was to represent the anointing of Aaron's head, reaching the ephod robe, and the names of Israel engraved on the ephod breastplate, linking on those names, by means of one stream of oil, with the head of the high priest. The only difficulty which arises to make one question this interpretation is, that *garments* is in the plural, and therefore implies that more than one garment of the high priest was reached by the oil.

Whichever way it be taken the truth prefigured is much the same. Aaron's garments were all representative, being worn by him as one who stood before God on behalf of others. This good oil wherewith he was anointed, flowed from his head down to these garments for glory and beauty, forming a connexion between his anointing, and the people whom he represented before God.

We as believers have received an unction from the Holy One, from Christ Jesus, our anointed Head. The Lord is called the " Holy One " in the following

Scriptures : Mark i. 24. ; Luke iv. 34. ; Acts iii. 14.
The title, "the Holy One" does not seem to be given
to the Spirit of God ; but when He is spoken of, the
word *Spirit* is always added.

This unction, (chrism,) 1st John ii. 20, teaches us all
things, enabling us to discern between truth and error :
"is truth and is no lie," abides in us, and teaches us to
abide in Him, Christ.    It is the spirit of unity and
of brotherhood, helping us to *dwell* together in unity,
(not merely to meet occasionally together,) but to abide
in one, and that with all saints.    Wherever separation
comes in and divides believers from one another, the
bond of brotherhood is made to yield to some other
bond ; the tie of life and union with Christ, witnessed
by the Holy Spirit's presence and power, is sacrificed
to some fleshly association.    A portion it may be of
God's truth is made the bond which links certain of
God's children together, or they gather round some
human leader or head, and the dwelling together in
unity of the "holy brethren" is set aside.    The apostle
saw the germs of all this schism working at Corinth,
and he spoke to them as *carnal* in consequence, although
they were distinguished for much manifestation of the
gifts of the Spirit.    Even the name of Christ may be
used in a sectarian way.    "I of Christ." 1st Cor. i. 12.
It may be adopted in the way of a boastful assertion, to
imply that others are not of Him, because they are not
taking precisely the same course, or viewing certain subjects of truth exactly in the same way.    This tendency
was early displayed in the disciples.    Even John rebuked
one who was clearly on the Lord's side ; "because he
followeth not with us."

The Spirit would, doubtless, lead us into all truth if
we were willing to be led ; but early prejudices, and
our own natural self-will and self-conceit, are grievous
hindrances to His power.    Division and dissension are
almost sanctioned now as of the Spirit, and are sometimes
gloried in as good for the church of God.    Thus the

Holy Spirit is grieved, and the word of God becomes of none effect; and *love*, that bond of perfectness is chilled in the heart. There is evidently a struggle in the church of God at this time after more manifested and conscious unity, and fellowship. May the Lord increase this desire a hundred-fold—and may we be more like little children, seeking to learn through that anointing and the word of God, how to keep "the unity of the Spirit in the bond of peace." "God hath not given us the spirit of cowardice, but of power, and of love, and of a sound mind." 2nd Tim. i. 7. "Where envy is, there is confusion and every evil work. But the wisdom that is from above, is first pure, then peaceable, gentle, easy to be entreated, full of mercy and good fruits, without partiality, without hypocrisy." James iii. 16, 17.

Believers have not to *form* a unity; but " with all lowliness and meekness, with long-suffering, forbearing one another in love," they are to endeavour " to keep the unity of the Spirit in the bond of peace."

The Spirit's unity is described in the seven unities which follow.

One body,
And one Spirit.
One hope of your calling.
One Lord.
One Faith.
One Baptism.
One God and Father of all,
Who is above all, and through all, and in you all. Eph. iv. 2—6.

To endeavour to keep the unity of the Spirit will consist in our endeavouring to hold fast these seven truths, in which every believer is supposed from the first to have been grounded and settled. God has already formed and defined the one body; and one Spirit dwells in and pervades that one body. The responsibility rests upon each member of that body, to use all diligence to keep the unity of the Spirit, by holding fast these great truths, these facts upon which the body is founded as one.

Let us remember that uniformity or confederacy is not unity. The unity of the Spirit must extend to the whole of the one body, and therefore anything which on our part hinders any member of that one body from manifesting the unity of the Spirit, or anything that hinders the edifying of the one body as a whole, is a breach of the unity of the Spirit.

Aaron having been clothed and anointed, his sons were next clothed with their garments for glory and beauty ; and the second part of the chapter ends with the words, " *as the Lord commanded Moses.*"

Aaron and his sons now stood arrayed in fitting garments for service. But the means whereby they had been separated off to God, had not yet been made manifest in the type. Neither had they as yet, any gifts or sacrifices which they could present. The subsequent part of the chapter therefore takes up the sacrifices in detail, which were the real power of their consecration, and with which their hands were filled for service.

## The Altar of Burnt Offering Partly Covered

# THE OFFERINGS

## THE BULLOCK FOR A SIN-OFFERING

"Thou shalt cause a bullock to be brought before the tabernacle of the congregation: and Aaron and his sons shall put their hands upon the head of the bullock.

"And thou shalt kill the bullock before the Lord by the door of the tabernacle of the congregation.

"And thou shalt take of the blood of the bullock, and put it upon the horns of the altar with thy finger, and pour all the blood beside the bottom of the altar.

"And thou shalt take all the fat that covereth the inwards, and the caul that is above the liver, and the two kidneys, and the fat that is upon them, and burn them upon the altar.

"But the flesh of the bullock, and his skin, and his dung, shalt thou burn with fire without the camp: it is a sin offering."

Exod. xxix 10—14

"And he brought the bullock for the sin-offering: and Aaron and his sons laid their hands upon the head of the bullock for the sin-offering.

"And he slew it: and Moses took the blood and put it upon the horns of the altar round about with his finger, and purified the altar, and poured the blood at the bottom of the altar, and sanctified it to make reconciliation upon it.

"And he took all the fat that was upon the inwards, and the caul above the liver, and the two kidneys, and their fat, and Moses burnt it upon the altar.

"But the bullock, and his hide, his flesh, and his dung, he burnt with fire without the camp, as the Lord commanded Moses."

Lev. viii 14—17

THE first offering brought by Moses was "the bullock for the sin-offering," or as it might be better rendered, "*the bullock the sin.*" The word "*offering*" is never found in the Hebrew, connected with the various sacrifices.

"And Aaron and his sons laid their hands upon the head of the bullock, the sin."

This word "*laid*" has sometimes the thought of laying, or leaning the hand heavily—thus in Psa. lxxxviii. 7, it is translated "thy wrath *lieth* hard upon me."

The priestly house had to become acquainted with the sin-offering. They were the first portion of Israel that ever knew an offering for sin. Hitherto every sacrifice which had been presented to God, from Abel

downwards, had been a burnt-offering ; and even when
the covenant was confirmed by the shedding of blood,
Exod. xxiv. that blood was procured from burnt-offerings
and peace offerings. Thus an offering solely and
peculiarly appropriated to sin, had never been known
until the consecration of the priests. We must remember
that this 8th chapter of Leviticus which we are consider
ing, in point of time, preceded the first seven chapters
of that book, for the events therein related took place
when the tabernacle was first set up. Exod. xl. 12—15.

Aaron and his sons by laying their hands heavily upon
the head of the victim, recognized their identification
with it, typically transferring their sin from off themselves,
to the bullock thus appointed to bear it. It was like the
act of faith in a sinner when he first trusts in Jesus, and
who believes that his sin has been borne by Christ ; like
the verse of our well-known hymn,

> " By faith I lay my hand,
>     On that dear head of thine,
> Whilst like a penitent I stand.
>     And there confess my sin."

Moses then slew the bullock. Death at once followed
the transfer of sin upon its head—death by the hand of
another. Throughout this scene Moses seems to take
the place of God—Aaron and his sons are completely
passive—he deals with them as God commands.

The grand aspect of Christ's death is that He
suffered at the hands of God. God provided the Lamb,
" and it pleased the Lord to bruise him." God made
" his soul an offering for sin."

Moses next took the blood, putting it on the horns of
the altar, (of burnt-offering) round about with his finger,
thereby purifying the altar—and poured the blood at the
bottom of the altar and sanctified it, to make reconciliation upon it.

This action of putting the blood with the *finger* on
the horns of the brazen altar is confined to the blood of
the sin-offering. Lev. iv. 25, 30, 34.

It is perhaps expressive of a knowledge of the value of the blood, as to its cleansing power—Moses the clean person handling it, and applying its value to the horns of the altar ; the horns representing the power, or the strength of the altar. The blood of the *sin-offering alone* was *poured* at the bottom of the altar. Exod. xxix. 12 ; Lev. iv. 7, 18, 25, 30, 34.

The altar was thus established upon blood—poured out blood was the very basis upon which it stood. It was Israel's place of access to God, where gifts also were presented. It was founded upon the blood shed. In Psa. xxii. 14, we have the blessed Lord on the cross uttering his deep sorrows in death to God, and saying, " I am *poured* out like water "—and again in Isa. liii. 12, " he hath *poured out* (or emptied) his soul unto death." To this also the Lord makes allusion when on the night of His betrayal, " He took the cup, and gave thanks, and gave it to them, (His disciples,) saying, drink ye all of it, for this is my blood of the new covenant, which is *shed* for many for the remission of sins." Matt. xxvi. 27, 28 ; Mark xiv. 24. And again, " this cup is the new covenant in my blood, which is *shed* for you." Luke xxii. 20.

The great canon of truth " without shedding of blood is no remission," is here typically declared.

Three chief uses of the blood are emphatically declared in this 15th verse of Lev. viii. purification, sanctification, and reconciliation.

The word which we translate cleanse, or purify, is the same as is elsewhere translated " *to sin* "—only a little varied in its inflection. How remarkably the Spirit of God calls our attention (even by the use of words) to the fact that we can only be cleansed from our *sins*, by the blood of Him who was *made sin*. A serpent of brass raised up upon a pole, was presented to the eye of a dying Israelite, as the only object that could give him life, when he was suffering from the bite of a fiery serpent. Num. xxi. 8.

The blood *put with the finger*, purified. The blood *poured out*, sanctified, and reconciled. So it is with the saved sinner. He is reconciled to God—atoned for by the shedding of the blood of Christ. Through that one offering also, he is sanctified ; and the blood applied to his heart purges him from an evil conscience.

The priests had themselves first to realize the value of the blood ; its power to purify, sanctify and atone, constituting them worshippers of God. After this they could present a sin-offering for other Israelites, with some appreciation of its value.

Portions of the bullock, all the fat that was upon the inwards, and the caul above the liver, and the two kidneys and their fat, were next burned upon the altar by Moses—but the bullock itself and his hide, his flesh, and his dung he burnt with fire without the camp.

Two distinct words are employed for these two burnings, and they are never interchanged. The one is always used when either the whole animal, or portions of it were burned upon the altar of burnt-offering ; the other, when the victim was burnt for sin outside the camp. In the first the thought of a sweet savour going up to God is connected with the word. Incense is derived from it—we find it in the following cases.

The burnt-offerings. Lev. i. 9, 13, 15, 17.

Meat-offering. Lev. ii. 2, 9, 16.

Parts of the peace sacrifice. Lev. iii. 5, 11, 16.

Parts of the sin-offering. Lev. iv. 10, 19, 26, 31, 35.

Incense. Exod. xxx. 7, 8 ; xl. 27.

In the second the idea of fierce consuming fire is attached to it. It is generally connected with the word fire ; and is used for burning in wrath. For instance, where Nadab and Abihu were burnt, Lev. x. 6 ; Korah's company, Num. xvi. 37.

Its use is confined (amongst the sacrifices) to the consuming of the sin-offering outside the camp. Exod. xxix. 14 ; Lev. iv. 12, 21 ; xvi. 27, 28 ; and the red heifer, Num. xix. 5.

In this beautiful type we have two thoughts inseparably connected together. The death of the Lord Jesus under the wrath of God on account of sin, consumed like the victim outside the camp, at the same time *that death* was the odour of a sweet savour to God ; like the portions burnt as incense on the altar of burnt-offering.

The third portion of the chapter closes here, with the words again repeated, " *as the Lord commanded Moses.*'

## THE RAM FOR THE BURNT-OFFERING

" Thou shalt also take one ram ; and Aaron and his sons shall put their hands upon the head of the ram.

" And thou shalt slay the ram, and thou shalt take his blood, and sprinkle it round about upon the altar.

" And thou shalt cut the ram in pieces, and wash the inwards of him and his legs, and put them unto his pieces, and unto his head.

" And thou shalt burn the whole ram upon the altar ; it is a burnt offering unto the Lord : it is a sweet savour, an offering made by fire unto the Lord."—Exod. xxix 15—18

" And he brought the ram for the burnt-offering : and Aaron and his sons laid their hands upon the head of the ram.

" And he killed it ; and Moses sprinkled the blood upon the altar round about.

" And he cut the ram into pieces ; and Moses burnt the head, and the pieces, and the fat.

" And he washed the inwards and the legs in water ; and Moses burnt the whole ram upon the altar : it was a burnt sacrifice for a sweet savour, and an offering made by fire unto the Lord ; as the Lord commanded Moses."— Lev. viii 18—21

NEXT " he brought the ram for the burnt-offering." The burnt-offering is the highest sacrifice in Scripture, for all of it ascended from off the fire of the altar as a sweet savour unto the Lord. The Hebrew word (ohlah) translated " *burnt-offering*," means in reality that which " *ascends*," or " *goes up*." It designates a sacrifice which entirely ascended in fragrance. Noah's offerings when he came out from the ark into the new world, were of this character. Gen. viii. 20, 22. " The Lord smelled a sweet savour," or as it is in the margin,

" a savour of rest," and said in His heart, I will not again curse the ground any more for man's sake ; for the imagination of man's heart is evil from his youth : neither will I again smite any more every thing living as I have done. While the earth remaineth, seed time and harvest, and cold and heat, and summer and winter, and day and night shall not cease." Abraham was also directed to offer Isaac for a *"burnt-offering."* Gen. xxii. 2—13.

Whilst God's perfect rest, satisfaction and delight in this sacrifice were expressed by its all ascending as a sweet savour; the devotedness also, and perfect obedience of Him whom it pourtrayed, are implied in the words recorded of the offerer, Lev. i. 3, *" he shall offer it of his own voluntary will."* And throughout this 8th chap. of Lev. the words *" and he brought,"* ver. 14, 18, 22, express the readiness of the victim to draw near the altar, like the phrase, Isa. liii. 7, " he is *brought* as a lamb to the slaughter ;" or as it is in Acts viii. 32, " he was *led* as a sheep to the slaughter."

In the Gospel of John we have this Scripture remarkably fulfilled. "And they *led* him away to Annas first—then *led* they Jesus from Caiaphas." Chap. xviii. 13, 28. " Then *came Jesus forth* wearing the crown of thorns. He *brought* Jesus *forth*. They took Jesus and *led* him away. And he, bearing his cross, *went forth*." xix. 5, 13, 16, 17.

" And Aaron and his sons laid their hands upon the head of the ram, and killed it," ver. 18, 19.

Again, they identified themselves with the victim. All their sins and failures in obedience being transferred from themselves to it. Immediately this was done, Moses killed the ram. Death instantly succeeded the laying of their hands upon its head.

" And Moses sprinkled the blood upon the altar round about." Thus the altar was completely conse-crated by blood. Blood had been put upon the horns of it round about ; had been poured at the bottom of it, and now was sprinkled round about it. The top, base, and sides presented in every direction the records of death ; for there can be no access to God, and no worship, save through death, the death of Christ.

" And he cut the ram into pieces, and Moses burnt the head, and the pieces, and the fat. And he washed the inwards and the legs in water ; and Moses burnt the whole ram upon the altar," ver. 20, 21.

Every portion of the ram came under the eye of Moses. The head, the seat of mind and intellect : the inwards, the seat of the will and affections : the legs, the tokens of the outward walk and conduct. All were scrutinized, and presented in perfect cleanness to God, upon the altar. The type this of the unblemished ways, and spotless intrinsic purity of Christ.

" In Him is no sin." 1st John iii. 5.

" He knew no sin." 2nd Cor. v. 21.

" He did no sin." 1st Pet. ii. 22.

And though tempted in all points like as we are, He was " without sin." Heb. iv. 15. A blessed fourfold testimony to the perfection of Christ. But this is not all. Not only sinless, so as to be personally ignorant of sin ; without it under every temptation ; and never doing it ; but actively devoting Himself to God throughout the whole course of His life on earth, and at last in perfect subjection and obedience, yielding up that life on the cross ; giving " Himself for us an offering and a sacrifice to God for a sweet smelling savour." Eph. v. 2. In all the full value of Him, who thus gave Himself, we are accepted. The same burnt-offering whose blood was poured out as an atonement for sin, was burnt as a sweet savour upon the altar. And the priests who laid their hands upon it, found remission of sin through the shedding of its blood, and at the same time perfect acceptance with God, according to the full value of the spotless victim consumed on the altar.

Although the sin-offering presented most strongly and vividly the aspect of Christ's death under wrath, because

of sin, yet even in that case portions of the sacrifice were
burnt as a sweet savour upon the altar.  And the burnt-
offering, which has regard more especially to the death
of Christ as that through which we are perfectly justified, and according to the value of which we are
accepted of God ; still keeps in view the fact, that *that*
death has also atoned for us as sinners.  In the shedding
of blood, *sin*, the cause of death, is always acknowledged.   And as without shedding of blood there could
be no remission ; so also, there can be no justification
but by the blood.   The song of (Rev. v. 9, 12) is, "Thou
art worthy . . . . . for thou wast slain, and hast redeemed
us to God by thy blood."

   "Worthy is the Lamb that was slain," seems especially to contemplate the death of the Lord Jesus, in all
the value of the burnt-offering.   We claim His worthiness, whilst we own our worthlessness.   We are
accepted in the Beloved, whilst in ourselves, " we were
by nature the children of wrath, even as others."

   The fourth part of the chapter here concludes with
the same words before repeated, " *as the Lord commanded
Moses.*"

# THE RAM OF CONSECRATION

"And thou shalt take the other ram; and Aaron and his sons shall put their hands upon the head of the ram.

"Then shalt thou kill the ram, and take of his blood, and put it upon the tip of the right ear of Aaron, and upon the tip of the right ear of his sons, and upon the thumb of their right hand, and upon the great toe of their right foot, and sprinkle the blood upon the altar round about."—Exod. xxix 19 20

"And he brought the other ram, the ram of consecration: and Aaron and his sons laid their hands upon the head of the ram.

"And he slew it; and Moses took of the blood of it, and put it upon the tip of Aaron's right ear, and upon the thumb of his right hand, and upon the great toe of his right foot.

"And he brought Aaron's sons, and Moses put of the blood upon the tip of their right ear, and upon the thumbs of their right hands, and upon the great toes of their right feet: and Moses sprinkled the blood upon the altar round about"—Lev. viii 22—24

THE last sacrifice offered was "the Ram of Consecration." Two rams were brought, (v. 1 ;) one was offered for a burnt-offering, and the other is called "the ram of consecrations;" or, of filling (the hands.) The word *consecrations* is in the plural, and is found in Exod. xxix. 22, 26, 27 : "for it is a ram of consecrations"—"the ram of Aaron's consecrations"—"the ram of the consecrations." Lev. viiii. 22, 29. In Exod. xxix. 34, the word occurs in the plural—"flesh of the consecrations," as it ought to be throughout.

Aaron and his sons laid their hands upon the head of this ram, and Moses slew it, as in the two former cases. The death of the victim following immediately upon this act of identification.

"And Moses took of the blood of it, and put it upon the tip of Aaron's right ear, and upon the thumb of his right hand, and upon the great toe of his right foot. And he brought Aaron's sons, and Moses put of the blood upon the tip of their right ear, and upon the thumbs of their right hands, and upon the great toes of their right feet." Thus the ear, the right hand, and the right foot of Aaron and his sons, were dedicated to God

by blood. From henceforth their ear was to listen to
no sounds, but such as might be heard in connection
with the blood of the sacrifice.

So also the believer at the present time. His ear has
been consecrated to God, through the death of Christ,
that he might hearken to His voice ; inclining his ear to
hear heavenly words ; and listening to the voice of the
Good Shepherd. He is to allow no whispers of temptation, and no sound of human revelry or ambition, to
enter his priestly ear : but to be deaf as his Lord was,
opening the ears of others, whilst He Himself heard not
the temptations of the enemy. Isa. xlii. 19, 20. That
perfect servant of Jehovah was blind and deaf—blind
to all fascinations of the world, and deaf to every
suggestion of Satan. And when at last led to the
slaughter, He was dumb, uttering no words of reviling
or threatening when falsely accused ; not opening His
mouth when buffetted, spit upon, mocked, and crucified.

May we set before ourselves the blessed example of
our Lord, and remember that by His blood we have a
priestly circumcised ear.

The thumbs of the right hand were also touched
with the blood. The *right hand* is in Scripture used to
express *power*. " Thy right hand, O Lord, is become
glorious in power ; thy right hand, O Lord, hath dashed
in pieces the enemy." " Thou stretchedst out thy right
hand, the earth swallowed them." Exod. xv. 6, 12.

And also *skill*. " A wise man's heart is at his *right
hand*, but a fool's heart, at his left." Eccl. x. 2. That is,
he guides the activities of his hand with wisdom : he is
prompt also to execute the counsels of his heart.

" If I forget thee, O Jerusalem, let my right hand
forget (her cunning.) Psa. cxxxvii. 5. The psalmist
finds it as impossible to forget Jerusalem, as it would
be impossible for his *right hand* not to act with rapidity
and skill at the prompting of his will.

The thumb is that part which peculiarly distinguishes
the human hand from the paw of those animals, which

in appearance most resemble the human form. It is the most valuable finger of the hand; without it, this member of the body would be comparatively useless.

The priestly hand touched with the blood was consecrated to handle gifts and sacrifices for God. Its skilfulness was devoted to the Lord's service, and the priest was not to touch any unclean or dead thing. Another beautiful type of the occupations of the believer, whose business in life is to serve God in all that he undertakes. Even when handling the things of this world, he is to do so to God's glory. His faculties, his powers of mind and body, are for the Lord; the precious blood has separated him off to God, and the most ordinary actions of life, which as an unbeliever he performed in self-will, and for mere self-pleasing, he is now to do "to the glory of God."

In all things he is to "seek first the kingdom of God and his righteousness;" and strange as it may seem, he is not to labour for the meat that perisheth, but for that meat which endureth unto everlasting life. This latter precept of the Lord Jesus has been softened down by some to mean, that "we are not to labour inordinately, or exclusively, for the meat which perisheth, and that if the text were taken without some qualification, it would encourage idleness." In answer to this, it may be said that we have no right to qualify the text. The words of the Lord are distinct and emphatic, "labour not for the meat which perisheth." The difficulty is easily solved. We are, even in the necessary occupations of life, to make the Lord's glory our object, and not to be labouring for the meat which perisheth, as if that were our *only* purpose. We are to do all things in such a way, that we may be exhibiting ourselves as sons of God without rebuke, shining as lights in the world. Phil. ii. 14, 15; and we are not to live as if we had two existences, a secular, and a religious.

Lastly, the blood was put upon the great toes of their right feet. The Hebrew word is the same for great toe as for thumb. The principal finger of the most active hand, and the principal toe of the most active foot, were alike touched with the blood. No pathway was to be followed, in which the priest could not walk with the blood anointed foot. His feet being holy, he was ever to tread upon holy ground, passing his life in the precincts of the sanctuary. So the priests to God of the present time are to be careful in their walk and conduct, lest they be found treading unholy paths, mingling themselves in the world's follies and amusements, forgetful of the blood whereby they have been sanctified. Our feet were naturally swift to shed blood—destruction and misery were in our ways—the way of peace we once knew not. Rom. iii. 15, 17. Now, our path is to be that of the righteous ; our feet are to be beautiful, as messengers of glad tidings ; our ways are to be ways of pleasantness and peace. May we avoid all companies into which we cannot go with the blood sprinkled feet ; into which we cannot carry the good news of the blessed name of Jesus. The ear, the hand, and the foot are the Lord's. " Ye are not your own, for ye are bought with a price, therefore glorify God in your body." 1st Cor. vi. 19, 20.

Moses next "sprinkled the blood upon the altar round about." ver 24. The same blood which had been put upon the priests, was sprinkled on the altar. Thus the vessel at which they habitually ministered was alike separated off to God with themselves. The patterns of things in the heavens being purified with these typical sacrifices, whilst the heavenly things themselves with better sacrifices than these. Heb. ix 23

"Also thou shalt take of the ram the fat and the rump, and the fat that covereth the inwards, and the caul above the liver, and the two kidneys, and the fat that is upon them, and the right shoulder ; for it is a ram of consecration :

"And he took the fat, and the rump, and all the fat that was upon the inwards, and the caul above the liver, and the two kidneys, and their fat, and the right shoulder :
"And out of the basket of unleavened bread, that was before

"And one loaf of bread, and one cake of oiled bread, and one wafer out of the basket of the unleavened bread that is before the Lord.

"And thou shalt put all in the hands of Aaron, and in the hands of his sons; and thou shalt wave them for a wave offering before the Lord.

"And thou shalt receive them of their hands, and burn them upon the altar for a burnt offering, for a sweet savour before the Lord: it is an offering made by fire unto the Lord.

"And thou shalt take the breast of the ram of Aaron's consecration, and wave it for a wave offering before the Lord: and it shall be thy part.

"And thou shalt sanctify the breast of the wave offering, and the shoulder of the heave offering, which is waved, and which is heaved up, of the ram of the consecration, even of that which is for Aaron, and of that which is for his sons:

"And it shall be Aaron's and his sons' by a statute for ever from the children of Israel; for it is an heave offering: and it shall be an heave offering from the children of Israel of the sacrifice of their peace offerings, even their heave offering unto the Lord.—Exod. xxix 22—28

the Lord, he took one unleavened cake, and a cake of oiled bread, and one wafer, and put them on the fat, and upon the right shoulder:

"And he put all upon Aaron's hands, and upon his sons' hands, and waved them for a wave offering before the Lord.

"And Moses took them from off their hands, and burnt them on the altar upon the burnt offering: they were consecrations for a sweet savour: it is an offering made by fire unto the Lord.

"And Moses took the breast, and waved it for a wave offering before the Lord: for of the ram of consecration it was Moses' part; as the Lord commanded Moses.—Lev. viii 25—29

SEVEN portions of the ram were thus taken by Moses: the fat, and the rump, and all the fat that was upon the inwards, and the caul above the liver, and the two kidneys, and their fat, and the right shoulder.

The word for "fat" has especial reference to the inside fat of the victim, and is in the margin of Lev. iii. 3, translated "suet." Three portions of fat were taken; the fat, all the fat that was upon the inwards, and the fat of the kidneys. This proved the healthiness, the inward vigour of the animal. No human eye could perceive this development of life, until the victim had been slain. Beautiful figure this of the complete devotedness of Christ, as to all His inward affections, and will, and desires, to please God ; He could say, " I delight to do thy will O my God—yea thy law is within my heart." Psa. xl. 8. The truth of this wonderful inner life, in all its richness and fulness dedicated to God, was made manifest when the Lord hung upon the tree, " obedient unto death, even the death of the cross." We can now look back upon the life and ways of the blessed Lord, and see in them that humbling of Himself ; that dedication to God ; that one object of pursuit, to glorify God ; the one motive of His heart, which He finally so marvellously displayed in laying down His life at the commandment of His Father. He that discerneth the thoughts and intents of the heart, could be appealed to by Christ in the words of Psa. cxxxix. 23, " search me, O God, and know my heart ; try me, and know my thoughts ; and see if there be any wicked way in me," or (margin) " way of pain or grief." He could challenge the eyes of Him to whom all things are naked and opened, to search His inmost soul, well knowing that there was not a thought within, which would grieve His Father, but that He would have the ready response, " my beloved Son in whom I am well pleased."—" mine elect in whom my soul delighteth." Love to God being the pure motive from which all His actions took their rise, He could with truth say, " I do always those things that please him." John viii. 29. Blessed perfectness, sinless purity, unswerving obedience ! How contrasted with the mixed motives, the unclean desires, the constant unbelief and disobedience which meet the eye of our heavenly Father, as He marks our thoughts and intents, as He searches our purposes and our ways.

" The caul above the liver." It will be perceived on referring to the margin of the Bible, that " midriff "

is substituted for "caul." Exod. xxix. 13 ; Lev. iii. 4.
And this probably is the right translation, midriff, or
diaphragm, being the portion here specified. This is a
muscular membrane, dividing the body into two parts,
and is the great organ by means of which the breath
is inhaled. It is in the type always mentioned in
close connection with the liver.

The word "*above*," or *upon* the liver is used in
Exod. xxix. 13 ; Lev iii. 4, 10, 15 ; iv. 9 ; vii. 4 ; ix, 10.
This word "*above*" is omitted in Exod. xxix. 22 ;
Lev. viii. 16, 25 ; ix. 19, in which passages, the caul
would almost seem to be identified with the liver.

Thus the organ by which the victim breathed, (the
midriff,) and which was closely connected with that
(the liver) wherein gall and bitterness were naturally
secreted,* was wholly presented to God. In the
Antitype the whole power of His inner life, every breath
He drew was altogether for God—and there was no
gall or bitterness in Him ; no envy or malice to taint
the inward feelings of His soul. He was "meek and
lowly in heart."

Two other portions, "the rump, and the two
kidneys," were also selected. The kidneys are elsewhere translated, *reins*. God is said to try, to search,
and to see the heart and reins. Psa. vii. 9 ; Jer. xi. 20 ;
xvii. 10 ; xx. 12. He searches the inward motive, and
the secret affection. The hidden desire is known to
Him. The Lord Jesus could appeal to the judgment
of God, and say, "Judge me, O Lord, for I have
walked in mine integrity : I have trusted also in the
Lord : I shall not slide. Examine me, O Lord, and
prove me; try my reins and my heart." Psa. xxvi. 1, 2.
He was the only one who could claim an integrity of
His own. And this word *integrity* is interesting,
because it is almost the same as the Thummim ; the

---

* Pliny says of the bile or gall secreted by the liver, "of all those things
which are generally to be found in every living creature, the gall is that which
is of greatest efficacy in operation; for power it hath naturally to heat, bite,
draw, discuss, and resolve."—*Richardson's Dict, under* "*gall.*"

perfections, the uprightnesses, placed in the breastplate
His inward perfections were the power of His outward
walk—like the upper and hinder part of the victim's
legs, presented with the kidneys. So also He could
say, " I shall not slide." His own integrity, and His
ceaseless trust in Jehovah preserved His foot in an even
place. And not only so, but when proved and tried,
yea, and scorched with the refining fire of God's
holiness, His reins and His heart were fit for the altar,
and yielded nothing but the sweetest savour to God.

The word, *try* my reins and my heart, is that used for
the refining of metals in the furnace. This blessed one
could also say, " I will bless the Lord who hath given
me counsel ; my reins also instruct me in the right
seasons." Psa. xvi. 7. The counsel He received from
Jehovah found an immediate response from His own will.
And in that one night of fearful sorrow, that unnatural
night—when the sun was darkened at noon-day, His
own desire to accomplish the commandment of God,
instructed Him to lay down His life of Himself, even
though in so doing He had to bear sin and shame, and
curse and wrath.

Wondrous perfection, when the inward will and
strength of the Son of Man, answered completely the
mind and purpose and counsel of God.

*The right shoulder* completed these precious portions of
the ram of consecrations, expressive of the power
patiently to endure, all that might be laid upon the victim
by the hands of another.

There was strength in Jesus adequate to the heavy
burden laid upon Him by God—in nothing did He fail.
He bore the weight of our sins upon the tree, till He
knew that the stripes of God upon His soul had reached
the appointed number, and till the bruising of Jehovah
ended in His yielding up the ghost. God could,
according to the infinite measure of His own holiness,
and His infinite judgment upon sin, say, " it is enough."
The burden had been borne—the chastisement of our

peace was completed. The strength of the blessed victim had sufficed, and the body of the Lord laid in the tomb in the helplessness of death, witnessed that sin was put away, and remitted—and that the great object which from all eternity had been in the counsels of God, was completed. The way of access for the sinner to the glory was made—the way into the holiest was laid open.

Moses next took out of the basket three sorts of bread—one unleavened cake—one unleavened cake mingled with oil—and one wafer, unleavened, anointed with oil.

Leaven is universally used in Scripture, as a type of sin spreading its corrupting influence. A secret working of evil, which may not be outwardly manifest, but which arises from a corrupt nature within. All types therefore of the blessed Lord, which refer to Him as the bread from heaven, are without leaven. No leaven could be burnt on the altar in any offering of the Lord made by fire ; because God could not accept a sacrifice in which there was the slightest taint or corruption.

Three aspects of Christ as the bread of life are presented to us in these three portions selected from the basket of unleavened bread :—

First, His sinless purity, the unleavened cake. Next, as the Christ of God—from His birth filled with the Holy Ghost, the unleavened cake mingled with oil ; and thirdly, as anointed by the Holy Ghost with power to accomplish the most minute precept of God, the unleavened wafer, anointed with oil. He is the unleavened bread of sincerity and truth—the true bread from heaven—the bread of life— the living bread—the bread of God—the bread which God has provided. The sixth chapter of John seems to be the Lord's exposition of the manna, and the meat-offerings. And we find in that chapter, He mingles the thought of flesh and blood with bread. " The bread that I will give is my flesh.".—" whoso eateth my flesh and drinketh my blood hath eternal life."—" for my flesh is true meat, and my blood is true drink."—" he that eateth me even he shall live by me."—" this is that bread which came down from heaven—he that eateth of this bread shall live for ever," verses 51, 54, 55, 57, 58. Thus the Lord closely connects the fact of His death, with His being the bread of life. Indeed there is no feeding on Christ except in close connection with His death on the cross. The contemplation of His life of perfect obedience, will not avail us, or strengthen our souls to follow His example, unless we connect such meditations with the sacrifice of Himself upon the tree. These cakes therefore were presented to God, already baken in the oven— a type of Christ contemplated in His death.

*Filling the hands.* Moses put these unleavened cakes " on the fat, and on the right shoulder, and put all upon Aaron's hands, and upon his sons' hands, and waved them for a wave offering before the Lord," verses 26, 27.

Here we have an explanation of the word *"consecrations"* —in the Hebrew literally—*"fillings."* (of the hand.)

The word is used in the following connections :

" The ram of consecrations." Exod. xxix. 22, 26, 27 ; Lev. viii. 22, 29.

" The flesh of the consecrations." Exod. xxix. 34.

" Basket of consecrations." Lev. viii. 31.

" Days of consecrations." Lev. viii. 33.

" Consecrations* for a sweet savour." Lev. viii. 28.

The peculiar meat-offering recorded in Lev. vi. 19— 23, which was offered by Aaron and his sons on the day when he was anointed, is also called " consecrations." Lev. vii. 37.

Aaron's hands and his sons' hands were filled with parts of the ram, and the unleavened cakes. They handled the most precious portions of the sacrifice—thus appreciating their value ; their hands had previously been laid upon the heads of the victims, and thereby they had in figure transferred their own sin, guilt, and need to those victims. So these hands thus emptied of their

---

* The word " consecration " is plural in all these passages.

own guiltiness, were then filled with peculiarly choice parts of the slain ram, and with unleavened cakes of fine wheat flour—wondrous transfer! May we behold by faith, all our sin and misery laid on Jesus crucified, and may we have our hearts filled with contemplations of His preciousness.

We may be assured that our hands and hearts will be occupied with one thing, or another. Either the world with its vanities, and the flesh with its lusts will take their place within—or Christ and His comeliness, His beauty, His perfections, will fill our souls.

It seems as if the priests were waved with their hands thus filled, as a wave-offering before God. The attention of Jehovah was called to contemplate them. His eyes might be invited to search them, because their hands were filled with the costly consecrations. They were identified with, and became one with the hallowed things which they handled. This was one peculiar and especial part of priestly consecration. The priests had to estimate for themselves the value of the sacrifices, and to handle various portions thereof, that they might know how to approach and worship God, and might stand in the place of intercession for others.

The apostle John opens his epistle with a declaration of somewhat of this priestly experience, " that which was from the beginning, which we have heard, which we have seen with our eyes, which we have looked upon, and our hands have handled of the word of life. For the life was manifested, and we have seen it, and bear witness, and shew unto you that eternal life which was with the Father, and was manifested unto us—that which we have seen and heard declare we unto you." 1st John i. 1—3.

We have first to know for ourselves, and to see for ourselves, and as it were to touch and handle for ourselves the sacrifice, in its sweet savour and acceptableness to God ; before we can testify to others of its value, or can worship God in spirit and in truth. A witness must not ground his testimony upon mere hearsay reports which he has received from others ; but must himself know and comprehend the facts to which he testifies. The Lord Himself in speaking to Nicodemus says, " verily, verily I say unto thee, we speak that we do know, and testify that we have seen, and ye receive not our witness." John iii. 11. He speaks in the plural number, including all true witnesses with Himself, the faithful and true witness.

Are our hands so filled with Christ, are our hearts so occupied with Him, that we have no desire to meddle with the things of the world, and that out of the abundance of the heart the mouth speaketh ?

All these parts of the sacrifice, and the unleavened bread, which had filled the hands of the priests were taken by Moses " from off their hands and burnt on the altar, upon the burnt offering : they were consecrations for a sweet savour, it is an offering made by fire unto the Lord," v. 28.

The priests were by this act identified before the Lord with the burnt-offering, and accepted according to its sweet savour. They had been cleansed, atoned for, personally dedicated, had their hands filled, and were accepted, in the full value of the offerings which had been presented on their behalf to God, and according to the preciousness of the blood shed for them. One portion of the ram of consecration was especially reserved for Moses : he " waved the breast before the Lord, for of the ram of consecration it was Moses' part," v. 29.

Throughout this scene Moses acted on the part of Jehovah—as a substitute accurately fulfilling His commands. And the breast of the ram of consecrations became his portion on that account. He was to enter with something like the estimate of God, into the love of Him, who was portrayed in these sacrifices. The breast is a type of the seat of the affections. To God alone primarily belong the affections of Christ. To the Son of God alone primarily belong the affections of God.

Who can estimate, save the Father, the love of His Son;
and who can enter, save the Son, into the full understanding of the love of the Father?

And yet, wondrous grace! we hear the Lord saying,
" thou hast loved them as thou hast loved me ".—and it
is said by the Holy Spirit of Him, " He loved us and
gave Himself for us." God has given to us to know the
love of Jesus towards us. He has given us His own
heart's affections, and the affections of His Son. And Jesus
has revealed to us the deep secret of the cross, viz., that it
was love for the Father, and love for us because we are
loved of the Father, that led Him to lay down His life.
O mystery of love! the subject for our everlasting
contemplation, and for our eternal fellowship and joy.

Here closes the fifth portion of the chapter with the
words again repeated, " *as the Lord commanded Moses.*"

"And thou shalt take of the blood that is upon the altar, and of the anointing oil, and sprinkle it upon Aaron, and upon his garments, and upon his sons, and upon the garments of his sons with him: and he shall be hallowed, and his garments, and his sons, and his sons' garments with him."—Exod, xxix 21

" And Moses took of the anointing oil, and of the blood which was upon the altar, and sprinkled it upon Aaron, and upon his garments, and upon his sons, and upon his sons' garments with him; and sanctified Aaron, and his garments, and his sons, and his sons' garments with him,"—Lev. viii 30

IF we compare the parallel passage in Exod. xxix. 21, we
shall find a remarkable alteration both in the arrangement
of the verses, and in the order in which the blood stands
It will be observed in the passage in Exodus, that this
sprinkling upon Aaron and his garments, is placed immediately after the blood is put upon Aaron's right ear, etc.;
and the filling of the hands of Aaron and his sons comes
afterwards.

In this chapter of Leviticus which we are contemplating, the hands of the priests are filled before the
sprinkling takes place ; and immediately after their
ears, etc., are touched with the blood. In Exodus also
the blood is mentioned before the oil. In Leviticus the
anointing oil precedes the blood.

There may be a purpose in this variation, to link so closely together the anointing oil and the blood, and the blood and the anointing oil, that we may not either sever the one from the other, or give precedence to one before the other.

There has been a thought expressed by some of the Lord's people, that there may be an interval of time, between the salvation of a sinner through the application of the precious blood of Christ to his heart and conscience, and the anointing of the Holy Ghost. There has also been a tendency in writers on the work of the Holy Spirit, to attribute redemption to Christ, and sanctification to the Holy Spirit exclusively. The type we are contemplating negatives both these suppositions.

Immediately the sinner believes on the Lord Jesus he is born again ; the power of the Holy Ghost communicating to him life and faith in Jesus Christ, and Him crucified. The same Spirit baptizes him at the same moment into the one body, and he receives the Holy Ghost as the indwelling Spirit of God, because he is a child of God, and is united to the living Christ, the Son of God, a member of His body, of His flesh, and of His bones. But besides this establishing of the believer in Christ, he is also anointed with the Spirit of God. He is united to a Christ, an anointed one, and therefore has the Spirit of God. And he also receives a special anointing of the Spirit, enabling him to fulfil his duties as a member of the body, and giving him a gift in accordance with that membership.

The Spirit of God is also the seal, or stamp of God, upon the believer, proving by His very presence with, and in the believer, that he is a child of God—that he is a new creation of God—a deed executed by God— a fiat of God's love and power. The Spirit also is the earnest in the believer's heart of the future glory—a pledge from the right hand of the throne of God—from the risen Christ, of the glorious resurrection which shall be his when Christ returns. An earnest of the bright inheritance which awaits him, and which will be his in possession when Jesus comes.

The anointing oil and the blood go together. Redemption through the blood of Christ, and the anointing of the Spirit, are simultaneous. "Now he which stablisheth us with you in Christ, and hath anointed us, is God ; who hath also sealed us, and given the earnest of the Spirit in our hearts." 2nd Cor. i. 21, 22.

"In whom (Christ) ye also trusted after that ye heard the word of truth, the Gospel of your salvation: in whom also, after that ye believed, ye were sealed with that Holy Spirit of promise, which is the earnest of our inheritance, until the redemption of the purchased possession, unto the praise of his glory." Eph. i. 13, 14.

In this passage the words "after ye believed," do not imply any interval of time: they might better be rendered, "in whom having believed, ye were sealed;" or, according to our English idiom, we should insert the word, "*and ;*" "in whom ye believed and were sealed." Here the presence of the Holy Ghost with, and in the believer as God's seal, and as the earnest of the glory, is immediate upon faith.

We have a striking illustration of this in the case of Cornelius and his household, recorded in Acts x. An interval *had* elapsed between the conversion of the Jewish believers, and the descent of the Holy Ghost upon them at Pentecost. But there was no such interval in the case of these first Gentile converts. Immediately Peter in his discourse had reached the point where he declared that "through his name *whosoever* believeth in him shall receive remission of sins; while he yet spake these words, the Holy Ghost fell on all them which heard the word." Or as Peter himself declares, when subsequently relating the circumstance—"And as I began to speak the Holy Ghost fell on them, as on us at the beginning." Acts xi. 15. The word of faith was heard and believed, and the Spirit of God at once attested the fact by His presence and anointing. It is also interesting to remark, that Peter made use of the words " *whosoever* believeth in him," the very words of the Lord Jesus Himself, when preaching the Gospel to Nicodemus.

*Sanctified.*—Let us turn now to the subject of sanctification. It may be observed that the object of the whole ritual described in Exod. xxix. and Lev. viii. was to sanctify Aaron and his sons, in order that they might be priests. "And this is the thing that thou shalt do to hallow (or sanctify) them." And this sanctification is expressly repeated in connection with the blood and the oil : " And he shall be hallowed, (sanctified,) and his garments, and his sons, and his sons' garments with him." Exod. xxix. 21. " And sanctified Aaron and his garments, and his sons, and his sons' garments, with him." Lev. viii. 30. The sacrifices, the blood, and the oil, were the means employed in this sanctification.

Sanctification implies separation "*from*," and separation " *to*." Separation *from* sin and sinners, *unto* a holy God. A very concise and yet full definition of this occurs in Lev. xx. 26. "And ye shall be holy unto me ; for I the Lord am holy, and have severed you from other people, that ye should be mine." Israel had been severed from Egypt, and set apart to God in distinctness from all other nations of the earth. This separation had been effected through judgment. They had been redeemed from wrath, through the blood of the Paschal Lamb ; and had been redeemed out of Egypt and from Pharaoh's power, through the waters of the Red Sea.

Thus they had been sanctified to God. The family of the priests were still further sanctified ; being separated from the rest of Israel, and brought peculiarly nigh to God. The believer is by the blood of the Lamb, separated from the flesh, from sin, from the world, to be a child of God, a king and priest ; quickened together with Christ, risen with Christ, one with Christ, and therefore holy unto God his Father.

The Word of God speaks of sanctification as effected either by the will of God ; by the Holy Spirit as the agent; by the offering of Christ as the means; or, by the Word of God, as the instrument.

By the will of God—"by the which will we are sanctified, through the offering of the body of Jesus Christ once for all." Heb. x. 10.

This passage attributes sanctification to the eternal purpose of God, whose will it was to separate to Himself a family of priests ; and the way in which He was able to accomplish His will was through Christ coming to do it, and offering up Himself as a sacrifice for sin.

Paul, when relating before Agrippa the history of his wonderful conversion, gives a striking summary of the commission he then received from the Lord, to preach the Gospel to the Gentiles : " To open their eyes, to turn them from darkness to light, and from the power of Satan unto God, that they may receive forgiveness of sins, and inheritance among them which are sanctified by faith that is in me." Acts xxvi. 18.

Faith in Christ is here declared, by the Lord Jesus Himself, to be the sanctifying power; separating off the Gentile to be holy to the Lord, and to an inheritance with the saints in light. It is a " most holy faith," through which we Gentile sinners have been severed from the world around us, to be God's holy ones; and it is a " most holy faith " upon which we, thus sanctified, are to be constantly building ourselves. Jude 20.

In Jude, ver. 1, we have sanctification attributed to God the Father, or rather, the passage may be rendered, " sanctified in God the Father; " the security of the believer is contemplated, for he is looked at as holy, because of his union with the Father and the Son.

We find the phrase *" called saints "* occurring more than once in the epistles. In our version the words *" to be "* are unhappily inserted; they tend to impair the real force of the expression. We are actually made " saints," or holy ones by God's call ; for we are " Holy brethren, *partakers* of a heavenly calling." " Who *hath saved us, and called us with an holy calling,* not according to our works, but according to His own purpose and grace, which was given us in Christ Jesus before the world began." 2nd Tim. i. 9. " Ye also are *the called* of Jesus Christ, beloved of God, *called saints*." Rom. i. 6, 7. " All things work together for good, to them that love God, to them who are *the called* according to his purpose." Rom. viii. 28. " To them that are sanctified in Christ Jesus, *called saints*." 1st Cor. i. 2. " Preserved in Jesus Christ, *called*." Jude I. From all these passages it is clear God's call is not an exhortation from Him to us, requiring us to accomplish a holiness of our own, but that His calling is His own effectual act, separating us as holy ones to Himself. We are partakers of His calling; we are saints, made so by His calling. The voice of His power sounding effectually in our hearts, has transformed us from sinners to saints, has created us anew in Christ Jesus. We cannot be too particular as to this truth—for on the one hand there is a kind of inherent notion that in some way or other death purifies the sinner and makes him holy; and on the other hand there is a common belief even amongst the children of God, that the work of the Holy Ghost in the believer gradually renders him more holy, and more fit for heaven. Both these very current opinions are contrary to God's truth. A believer in Jesus is not sanctified by death, but he is sanctified in Christ Jesus. Neither is it any gradual operation of the Holy Ghost in us that makes us holy, so as to render us fit for God and His glory. The song in the glory will be " Worthy is the Lamb that was slain," and has " redeemed us to God by His blood."

The sinner is already saved through faith in the Lord Jesus, and has to give thanks to the Father that already "He hath made him meet to be a partaker of the inheritance of the saints in light;" that already "He hath delivered him from the power of darkness, and hath translated him into the kingdom of his dear Son;" " In whom" (His Son) already "he hath redemption through his blood, the forgiveness of sin." Col. i. 12—14.

Sanctification attributed to the Holy Spirit—"that the offering up of the Gentiles might be acceptable, being sanctified by the Holy Ghost." Rom. xv. 16. The apostle speaks of himself as a priest presenting to God a meat-offering of the Gentiles; like the new meat-offering on the day of Pentecost, when two wave loaves were waved before God as bread of first-fruits.

This type of first-fruits was fulfilled as regards the Jews on the day of Pentecost. There were no Gentiles present when the Holy Ghost was poured out. Paul being especially the apostle to the Gentiles, and writing his epistle to believers dwelling in the ruling Gentile city of the world, speaks of the presentation to God of Gentiles converted through his preaching, as a similar meat-offering; sanctified by the Holy Ghost; manifested as holy, by the presence and indwelling of that blessed Spirit. Like the oil poured upon a meat-offering.

Again, "God hath from the beginning chosen you to salvation through sanctification of the Spirit and belief of the truth." 2nd Thess. ii. 13.

And, "Elect according to the foreknowledge of God the Father, through sanctification of the Spirit, unto obedience, and sprinkling of the blood of Jesus Christ." 1st Peter i. 2.

In both these texts, the Spirit is presented as separating off in holiness the believer through belief in the truth in the first case; and in the latter, separating him off unto the obedience of faith, and unto the sprinkling of the blood of Jesus Christ. The Holy Spirit being the agent employed by God the Father to accomplish His will, in communicating faith in the precious blood of Christ to the sinner, in order to his salvation.

Sanctification is attributed to Christ. "Christ loved the Church and gave himself for it; that he might sanctify and cleanse it, with the washing of water by the word." Eph. v. 25, 26.

The Lord's death is presented to us in this passage as accomplished by Himself, that He might thereby sanctify and cleanse the Church. The cleansing power of the blood being applied by the word of God.

The Lord Jesus is also called the Sanctifier, "both he that sanctifieth, and they who are sanctified are all of one—for which cause he is not ashamed to call them brethren." Heb. ii. 11. And the means whereby He accomplishes this is His own precious blood—"Jesus also that he might sanctify the people with his own blood suffered without the gate." Heb. xiii. 12.

And believers are of God, "in Christ Jesus, who of God is made unto us wisdom, and righteousness, and sanctification, and redemption." A very blessed passage tracing our new creation up to God, in union with Christ, and telling us that Christ is made to us the full and blessed treasury of all wisdom, righteousness, holiness, and redemption. If we lack wisdom, God has given us all wisdom in Jesus. If we are conscious of unrighteousness, Christ is our righteousness. If we are conscious of our unholiness, He is our sanctification. If we look around us upon the world and find ourselves differing but little from the unredeemed, He is our redemption. We are in God's sight severed as far from this world, and as distinct from it, as the Lord Jesus Himself is at the right hand of God.

The Lord Jesus Himself was separated off as God's elect and sent into the world—that holy one, the Son of God. John x. 36. And He sanctified Himself for our sakes—separating Himself unto God through the death of the cross, that we might be sanctified through the truth. His prayer to the Father was, "sanctify them through thy truth, thy word is truth." John xvii. 17.

The Holy Spirit uses the word of God, first to communicate life in separation to God; and next, to cleanse us practically from the defilements and uncleannesses constantly attaching to us through the flesh, and the world. Practical holiness in our walk and conver-

sation is only to be obtained through the word of God
under the power of the Spirit of God. We are saints,
we are holy, we are washed, we are sanctified, we are
justified in the name of the Lord Jesus, and by the Spirit
of our God. We have to be practically clean, and
practically holy—and that through the same power and
means by which we have been already saved. The
word of God, testifying to the precious blood of Christ,
applied by the Spirit of God. Thus the oil and the
blood are inseparable. The Holy Ghost testifies to
Jesus and His Cross.

We should aim *to be* what we *really are.* Our
struggles, our conflicts should result from the fact that
we are children of God, that we are seated in heavenly
places in Christ, that we are alive in the Spirit, that we
are God's holy ones. If we turn the eye within, we
have no power ; we shall only discover unworthiness,
weakness, and sin ; and this will give us no strength for
conflict. We must keep our eye fixed on Jesus.
Looking away from all other objects unto Him, the
Author and Finisher of faith. And as we contemplate
Him, we gain strength, we become practically more
holy; we are changed into His likeness, we grow up
into Him.

This was the last act of Moses, sprinkling the oil and
the blood upon Aaron and his sons, and upon their
garments. They and their garments were sanctified.
It is to be observed that Aaron's sons, and his sons'
garments are closely linked in this sprinkling with Aaron
himself—" upon his sons, and upon his sons' garments
*with* him."—This is four times repeated. Exod. xxix.
21 ; Lev. viii. 30.

Their persons were first sanctified, then their garments.
And thus they stood a hallowed family in connection
with Aaron their head.

May we not see in this a little figure of the truths
expressed in the epist'e to the Hebrews, though at the
same time there is a contrast.

Aaron and his garments had to be sanctified. Christ sanctified Himself for our sakes. Aaron's sons derived no sanctification from any act of Aaron. Christ's house derive *all* their sanctification from Christ their Head, and High Priest.

Thus far there is a contrast—but we read, " he who sanctifieth, and they who are sanctified are all of one, for which cause he is not ashamed to call them brethren." and, " holy brethren, partakers of the heavenly calling, consider the Apostle and High Priest of our profession, Christ Jesus." Heb. ii. 11; iii. 1. Here is the fulfilment of those little words " *with him*," we are all of one with Him that sanctifieth us. We are partakers of that wondrous calling of which He is the High Priest. We are " holy brethren," and " He is not ashamed to call us brethren "—a priestly family—a spiritual house, builded by God, belonging to the Son of God, over which He is the Head.

Wondrous calling! accomplished by a wondrous God, Father, Son, and Holy Ghost. A family, named of the Father ; children and heirs of God, and joint-heirs with Christ : brethren whom Jesus is not ashamed to own as His brethren. An assembly in the midst of which He will sing praise to God—a congregation of priests anointed with the Holy Ghost—an holy priesthood, a royal priesthood, "to offer up spiritual sacrifices, acceptable to God by Jesus Christ," and " to shew forth the praises (virtues) of him who hath called us out of darkness into his marvellous light." 1st Pet. ii 5, 9

# THE FOOD OF THE PRIESTS

"And thou shalt take the ram of the consecration and seethe his flesh in the holy place.

"And Aaron and his sons shall eat the flesh of the ram, and the bread that is in the basket, by the door of the tabernacle of the congregation.

"And they shall eat those things wherewith the atonement was made, to consecrate and to sanctify them : but a stranger shall not eat thereof because they are holy.

"And if ought of the flesh of the consecrations, or of the bread, remain unto the morning, then thou shalt burn the remainder with fire : it shall not be eaten, because it is holy.

"And thus shalt thou do unto Aaron, and to his sons, according to all things which I have commanded thee : seven days shalt thou consecrate them.

"And thou shalt offer every day a bullock for a sin offering for atonement : and thou shalt cleanse the altar, when thou hast made an atonement for it, and thou shalt anoint it, to sanctify it.

"Seven days thou shalt make an atonement for the altar, and sanctify it ; and it shall be an altar most holy : whatsoever toucheth the altar shall be holy."
—Exod. xxix 31—37

"And Moses said unto Aaron and to his sons, boil the flesh at the door of the tabernacle of the congregation ; and there eat it with the bread that is in the basket of consecrations, as I commanded, saying, Aaron and his sons shall eat it.

"And that which remaineth of the flesh and of the bread shall ye burn with fire.

"And ye shall not go out of the door of the tabernacle of the congregation seven days, until the days of your consecration be at an end : for seven days shall he consecrate you.

"As he hath done this day, so the Lord hath commanded to do, to make an atonement for you.

"Therefore shall ye abide at the door of the tabernacle of the congregation day and night seven days, and keep the charge of the Lord, that ye die not : for so I am commanded.

"So Aaron and his sons did all things which the Lord commanded by the hand of Moses."
—Lev. viii 31—36

HITHERTO Aaron and his sons had been comparatively passive ; the only action on their part was the laying their hands upon the heads of the various sacrifices. They were now however commanded to eat the flesh of the ram of consecration, (the ram with which their hands had been filled,) and the remainder of the bread of consecrations, (with which also their hands had been filled.) They were to be strengthened for the Lord's service by feeding on "those things wherewith the atonement was made, to fill their hand, to sanctify them." Exod. xxix. 33. Atonement, consecration, and sanctification were all included under the one sacrifice of the ram, and the bread which now became their food, or as it were the source of life to them.

So it is also with the believer. He recognizes Christ as having in His death made a full atonement for his sin, and as having thereby consecrated and sanctified him as a king and priest to God ; and the very act of thus contemplating Christ by faith, is *life*, is Christ *within* him. Paul as Saul of Tarsus had a revelation of Christ from heaven *to* him, and this was by the operation of God the revelation of Christ *in* him. Gal. i. 15, 16. If Jesus be the object to which as sinners we turn, then we receive him by faith, and " Christ is in us the hope of glory." Col. i. 27. Faith and life go together. They are synchronous, we cannot place one before or after the other. Christ as our object, becomes Christ in us. And so also as to the nourishment of that life afterwards. We grow, and are strengthened, exactly in the same way in which life was originally communicated to us ; that is by contemplating the same object, Jesus Christ, and Him crucified. Looking at Him as an *external* object, moulds and fashions *within* into His likeness. " We all, with unveiled face beholding as in a glass the glory of the Lord, are changed into the same image from glory to glory, even as by the Spirit of the Lord." 2nd Cor. iii. 18. Moses wist not that his face shone, when he came down from the mount. He had been in converse with God, and had unconsciously to himself, caught some of the glory of the Lord upon his countenance. We shall as surely, though perhaps imperceptibly to ourselves, be transformed into the image of Christ if we keep him constantly before us. Looking within ourselves will not advance us in spiritual growth ; neither will mental efforts of our own advantage us ; *looking off* ourselves unto Jesus, will have a transforming power.

The eating of those things wherewith the atonement
was made, may have this truth in type. The Lord in
John vi., to which reference has already been made,
identifies his flesh and blood with bread ; and identifies
*faith*, and *coming* to Him with *eating*. "I am the bread
of life ; he that *cometh* to me shall never hunger ; and he
that *believeth* on me shall never thirst." John vi. 35.
"That he that *seeth* the Son and *believeth* on Him may
have everlasting life," 40. "Verily, verily, I say unto
you, he that *believeth* on me hath everlasting life," 47.
"I am that bread of life"—"that a man may *eat*
thereof, and not die"—"if any man *eat* of this bread he
shall live for ever." "Whoso *eateth* my flesh, and
drinketh my blood, hath eternal life." "He that *eateth*
of this bread shall live for ever," ver. 48, 50, 51, 54,
58. * Thus the appropriation of Christ to oneself by
faith, believing on Him, is eating His flesh and drinking
His blood. It is "to taste that the Lord is gracious."
1st Pet. ii 3.

Eating is also a type of communion, or fellowship.
It is so used in 1st Cor. x. 18—21. "Behold Israel
after the flesh : are not they which eat of the sacrifices
partakers of the altar ? ' They typically partook of the
same sacrifices of which God had partaken from off the
altar. There can be no partaking with another of the
same food, unless there be peace and friendship between
the two.

---

* An interesting question occurs in reading this chapter. Why does the Lord
suddenly make use of another Greek word not commonly employed, when He
speaks of *eating* His flesh? The word *trogo*. v. 54. "Whoso *eateth* my flesh."
56. "He that *eateth* my flesh," 57. "So he that *eateth* me," 58. "He that
*eateth* of this bread." The Lord has all through this chapter previously
employed another word, *phago ;* and once only uses this latter word when
speaking of *eating* His flesh. 53. "Except ye *eat* the flesh of the Son of Man."
The word *trogo* in Liddell and Scott's Greek Dictionary, is translated to *gnaw* or
*chew*, especially of herbivorous animals ; and when used "of men, to eat *raw*
vegetables, opposed to eating *dressed* food.' Is this word selected by the Lord,
in order to connect more intimately His flesh and blood with the word *Bread*,
and with the manna ?
It may be proper to observe the use of the participles in the Greek,
throughout this chapter. "He that believeth on me," ver. 35. 40, 47. "He that
*eateth*," ver. 54, 56, 57, 58. "He that drinketh," ver. 54, 56. In all which
instances the present active participle is used to express a continuous action.
Not a mere eating and drinking once for all, but a habit. Faith is an active,
continuous habit of the soul; it is the constant expression of life—and life is eternal.

Atonement having been made, and perfect reconciliation established, the priests could eat of the sacrifices in
the presence of God ; could have fellowship with Him
in those very things with which that atonement had been
effected. In like manner the Lord's table becomes to the
believer a place of fellowship with the Father and the
Son. As a saved sinner he takes a place at that table, to
remember Christ in God's presence, to worship and bless
God for the gift of His Son, and in some measure to enter
into God's joy and God's thoughts respecting that Great
Salvation effected by Christ. What a wondrous invita-
ation is that given by the Father in Luke xv. 23 : "*Let us*
eat and be merry." And again, "It was *meet* that *we*
should make merry, and be glad ; for this thy brother
was dead, and is alive again ; and was lost, and is
found," ver. 32.

Do we as we might, and as we ought, enter even
now into the joy of our Lord ? Do we believe that
God has greater delight in saving us, than we have in
being saved ? Do we gather round the Lord's table
that we may rejoice with God in the death of His Son,
and delight ourselves in Christ ?

Peter in the vision of the sheet let down, had
instruction conveyed to him respecting intercourse and
fellowship with the Gentiles, under the type of *eating*
He said to Cornelius and those assembled, "Ye know
how that it is an unlawful thing for a man that is a Jew
to keep company, or come unto one of another nation ;
but God hath shewed me that I should not call any
man common or unclean." Act x. 28. And he subsequently related the vision to the saints at Jerusalem, in
answer to their objection to his having gone to men
uncircumcised and having eaten with them. Acts xi.
Here again *eating* is employed as a type of intercourse.

We have also a very distinct reference to the same
truth in Heb. xiii. 10—14. "We have an altar,
whereof they have no right to eat which serve the
tabernacle. For the bodies of those beasts, whose

blood is brought into the sanctuary by the high priest
for sin, are burned without the camp. Wherefore
Jesus also, that he might sanctify the people with his
own blood, suffered without the gate. Let us go forth
therefore unto him without the camp, bearing his reproach. For here we have no continuing city, but we
seek one to come."

A very full and remarkable passage, to which reference has already been made in page 322, but which it
may be well to enter into more fully. We are first told
that we have an altar, in contrast with those who serve
the tabernacle, and who have no right to eat of our
altar. The altar here seems to be identical with the
cross—the cross (if we may so say) transferred to the
glory. We have a right to eat of the flesh and blood
of the Son of Man, slain upon the tree. That flesh and
blood was first eternal life to us, and next becomes the
sustainment of that life, and enables us to abide in
Christ. "He that eateth my flesh, and drinketh my
blood, dwelleth in me, and I in him." John vi. 56.
The word here translated *dwelleth* is the same that is
elsewhere translated *abideth*. See John xv. throughout.

The secret of abiding in Christ is to be feeding on
Christ, especially as crucified for us. Some of the
Lord's own people, it may be, desire to abide in Him,
and yet know not how to arrive at that blessing. Two
things were apparently in the mind of the Lord in
John xv. First, that we should abide in Him; and
next, that His words should abide in us, so that we
might keep them. John xv. 4, 7, 10. The former is
practically attained by constantly eating His flesh, and
drinking His blood; the latter will result from a frequent meditation on His life and words. Ever remembering that we have the words of the Lord expanded, if
we may so say, in the Epistles.

They who serve the tabernacle have no right to eat
of our altar. They have no right nor power to eat of
the flesh and blood of Christ. And who, it may be

asked, answer at the present day to those to whom the apostle thus alludes in his day? As a matter of fact there were none, even in Paul's day, who were serving the *tabernacle;* for the tabernacle had for some centuries been superseded by the *temple.* But the Spirit of God writes, throughout the Epistle to the Hebrews, as if the tabernacle were still in existence; because the principles to be maintained were such as had their more correct types during the tabernacle dispensation, and the sins to be avoided had been brought out in Israel's history during their sojourn in the wilderness, whilst the tabernacle was standing.

So at this present time, although both tabernacle and temple are gone, yet we as believers are looked upon as in the wilderness on our way to our rest; and the same errors are continued, the same false principles openly advocated, as if the tabernacle and temple were still standing. Any that proclaim efficacy in sacraments; any that uphold an order of priesthood distinct from all who are truly believers; any that arrogate to themselves or on behalf of others, the power to convey the Holy Ghost, or to qualify others for spiritual offices in the Church of God; are still serving the tabernacle. They have no right to eat of our altar. And for this reason, they have not owned a sacrifice sufficient to sanctify the people. They contend that something *more* than " Christ and Him crucified " is needful. They seem to think that the anointing of the Holy Ghost is *not* solely the consequence of a believer being at his conversion baptized into the body of Christ. They practically deny that " Christ hath loved us, and washed us from our sins in His own blood, and hath made us kings and priests to God and his Father." And they think that priests are to be made after a tabernacle fashion; a human consecration.

The apostle enforces his argument upon the ground that in the tabernacle service, " the bodies of those beasts, whose blood is brought into the sanctuary for sin, are burned without the camp." When a sin-offering was slain of such a high character that its blood was carried either into the holy or most holy places, then the body of the victim was burned outside the camp—no portion was eaten by the priests—all was consumed. In the Antitype, "Jesus that he might sanctify the people with his own blood suffered without the gate." He was the true offering for sin. He suffered outside the gate of Jerusalem; outside that city of solemnities, in reproach and dishonour—outside all ceremonial religion, all observances of fleshly religiousness; outside all formalities. A wondrous reality; not a type or shadow; but the substance of all type and shadow. A true Christ; a true sacrifice; the true "Lamb of God." No human priest had to do with that sacrifice—no fleshly ceremonial was connected with it. Man in all his true-hearted hatred to God was there, an active agent in the work of slaughter. The serpent was present to bruise the heel of the woman's seed; the "sword of Jehovah of hosts smote the man that was his fellow." The marvellous reality made all rituals of priestly service, all sacrifices of old, all type and shadow fade away into insignificance.

The victim on that tree of curse, who shed His own blood of such unspeakable value, made the blood of bulls and of goats utterly worthless. "Lebanon was not sufficient to burn, nor the beasts thereof sufficient for a burnt-offering." The offerer who "offered up himself," for ever set aside the Aaronic high priest with all his outward glory and beauty, and all his offerings. The stripes upon the soul of Jesus, which extracted healing virtue for us poor sinners, for ever made of none effect, even "ten thousand rivers of oil." The precious blood was borne into heaven itself by the great High Priest in resurrection, and all holy places made with hands were set aside. Henceforth the true worshipper enters with confidence through the blood into the holiest of all, the very presence of the living God, and finds the only Priest he needs already there for him. Sanctified once for all by that one offering, and perfected for ever by it, the believer, a true priest himself to God, feeds on the flesh and blood of Him who is the sin-offering; setting aside by that act, even the very form of the Jewish ritual. He needs no outward dress to make him holy; no imposition of human hands to separate him to God; no license from man " to serve the living God." He claims his sanctification, his separation, his consecration, his priesthood, his salvation from Him who suffered without the gate; the Son of God Himself—who has shed *His own* blood ; and he boldly says to all mere human pretenders, to all who trust in carnal ordinances, " you have no right to eat off our altar."*

But what follows this simple dependence upon Christ, this full reliance on His death, and on His death alone as all sufficient ; " Let us go forth therefore unto him without the camp, bearing his reproach." Outside the gate of Jerusalem where the blessed Lord suffered is again exchanged for "*outside the camp.*" The church is looked upon like the camp of Israel of old, with the golden calf in the midst. A worldly religion, suited to the flesh, and adapted to keep the consciences of unregenerate sinners lulled in the sleep of death, has been universally adopted. The people can " sit down to eat and drink, and rise up to play," and have their religious ceremonies, and prayers, and ordinances, and priesthood, at the same time; and with the name of Jesus mixed with it all. What then is to be the course pursued by the true-hearted worshipper? " To gò to Jesus without the camp bearing his reproach " We have been brought nigh to God by His blood *within the vail ;* our path *here* below is to be outside all human

---

* The attention of the reader is requested to the fact, that the word *"atonement"* is used in Lev. viii. 34, to include the whole of consecration for the priesthood; as the word "*to hallow*" is also employed in Exod. xxix 1. So that a person atoned for is a consecrated priest; so also is a person *sanctified*. Thus we find the word *sanctified* used in Heb. x. 10, 14, as including priestly consecration.

order, all mixed worship, all priestly ceremonial.  But
it is *to Him;* it is to Jesus the crucified, the risen one,
that we go ; to walk with Him in holy, happy fellowship ; to learn from Him the ever deep mysteries of
His cross ; to glory in that cross, whereby " the world
has been crucified to us, and we to the world ; " to
lean on Him for support and strength, and to bear His
reproach.

From whence did that reproach come upon Him ?
Not only from the openly profane ; Herod and his
men of war did indeed set him at nought ; but chiefly
from the temple worshippers, from the established
priests and religious sects of the day.  They cast Him
out ; they crucified Him in a place to which they
would on no account themselves go, lest it should
defile them—"the place of a skull."  They preferred
to keep the shadow, to trusting the substance.  They
were careful not to enter the hall of judgment lest they
should defile themselves, " but that they might eat the
passover," whilst the Lamb of God was in reality
suffering on the tree outside the gate.  A solemn
thought this.  The shadow may and does at this very
day in ten thousand cases supersede the substance.
Men will earnestly contend for a form, a ceremony, a
shadow, whilst they utterly reject Him to whom the
shadow points.  We are exhorted " earnestly to contend
for *the faith;* " " to hold fast the *common* salvation," the
" *great* salvation."  *Common* alike to all the Lord's
people ; alike *great* to all that receive it.  Men will be
valiant on behalf of a sacrament, or of a holy day,
when they trample at the same time, on the precious
blood of Christ, and shrink in every respect from
" His reproach."

When superstition is exposed, or when the believer
ceases to consent to belong to a worldly church, he
will suffer the reproach of Christ.  Let but a trifle be
added to the truth, and the reproach of Christ will
cease.  If Paul would only have added an ordinance to

justification by faith, the offence of the cross would have been at an end, and he would no longer have suffered persecution.   Gal. v. 11.

Oh may we be ever in the holiest true worshippers of the Father, and feeding on the Lamb ; and know the companionship of Jesus here with us outside the camp ; and have the honour and glory of bearing somewhat of His reproach.

" For here have we no continuing city, but we seek one to come." When the worship of Israel became mixed with idolatry, they made the wilderness their home. " They sat down to eat and drink, and rose up to play." A religion of form and ceremony, which is in truth a religion mixed with idolatry, will always consist well with worldliness. But *we* have no continuing city here ; this is not our rest ; the wilderness is no place for pastime ; we are strangers and pilgrims. The blood of the Lamb has separated us to God and to glory. May it be so in truth ! May our lives belie our words ! Let us remember the beautiful order of these truths. Eat of the altar in the holiest *first ;* go outside *to Christ* next, and we shall have His reproach ; lastly, seek the future city ; look earnestly onwards to the coming of the Lord, when that glorious heavenly city will be revealed.

Aaron and his sons were finally directed to abide seven days, day and night, at the door of the tabernacle, and to keep the charge of the Lord. During all this time, a bullock for sin was daily offered upon the altar for atonement. Exod. xxix 36. They were to be habituated to abide before the Lord ; and they were to realize the value of the sin-offering, as thus enabling them so to abide there. The seven days of their week of consecration, may in type prefigure the whole of our earthly life. Our whole week of service. We are to accustom ourselves to be in the presence of our God. Our life is to be spent there ; only *we* have the privilege of abiding, not at the *door*, but in the very *holiest* of all.

May we rejoice to use this wondous liberty of access, and not only " draw near," but " abide under the shadow of the Almighty ; " " trusting under his wings." And what will be our help and power for this ? The sin-offering of atonement constantly realized, by the help of the Holy Spirit. The precious blood recognized as upon the mercy-seat, and before the mercy-seat, carried into the holy of holies.

The chapter concludes with a change of the oft-repeated sentence, " *as the Lord commanded Moses,*" to " *So Aaron and his sons did all things which the Lord commanded by the hand of Moses.*" They had themselves, through their consecration and the feeding on the sacrifice, power to fulfil God's commands, and to act independently of Moses. The power and intelligence of priests.

## THE EIGHTH DAY SERVICE

THE next chapter of Leviticus, the 9th, opens with " *the eighth day.*" This is a singular expression, because it is an additional day to a week already ended. And this *eighth day* would necessarily be the *first day* of a new week. Thus we have a type of resurrection. For resurrection could not be unless there had been a preceding creation, which had failed, having been ruined by sin. Resurrection is something entirely *new*, and yet it comes in upon that which is old.

The only feast which had an eighth day was the feast of Tabernacles. Lev. xxiii. 36, 39 ; Num. xxix. 35. (See page 55 of this work.) Circumcision was on the eighth day. Lev. xii. 3. In this rite there was evidently a shadow of what resurrection effects. The true circumcision ; " the putting off the body of the sins of the flesh." Col. ii. 11—13. "We are the circumcision, which worship God in the Spirit, and rejoice in Christ Jesus, and have no confidence in the flesh." Phil. iii. 3. As the man-child was on the eighth day circumcised, so on that day the firstling of oxen and sheep were given to God. Exod. xxii. 30 ; Lev. xxii. 27. Another shadow of death and resurrection. It is also deeply interesting to observe that the leper, when healed of his disease of leprosy, and fulfilling the ritual appointed for his ceremonial cleansing, had an eighth day service, which in many respects approached very nearly to the ritual appointed for the consecration of the priests. Blood and oil were put upon the leper's right ear, and thumb, and great toe. Oil also was put upon his head. See also the sacrifices offered. Lev. xiv. 10—20, 23—31 A cleansed leper obtained that to which no ordinary Israelite who had never suffered under the fearful disease of leprosy, was entitled. A saved sinner is raised by the grace of God to an infinitely higher position, and is a far higher being in the scale of existence, than was Adam before his fall

A man or woman who might have suffered under an issue, and been healed, presented sacrifices to the Lord on the eighth day. Lev. xv. 14, 29. In both these types we have evidently allusions to the great fact. brought out in all distinctness at length in the teaching and death and resurrection of the Lord Jesus ; namely, that there can be no real cleanness before God, except through being born again. Put to death with Christ upon the tree, and quickened together with Him into life eternal.

There is one more remarkable instance of an eighth day. The Nazarite was to bring his offering on that day under certain circumstances. Num. vi. 10. The Nazarite, the cleansed leper, and the priest, had each an eighth day, and had certain ceremonies remarkably in common. The saved sinner, a priest to God,

separated off to God, combines all the three types ; and
stands ever able to serve God, because he is, '' risen
with Christ." Col. iii. 1—5.

The priests at the close of their seven days consecration were in an anomalous state.   They were priests
for themselves, but not for others.   They had no
power to offer on behalf of Israel.   On the eighth day
they were enabled to present sacrifices not only for
themselves, but for the people.   All our power to
serve God ; all our power to intercede for others ; all
our ability to walk here as strangers and pilgrims, is
the result of resurrection.   We are priests, because
" partakers of a heavenly calling."   Christ is " not
ashamed to call us brethren," because we are " risen
together with him."   We can worship God, because
we are " not in the flesh."   We can intercede for
others, because we are ourselves saved. and have life in
common with the risen Lord.   We can present to God
the precious blood of His son on our own behalf as
worshippers already saved, and plead it on behalf of
the unsaved, because we have in ourselves trusted in its
value, and are accepted and justified, and risen as the
evidence of its preciousness.

Let us trace from the Scriptures some of our
responsibilities and power as priests to God.

First.—Our food for life and abiding fellowship with
Christ is priestly ; it is His flesh and blood.   Heb, xiii.
10 ; John vi. 54—58.

Next.—We have access into the holiest by His blood,
and can worship God in Spirit and in truth.   Heb. x.
19—22 ; John iv. 21—23 ; 1st Peter ii. 5, 9.

Again.—We are to assemble ourselves together, and
to exhort one another, and so much the more because
the day of the Lord's coming is approaching.   Heb.
x. 25.

Then we are " to present our bodies a living sacrifice,
holy, acceptable to God, our reasonable (priestly)
*service.*"   Rom. xii. 1.

We are to discern, and put " difference between holy
and unholy, and between unclean and clean." Lev. x.
10 ; xi. 47.   To separate the precious from the vile.
Jer. xv. 19 ; 2nd Cor. vi. 14—18.

The real knowledge of sin and estimate of its fearful
evil in the sight of God, is a priestly knowledge to be
deepened and increased by daily communings with God
respecting the sacrifice of His dear Son.   The priest
alone could decide in days of old as to the fearful
plague of leprosy and all its manifested tokens.

The priests have also to instruct others in God's
word, and God's thoughts, gathered from His word.
Deut. xxxiii. 10 ; Lev. x. 11.   See also Neh, viii. 18,
as an example.

Wisdom should be kept in their lips.   Mal. ii. 7.
" Let the word of Christ dwell in you richly, in all
wisdom." Col. iii. 16.   " Let no corrupt communication
proceed out of your mouth, but that which is good to
the use of edifying, that it may minister grace unto the
hearers." Eph. iv. 29.   " Let your speech be alway
with grace, seasoned with salt, that ye may know how
ye ought to answer every man." Col. iv. 6.

Praise to God is a priestly service.   " By him (Christ)
therefore let us offer the sacrifices of praise to God continually, that is, the fruit of our lips, giving thanks to
his name ; " or, as the margin has it, " *confessing* to his
name." Heb. xiii. 15.

Let us remark the *therefore* of this verse.   Praise must
result from a heart fully confident of the entire and
eternal salvation and sanctification, accomplished by the
sufferings of the Lord Jesus on the cross.   The word
*therefore* is inserted because of this fact having been
stated before.   Also the word *continually*.   All through
our life, all through our circumstances, continuous
praise.   Also in intercourse with other priests, " teaching and admonishing one another in psalms and hymns
and spiritual songs, singing with grace in your hearts to
the Lord." Col. iii. 16.   " Speaking to yourselves in

psalms and hymns and spiritual songs, singing and making melody in your hearts to the Lord." Eph. v. 19.*

To *give* is a priestly action. "But to do good, and to communicate, forget not; for with such sacrifices God is well pleased." Heb. xiii. 16. The gifts of the Phillippians to Paul, assisting him thereby to continue in his work of preaching the Gospel, were priestly offerings to God; "an odour of a sweet smell, a sacrifice acceptable, well pleasing to God." Phil. iv. 15—18.

Prayer and intercession mingled ever with thanksgiving are true priestly exercises of soul. See Rev. v. 8.

These are some of the chief services of priests to God, who have been washed in the blood of the Lamb. In this 9th chap. of Lev. we find Aaron and his sons exercising on this eighth day their priestly calling; killing the sacrifices, handling the blood, selecting the pieces for the altar; in short, going through the whole routine with the necessary accuracy, and according to the precise directions given by God, in the power of the eighth day.

One sacrifice is added to the list, which had not been offered in their consecration; "a bullock and a ram for peace-offerings." It is worthy of remark that the word " *sacrifice* " in the Hebrew is confined to this peace-offering, or as it should be called " *peace-sacrifice.*" So in Psalm xl. 6, (where all the four offerings of the first four chapters of Leviticus are enumerated, as set aside by being fulfilled in Christ Himself,) the word "sacrifice" stands for *peace*-sacrifice. The word " *peace* " is in the plural number, as if to betoken peace of every kind— " perfect peace." Peace that shall answer every question of doubt or uncertainty; every opposing thought;

---

* The text, "that ye should shew forth the *praises* of him who hath called you out of darkuess into his marvellous light," (1st Pet. ii. 9,) may be read " *virtues* ' instead of *praises*," as in the margin; and this may be the better rendering, as " a royal priesthood," "a peculiar people," purchased to God by the blood of His Son, born of God as our Father, we are to shew forth the character and ways of God in our lives; imitators of God as dear children ;" following the example of Jesus. A priestly walk will be a Christ-like walk.

whether of sin in the nature, sins committed, unworthiness, weakness, helplessness, infirmity. It was peculiarly a sacrifice of fellowship : the offerer eating the greater part of it in his own dwelling A kind of celebration of peace made between two parties, before opposed to one another.

As the word "*peace*" was the friendly salutation between persons greeting one another ; so this sacrifice was like a salutation of peace between God and the offerer. A striking type of Christ as the one through whom God is able to salute us with the blessed word *peace*. "He is our peace." Eph. ii. 14. "We have peace with God through our Lord Jesus Christ." Rom. v. 1. "And you that were sometime alienated, and enemies in your mind by wicked works, yet now hath he reconciled in the body of his flesh through death." Col. i. 21, 22. "God hath reconciled us to himself by Jesus Christ." 2nd Cor. v. 18.

This was the concluding sacrifice. "And Aaron lifted up his hand towards the people and blessed them." Lev. ix. 22. He wafted towards them and upon them, the rich mercies procured by the sacrifices. Sin atoned for by the sin-offering. Acceptance with God in the sweet savour of the burnt-offering. Life through the bread of life the meat offering. And full reconciliation peace and fellowship with God, through the peace-sacrifice. And he uttered the priestly blessing.

" The Lord bless thee, and keep thee ;

" The Lord make his face shine upon thee, and be gracious unto thee ;

" The Lord lift up his countenance upon thee, and give thee peace.

" And they shall put my name upon the children of Israel ; and I will bless them." Num. vi. 24—27.

Or, as it might be rendered—

Jehovah bless thee, and keep thee ;

Jehovah cause his face to shine upon thee, and be gracious unto thee ;

Jehovah lift up his face upon thee, and place upon thee peace.

It is remarkable that the last sacrifice was that which was for peace : and the conclusion of the priestly blessing is, " Jehovah place upon thee peace."

What a precious thing is peace *with* God, derived *from* God. Perfect reconciliation with Him. Unhindered intercourse with Him. No reserves—no reason for having any concealment with Him. A " spirit in which there is no guile "—no hypocrisy—no false pretences ; because every defect, every sin, every evil corruption within and without, has been fully met, atoned for, and set aside in the death of the Lord Jesus.

But the priestly blessing goes further than this. " Jehovah lift up his face upon thee, and place upon thee peace." Great as is the blessing, and beyond all price of having peace *with* God ; yet there is a peace even beyond this—" *the peace of God.*" The peace which God Himself enjoys : the peace which Christ can call " *my* peace." Undisturbed by opposing powers of evil ; unruffled by the violence and seeming triumphs of Satan, the peace of God like the calm crystal sea before the throne, remains firm and unshaken in the soul of the believer. It passeth all understanding ; " for the very opposing elements that would seem to have the power to disturb it, only in fact confirm it. God sees the end from the beginning : He makes all things work out the counsels of His own will. The believer knows this ; he sees also the end that must in due time come, when all things shall terminate to the glory of God ; thus the peace of God rules or garrisons his heart and mind through Jesus Christ. Phil. iv. 7. " If the foundations be destroyed, what can the righteous do ? The Lord is in his holy temple, the Lord's throne is in heaven." Psa. xi. 3, 4. Perfect peace is there, and the dwelling place of the righteous is there. The promise, " thou wilt keep him in perfect peace whose

mind is stayed on thee, because he trusteth in thee," (Isa.
xxvi. 3,) seems to allude to the plural of the peace-
sacrifice, the word peace being doubled, (see margin,)
" abundance of peace," " peace always by all means."

There are two portions of this priestly blessing which
especially demand our attention.

" Jehovah cause his face to shine upon thee ; " Jehovah lift up his face upon thee." So deeply important is
it for the soul to realise the unclouded countenance of
the Lord, that this portion of the blessing is twice
repeated. One great object of the priesthood of the
blessed Lord is that we may at all times enjoy free
unhindered access to God : that we may never have to
say He hides His face from us

The fearfulness of that time when God was, we may
say compelled, to withdraw the light of His countenance
from His blessed Son, was to Christ the great ingredient
of woe in the cup He had to drink for us. In some of
the Psalms we find that terrible time of darkness anticipated by Him.

" Hide not thy face from me in the day when I am
in trouble ; incline thine ear unto me : in the day when
I call answer me speedily." Psa. cii. 2.

" Hide not thy face from me ; put not thy servant
away in anger : thou hast been my help ; leave me not,
neither forsake me, O God of my Salvation." Psa. xxvii. 9.

" Lord, why casteth thou off my soul ? why hidest
thou thy face from me ? " Psa. lxxxviii. 14.

" Hear me speedily, O Lord : my spirit faileth : hide
not thy face from me, lest I be like unto them that go
down into the pit." Psa. cxliii. 7.

" Hide not thy face from thy servant ; for I am in
trouble : hear me speedily." Psa. lxix. 17.

And who but the Lord Jesus could really estimate
what it was to be forsaken of God ? He who was the
only begotten Son in the bosom of the Father, and who
had walked all His days on earth in the unclouded light
of the blessed countenance of God : He who had known

and dwelt in the fulness of joy which is in God's presence, (in God's countenance.) In the same Psalm, which begins with His deepest cry of agony, " my God, my God, why hast thou forsaken me," He still looked forward to the restoration of the light of God's countenance as His great joy—" for he hath not despised nor abhorred the affliction of the afflicted, neither hath he hid his face from him, but when he cried unto him he heard." Psa. xxii. 24. And in the prospect of resurrection, He says, " as for me I will behold thy face in righteousness." Psa. xvii. 15. " Thou hast made him exceeding glad with thy countenance." Psa. xxi. 6.

Clouds of darkness and unbelief may come up in our souls, but the face of our God is unclouded. Satan may suggest that there is a hindrance to our approaching Him; but the precious blood and the High Priest over the House are complete answers to Satan's lie. We may be conscious of some allowed failure—or may be overtaken in some fault—the adversary will then tempt the soul, suggesting that our unfaithfulness has closed the door of entrance into the Holiest. But in truth, the place of confession is the mercy-seat. In the presence of God alone can we really pour out our hearts in self-abasement, and it is the assurance of His unabated love, and that the way into the holiest is still open, that will really melt the heart into contrition.

Aaron having blessed the people, went with Moses into the tabernacle. There may be in this a little shadow of the Lord's action as related in the end of the Gospel by Luke. "And he led them out as far as to Bethany, and he lifted up his hands and blessed them. And it came to pass, while he blessed them, he was parted from them, and carried up into heaven." chap. xxiv. 50, 51. Our great High Priest with uplifted hands, blessing His people with all the full results of His wondrous sacrifice, was parted from them, and still perpetuates the same streams of blessing, pouring them down upon them from heaven. For a little while He is concealed from our

view.   For a little time Moses and Aaron were together
in the tabernacle, hidden from the eyes of the people.
But they soon came out and *together* blessed the people,
" and the glory of the Lord appeared unto all the
people." Lev. ix. 23.   This was a second blessing
direct from the holy places, and in this blessing Moses
took the lead, combining with Aaron.   " Moses was
king in Jeshurun." Deut. xxxiii. 5.   Thus a kingly as
well as priestly blessing flowed from the two, a kind of
Melchizedeck blessing.   Gen. xiv. 18—24.

This " king of righteousness and king of peace,"
combining in his own person king and priest, brought
forth bread and wine to Abraham, after the latter had
gained the first victory recorded in Scripture over five
confederate kings.   The whole scene of this remarkable
meeting between the priest of the Most High God, and
the father of many nations, is surrounded with emblems
of royalty.   The king of Sodom was there—it took
place in the king's dale—the spoils won from the
vanquished kings lay in profusion all around—and the
first king who had a royal title from the Most High was
present.   He was also *the priest* of the Most High God
—and four times is the remarkable title "the Most High
God" repeated.   God is acknowledged by this priest to
be " the Most High, possessor of heaven and earth,"
and the blessing he bestows is *from* " the Most High
God, possessor of heaven and earth."   A striking
anticipation this of the time when the Lord Jesus shall
come from heaven in all " His own glory, and in the
glory of the Father, and in the glory of the holy angels,"
to bless with resurrection glory, His own victorious
saints, and to claim the kingdoms of the world on behalf
of the Most High God, who will then be manifestly
" possessor of heaven and earth."

"And there came a fire out from before the Lord,
and consumed upon the altar the burnt-offering and the
fat : which when all the people saw, they shouted and
fell on their faces." Lev. ix. 24.

They did not shout at the sight of the glory, nor fall on their faces in worship, although that sight must have been an unlooked for manifestation of the presence of God—but God's acceptance of the burnt-offering and the fat upon the altar, witnessed by the fire from before Him consuming them, raised a shout of gratitude and thanksgiving from their hearts, and bowed them down in reverence before Him.

It will not be " the appearing of the *glory* of the great God, and our Saviour Jesus Christ, which will raise our shout of joy and our song of worship and of praise, but it will be the sight of *Himself*, " *the Lamb as it had been slain*," which will be the great cause of our joy and thanksgiving. It is that beautiful word "*Himself*" which is so comforting, and which so gladdens the heart, " the Lord *Himself* shall descend from heaven with a shout," our hope is in *Him*, to see *Him* as He is: (1st John iii. 2.) and then shall we realize the value of that sacrifice, of that gift of God which is unspeakable. Then will true unhindered worship begin. Then shall we be truly humbled when we reach the exceeding height of glory.*

---

\* In concluding this portion of the subject it may be well to notice a mistake which often occurs both in writing and speaking of it.

Aaron the high priest is frequently alluded to, as coming out and blessing the people at the close of the day of atonement—as also he is represented as going in to make atonement, clothed in the blue robe, with the bells sounding on his going in and coming out. Neither of these statements is correct—Aaron did *not* bless the people at the conclusion of the day of atonement, neither did he enter the holiest on that occasion with the bells upon his vesture. He blessed the people as above related on the day of his consecration, and there is no other occasion recorded of his doing so. On this occasion he was clothed in his garments for glory and beauty, with the golden bells, &c.

On the day of atonement he went into the holiest, and came out, clothed in distinct dress used only for that occasion, to which reference will be made hereafter.

# THE LAW OF THE BURNT-OFFERING

"And the Lord spake unto Moses, saying,

"Command Aaron and his sons, saying, this is the law of the burnt-offering: it is the burnt-offering, because of the burning upon the altar all night unto the morning, and the fire of the altar shall be burning in it.

"And the priest shall put on his linen garment, and his linen breeches shall he put upon his flesh, and take up the ashes which the fire hath consumed with the burnt-offering on the altar, and he shall put them beside the altar.

"And he shall put off his garments, and put on other garments, and carry forth the ashes without the camp unto a clean place.

"And the fire upon the altar shall be burning in it, it shall not be put out: and the priest shall burn wood on it every morning, and lay the burnt-offering in order upon it, and he shall burn thereon the fat of the peace-offerings.

"The fire shall ever be burning upon the altar; it shall never go out."—Lev. vi 8—13

THE law of the burnt-offering is introduced here because there are peculiar directions given to the priest respecting the removing of the ashes; and a peculiar dress worn by him on that occasion. The burnt-offering, or, "ascending-offering," is here defined to be such, "because of the burning upon the altar all night unto the morning, and the fire of the altar shall be burning in it." An unusual word is here used for *burning*, (Heb. *yahkad*,) and found only in this chapter, verses 9, 12, 13, with respect to sacrifice. It is elsewhere used in Scripture, but always in connection with the thought of burning in judgment. See Deut. xxxii. 22; Isa. x. 16; Jer. xv. 14; xvii. 4. It may be, that the reason of its being introduced in connection with the altar of burnt-offering, is to include the thought of that altar being a place of judgment with respect to the victims consumed on it; although the *great* thought connected with this altar, is that it was an altar from which a sweet savour ascended to God. As to the other words used in the Hebrew for *burning*, see page 366 of this work. The Spirit of God would have us ever remember the solemn fact, that the death of our blessed Lord was a death under judgment, although at the same time it was the perfection of obedience, and most acceptable as a sweet savour to God.

Twice are the words repeated, " the fire of the altar shall be burning in it," ver. 9 and 12. This apparently refers to the victim: the fire of the altar shall always be burning in the burnt-offering; all night unto the morning. The camp of Israel rested securely all night under the shelter of the evening lamb upon the altar. They could repose without fear, for there was a sweet savour on their behalf ever ascending to God. There was a beacon fire kept burning for the eye of God to rest upon, and no enemy could prevail—no power of darkness could harm them, because of the protection afforded them through that sacrifice.

Throughout the night of this world until the morning of the resurrection dawns, our shelter, our protection is the sweet savour of the sacrifice of Christ. Our watchful High Priest ever perpetuates the fragrance of His death in the glory for us. And thus we securely rest under the shadow of the Almighty.

The priest had a peculiar linen garment which he put on, and his linen breeches upon his flesh when he took up the ashes which the fire had consumed, the ashes of the burnt-offering. This garment was of linen, *(bad)* the same material as was used for the linen breeches— see page 304 of this work. What the difference was between the linen *(shesh)* used in the curtains, etc., of the tabernacle, and also in the high priest's dress for glory and beauty; and the linen *(bad)* of which this garment and the garments for atonement (Lev. xvi.) were made, cannot now be satisfactorily ascertained. It may be that the *"shesh,"* was a fine cotton, like the muslin of modern days—whilst the *"bad"* was fine flax, the linen of our time.

But whatever may have been the material, it would seem that a special, fine white garment was required when the priest was brought into close contact with the death of the victim. The ashes removed from the altar were evidence of death having wrought its utmost. The fire from God had consumed to ashes the lamb, and nothing remained of the sacrifice but that which manifested that the whole of it had been fed upon by the fire, and all had ascended to God as a sweet savour.* The priest in this especial white linen dress carefully removed the ashes from the altar, and put them beside the altar. This expression, "beside the altar" occurs also in Leviticus i. 16; and x. 12. In the 1st chap. ver. 16, "the place of ashes," is said to be "beside the altar on the east part." The rising sun would cast its light upon "the place of ashes," where the priest was pouring out the fresh ashes just taken from the altar.

Does not this type allude to the death of Christ, evidenced by His lifeless body being taken down from the cross. If we read the Gospels on the subject, we shall find how carefully the Spirit of God marks the complete extinction of life in the blessed Lord. Joseph of Arimathea came to Pilate and begged the body of Jesus. "Pilate marvelled, if he were already dead: and calling unto him the Centurion, he asked him whether he had been anywhile dead." This Centurion was evidently the one in command at the crucifixion of the Lord, who had witnessed all the circumstances of the Lord's death; and who had heard His expiring cry, and had been led thereby to exclaim, "truly this man was the Son of God." He had also

---

* The word for ashes (dehshen) is used only for the ashes of the burnt-offering It is derived from a verb signifying, to be fat, or, to make fat.

In Psa. xx. 3, "remember all thy offerings, and accept thy burnt sacrifice "— the margin has it, "*turn to ashes*, or *make fat*, the burnt sacrifice," In Psa. xxiii. 5, "thou anointest my head with oil"—margin, "thou *makest fat* my head with oil," the same verb occurs. May not this word, *to make fat*, be used in this latter Psalm in connexion with the oil poured on the head, by way of contrast with the sackcloth and ashes put upon the head of the mourner? The word for *ashes* in such case being quite different.

The burnt-offering ashes were fat, because they were the result of the fire feeding especially on the inwards and fat of the burnt-offering and peace-sacrifice.

seen the fact of the death of Jesus doubly confirmed by the act of one of the soldiers piercing the side of the Lord, so that he could give full evidence to Pilate as to the death of Christ.

"And when he knew it of the Centurion he gave the body to Joseph."

The early morning light of the rising sun shining on the ashes, made it manifest that the Lamb had been entirely consumed. The sun arose as usual upon the morning of the sabbath which succeeded the day of Christ's crucifixion, and shone upon a cross, from which the slain Lamb of God had been taken away; and upon a sepulchre, wherein lay the body of Jesus. The sun in the heavens is witness to the death of its Creator.

The priest having laid the ashes beside the altar, in the place of ashes on the east part, then put off his linen garments and put on other garments, and carried forth the ashes without the camp unto a clean place.

This *clean place* outside the camp is the same as that in which the sin-offerings were burnt. "The whole bullock shall he carry forth without the camp unto a clean place, *where the ashes are poured out*, and burn him on the wood with fire : where the ashes are poured out shall he be burnt." Lev. iv. 12.

The word *poured* with respect to the ashes, is the substantive of the verb used for the pouring all the blood of the sin-offerings at the bottom of the altar. Exod. xxix. 12 ; Lev. iv. 7, 18, 25, 30, 34. Thus the *pouring out* of the ashes outside the camp would be connected with the *pouring out* of the blood at the bottom of the altar, and the burning of the sin-offering outside the camp. It would be another mode of expressing the entire pouring out of the life of the blessed Lord ; the shedding of His blood as the atoning sacrifice ; the sin-offering outside the camp.

This command to carry forth the ashes without the camp unto a clean place, may have some reference to

the *burial* of the Lord.   His burial was the fullest
evidence of His death.   The place where He was
buried was a garden, in the place where He was
crucified.   In the garden there was a new sepulchre
hewn out of a rock, " hewn in stone, wherein never
man before was laid."   " Wherein was never man yet
laid."  Luke xxiii. 53 ;  John xix. 41.

The sepulchre wherein the Lord lay answered the
requirements of a clean place.   No corrupt body of
fallen man had ever lain there.   And such being the
case, the resurrection of the Lord could not be
blasphemously attributed to the resurrection of another
person.

The burial of the Lord Jesus is part of the Gospel.
" Moreover, brethren, I declare unto you the gospel
which I preached unto you, which also ye have received,
and wherein ye stand ;  by which also ye are saved, if
ye keep in memory what I preached unto you, unless
ye have believed in vain.   For I delivered unto you
first of all that which I also received, how that
Christ died for our sins according to the scriptures ;
and that he was *buried*, and that he rose again the third
day according to the scriptures.  1 Cor. xv. 1—4.

It was foretold by Isaiah, "and he made his grave
with the wicked, and with the rich in his death." liii. 9.
His grave was in a garden which was close to, and
seems to have formed part of Golgotha, the place
where He was crucified, so described in John xix. 41 ;
it is also added, " the sepulchre was nigh at hand."
ver. 42, so that His body could be interred quickly.

This will account for the portion of the verse where
it is said " he made his grave with the wicked ;" the
word wicked being in the plural number.   The graves
of the malefactors who suffered on Golgotha being
probably dug close to the place of their execution, and
therefore near the garden in which was Joseph's new
tomb.   It is added, " and with the rich."   And here
we may observe the accuracy of prophetic Scripture.

The word *rich* is in the singular—" the rich one "—
whereas the word wicked *is* in the plural—" wicked
ones." It was in the sepulchre of a rich man—(" when
the even was come there came a *rich man* of Arimathæa
named Joseph," Matt. xxvii. 57,)—that the Lord made
His grave.

"In His death,"or as the margin has it, "in His *deaths,*"
the only place in the Scripture where the word *death*
occurs in the plural. Is it not so expressed because the
Lord Jesus suffered death according to all the fearful
variety of pain and judgment which can be inflicted by
the King of Terrors ?

The only direct allusions to the burial of the Lord
uttered by Himself during His lifetime are, when
speaking of Jonah as a sign. He said " As Jonah
was three days and three nights in the whale's belly;
so shall the Son of Man be three days and three
nights in the heart of the earth." Matt. xii. 40. And
when anointed in Bethany, recorded in three of the
Gospels, Matt. xxvi. 6—13 ; Mark xiv. 3—9 ; John
xii. 1—8 ; He speaks of it, as for His burial. On
comparing the Gospels which relate the circumstances
of the Lord being anointed, according to Matthew and
Mark, the woman anointed His *head.* According to
the account in John, Mary anointed His *feet.* In the
two former Gospels the Lord speaks of the ointment as
having been poured on His *body.* " For in that she
hath poured this ointment on my body, she did it for
my burial." " She hath done what she could, she is
come aforehand to anoint my body to the burying."
And in John, " Then said Jesus, let her alone, against
the day of my burying hath she kept this." This was
the only anointing for the tomb which the Lord had ;
for although we read in John xix that Nicodemus
brought a mixture of myrrh and aloes, and that the
body of Jesus was wound in linen clothes with the
spices, yet this was not anointing the body. And we
find that the women from Galilee prepared spices and

ointments, and brought them to anoint Him on the first day of the week, but found the sepulchre empty, and were told that He was risen.

May there not have been in this act of anointing the Lord's head and feet, (and in so doing His body,) a foreshadowing of the costly value and sweet savour of His death which belongs to every member of the body of Christ in resurrection. The odour of that very precious sacrifice fills the house of God ; and each member of Christ's body, of His flesh and of His bones, from the foot to the head, is accepted and loved by God according to the unspeakable value of Him " who gave Himself for us, an offering and a sacrifice to God for a sweet smelling savour."

How we see the old things of the law rapidly coming to their close as the death of the Lord Jesus, the Lamb of God, drew nigh ; as the new eternal things were about to be established. Caiaphas breathes out a last utterance of wondrous import, in which all *prophetic* power of the Aaronic priesthood finally ceased. " Ye know nothing at all, nor consider that it is expedient for us, that one man should die for the people, and that the whole nation perish not." John xi. 49, 50.

Subsequently it would seem that the high priest committed a breach of the very law that constituted him priest ; so that he not only made void his priesthood, but even exposed himself to the sentence of death. He rent his priestly clothes in the act of condemning Him, who through that very death to which he condemned Him, was to be raised up a High Priest for ever, after a new and eternal order.

" And the high priest answered and said unto him, I adjure thee by the living God, that thou tell us whether thou be the Christ, the Son of God.

" Jesus saith unto him, Thou hast said : nevertheless I say unto you, Hereafter shall ye see the Son of man sitting on the right hand of power, and coming in the clouds of heaven.

" Then the high priest rent his clothes, saying, He hath spoken blasphemy ; what further need have we of witnesses ? behold, now ye have heard his blasphemy.

" What think ye ? They answered and said, He is guilty of death."—Matt. xxvi. 63—66.

" Again the high priest asked him, and said unto him, Art thou the Christ, the Son of the Blessed ?

" And Jesus said, I am : and ye shall see the Son of man sitting on the right hand of power, and coming in the clouds of heaven.

" Then the high priest rent his clothes, and saith, What need we any further witnesses ?

" Ye have heard the blasphemy : what think ye ? And they all condemned him to be guilty of death."— Mark xiv. 61—64.

This rending of the high priest's clothes was forbidden : first, in Lev. x. 6, " uncover not your heads neither rend your clothes, lest ye die," and subsequently a distinct precept was given to that effect—" the high priest among his brethren, upon whose head the anointing oil was poured, and that is consecrated to put on the garments, shall not uncover his head, nor rend his clothes."— Lev. xxi. 10.

Although in both these cases the prohibition is made in connexion with mourning for the dead, yet the very fact of such being the case, would seem to imply that he must not do so on any other occasion. If in the first natural outburst of grief, because of a deep domestic sorrow, he was threatened with death if he rent his clothes, surely such an act could not be permitted under any other circumstances.

Whilst the Lord lay in the tomb, the last Sabbath day under the law was observed. We read no more of the keeping of that day in the Acts or in the Epistles. It is emphatically said in Luke xxiii. 56, " that the women returned (from the sepulchre) and prepared spices and ointments ; and rested the Sabbath day, according to the commandment." The chief Priests and

Pharisees on the other hand broke the Sabbath by sealing the stone and setting the watch over the sepulchre of Jesus.   It is distinctly said that they came to Pilate the day that followed the day of preparation, the day of preparation being the day before the Sabbath. Matt. xxvii. 62—66 ; Mark xv. 42.   What a strange rest was this last Sabbath !   The last day of a creation week, when originally the morning stars had sung together, and the Sons of God had shouted for joy, at beholding the handy work of the Son of God.   But how still, how silent all song and shout, whether in heaven or in earth. What a strange pause, an interval between the passing away of the old things and the beginning of the new : not a real Sabbath of rest and joy.*   Truly old things have now passed away : the Lord is risen indeed, and the law which made nothing perfect has been changed. A better hope has been brought in, established upon an entire change of priesthood.   We have an everlasting High Priest, an everlasting righteousness, an everlasting salvation, an everlasting covenant, an everlasting redemption, everlasting life.   We are dwelt in by an eternal Spirit, and we are entering into God's eternal rest.

---

* The words, *and they rested* (Luke xxiii. 56) has in the Greek, rather the sense of silence and stillness, than the thought of rest from labour, or work.   A participle of the same verb is used for "the *dead* of night."   It was indeed a time of stillness like the dead of night, and yet what a mighty victory was won, "through death he (Jesus) destroyed him that had the power of death, that is the devil."— Heb. ii. 14.

Twice only in Scripture is it said, "they rested on the seventh," or "sabbath day."   Exod. xvi. 30, when the manna was given; and the above verse, in Luke xxiii.

# THE DAY OF ATONEMENT

"And the Lord spake unto Moses after the death of the two sons of Aaron, when they offered before the Lord, and died;

"And the Lord said unto Moses, Speak unto Aaron thy brother, that he come not at all times into the holy place within the vail before the mercy-seat, which is upon the ark, that he die not: for I will appear in the cloud upon the mercy seat.

"Thus shall Aaron come into the holy place: with a young bullock for a sin-offering, and a ram for a burnt offering."—Lev. xvi 1—3

THE book of Leviticus seems to change its character and mode of teaching, after the 10th chapter. The sacrifices and consecration of the priesthood, which we have been considering occupy the first nine chapters. But when, as in the case of Nadab and Abihu, the priesthood had proved itself an utter failure, another course of instruction is pursued by the Lord, and we have first, descriptions of unclean animals, and next, chapter upon chapter detailing various uncleannesses—leprosy, issues, and the like. It is as if the higher mode of instruction had been first adopted by God, namely, to teach His holiness and hatred to sin, through the purity, and preciousness, and value of the sacrifices: and the priests having failed thus to learn that they had to deal with a Holy God, a lower course of instruction is adopted, teaching what man is, and what the world is; filled with iniquity and uncleanness. Then follows this grand chapter of the book.

In each of the first four books of the Word of God, there occurs one striking chapter to which we instinctively turn for typical instruction, respecting the great truths of salvation. The 22nd chapter of Genesis, Abraham offering up "his only begotten son," directs our thoughts to the Lamb of God. God's blessed Son, revealed to us in the Gospel by John.

The 12th of Exodus, is a foundation chapter from whence we gather the great truth of redemption by the blood, there for the first time prefigured.

This 16th of Leviticus which we are about to consider

is the great chapter depicting atonement and its results. It is frequently referred to in the Epistle to the Hebrews. Whilst in the book of Numbers we have the ashes of the red heifer and the water of purification in the 19th chapter, which affords us deep lessons respecting the constant defilements we incur, and the constant need of the blood of cleansing.

God gave the directions contained in this chapter of Lev. respecting the day of atonement, after the death of Nadab and Abihu. On the very day* of their consecration (elated perhaps by the high position into which they had been brought) they " took either of them his censer, and put fire therein, and put incense thereon, and offered strange fire before the Lord." chap. x. i.

Fire had come out from before the Lord and had consumed the sacrifices upon the altar. These two eldest sons of Aaron should have taken coals of burning fire from off that altar fire which had come from the Lord. But instead of this, they put fire in their censers which was *common* to them, but *strange* to the Lord. May we not regard this as another form of Cain worship? Another warning against the unitarianism, or socinianism of the day? Cain offered an offering without the shedding of blood. His was a religion of works, though the name of the Lord was in it. His was not the worship of a false God—but it was false worship of the true God, worship which was not preceded by salvation.

Nadab and Abihu were quite correct as to censer, incense, and the holy place : but they did not recognize that it was the fire *from God* which had fed upon the sacrifices, and that no fragrance could come up to God from the hands even of His priests, unless through the sacrifice consumed in judgment on the altar. Christ may be owned as a true Christ. He may even be

* This, it would seem, was the case, from Lev. x. 19. "Aaron said, Behold *this day* have they offered their sin-offering and their burnt-offering before the Lord, and such things have befallen me." The sin-offering and burnt-offering to which Aaron here alludes, are those mentioned in Lev. ix. 2, 8—14, which were therefore offered on the same day that Nadab and Abihu perished

confessed with the lip as the Son of God. Prayer and
worship may be conducted in His name—but unless His
death be acknowledged and trusted in, as a death in the
way of atonement, a death not meritorious only because
of His fortitude and meekness and grace, but of
unspeakable value because God laid iniquity upon Him,
and he suffered at the hands of God who made His soul
an offering for sin—unless this be owned, the worshipper
whoever he be is offering strange fire, mingled though
it be with the name of Christ.

This sin of Nadab and Abihu is stamped upon them.
See Numbers iii. 4 ; xxvi. 61.

" Our God is a consuming fire." Heb. xii. 29. Some
believers are wont to say that " God out of Christ is a
consuming fire"—but the word says, " *our* God." God
known in Christ is a consuming fire. We read the
consuming fire of His holiness nowhere so plainly and
forcibly as in the death of His own Son upon the cross.
We reverence Him and serve Him with godly fear
because we know His solemn judgment of sin and of
ourselves as sinners, in the sacrifice of the Lamb of God
upon the tree. Nadab and Abihu were devoured by
the fire from the Lord, and died before the Lord, instead
of living before Him, because they had neglected to
observe and use the fire from before the Lord which had
consumed the victim on the altar. The judgment of
God must be seen poured out upon Christ as the sinner's
substitute in death ; or, the sinner himself will have to
know and realize the fearfulness of it throughout eternity.

The words " *before the Lord*," often repeated in the
chapters we have been considering, and in this 16th
chapter, are solemn words. Solemn and blessed if we
have everlasting life, and live and serve before Him now
and for ever. Solemn and terrible if we look at the
judgment upon the sinner who has neglected or mis-
used the great salvation presented in Christ, and who
will receive his judgment from " *before the Lord*,"
and will be " punished with everlasting destruction

from the presence of the Lord, and the glory of his power." 2nd Thess. i. 8, 9.

" Speak unto Aaron thy brother." This is the only occasion on which Moses was directed to speak to Aaron his *brother*. The Lord does not say, Aaron the high priest : indeed throughout the whole ceremony of the day of atonement the word *priest* does not occur. It is only mentioned at the close of the chapter, ver. 32, 33. The death of Nadab and Abihu had made manifest the insufficiency of the whole family of Levi to perpetuate any real lasting blessing. This day of atonement was the establishment of an entirely new ritual, both as regarded Aaron and his house, and the people Israel. Aaron sinks back to the mere brother of Moses. God had before spoken of him in the same way when giving directions for separating him and his sons off for the priests' office ; and also for making the garments for glory and beauty in which they were to be consecrated. Exod. xxviii. 1, 2, 4. Subsequently to this day of atonement the same expression is significantly used by the Lord when He directed Moses and Aaron to speak to the rock, (Num. xx. 8 ;) and when by their joint failure, they proved indeed that they were brethren. Also God calls Aaron the brother of Moses, when He tells Moses that he shall die. Numb. xxvii. 13 ; Deut. xxxii. 50. It was altogether a failing family. Like the law itself, those who had to carry it out were weak and unprofitable. Heb. vii. 18. And this very addition to the law of another day, only the more evidenced the necessity that another priest should rise after another order, and not after the order of Aaron. Heb. vii. 11.

" That he come not at all times into the holy place within the vail, before the mercy-seat, which is upon the ark ; that he die not : for I will appear in the cloud upon the mercy-seat." Before this, it would appear that Aaron as the high priest was to have unrestricted access into the holy of holies. But from henceforth he could not enter there except " once every year, and then not without blood, which he offered for himself and for the errors of the people." This we are told in Heb. ix. 7, is an intimation by the Holy Ghost that the way into the holiest was not made manifest. No one had access there save the high priest, and he was forbidden to enter, save once a year ; and even then his service there was of a very limited character. He could have no constant intercourse with God concerning his own necessities or those of others.

" *Within the vail*," (an expression thrice repeated in this chapter, is a sentence which raises in *our* hearts thoughts of blessed nearness, and happy confidence and fellowship with God our Father. To the high priest of those days, "within the vail," must have sounded somewhat fearfully upon the ear, since " that he die not" is twice connected with them, (ver. 2, 12, 13.)

Aaron is next directed to come into the holy place with a bullock for a sin-offering and a ram for a burnt-offering. A dress also worn only on this occasion is for the first time mentioned.

## THE HOLY LINEN GARMENTS

"He shall put on the holy linen coat, and he shall have the linen breeches upon his flesh, and shall be girded with a linen girdle, and with the linen mitre shall he be attired : these are holy garments ; therefore shall he wash his flesh in water, and so put them on."– Lev. xvi 4

THESE garments **are** all of the same materials *(bad)* before referred to pp. 304, 415. No directions are given as to their being made : they are rather abruptly introduced, as if the high priest had understanding respecting them. They are also peculiarly specified as *holy* garments : and the coat is called a *holy* linen coat, or tunic ver. 4, 32. Therefore the high priest was to wash his flesh in water before he put them on.

These *holy* linen garments, seem to prefigure the perfectly holy and righteous standing of the high priest before God—clean and spotless from head to foot—a foreshadowing of Him, whom God raised from the dead, and who would enter the holiest as the justified and righteous One, standing in His own intrinsic holiness before God, in order to make atonement for the sins of others. These garments for atonement were not of a representative character. The names of Israel were not upon the shoulders or breast of the High Priest graven in precious stones ; and no golden plate on behalf of others adorned His forehead. It was like the commencement of a new order of priesthood in which the High Priest should first accomplish full atonement, and afterwards take a representative standing for glory and beauty on behalf of others.

## THE OFFERINGS FOR SIN

"And he shall take of the congregation of the children of Israel two kids of the goats for a sin offering, and one ram for a burnt offering.

"And Aaron shall offer his bullock of the sin offering, which is for himself, and make an atonement for himself, and for his house.

"And he shall take the two goats, and present them before the LORD at the door of the tabernacle of the congregation.

"And Aaron shall cast lots upon the two goats; one lot for the LORD, and the other lot for the scapegoat.

"And Aaron shall bring the goat upon which the LORD'S lot fell, and offer him for a sin offering.

" But the goat, on which the lot fell to be the scapegoat, shall be presented alive before the LORD, to make an atonement with him, and to let him go for a scapegoat into the wilderness." Lev. xvi. 5—10.

AFTER being thus clothed, Aaron was to " take of the congregation of the children of Israel two kids of the goats for a sin-offering, and one ram for a burnt-offering." These two goats he presented before the Lord at the door of the tabernacle of the congregation, and cast lots upon them ; one lot for the Lord, and the other lot for the scapegoat. The goat upon which the Lord's lot fell, was to be offered for a sin-offering, but the scapegoat was to be presented alive before the Lord to make an atonement, to send him for a scapegoat into the wilderness. It is important here to remark that the two goats were *one* sin-offering, and the apparent object of having *two* was, to present two aspects of the same offering for sin. An atonement accomplished for the Lord to satisfy Him ; and this atonement made manifest to the people in the scapegoat sent into the wilderness. So that the one goat is directed to be offered for sin, viz : that upon which Jehovah's lot fell ; and the other is spoken of as making atonement by being let go as a scapegoat into the wilderness. And here on consulting the Hebrew, we shall find a remarkable and important expression. If the 9th verse were literally translated, it would read thus, " and Aaron shall bring the goat upon which Jehovah's lot went up, *and shall make it sin.**

Do we not find here the source from which that blessed sentence in the New Testament is derived, " he hath made him sin for us who knew no sin, that we might be made the righteousness of God in him." 2nd Cor. v. 21.

The goat on which the Lord's lot fell, and which therefore peculiarly belonged to the Lord, was killed as bearing the sin of the people. see ver. 15. No audible voice of the high priest laid the sin of the people upon its head ; but in the act of killing the goat, he laid the judgment of death upon it because it represented the people's sin.

---

* In some versions of the Sept. this Hebrew word is translated "*make*" (poiesei) in this passage. Lev. xvi. 9. See Trommius, vol. 1, page 336, under the word *prosphero*. Montanus in his Latin translation of the Bible, renders the passage thus, " et faciet eum peccatum;" " and shall make him sin ;" almost word for word the same rendering as the vulgate adopts for 2nd Cor. v. 21, " eum pro nobis peccatum fecit," " He made him sin for us."

In the other passages of the Bible where this Hebrew word (*ahsah*) occurs in connection with sacrifices, (which are not many,) it is translated "*offer*;" although it is not the usual word for *offer*. These occurrences are Lev. xiv. 19, 30· xv. 15, 30; xvi. 9, 24; xxiii. 12, 19; Num. vi. 11, 16, 17; xv. 14, 24; xxix. 2, Deut. xii. 27. In all which passages we might substitute the word "*make*" for "*offer*."

When the Lamb of God was nailed to the tree, He fell under the whole weight of God's judgment upon sin. God made Him who knew no sin, to be sin on our behalf—dealing with Him according to His own holy and just indignation against sin. Christ became a curse for us—according to the solemn words of Deut. xxi. 23, "he that is hanged is the curse of God." Jesus was then our substitute—for what are we by nature but children of wrath? Jehovah's lot had fallen upon Him. God had selected Him in His own eternal counsels as the only one who could (because without sin) be the substitute for the sinner; and because He was the Son of man, the Son of God, the mighty God, He alone could endure the fearful penalty due to sin.

And what a wonderful result is deduced in that verse in the epistle to the Corinthians, from the fact of the Lord Jesus having been made sin—"that we might be made the righteousness of God in Him." A different word is here used for *made*, that we might *become* the righteousness of God in Him. The righteousness of God —what a glorious manifestation will the church be hereafter as a whole, and every living member of it, of the righteousness of God—the full expression of His perfect righteousness, because one in life, in glory with Christ—"in Him"—deriving all from Him, and united to Him. Receiving out of His fulness; and manifesting His fulness.

# SPRINKLING THE BLOOD UPON THE MERCY-SEAT

"And Aaron shall bring the bullock of the sin offering which is for himself, and shall make an atonement for himself, and for his house, and shall kill the bullock of the sin offering which is for himself.

"And he shall take a censer full of burning coals of fire from off the altar before the LORD, and his hands full of sweet incense, beaten small, and bring it within the vail.

"And he shall put the incense upon the fire before the LORD, that the cloud of the incense may cover the mercy seat that is upon the testimony, that he die not.

"And he shall take of the blood of the bullock, and sprinkle it with his finger upon the mercy seat eastward; and before the mercy-seat shall he sprinkle of the blood with his finger seven times.

"Then shall he kill the goat of the sin offering, that is for the people, and bring his blood within the vail, and do with that blood as he did with the blood of the bullock, and sprinkle it upon the mercy seat, and before the mercy seat.

"And he shall make an atonement for the holy place, because of the uncleanness of the children of Israel, and because of their transgressions in all their sins: and so shall he do for the tabernacle of the congregation, that remaineth among them in the midst of their uncleanness.

"And there shall be no man in the tabernacle of the congregation when he goeth in to make an atonement in the holy place, until he come out, and have made an atonement for himself, and for his household, and for all the congregation of Israel. Lev. xvi. 11—17.

IN the order of the sacrifices Aaron first killed the bullock, the sin offering which was for himself to make atonement for himself and for his house. This bullock is three times recorded as the sin-offering for *himself*, ver. 6, 11; and wherever the atonement made by it is mentioned it is said to be for himself and his house, ver. 6, 11, 17. So closely are the high priest and his house linked on together; doubtless to draw our attention to the oneness between Christ and His house— only with a striking contrast also—Aaron's bullock for sin suffered for himself and his house—he being *himself* a sinner, and his house composed of sinners *like himself*.*

* Throughout the Epistle to the Hebrews, the high priest and the people are alone alluded to; there is no mention made "of *his* house." Heb. v. 3; vii. 27; ix. 7. *The house* when spoken of is God's house, and Moses, not Aaron, the head over it; the whole assembly of Israel being included in "the house." Heb. iii. 2.

Our High Priest knew no sin, and offered up Himself solely therefore on behalf of others.

Aaron next took the censer full of coals of fire from off the altar before the Lord, and his hands full of sweet incense beaten small, and brought all within the vail, and put the incense upon the fire before the Lord, that the cloud of the incense might cover the mercy-seat upon the testimony, that he might not die.

The censer was apparently a golden censer. If we refer to the Epistle to the Hebrews, chap. ix. a description of the tabernacle is given us on this day of atonement. No incense altar is mentioned standing in the holy place; but the golden censer in the holiest. The cherubim also, shadowing the mercy-seat are called " cherubim of *glory*." On this day of atonement the coals of fire were moved from off the incense altar, and the golden censer being filled with them was carried within the vail. For the time therefore, the incense altar was inactive, and is not alluded to probably on that account in the 9th chapter of Hebrews. Jehovah appeared in the cloud upon the mercy-seat—the cloud of *glory*—and this may be the reason why the cherubim are called " cherubim of *glory*." Aaron notwithstanding the washing of his flesh, and the linen garments with which he was clothed, could not enter the holiest with the blood of atonement unless he could personally shelter himself under a cloud of incense. A perfume, not his own, but provided according to minute directions given by God.

Two epithets are especially attached to the incense, '*pure*," and " *holy*"—and it was to be holy for the Lord. Exod. xxx. 35, 37. The frankincense, which was one ingredient of the incense, betokened purity. The word " pure" is connected with it. Exod. xxx. 34; Lev. xxiv. 7; and the Hebrew word " *Levohnah*" has the appropriate signification of whiteness. One of the Hebrew words for the moon is almost the same as that for frankincense—"fair as the moon." Cant. vi. 10. There

is one of whom it is truly said, " Thou art fairer than
the children of men ;" whose unsullied purity formed a
wondrous contrast with every other human being. A
purity, a righteousness so made manifest upon the cross
that even a Roman Centurion exclaimed, " Certainly
this was a righteous man." Luke xxiii. 47. The cloud
of incense beaten small, as it wafted itself up to God,
attracted with its singular perfume that Gentile soldier.
Purity and holiness are not to be found here except
in one whose graces were fully displayed before God.

The incense was compounded of three sweet spices
besides the frankincense, " stacte, onycha, and galba-
num." The two last are not known ; but the stacte is
manifestly derived from a word signifying " *to drop*,"
both in the Hebrew, and in the Greek translation. A
sweet spice that spontaneously dropped from the tree
which produced it. Another emblem of the grace of
the Lord Jesus, the Son of Man. Grace and truth came
by Jesus Christ. His paths dropped fatness ; wherever
He went, true love, sympathy, and pity flowed from His
heart towards the weak, the weary, and the afflicted.
He was the true Man in the midst of falsehood and
deceit in human beings all around Him. True in His
affection ; true in His words ; true in His sympathies ;
true in His rebukes of evil as well as in His forgiveness
of sin. It is blessed to turn from the hypocrisies of our
own hearts, and of men around us, and contemplate
Him " who did no violence," " neither was guile found
in his mouth." Isa. liii. 9 ; 1st Pet. ii. 22. There was no
*effort* in Him ; He simply lived, manifesting life in all
He did and said. There was no affectation of spirituality ; He *was* what He *appeared to be*. Thus His
words and ways were not forced. His sanctity was
not assumed. He had nothing to lay aside when He
came into the presence of others. He put on nothing
to gain their admiration. He was always Himself,
living in the presence of God, ever pleasing God
Blessed contrast with men who have to assume religi-

ousness to hide their own evil, who think that rough-
ness is sincerity, and who are unnatural oft-times even in
the very presence of God.

The incense " tempered together pure and holy" may
have reference to the sweet fragrance which the Man
Christ Jesus ever presented to God.    The Israelites
were forbidden to make a perfume like it, " to smell
thereto."    Christ is not to be imitated by a false humility to gratify one's own self-conceit.    There may be
a shew of wisdom and humility by which men satisfy
their own flesh, but this is like an imitation of the holy
perfume to smell thereto.    If we are imitators indeed
of Him we must first have been washed in His precious
blood, and be born of God.    To follow Him would
involve self-crucifixion instead of self-admiration.

The golden censer was *filled* with burning coals, and
Aaron's hands were *filled* with incense.    The vessel that
held the fire—type of the holiness of God—was full.
The altar from which that fire had originally been
taken was a place where the holiness of God was
exhibited in no scanty measure ; and the censer was
also filled, that in the very holiest itself that consuming
fire might again be presented according to the divine
estimate.

The high priest's hands were also full of sweet
incense.    He had to grasp that holy compound to the
full extent of his ability, that his filled hands might
answer to the filled censer.    He then put the incense on
the fire before the Lord, and the cloud of the incense
covered the mercy-seat, and mingled with the cloud of
glory upon the mercy-seat, in which Jehovah appeared.

We must here draw a contrast betwixt Aaron and
Christ.    The Lord Jesus presented Himself to God on
the morning of His resurrection—called of God an High
Priest, after the order of Melchizedek.    His entrance
into heaven itself was like the bringing in of fresh
incense before God ; for He entered on the ground of
His perfect obedience unto death, even the death of the

cross. God had been glorified in Him, on that very
earth where God had been so dishonoured by man ; and
when for the first time a Man stood in the presence of the
glory of God before " the throne of the Majesty in the
heavens," a cloud of human fragrance (may we not say ?)
mingled itself with the cloud of Divine glory. What a
wondrous addition to the heaven of heavens ! What an
added glory was the entrance of the risen Man there for
the first time as the risen man—a man able to stand before
God on the ground of His own righteousness, His own
obedience, His own purity, His own holiness ; and also
able to say to God, " I have glorified thee on the
earth, I have finished the work which thou gavest me
to do."

May we not with reverence contemplate this resurrec
tion of Jesus, and His thus presenting Himself before God
in heaven itself, as a marvellous change in the economy of
the heavens. One who bore the likeness of the creature,
standing in the midst of the throne of the Most High in
such nearness to God ? What indeed has God wrought !
What marvels has He accomplished through His blessed
Son !

Aaron next took of the blood of the bullock and
sprinkled it with his finger upon the mercy-seat, and
before the mercy-seat, seven times. So also he did
with the blood of the goat, the sin-offering for the
people. Having sheltered himself under the cloud of
incense, he was able to bring this record of death, the
blood, and sprinkle it under the glory of God upon the
mercy-seat, and upon the ground before the mercy-
seat ; first by way of atonement for himself and his
house ; and next on behalf of the people.

What a singular ritual this. The emblem of death
placed where God in His glory manifested Himself.
What a wondrous coming together of things in themselves opposed to one another. A record of life *poured
out on account of sin*, brought into the holy of holies.
And yet how this shadowy ritual pourtrays to us the

truth in which our souls rejoice. The great enigma of truth solved to faith in the death of God's Son.

It was said of the Aaronic high priest that "he entereth into the holy place every year with blood of *others*," (Heb. ix. 25 ;) or, as it might be rendered, *strange* or *foreign* blood, (*alotrio*,) seeing there was no affinity between the blood of a bullock, and a goat, and himself, a human being. It is written of Christ that " he by his *own* (*idiou*) blood entered in once into the holy places," Heb. ix. 12 ; and, the word " *his own*" is again repeated, Heb. xiii. 12.

Aaron had to make atonement for himself as well as for his house. His own blood would have been of no avail for others, or for himself, for he was a sinner. Our High Priest is " holy, harmless, undefiled, separate from sinners, and made higher than the heavens ;" and what He is now in the glory that He was when on earth, as far as regards holiness and harmlessness. Free from all human infirmity—the Son—who offered up Himself.

Aaron had to sprinkle the mercy-seat *eastward*, because his approach into the holiest was from the east, and he had to sprinkle before the mercy-seat, to establish a footing for himself before God ; for his own feet would have defiled the ground before the mercy-seat. The Lord Jesus, has His own rightful place—the Lamb as it had been slain in the midst of the throne—and He enables us *sinners* by nature, to enter into the holiest by His blood, "by a new and living way, which he hath new made for us, through the vail, that is to say, His flesh."

We have no threat of " *lest he die*" held out to us in our approaches to God ; but our very way is a *living* way, made *new* in contrast to all other ways of old, and ever new with the fresh sprinkled blood, in contrast with the blood only sprinkled once a year. The sacrifice of Christ is as fresh in all its life-giving value, and in all its cleansing power to-day, as it was on the very day it was first offered. The blood of Christ has ever its full, and fresh, and living value, in contrast with the blood of victims which had to be renewed daily and yearly.*

Aaron had to make atonement for the holy place, and for himself, his household, and the congregation of Israel. " *The holy place*," throughout this chapter where the word "*place*" is in italics, signifies the "*most holy*," ver. 2, 16, 17, 20, 23, 27. Called " the holy sanctuary" in verse 33. No one was to be with him, or enter the tabernacle until he had completed that important work of atonement. Atonement properly speaking is all Godward ; and is accomplished by one alone. The sinner who is atoned for has no part in the work. It is accomplished entirely by another. He is passive, and ignorant of the fact, until God reveals it to him by His Spirit through the Word. It is most important for the peace of the soul that this should be fully understood. And this type makes it very plain. Not one of the congregation, nor one of Aaron's house was with him whilst he thus acted for them before God. They could not be aware whether even he was alive in the sanctuary, or what he had accomplished there. They were not in any attitude of prayer or supplication outside ; but they silently waited in suspense till he came out ; then they knew he had fulfilled all God's requirements ; this being proved by the fact that he was alive.

The whole work of atonement, from beginning to end, has been accomplished by Christ alone ; whether we look at the commencement of the work in the shedding of His blood on the cross, or at its completion in His resurrection as the great High Priest, and entering in, "once for all, by His own blood into the holy places,

---

* The word translated "*consecrated*," is as the margin of the Bible has it, "*new made*." The word "*new*" is a remarkable one, literally meaning "fresh slain," (*prosph ton*,) and is used by the Spirit of God apparently to mark the contrast between the way on the day of atonement of old, when the blood must have at once ceased to keep its value, because it became stale, and had to be renewed every year ; and the constant fresh value of the precious blood of Christ, as of a lamb just slain.

having obtained eternal redemption." Heb. ix. 12. This is emphatically stated in the Epistle to the Hebrews : " when he had by *himself* purged our sins," i. 3 ; " this he did once when he offered up *himself*," vii. 27. " he hath appeared to put away sin by the sacrifice of *himself*," ix. 26. Alone upon the cross, the Lamb of God slain on account of sin. Alone in resurrection, the first-fruits of them that slept. Alone in the holiest with God, the great High Priest. He has offered one sacrifice for sins for ever, and has by Himself perfected the whole work of reconciliation which God committed to Him.

The sinner troubled in conscience on account of his sins, is not called upon by efforts of his own to reconcile God to himself. Every attempt of his own of this kind is the expression of an unbelieving heart, calling in question the full eternal redemption which Christ has obtained for us. He has to believe in a reconciliation accomplished. An atonement completed. A salvation finished. And that by the Lord Jesus Himself alone.

The " atonement for the holy place was because of the uncleanness of the children of Israel, and because of all their transgressions in all their sins ;" or it might perhaps be rendered, " he shall make atonement upon the holy place, *from* the uncleanness of the children of Israel, and *from* their transgressions *in respect to*, or *on account of* all their sins." *

Throughout this chapter uncleanness is in the plural. (Heb. *tumoth.*) *Uncleannesses* twice in ver. 16, and once in ver. 19. It seems especially to refer to personal defilements originating from man's very nature, the constitution of his body, or from disease. Transgressions are also mentioned. Sin is that evil thing in which we are conceived, which renders us utterly unclean from our very birth ; children of wrath by nature. The corrupt body is an outward evidence of the evil taint

---

* This would appear to be the meaning of the Hebrew preposition " *Lamed*," placed before "all their sins." It is frequently used in this sense in other parts of Scripture

which pervades us. Our mortal flesh, mortal as to every part ; without a spot of it free from death and corruption, is a proof of what we are by nature as regards our whole being, unclean perishing sinners.

Transgressions are sins made manifest in direct acts contrary to the revealed mind of God. Atonement had to be made with reference to the uncleannesses of Israel, and their transgressions. These two manifestations of evil indicating their sins.

The law had no full type of the entire corruption of man. One of the objects for which it was given, was to develope that corruption in overt acts : "wherefore then the law? It was added because of transgressions." Gal. iii. 19.

" Moreover the law entered that the offence might abound." Rom. v. 20. It was "the strength of sin." 1st Cor. xv. 56. In the types therefore which form part of the law, we do not discover that great truth, that a man is so irremediably a sinner by nature as to need new birth, a new existence.

Perhaps *leprosy* affords the nearest type of the entire uncleanness of the human being. But even here the priest could only deal with the *manifestations* of the disease. In interpreting these shadows therefore we have to go deeper than the types themselves. The atonement made by Christ does not only answer to God for *us* as regards *our* uncleannesses, but also in respect to the unclean nature itself, in which we entered this world as children of the first Adam. Our unclean selves ; and here we must be careful to distinguish between *ourselves* and our corrupt *nature*. The atonement made by Christ has not in any way cleansed, improved, or reconciled our flesh, our evil nature ; for that is so irremediably bad, that all that God could do with it was utterly to condemn it. In the death of Christ for sin, God has " condemned (damned) sin in the flesh." Rom. viii. 3. " Our old man is crucified with him that the body of sin might be destroyed," vi. 6. The body of the sins of the flesh have been put off from us as regards all judgment and wrath of God. *We* (not our evil nature) have been reconciled to God (2 Cor. v. 18; Col. i. 21).

This is the great aspect of atonement. For what troubles us most is the constant presence of an evil heart, an evil nature ; an inclination for sin, which will make itself to be felt notwithstanding all our efforts towards practical holiness, and notwithstanding we are new creatures in Christ, and notwithstanding the presence of the Holy Spirit dwelling in us. As believers we have a right to look at this, the old man, and say, it has been crucified ; it has been condemned once for all ; it has been judged under the full wrath of God, poured out upon His own Son for us. And there is " now no condemnation " of any kind to us—no condemnation on account of this evil nature which we still know to exist—no condemnation on account of weakness, failures, ignorances, sins. The uncleannesses and transgressions of the people entered the sanctuary of God, and had to be met by the blood of atonement; or otherwise wrath must have burst forth from before the Lord upon the people, or God must remove His dwelling-place from the midst of them.

" The patterns of things in the heavens were purified with these (sacrifices), but the heavenly things themselves with better sacrifices* than these. For Christ is not entered into the holy places made with hands, the figures of the true ; but into heaven itself, now to appear in the presence of God for us " (Heb. ix. 23, 24).

Notwithstanding our manifest sins and uncleannesses, of which to a great extent we are unconscious, Christ has opened the way for us into the very glory of God— He has preceded us there with His own most precious blood—and now we can draw near with confidence,

---

* This is the only place where the word *sacrifices* occurs in the plural, when the death of the Lord Jesus is spoken of. In all probability it is used to express the fact of His one sacrifice embracing every varied aspect of the *many sacrifices* offered under the law.

without defiling with our presence the holiest of all.
We can confess our sins before the mercy-seat itself.
We can bring our deep necessities, and find mercy and
grace to help us. We can offer thanksgiving, praise
and worship which God can accept because of the
sweet savour of that precious blood. We can say,
without fear, "thou hast set our iniquities before thee,
our secret (sins) in the light of thy countenance,"
(Psa. xc. 8.) because we know Christ is in the presence
of God for us ; His precious blood is in the very light
of the glory of God on our behalf. The sins which
have reached to heaven have been covered ; blotted out
by that sprinkled blood. "We have come to God, the
judge of all." We have heard His sentence pronounced
upon us as guilty and defiled sinners. We have seen
that sentence executed in the death of His own Son.
We have been justified from sin through that death,
"justified by his blood." Rom. v. 9; vi. 7.

We have come "to Jesus the mediator of the new
covenant ;" the High Priest in the presence of God for
us, ministering to us all the blessings of that new
covenant. We have come "to the blood of sprinkling
that speaketh better things than that of Abel ;" the
blood of sprinkling *upon* the mercy-seat, and *before* the
mercy-seat. God said to Cain respecting the blood of
Abel, "the voice of thy brother's blood crieth unto me
from the ground, which hath opened her mouth to
receive thy brother's blood from thy hand." Gen. iv.
10, 11. The blood cried for vengeance. The blood
of sprinkling to which we have come, speaketh incessantly mercy and grace; answers every accusation; calls
down ceaseless blessings ; cleanseth from all sin ; utters
a voice which delights the ear of God ; and which
enables Him to open His hand and fill us with good.
The word "*speaketh*" is a blessed word, in contrast
not only with the blood of Abel which cried for
vengeance, but with the blood of bulls and of goats,
which spoke but for a moment, and effected nothing in

reality.   Whereas this blood speaketh on and on with
a ceaseless still small voice of power, until the day of
full redemption, when the resurrection of the Church
in glory will manifest for ever its mighty efficacy : and
the voice of the precious blood will continue to sound
until Israel, God's *chosen nation*, and others redeemed out
of the world during the 1000 years reign of Christ,
are clothed with immortality.


## SPRINKLING THE INCENSE ALTAR

"And he shall go out unto the altar that is before the LORD, and
make an atonement for it; and shall take of the blood of the bullock,
and of the blood of the goat, and put it upon the horns of the altar
round about.
   "And he shall sprinkle of the blood upon it with his finger seven
times, and cleanse it, and hallow it from the uncleanness of the
children of Israel.—Lev. xvi 18, 19

THE words *"until he come* out and have made an
atonement," see ver. 17, seem at first to be violated by
the beginning of the above passage, *" and he shall go
out unto the altar that is before the Lord."*
   " The altar before the Lord " is not the altar of
burnt-offering in the court of the tabernacle, but the
altar of incense in the holy place ; so that Aaron did
not go out of the tabernacle itself, he only went out
from the holy of holies where the ark stood into the
holy place.   He did not go out into the court of the
tabernacle until he had finished the work of atonement
towards God, for himself, and the people ; and also
had cleansed the holy places.
   The blood of the bullock, the sin-offering for
himself, and for his house ; and the blood of the goat,
the sin-offering for the people, was put upon the horns,
and sprinkled seven times upon the altar of incense, as the
blood of the same sin-offerings had been before sprinkled

on the mercy-seat and ark. By this means the altar was cleansed and hallowed from the uncleannesses of the children of Israel. In Exod. xxx. 10, this atonement is anticipated. "Aaron shall make an atonement upon the horns of it once in a year with the blood of the sin offering of atonements : once in the year shall he make atonement upon it throughout your generations : it is most holy unto the Lord."

The mercy-seat was the throne of glory where God manifested His presence—He dwelt between the Cherubim. The incense altar was the holy vessel from which, day and night, the holy perfume ascended from burning coals of fire, filling the tabernacle with fragrance. It was, we may say, the *active* vessel of the tabernacle. The blood of atonement accomplished a double purpose : the uncleannesses, transgressions, and sins of Israel were purged away from before God in the holiest ; and the altar of incense was cleansed from all defilement attaching to it through their uncleannesses, and was made ready to receive the burning coals and incense as if it had been for the first time made and hallowed for that purpose.

We see in this type a figure of the atonement completed by the Lord Jesus with regard to the purging of our sins, and the consequent exercise of His priesthood in ceaseless intercession, like the golden altar before the Lord, continually sending up its cloud of sweet incense. In the Epistle to the Hebrews, these two blessed services of our great High Priest are clearly distinguished from one another. If we regard the question of atonement for sin, the Lord Jesus has sat down, having completed that work. Four times in this Epistle are the words "sat down" repeated.

"When he had by himself purged our sins, *sat down* on the right hand of the majesty on high," i. 3.

"We have such an high priest who is *set on the right hand* of the throne of the majesty in the heavens," viii. 1.

"Every priest standeth daily ministering and offering oftentimes the same sacrifices, which can never take

away sins : but this one, after he had offered one sacrifice for sins for ever, *sat down* on the right hand of
God," x. 11, 12.

" Looking unto Jesus the author and finisher of faith,
who, for the joy that was set before him, endured the
cross, despising the shame, and is *set down* at the right
hand of the throne of God," xii. 2.

The expressions are remarkably varied in these four
passages as to where the Lord has sat down.

" *On the right hand of the Majesty on high.*"

" *On the right hand of God.*"

" *On the right hand of the throne of the Majesty in the
heavens.*"

" *On the right hand of the throne of God.*"

We may gather some instruction from these changes
of expression. In the first quotation there seems to be
a striking contrast between *purging sins*, and *the Majesty
on high*. Who could have expected that one who had
been engaged in such a work as cleansing away sins,
with all their guilt and defilements, would have immediately taken His place at the right hand of the highest
glory ? Yet such is the dignity of His person, and such
was the greatness of His work—such the lowliness
of His obedience, that He was exalted to the highest
place of glory, from the lowest place of suffering and
humiliation.

A cross of curse and shame where He purged our
sins, followed by a grave in which His body lay in the
helplessness of death, was the pathway taken by the
Lord Jesus to reach His place of super-exaltation.

In the second quotation we have Jesus as the High
Priest sat down on *the right hand of God*, after He had
offered one sacrifice for sins for ever. In many of our
Bibles the stopping of this verse is different, reading
thus—" when he had offered one sacrifice for sins, for
ever sat down." And this perhaps is the more correct
punctuation. The purport of the passage being to tell
us that Christ has sat down in perpetuity, or for ever, in

respect to the fact of His having offered one sacrifice for sins. He has officially taken His seat at the right hand of God with regard to a work that is finished. He will never rise from that seat about sacrifice for sins, for that is accomplished once for all. Other priests had to stand daily and yearly. No seat was provided for them in the tabernacle, or in the court of the tabernacle, for their work was never finished. Sins were never put away—the worshippers were never purged. God was never satisfied. Atonement was never perfected. But our High Priest has sat down on the right hand of God, for atonement has been made to God. God's will has been accomplished—God's holiness has been for ever satisfied. God's indignation against sin has been for ever appeased. And He has received His Son, and has said to Him, " sit Thou at my right hand " in token of His delight in Him, and in His completed work, and as an evidence to us, that all wrath and judgment against sin has been completely poured out and ended in the death of Jesus.

Thus the fact that Christ is seated at the right hand of God is the sure ground of peace to the soul of the believer. Salvation is accomplished, and Christ can henceforth expect " that his enemies shall be made his footstool," when He rises from the right hand of God, and comes to take vengeance on them. His heart is at rest respecting those who believe in Him, for " by one offering He hath perfected for ever them that are sanctified."

In the third quotation the Lord is looked upon in the greatness and glory of His priesthood. " We have *such an High Priest*." A glory and excellency which are His own. A priesthood which derives all its dignity and power from Him who is the great High Priest. His being seated " on the right hand of *the throne* of the Majesty in the heavens" witnesses to the power as well as the dignity of the High Priest. He can exercise the might of that throne on behalf of His people. He can bring us, and keep us nigh to that throne of Majesty in the heavens.

In the last passage, " Jesus the author and finisher of faith," is presented to us as the great example to whom we are to look in running our race. He " endured the cross despising the shame." And where is He now ? What is the goal which He has reached ? What is the joy which was set before Him, and which He has attained ? He is " set down at the right hand of *the throne of God.*" Rejected, and despised, and crucified by man ; God has received Him, God has counted Him worthy of the highest place of glory on His throne.

He has fought the fight for us. He is the " Captain of our salvation." He is the " forerunner" who has entered in for us. And if we keep our eye on Him we shall find grace and faith ministered to follow Him ; and He will come again and receive us to Himself, and will grant us to sit with him in his throne, even as he also hath overcome, and is set down with his Father in his throne. Rev. iii. 2 1.

Thus by Himself He hath purged our sins—by one offering He hath perfected us for ever as holy ones to God. He has also made a way for us into the very presence of God, to the throne of glory, the throne of grace in the holiest where He Himself has entered. So far He has " *sat down,*" having " put away sin by the sacrifice of Himself." All obstructions, all hindrances are put away, and we can have confidence of access into the holiest.

But there is another ministration of our High Priest which is perpetual, and in respect of which the words " *sat down*" do not apply. That is, His ministry of intercession ; of which it is said, " this one because he continueth ever hath an unchangeable priesthood : wherefore he is able also to save them to the uttermost that come unto God by him, seeing he ever liveth to make intercession for them," vii. 24, 2 5. And " Christ is not entered into the holy places made with hands, the figures of the true ; but into heaven itself, now to appear in the presence of God for us," ix. 24. And, "Who is he that condemneth ? It is Christ that died, yea rather, that is risen again, who is even at the right hand of God, who also maketh intercession for us." Rom. viii. 34.

This incessant service of intercession is the result of, and is grounded upon, the shedding of His blood. It is the perpetuating the voice of that precious blood in God's presence ; and it shelters those who have been atoned for by that blood under the full fragrance of Him that shed it. As the incense altar was established on the ground of the sprinkled blood on the day of atonement, so the Lord Jesus takes His place as the interceding High Priest, because He has fully answered for sin by the sacrifice of Himself. His death has met the wrath of God, and saved His people from all condemnation, whether due to them "as children of wrath by nature," or on account of their sins. His intercession covers every failure of which they may be guilty as the children God, and continues on their great salvation in all its completeness until the very end—the day of their redemption ; when they will stand in resurrection glory around the Lamb, and when their salvation in the fullest sense of the word will be perfected.

We have in the passage above quoted from the Romans a fourfold answer to all condemnation. The Apostle having answered the question, "Who shall lay any thing to the charge of God's elect," by the declaration that "it is GOD that justifieth ;" next asks "Who is he that condemneth ?" Who can condemn us as sinners ? *Christ* has died. He has answered in His death entirely for our sins. Yea, rather He is risen again : a full proof that His death was all sufficient. He has paid the penalty of which His resurrection is the evidence. He is even at the right of God. God therefore has been fully satisfied—God is well pleased with what His blessed Son has accomplished ; and has raised Him in consequence to the highest place of dignity and power.

And who shall condemn us as saints ? We are indeed most weak, most feeble ; poor specimens of saved sinners ; and but indifferent followers of the Lamb ; and very distant imitators of God as His children. But who can condemn ? for Christ is not only in the presence of God for us, but " also maketh intercession for us." " We have an advocate with the Father, Jesus Christ the righteous," who has identified Himself with our cause, who will maintain our cause to the end. And " He is the propitiation for our sins." Not only *has been* in His death, but is Himself by virtue of that death, the one who can answer for all our sins. According to another passage in the Epistle to the Romans, " God commendeth his love toward us, in that while we were yet sinners, Christ died for us. Much more then, being now justified by His blood, we shall be saved from wrath through Him. For if when we were enemies, we were reconciled to God by the death of His Son, much more, being reconciled, we shall be saved by His life." (Rom. v. 8, 10.)

Here we have Christ dying for us as sinners, and complete justification through that death; and all wrath which might break forth against us (because of our disobedience even as justified persons) averted through Him in resurrection : for if when we were *enemies,* the death of God's Son for us reconciled us to God— much more now that we have been reconciled, and are friends and children of God, shall we have salvation continued to the end, and perfected in the life of Christ for us at the right hand of God, in Him who ever liveth to make intercession for us.

The intercession of Christ also covers over all defects of our worship and prayers, like the incense which was added to the prayers of all saints upon the golden altar before the throne, and the smoke of which mingling with the prayers of the saints ascended up before God. Rev. viii. 3, 4. So the full value of Christ, the propitiation for our sins, and the sweet odour of His obedience in death render our worship acceptable to God.

Two great objects were accomplished by Aaron on the day of atonement : blood was sprinkled *on* the mercy-seat, and *before* the mercy-seat in the holiest. Thus atonement was made for himself and the sins of the people before God. And the incense altar was *also* established in the holy place in fresh purity, through the blood, so that a perpetual incense could thenceforth ascend from it to God. At that time the vail separated the holy place from the most holy. The vail is now rent ; the holy places are thereby thrown into one. The intercession of Christ is therefore in the holiest of all, and we as priests have access into the holiest.

This work of Aaron in the holy places being accomplished by himself alone ; he then came out ; and we have next the service of Aaron in the court of the tabernacle where the people were assembled.

# THE SCAPEGOAT

"And when he hath made an end of reconciling the holy place, and the tabernacle of the congregation, and the altar, he shall bring the live goat:

"And Aaron shall lay both his hands upon the head of the live goat, and confess over him all the iniquities of the children of Israel, and all their transgressions in all their sins, putting them upon the head of the goat, and shall send him away by the hand of a fit man into the wilderness.

"And the goat shall bear upon him all their iniquities unto a land not inhabited: and he shall let go the goat in the wilderness.

"And he that let go the goat for the scapegoat shall wash his clothes, and bathe his flesh in water, and afterward come into the camp.—Lev. xvi 20—22, 26

THREE times is the word "alive" connected with this goat, ver. 10, 20, 21, probably to convey to our minds the thought that the blessed Lord was in the full vigour of life when He presented Himself to God, to make atonement for our sins on the cross, according to His own words, "I lay down my life." "I lay it down of myself." John x. 17, 18.

Aaron having presented the scapegoat alive before the Lord to make an atonement with him, ver. 10, 20, next laid both his hands upon the head of the live goat, and confessed over him all the iniquities of the children of Israel, and all their transgressions in all their sins, putting them upon the head of the goat.

This was done in the presence and hearing of the congregation of Israel; the congregation for which he had previously made atonement in the holiest.* The

* In this Chapter the Hebrew word *kah-hal*, (sometimes translated *congregation*, sometimes *assembly*,) occurs twice. "And have made atonement . . . for all *the congregation* of Israel; and "for all the people of *the congregation*," ver. 17, 33. In the last passage the word "of" is not in the original, so that it should be, "for all the people, the congregation." All the people being thus defined as *the congregation*, or *assembly*.

This word is translated *ecclessia* (church) in the Sept., and is so quoted in the New Testament. "In the midst of the *church* will I sing praise unto thee." Heb. ii. 12. See also Psa. xxii. 22; lxxxix. 5; cvii. 32; cxlix. 1. The word *kah-hal*, *assembly*, occurs first in the blessing of Jacob; "that thou mayest be *a multitude* (margin, *assembly*) of nations;" and again, "a nation and *an assembly* of nations shall be of thee;" and "I will make of thee *an assembly* of nations." Gen. xxviii. 3;

high priest's hands, *both* hands, which had previously
been filled with sweet incense, were now, as it were,
filled with sins, which he transferred to the head of the
goat, whilst the assembly heard him confess over the
goat all their iniquities and transgressions, and saw him
"*give*" them upon the head of the goat.

No mere man like Aaron has put our sins upon the
Victim's head. Jehovah Himself "has laid upon him
(Jesus) the iniquity of us all." No human high priest
has confessed our iniquities, transgressions, and sins
over a scapegoat ; but the Lord Himself whilst hanging
on the cross, made full confession of our iniquities, our
folly, and our guilt ; suffering under the judgment of
them as if they had been His own. "Innumerable evils
have compassed me about : mine iniquities have taken
hold upon me, so that I am not able to look up, they
are more than the hairs of mine head ; therefore my
heart faileth me." Psa. xl. 12. "O God thou knowest
my foolishness, and my sins (margin, guiltiness) are not
hid from thee." lxix. 5.

Israel was constituted one assembly in redemption
through the blood of the Paschal Lamb in Egypt.
Though many lambs were slain, ("a lamb for an house,")
yet they were considered as one lamb : "the whole
assembly of the congregation shall kill *it* in the evening."
Exod. xii. 6. Israel subsequently met as sinners alike
before the Lord on this day of atonement, and heard
their various sins confessed over, and laid upon the
head of the one victim.

"All we (in like manner) as sheep have gone astray :
we have turned every one to his own way." Each of
us has had his own path of self-willed sin and departure from God. Some of us have taken a religious way

xxxv. 11 ; xlviii. 4. May not these passages look forward to the "*great assembly*"
again prophesied of in the Psalms xxii. 25 ; xxxv. 18 ; cix. 30.

The first occurrence of the word in respect to Israel as a nation, is when the
Passover was established : "the whole *assembly* of the congregation of Israel shall
kill it in the evening." Exod. xii. 6. Israel then for the first time was recognized
by God as having a corporate, and national existence.

Thus the passover lamb, and the goat for the sin-offering were for the *whole
assembly* as a corporate body.

of our own in wandering from the Lord. Others of us have trodden paths of more open uncleanness and sin ; but in either case iniquity, lawlessness, independence of God and His Word have marked our ways ; and Jehovah has made these our varied iniquities to meet on Christ.* We have each of us seen ourselves fully estimated by God as sinners, condemned and put to death in our substitute on that cross. Wonderful meeting place of our iniquities, and of wrath and judgment, which ever forbids one saying to another, "stand by, I am holier than thou." Each having been under "the same condemnation," and each therefore owning a "common salvation."

The assembly of Israel having thus heard their sins confessed, and having seen them transferred by Aaron to the head of the goat, next saw that goat sent away by the hand of a fit man into the wilderness. The victim with its load of iniquities disappeared from their sight. They knew that "*a fit man*," "a man of opportunity," had been selected for the occasion. And what rendered a man fit for this service ? Surely his knowledge of the desolate places, the fearful pits and precipices of the wilderness. That wilderness is described as "great and terrible"—" a desert land"—" a waste howling wilderness." Deut. i. 19 ; viii. 15 ; xxxii. 10. But the "fit man" had discovered some part of that desert of more than ordinary dreariness and fearful isolation ; some deep "valley of the shadow of death" from which there could be no return.

"And the goat shall bear upon him all their iniquities to a land not inhabited : and he shall let go the goat into the wilderness." Throughout this passage the word "*scapegoat*" does not occur ; that remarkable expression is used in three other places in the chapter— "the goat on which the lot fell, to be the scapegoat— to make an atonement with him to let him go for a

---

* It will be seen on reference to the margin of the Bible, that the way in which Isa. liii. 6. is there rendered, is "and the Lord hath *made the iniquities of us all to meet on him;*" instead of, "and the Lord hath *laid on* him the iniquities of us all"

scapegoat into the wilderness"—and, "he that let go the goat for the scapegoat," ver. 10, 26. Thus the goat was first *selected* to be the scapegoat by lot, and subsequently *became* the scapegoat when let go *for* the scapegoat into the wilderness ; and that letting him go for a scapegoat was making an atonement with him.

The lot fell upon the Lord Jesus ; He was elected of God to bear our sins. His entrance into the world was to that end. He partook of flesh and blood, "that through death he might destroy him that had the power of death." He was sent "in the likeness of sinful flesh" in order that God might condemn sin in the flesh, when He made His own Son to be sin for us upon the cross. But our iniquities were *not* laid upon Him, nor did He bear them until He was nailed to the tree. He *there* became the antitype to the scapegoat.

The word *azazel* in the Heb., about which there has been much profitless discussion, is translated in the Septuagint *apopompaios*, (Lev. xvi. 8, 10,) and "*eis teen apopompee,*" "to let him go for *the dismissal,*" ver. 10 ; our rendering of it *scapegoat*, or *goat sent away*, seems to be a correct one. It was a victim *dismissed* into the wilderness, into a land uninhabited, a land of separation, where it would perish with the fearful load which had been laid upon it. It could never return, and therefore the iniquities laid upon its head would never reappear. The goat was banished into a place of utter desolation, where no sound of life could reach its ear, and where it could find no green pasture or still waters to sustain life : it was consigned to a waste howling desert, a place of darkness and of death. The people must have had confidence in the hand of him who let go the goat for the scapegoat, that he would provide against its ever returning.

God has laid on Christ our iniquity, and Christ "*bare* the sin of many ;" "He shall *bear* their iniquities," "who his own self *bare* our sins in his own body on the tree." Isa. liii. 11, 12 ; 1st Pet. ii. 24. "Christ was

once offered to *bear* the sins of many." Heb. ix. 28.*
That tree of curse, the tree of judgment was chosen by
God as the place and manner of His death.

It was the place of isolation, of fearful separation to
which the Lord was led. He was lifted up there. The
storm of judgment beat with unmitigated fury upon Him.

* The passage 1st Pet. ii. 24, quoted above, has evidently been taken by the
Spirit of God from Isa. liii. 12. "He *bare* the sin of many." The Sept. in that
passage has " *sins*" for *sin*, and has the same Greek word for *bear* as that in Peter.
Dean Alford says that " by that passage of Isaiah our rendering in 1st Pet. ii. 24,
must be regulated." The same Greek word for *bear* occurs again in precisely the
same sense Heb. ix. 28, "Christ was once offered to *bear* the sins of many." The
passage in Isaiah seems also to allude to the Scapegoat; the same Hebrew word
(nahsah) *bear*, being in both places. Isa. liii. 12, and Lev. xvi. 22. Two words for
*bear* occur in Isa. liii, the ordinary one *nahsah*, and another, *sahral*; the latter
conveys the meaning of bearing a burthen, and is found in ver. 4, *carried* our
sorrows," and ver. 11, "He shall *bear* their iniquities." The *burdens* in Egypt are
expressed by this word; and in Isa. ix. 4, we have "the yoke of his *burden*."
May not the Lord have had some reference to this passage in Isaiah liii. respecting
the *burden* borne by Him, when He invited those that labour and are heavy laden
to come to Him for rest, (Matt. xi. 28, 30,) and offers His *easy* yoke and light burden,
instead of the heavy yoke and burden of sins. Some statements have of late appeared in print asserting that the Lord Jesus
was bearing sin all His life, from the moment of His birth; and this passage in
1st Pet. ii. 24, is altered (in order to meet these views) from the way it is rendered
in our version, "in His own body *on* the tree," to "in His own body *up* to the tree."
Like most errors in doctrine this weakens and lessens the value of the Cross;
because it spreads out over the whole life of the Lord, sufferings peculiar to the
cross, and it makes those sufferings of no avail. If these statements were true, the
Blessed Lord must have been forsaken of God all His days on earth. He could not
have walked in the light of God's countenance, for God could not deal with Him
as a sin-bearer, except in wrath. He could not have "rejoiced in spirit," He could
not have appeared in glory on the mount of transfiguration He could not have
uttered that blessed chapter, John xvii; indeed His whole life must have been an
existence of dark fearful gloom, far off from God, with the wrath of God afflicting
His soul without intermission. And all this suffering to no end, for no purpose—
for one sin could not have been in any way *remitted* by Christ, thus bearing them,
seeing that "without shedding of blood there is *no* remission." But to the true-
hearted believer the cross stands out in the word of God in all its solitary grandeur
of woe and suffering and blood. When Jesus was nailed to the tree *then* "was He
made a curse for us;" then He knew the desolation of the far off place of death;
then God laid our sins upon Him; then He bare our iniquities, then He bare the
sin of many. The glorious Gospel begins with Christ "made sin for us." "Christ
died for our sins according to the Scriptures." 1st Cor. xv. 1—3. The Scriptures
do not say He *lived* for our sins. "Christ was *once* offered to *bear* the sins of many."
Heb. ix. 28. Not all His life offered as some would have it. But the Spirit of God
has not allowed so great a truth as to *when* Christ bare our sins to be doubtful;
the very text itself 1st Pet. ii. 24, decides it. As if foreseeing the way in which
the mighty sorrows of the cross would be lessened, the Spirit of God has inserted
the all important words "*in His own body*." These significant words can refer to
nothing but the *death* of the Lord. They teach us to turn at once to the sufferings
of Christ on the cross—when His *body* was pierced, when He was "wounded for
our transgressions, bruised for our iniquities;" when His precious blood was shed
for our sins. And we find it said in Col. i. 22, "*In the body of his flesh*
through *death*;" "the offering of the *body* of Jesus Christ once" Heb. x. 10; "by
the *body* of Christ," Rom. vii. 4; all which passages clearly refer to the death of
the Lord upon the tree, when God did indeed "make him to be sin for us," when
God "made His soul an offering for sin" and when "He poured out His soul unto
death." Isa. liii. 10, 12. The word *bare (anaphero)* used in 1st Pet. ii. 24, is the
same as occurs in other passages of the New Testament respecting the *offering up*

We hear Him exclaiming, " Thou hast laid me in the lowest pit in darkness in the deeps. Thy wrath lieth hard upon me, and thou hast afflicted me with all thy waves." Psa. lxxxviii. 6, 7. " Save me, O God, for the waters are come in unto my soul. I sink in deep mire where there is no standing : I am come into deep waters, where the floods overflow me. Deliver me out of the mire and let me not sink : let me be delivered from them that hate me, and out of the deep waters. Let not the waterflood overflow me, neither let the deep swallow me up, and let not the pit shut her mouth upon me." Psa. lxix. 1, 2, 14, 15. " Deep calleth unto deep at the noise of thy waterspouts ; all thy waves and thy billows are gone over me." Psa. xlii. 7.

Who can comprehend these deep utterances of the soul of Christ ? The Spirit of God seems in the above passages to have selected emblems, gathered from the mighty deluge, as it rolled with increased fearfulness and noise over the buried world : and in the quotations which follow, imagery has been taken from the howling desert with its drought and deep desolate ravines, to express the experiences of the soul of Christ when He tasted death. For instance—" my life draweth nigh unto the grave. I am counted with them that go down into the pit: I am as a man that hath no strength: Free among the dead, like the slain that lie in the grave, whom thou rememberest no more: and they are cut off from thy hand. Shall thy wonders be known in the dark ? and thy righteousness in the land of forgetfulness ?" Psa. lxxxviii. 3—5, 12. " My heart is smitten and withered like grass. My days are like a shadow that

a sacrifice in *death*. "Who needeth not daily. as those high priests, *to offer up* sacrifice, first for his own sins, and then for the people's; for this He did once when He *offered up* Himself." "Christ was once offered *to bear* the sins of many." Heb. vii. 27: ix. 28. "When he had *offered* Isaac his son upon the altar." Jas. ii. 21. In all which passages the fact of *death* is the offering up alluded to. Let us remember also that our eternal life is the result of eating "His flesh and drinking His blood." "His flesh is the true meat, and His blood is the true drink." John vi. 53—56. The soul will derive no life and no sustenance from these speculations about the Lord Jesus bearing sin apart from the shedding of His blood. They are mere human theories, and draw away the soul from that which can alone help and nourish it—" Jesus Christ and Him *crucified*."

declineth, and I am withered like grass." Psa. cii. 4, 11 " My strength is dried up like a potsherd, and my tongue cleaveth to my jaws; and thou hast brought me into the dust of death." Psa. xxii. 15.

" A land not inhabited," or according to the margin, " a land of *separation*," into which the scapegoat was led that it might perish, means a land of *cutting off*. The same word in Hebrew is used in Isa. liii. 8 : " For he was *cut off* out of the land of the living ;* for the transgression of my people was he stricken." Manifestly this prophecy in Isaiah respecting the Lord's death has reference to the scapegoat. " Cut off from the land of the living," by being taken into the land of separation, the desolate, solitary desert. And some of the passages of the Psalms quoted above have expressions of the same kind. " Like the slain that lie in the grave *whom thou rememberest no more*," " and they are *cut off* from thy hand." And again, we have " *the dark*" mentioned—" the land of forgetfulness." Psa. lxxxviii. 5. 12.

On the cross the Lord was cut off out of the land of the living. It was a place of far off separation, in distance from God, and it was a land of forgetfulness, so that God is able to say to the sinner who looks at the death of Jesus, " Thy sins and iniquities will I remember no more." In Christ on the tree God *dismissed* our sins and our iniquities from His memory, as regards all the wrath due to them.

But we have again a remarkable contrast between the shadow and the substance. Israel had the sins of a *past year* put away in the type we have been considering. On the very next day after the day of atonement, uncleannesses, iniquities and transgressions began afresh to accumulate, and rolled on until the seventh month again came round, and the service of the

---

* *Cut off*, this word occurs also 2nd Chron. xxvi. 21, "He was *cut off* from the house of the Lord:" and Lam. iii. 54, "Waters flowed over mine head; I said, I am *cut off*;" and Ezek. xxxvii. 11, "We are *cut off* for our parts."

day of atonement was repeated. It would avail us nothing to have the sins of our past life blotted out ; for we are daily and hourly contracting guilt and defilement, and that often unconsciously. The redemption therefore that Christ has procured for us through His death is eternal. Instead of there being a remembrance made of sins every year, the Spirit of God is a witness to us in the Word, that God remembers our sins and our iniquities no more : there is a perfect remission of them, and therefore " there is no more offering for sin." " There remaineth no more sacrifice for sins." Heb. x. 18, 26.

The " once every year," " the sacrifices offered year by year continually," and the sacrifices offered " daily," (Heb. ix. 7 ; x. 1 ; vii. 27 ; x. 11;) were all " taken away" when the Lord Jesus offered Himself " once for all." This word " *once*" is the key note of the Gospel. " He died unto sin *once*." Rom. vi. 10. " Christ hath *once* suffered for sins." 1st Pet. iii. 18. " Now *once* in the end of the world hath he appeared to put away sin by the sacrifice of himself." " Christ was *once* offered to bear the sins of many." Heb. ix. 26, 28. " This he did *once* when he offered up himself," vii. 27. " By his own blood he entered in *once* into the holy places having obtained eternal redemption," ix. 12. " By the which will we are sanctified through the offering of the body of Jesus *once*," x. 10.

The result of this *one* offering, once offered, is that " the worshippers *once* purged should have no more conscience of sins," x. 2. The death of Christ instead of standing as the sin-offering of atonement at the end of a year's sins ; stands at " the *end* of the *world*;" or, as it might be rendered, *at the end of the ages*.

The ages of the world's history had rolled on to their climax when the Lord Jesus died. Man had been tested age after age under every variety of circumstances. He had fallen from innocence in the garden upon the very first temptation. He had manifested nothing but

self-will, corruption, and violence, when left to himself
in the ages before the flood.  Notwithstanding the
fearful judgment poured out in the deluge, self-will,
pride of heart, and insubjection to God afterwards were
again fully displayed in the building of the tower of
Babel.  Dispersed from thence by the confounding of
their language, men associated together according to
their speech ; thus forming distinct nations, giving themselves up to every species of idolatry.

A peculiar nation was then called out by God, and
separated off to himself : placed in a land of peculiar
fertility, and tutored under a law that was holy, just,
and good.  But the history of that nation is a history of
ceaseless backslidings and departures from the living
God.  Whether dealt with in judgment, or in mercy ;
by warnings or pleadings of grace and pity—or whether
spoken to by prophets or wise men, man proved
himself incorrigible : age after age only increased his
guilt.  Sacrifices, priesthood and law, had availed
nothing.  "But when the fulness of the time was come
God sent forth his Son ;" and, "now once in the
end of the ages hath he appeared to put away sin by
the sacrifice of himself."

Believers in the Lord thus recognize the cross as
sentencing all that is past, and standing on the very
brink of a glorious future ; they see that any progress or
improvement in man is hopeless.  A crucified Christ
proclaims "an end of all perfection."  But there is a
world to come "whereof we speak," which engages
our thoughts, and which will be commenced when the
kingdoms of this world will become the kingdoms of
our Lord, and of His Christ.  The Church itself having
been previously raised to be for ever with the Lord,
to reign with Him gloriously over this future world.

It is important to distinguish between "*no more
conscience of sins*," and "*no more consciousness of sin*."
An "evil conscience," is a conscience not at ease with
God : a conscience that thinks God has some demands,

some requirements unsatisfied. And therefore he that has an evil conscience, has a conscience of sins which have not been, as he thinks, fully purged by the blood of Christ. Such an one cannot have the heart of a worshipper. He cannot have love for God. His heart is more or less the heart of a slave, dreading the demands of an austere master, instead of the heart of a child trusting a loving father. The believer is conscious of sin and imperfection in everything he does ; and the longer he lives in this world as a child and servant of God, the deeper his acquaintance with his own unworthiness ; and the more conscious he is of an evil heart within, and of the temptations of Satan which he has to keep under and resist. But this consciousness is not "a conscience of sins." He knows that "through the offering of the body of Christ," he has been sanctified and perfected, so that he can draw near to God with confidence ; and he is a purged worshipper, never again needing to be re-sprinkled with the blood of Christ. His heart has been once for all, sprinkled from an evil conscience.

In the consecration of the priests of old, the blood was sprinkled outwardly upon their persons and garments. The precious blood of Christ is now sprinkled within, upon the *heart*. The Holy Spirit, applying the word of God touching the death of Christ to the heart of the sinner, sprinkles it from an evil conscience. The heart and conscience are intimately connected. If our hearts recognize the love of God in the gift of Christ, we cannot any more doubt the complete atonement made for sin. The heart and conscience will be at rest, because God is fully trusted.

The people gathered in holy convocation, looked on in silence at this scene respecting the scapegoat ; they did nothing, they said nothing. They uttered no prayer, nor petition. The stillness was only broken by the voice of another confessing their sins, and laying them upon the head of the victim. From beginning to end, the work of atonement was accomplished *for* them, and not by them ; they had no hand in it all. The only precepts laid upon them on this occasion were to afflict their souls, and to rest.

" This shall be a statute for ever unto you, that in the seventh month, on the tenth day of the month, ye shall afflict your souls, and do no work at all : for on that day shall he make an atonement for you, to cleanse you, that ye may be clean from all your sins before the Lord. It shall be a sabbath of rest unto you, and ye shall afflict your souls, by a statute for ever." Lev. xvi. 29—31.

" On the tenth day of this seventh month there shall be a day of atonement : it shall be an holy convocation unto you ; and ye shall afflict your souls, and offer an offering made by fire unto the Lord. And ye shall do no work in that same day : for it is a day of atonement, to make an atonement for you before the Lord your God. For whatsoever soul it be that shall not be afflicted in that same day, he shall be cut off from among his people. And whatsoever soul it be that doeth any work in that same day, the same soul will I destroy from among his people. Ye shall do no manner of work : it shall be a statute for ever throughout your generations in all your dwellings. It shall be unto you a sabbath of rest, and ye shall afflict your souls : in the ninth day of the month at even, from even unto even, shall ye celebrate your sabbath." Lev. xxiii. 27—32.

" Ye shall have on the tenth day of this seventh month an holy convocation ; and ye shall afflict your souls : ye shall not do any work therein." Num. xxix. 7.

These commands are very stringent—whatsoever soul was not afflicted should be cut off from his people; and whatsoever soul did any manner of work, God would destroy him from among His people. Affliction of soul and rest are remarkably associated together. Surely this is an eternal statute, which is still in force. All that God requires of the sinner is, to know himself to be a sinner ; to do no manner of work as regards his salvation ; but to see the whole work of the putting away of sin completed by another. Affliction of soul answers to the contrite heart.

"The Lord is nigh unto them that are of a broken heart ; and saveth such as be of a contrite spirit." "He healeth the broken in heart, and bindeth up their wounds."

"The sacrifices of God are a broken spirit ; a broken and a contrite heart O God thou wilt not despise." Psa. xxxiv. 18 ; cxlvii. 3 ; li. 17.

"Thus saith the high and lofty One that inhabiteth eternity, whose name is holy ; I dwell in the high and holy place, with him that is of a contrite and humble spirit, to revive the spirit of the humble, and to revive the heart of the contrite ones "

"Thus saith the Lord, the heaven is my throne, and the earth is my footstool : where is the house that ye build unto me ? and where is the place of my rest ? for all those things hath mine hand made, and all those things have been, saith the Lord : but to this man will I look, even to him that is poor and of a contrite spirit, and trembleth at my word." Isa. lvii. 15 ; lxvi. 1, 2.

Wherever therefore there is real consciousness of irremediable sinfulness and helplessness, there the soul may at once trust in God for the remission of sins through the death of His blessed Son. But alas ! we naturally attempt by some work or effort of our own to accomplish a salvation already finished, or to render ourselves fitting objects, when our very fitness for it really depends upon our total unworthiness and uncleanness.

Strange that when God commands us to rest we should be so unwilling to obey, and when God requires us to recognize our own worthlessness we should make so many attempts to improve ourselves. What would nave befallen an Israelite if he had abstained on the day of atonement from coming to the tabernacle to hear his sins confessed, and see them borne away by the scapegoat; and instead thereof had satisfied himself with going through a ceremonial of his own devising, seeking thereby to appease God? What will befall those who are not content to take God at His word; not assured that the death of Christ is all sufficient, but who seek to approve themselves to God, by some effort of their own, or mingle their own works with a kind of acknowledgment of the name of Jesus?

This day of atonement was also a time appropriated for a holy convocation. The people were called to assemble before God to witness the putting away of their sins. It is remarkable how all the holy convocations of Israel were feasts of the Lord, and how attached to them all is the command that no *servile* work was to be done. See Lev. xxiii. 7, 8, 21, 25, 35, 36; Num. xxviii. 18, 25, 26; xxix. 1, 12, 35. The spirit of *bondage* can have no connection with worshipping the Father in spirit and in truth. In beautiful accordance with this we read in Heb. x., first, of our own individual standing as purged worshippers, having confidence to enter into the holiest, and holding fast the profession of our hope without wavering, and then we are exhorted to consider one another to provoke unto love and to good works, and to meet as it were in holy convocation— "*not forsaking the assembling of ourselves together* as the manner of some is, but exhorting one another, and so much the more as ye see the day approaching."

One beautiful contrast remains to be considered. Israel when waiting outside the tabernacle for the high priest to come out after he had presented the blood to God, were yet uncertain about the remission of their sins, and were not assured of it until the scapegoat had been sent away. Moreover it would have been destruction to them had the victim which had borne their sins reappeared. In contrast with this we *look for* our High Priest " who his own self bare our sins in his own body on the tree," to come again, to reappear, " Christ was once offered to bear the sins of many; and unto them

that *look for him* shall he appear the second time, without
sin, unto salvation." This expression " without sin "
has in this place no reference to the sinlessness of Christ
—but to the fact of His coming again apart from all
dealing with sin in the way of remission, or in the way
of intercession. He has already sat down as far as the
remission of our sins is concerned, and by His own
offering on the cross He has perfected us as saints in
the presence of God. He is now also in the presence
of God for us, ever living to make intercession for us—
preserving us in the fulness of our redemption standing
before God, and keeping an unobstructed way open for
our approach to God—unobstructed by our sins, failures,
and shortcomings. But when He comes out from the
holiest in a little while, He will appear unto our
complete salvation—the salvation of our bodies as well
as our souls—the redemption of our bodies. We are
as believers in a strange and if we may so say, unnatural
state—by grace already saved, and yet expecting salvation
with perfect peace in our souls and rejoicing always, but
groaning still within ourselves. Sons of God, heirs of
God, and joint-heirs with Christ, with the spirit of
sonship in us, enabling us to say " abba Father," and
yet " waiting for the sonship, the redemption of our
body." Not in the flesh but in the spirit—yet cumbered
with the flesh and groaning for deliverance. We look
not for death, and we fear not that which is after death,
the judgment; for both death and judgment have been
met in the one offering of Christ on the tree—but we
expect Him, we look for Him, we shall see Him as He
is, and we shall be like Him. As surely as He was
seen at His first coming, when He came in order to put
away sin by the sacrifice of Himself, so surely shall He
be seen by us at His second coming when He shall come
not in weakness but in power—not in humiliation but
in glory—not with a cry of woe from a cross of shame
and curse, but with a shout of triumph and of gladness
to quicken our mortal bodies, and to raise us up into

His own likeness. We rejoice in hope of the return of our High Priest. God has raised Him from the dead in proof of the complete putting away of our sins accomplished in that death.

The day of atonement effected no change in the state of an Israelite personally. There was not even a shadow of resurrection in the types of that day. But the reconciliation we have received ; the justification we have through the blood of Christ, is a justification of life. We are born again—we are new creatures in Christ Jesus. Our place of worship, our place of rest and our citizenship are in heaven, " from whence also we look for the Saviour, the Lord Jesus Christ, who shall change our body of humiliation that it may be fashioned like unto His body of glory, according to the working whereby He is able even to subdue all things unto himself " Phil. iii. 20, 21.

**The Altar of Burnt Offering or Brazen Altar**

The Scapegoat

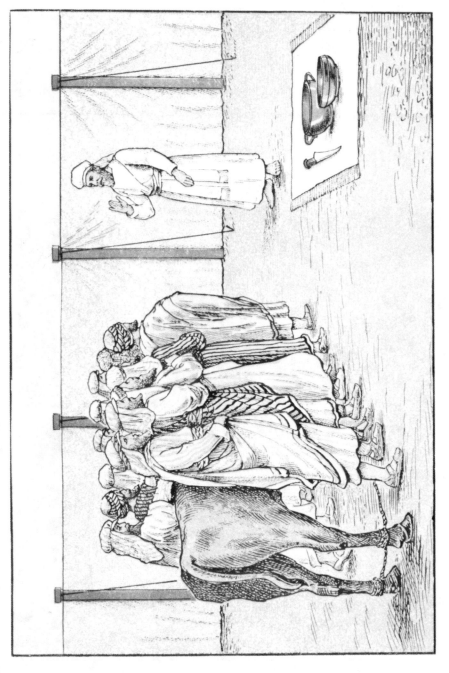

The Sin Offering

# THE BURNT-OFFERING

"And Aaron shall come into the tabernacle of the congregation, and shall put off the linen garments, which he put on when he went into the holy place, and shall leave them there:

"And he shall wash his flesh with water in the holy place, and put on his garments, and come forth, and offer his burnt offering, and the burnt offering of the people, and make atonement for himself, and for the people.

"And the fat of the sin offering shall he burn upon the altar.

"And he that let go the goat for the scapegoat shall wash his clothes, and bathe his flesh in water, and afterward come into the camp.

"And the bullock for the sin offering, and the goat for the sin offering, whose blood was brought in to make atonement in the holy place, shall one carry forth without the camp; and they shall burn in the fire their skins, and their flesh, and their dung.

"And he that burneth them shall wash his clothes, and bathe his flesh in water, and afterward he shall come into the camp." Lev. xvi 23—28

THIS change of garments of the high priest, implies a change of ministration. The whole of the service which he had conducted in the fine linen garments, was connected with one aspect of atonement, the putting away of sins in respect to God's judgment of wrath. The offering of the burnt-offering presents another aspect of atonement, viz : the *acceptance* of the worshipper according to the sweet savour of the sacrifice. Aaron therefore left the holy garments in the tabernacle where he had sprinkled the blood, and put on *his own* garments which were the garments for glory and beauty. This may be seen on referring to Exod. xxviii. 2, 4, 41 ; xxix. 21, 29; Lev. viii. 30 ; xxi. 10. It has been before observed, that these garments bore a representative character, and identified the high priest himself with the people Israel, in glory and beauty. Thus once a year, that nation had its sins numbered before God in order to be put away, and it stood in acceptance according to the sweet savour of the burnt-offering. The holy places were also cleansed, so that the Levitical routine of service could be conducted in them.

The man that led away the scapegoat, and he also who burnt the sin-offerings outside the camp, had to wash themselves and their clothes in water before they could return into the camp. This command proves how closely the scapegoat was allied to the sin-offering. In either case, all the uncleanness or defilement which attached substitutionally to the victim, was in no sense to be brought back again into the camp : for the time all sin had been borne away, and all traces of its defilement were to be obliterated.*

The 50th year called "the year of jubilee," began on the day of atonement. The trumpet was then blown, and the holy year of rest and liberty began, when also every man returned to the possession God had given him in the land. Lev. xxv. 9—13. Have we not in this abundant instruction for our souls ? We can have no holiness ; we cannot be "holy brethren" except through the blood of atonement ; we cannot walk at liberty with God ; at liberty from the dominion of sin ; at liberty from the bondage of law, unless we trust in the full grace of God in the gift of His blessed Son, as having answered for us as sinners, and given us life eternal. We shall enter "every man into his possession" in a little while, when the great trumpet of redemption is blown at the return of Christ, and when the full value of His atoning blood is made manifest on the resurrection morning, and the new song, "Thou wast slain and hast redeemed us to God by thy blood," (which even now faith anticipates,) is sung in all its fulness.

Space will not allow of a more lengthened exposition of this beautiful type of the day of atonement ; or of a more distinct consideration of its future application to the nation of Israel for which the Lord died. John xi. 50. The two chapters in the New Testament which have especial reference to it are John xx., when the Lord appeared to Mary Magdalene early in the morning, and

---

* It will be observed in turning to Exod. xxx. 10, that the word "atonement" is in the plural, ("*atonements.*") It ought to be in the plural also in Lev. xxiii ; 27, 28 ; Num. xxix. 11. The day is "*a day of atonements.*" Lev. xxiii. 27, 28 ; xxv. 9. Probably the use of the plural arises from the various aspects of atonement embraced on this occasion.

spoke of His ascending to His Father and His God, and returned in the evening to speak peace to His disciples ; and Heb. x., which is almost a running commentary by way of contrast. It will be seen by what has been already written, that the day of atonement comprised four great actions of the high priest—making atonement by blood in the holiest ; establishing the altar of incense — intercession, upon the ground of the blood of atonement ; giving to the people the *knowledge* of the remission of their sins under the type of the scapegoat ; and lastly, taking his full representative character in glory and beauty on the ground of acceptance through the sacrifice for a sweet savour. The great truths illustrated are— Christ made sin for us. 2nd Cor. v. 21. " The Lord hath laid on him the iniquity of us all." Isa. liii. 6. " He bare the sin of many." Isa. liii. 12. " Who himself bare our sins in his own body on the tree." 1st Pet. ii. 24. " Their sins and their iniquities will I remember no more." Heb. x. 17.

## CONCLUDING ADDRESS

In bringing the present portion of this work on the tabernacle to a conclusion, the writer desires to address a few words to any unsaved, unconverted reader, under whose eye it may fall. It will be seen that the truths heretofore enumerated have chiefly been for believers, for those who *are* saved and who *know* they are saved, because they believe what God says in His Word. But some one may take up this book who is not saved, or who questions or doubts his salvation. To such an one the writer would appeal in the language of God Himself. " What could have been done more that I have not done ?" Is it possible for God to do more than He has done ? Or can He express more clearly, more plainly what He has done than He has expressed it over and over again in His Word ? What more can be done ? Hear the word of the Lord. " Thou shalt call his name JESUS, for he shall *save* his people *from their sins.*" Mat. i. 21. "Behold the Lamb of God which *taketh away* the sin of the world." John i. 29. "When I shall *take away* their sins." Rom. xi. 27. "Ye know that he was manifested to *take away* our sins." 1st John iii. 5. "Now once in the end of the world hath he appeared *to put away sin* by the sacrifice of himself." Heb. ix. 26. "To give knowledge of salvation unto his people by the *remission* of their sins." Luke i. 77. "That repentance and *remission of sins* should be *preached* among all nations," Luke xxiv. 47. "Him hath God exalted with his right hand, to be a Prince and a *Saviour;* for to *give* repentance to Israel, and *forgiveness* of sins." Acts v. 31. "Through this man is preached unto you the *forgiveness* of sins." Acts xiii. 38. "That they may *receive forgiveness* of sins, and inheritance amongst them that are sanctified through faith that is in me" (Jesus.) Acts xxvi. 18. "Through his name whosoever believeth in him shall receive *remission* of sin." Acts x. 43. "Now where *remission* of these is there is no more offering for sin." Heb. x. 18. "Christ died for the *ungodly*." Rom. v. 6. "Christ died for *our sins* according to the Scriptures." 1st Cor. xv. 3. "To give his life a *ransom* for many." Matt. xx. 28. "He laid down his life *for* us." 1st John iii. 16. "Who *gave himself* for our sins." Gal. i. 4. "Christ hath once *suffered* for sins, the just one instead of unjust ones, that he might bring us to God." 1st Pet. iii. 18. "Who was *delivered* for our offences." Rom. iv. 25. "Who his own self *bare* our sins in his own body on the tree." 1st. Pet. ii. 24. "He *bare* the sin of many." Isa. liii. 12. "Christ was once offered to *bear* the sins of many." Heb. ix. 28. "When he had by himself *purged* our sins sat down." Heb. i. 3. "After he had *offered one sacrifice* for sins for ever sat down." Heb. x. 12. "He is the *propitiation* for our sins." 1st John ii. 2. "I write unto you little children, because your sins are *forgiven you* for his name's sake." 1st John ii. 12. "It is the blood that maketh *atonement* for the soul." Lev. xvii. 11. "Without shedding of blood is no *remission*." Heb. ix. 22. "The blood of Jesus Christ his son *cleanseth* us from *all* sin." 1st John i. 7. "Unto him that loved us and *washed* us from our sins in his own blood." Rev. i. 5. "They have *washed their robes* and made them white in the blood of the Lamb," vii 14. "Being now *just:fied* by his blood." Rom. v. 9. "Thou wast slain and hast *redeemed* us to God by thy blood." Rev. v. 9. "In whom we *have redemption* through his blood, *the forgiveness* of sins." Eph. i. 7. "In whom we *have redemption* through his blood, *the forgiveness* of sins." Col. i. 14. "This is my blood of the new covenant which is shed for many for the *remission* of sins." Matt. xxvi. 28 ; Mark xiv. 24. "Whom God hath set forth to be a *propitiation* through *faith* in his blood." Rom. iii. 25. "Made *nigh* by the blood of Christ." Eph. ii. 13. "That he might *sanctify* the people with his own blood." Heb. xiii. 12. "Not *redeemed* with corruptible things as silver and gold, but with the precious blood of Christ." 1st Pet. i. 18. "Having made *peace* through the blood of his cross." Col. i. 20. "*Purchased* with his own blood." Acts xx. 28.

"God is said to *pardon*." Isa. lv. 7. "To *pass by* transgression : not to *retain* his anger : to *delight* in mercy : to *subdue* iniquities : to cast all sins into the depths of the sea." Micah vii. 18, 19. "To *cast* sins *behind his back*." Isa. xxxviii. 17. To "*remember* them *no more*." Jer. xxxi. 34. To *blot out* sins and transgressions. Acts iii. 19 ; Isa. xliii. 25 ; xliv. 22. "Not to *impute* iniquity— to *cover* sin." Psa. xxxii. 2. "To *justify* the ungodly." Rom. iv. 5. "To *finish* the transgression and to *make an end* of sins." Dan. ix. 24. "God *commendeth* his love toward us in that while we were yet *sinners* Christ died for us." "When we were *enemies* we were *reconciled* to God by the death of his Son." Rom. v. 8, 10.

"This is a faithful saying, and worthy of all accept-ation that Christ Jesus came into the world to *save sinners*." 1st Tim. i. 15.

Texts such as these might be multiplied—the whole Bible is full of the testimony of the helplessness, worthlessness and complete ruin of every sinner—of the love and mercy and grace of God towards such vile and impotent sinners ; and of salvation present, completed, and eternal, provided by God in the death of His own Son, and freely offered by Him to the ruined and lost. The hard heart doubts and mistrusts the full and free manifestation of God's love in the death of His Son, and the consequence is, that recourse is had to some efforts of one's own to render oneself more acceptable to God ; and to religious ceremonies, with which the name of Christ is mixed.    Promises, resolutions, prayers, and outward reformations are resorted to, and God is not trusted, and the full efficacy of the precious blood. of Christ is not relied on.    Many an one says, "I know I can do nothing of myself," who is yet seeking to do a great deal of and for himself.    Many an one speaks of the finished work of Christ, who yet proves by his own actions and thoughts that he does not believe it to be finished.

God has exalted Christ to be a Prince and a Saviour, and we may rest assured that He will allow of no interference with that Saviour and His work. He commands all men everywhere to change their minds ; for the minds of all men everywhere are mistaken, both as to themselves and as to God.    Change your mind therefore as to yourself.    Cease from your own works. Cease from expecting improvement or amendment by your own efforts.    Cease from hoping to feel better or to be better.    Change your mind also as to God. Cease from doubting or mistrusting Him or His love. Behold the wonderful manner of His love, seen in the death of His Son upon the cross, and hear His universal proclamation of His love, "that whosoever believeth in Him shall not perish but have everlasting life"—shall have it at once, and shall have it for ever.

# Index

# Books on the Tabernacle

### Outline Studies of the Tabernacle                   Ada R. Habershon

A thought-provoking outline study on the construction, erection and service of the tabernacle.

**ISBN 0-8254-2820-3**               64 pp.                              **paper**

### Tabernacle in the Wilderness                          John Ritchie

A concise, practical study of the tabernacle, the offerings and the priesthood which all typify the person and work of Christ. A thrilling parallel between the Old Testament tabernacle and a Christian's daily walk is presented. Illustrated.

**ISBN 0-8254-3616-8**               120 pp.                             **paper**

### Thoughts on the Tabernacle                           J. Denham Smith

Beautiful, devotional reflections full of practical truths for believers. These meditations will draw out worship and marvel at the Lord's wonderful revelation of Jesus Christ and His work as prefigured in the Tabernacle. Illustrated.

**ISBN 0-8254-3756-3**               304 pp.                             **paper**

### The Tabernacle, Priesthood, and the Offerings    Henry W. Soltau

This exhaustive, richly suggestive treatment is a classic in its field. Charles H. Spurgeon evaluated this work by saying that it was "exceedingly well worked out in details, but not so wiredrawn as to prevent thought on the reader's part." Illustrated.

**ISBN 0-8254-3750-4**               496 pp.                             **paper**

### The Tabernacle of Israel: Its Structure
###   and Symbolism                                       James Strong

An exhaustive, scholarly investigation of the structure and components of the tabernacle. Contains a wealth of carefully examined symbolism which offers valuable insight and practical applications by the renowned author of *Strong's Exhaustive Concordance*.

**ISBN 0-8254-3745-8**               168 pp.                             **paper**

Available at your local Christian bookseller, or:

**kregel**
PUBLICATIONS

P. O. Box 2607 • Grand Rapids, MI  49501-2607